MILFORD MOONS

MILFORD

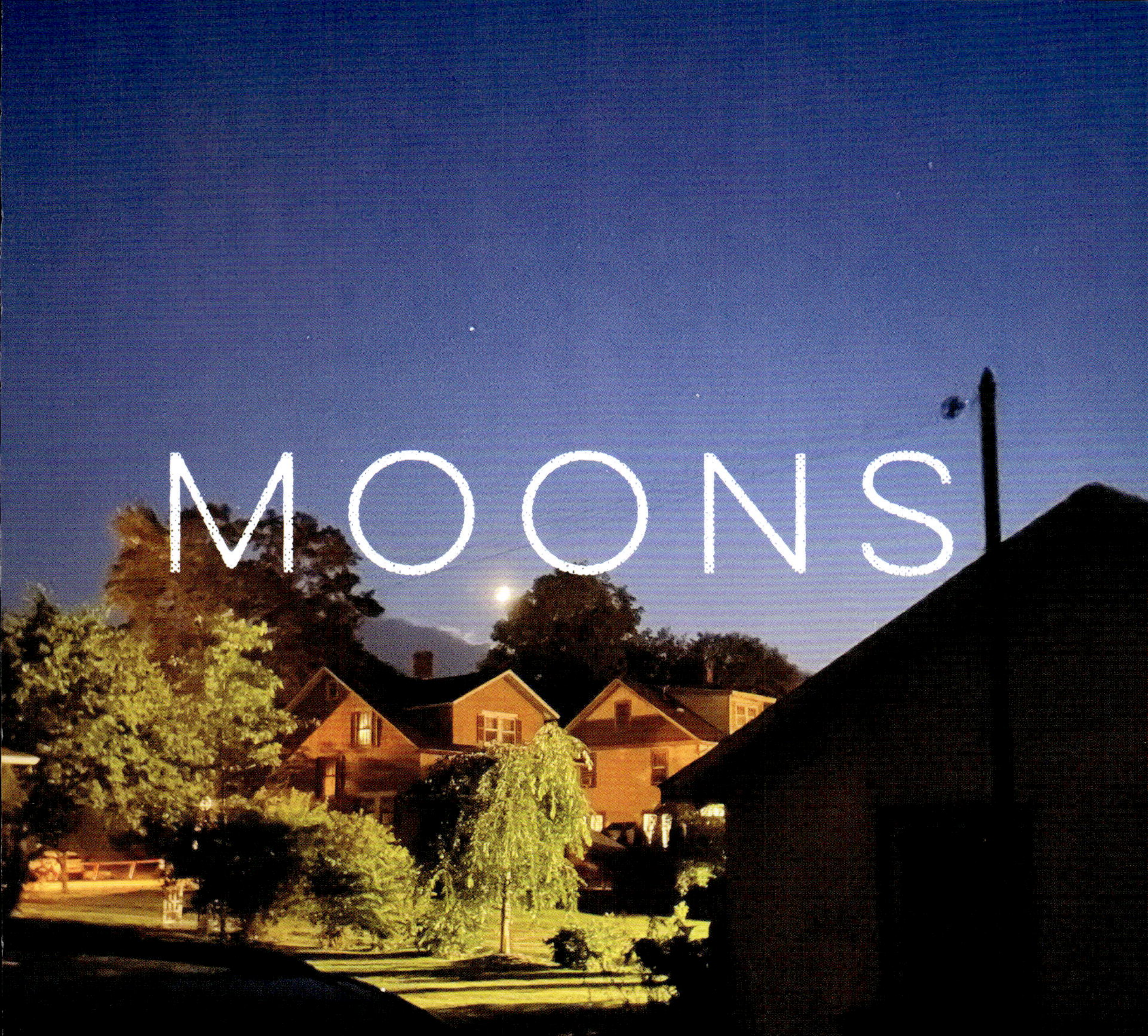

MOONS

A WRITER'S VISUAL LOVE LETTER TO HIS ANCESTRAL VILLAGE

RICHARD C. MORAIS

FOREWORD BY SEAN STRUB

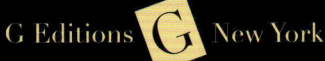
G Editions G New York

First published in 2025 by

G Editions
500 Seventh Avenue
New York, New York 10018
Telephone: 929.232.2472

www.geditions.com | media@geditions.com for inquiries

First edition, 2025

Library of Congress Cataloging-in-Publication Data is available from
the Publisher.

Hardcover edition ISBN: 978-1-943876-64-8
Printed and Bound in China

For further information contact Foliofina@gmail.com

10 9 8 7 6 5 4 3 2 1

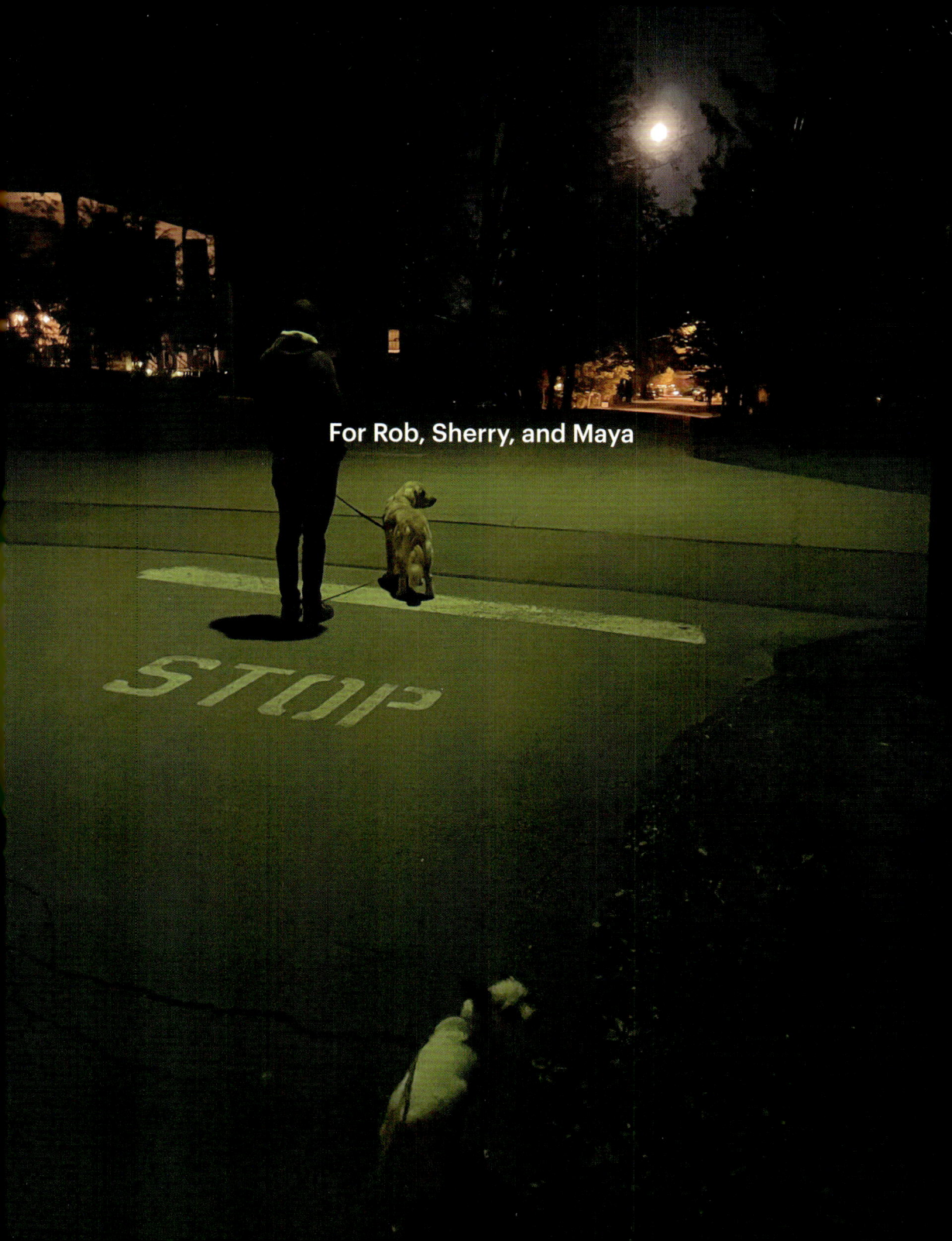

For Rob, Sherry, and Maya

CONTENTS

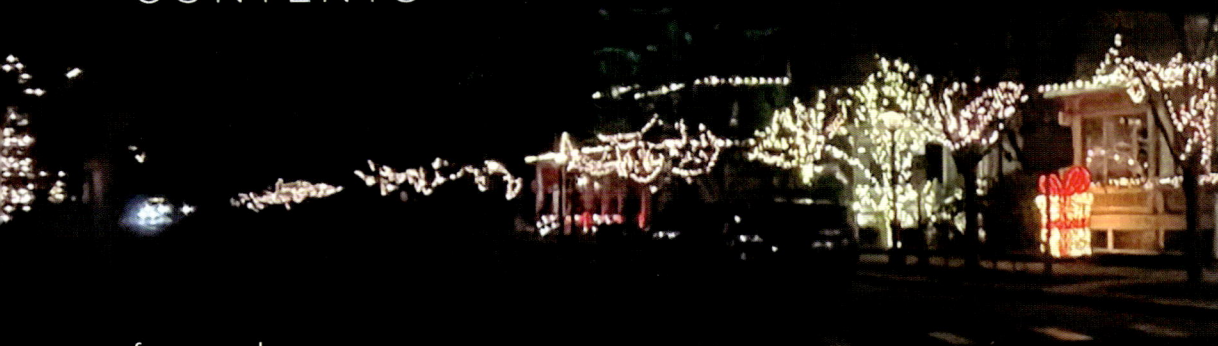

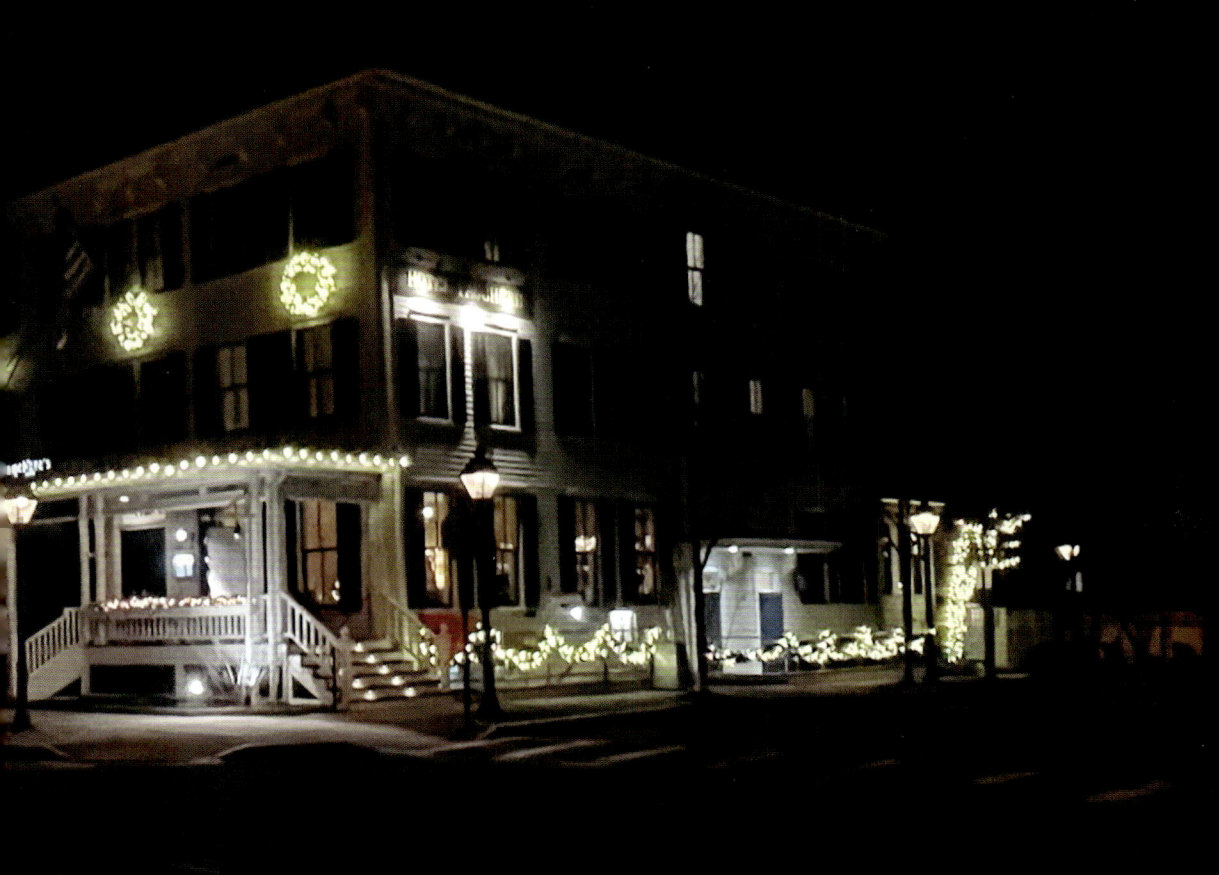

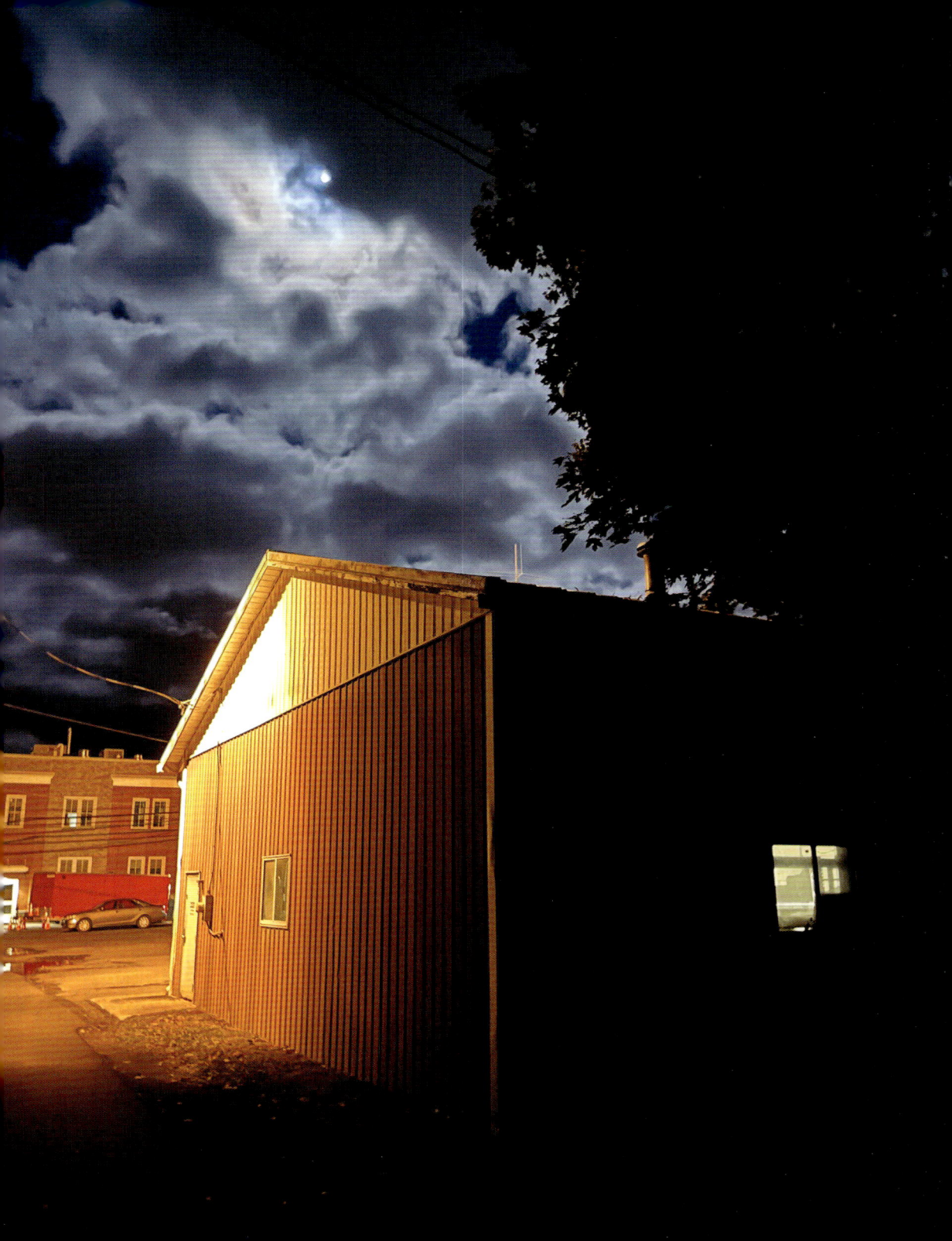

FOREWORD

Richard C. Morais excels at crafting lush, vivid imagery. His richly atmospheric and masterfully observational descriptions of food, landscapes, and intricate cultural settings in *The Hundred-Foot Journey* and *The Man With No Borders* transported my imagination to scenes and circumstances far beyond my experience.

Milford, Pennsylvania, however, is my experience; I know its residents—my neighbors—very well. I have studied Milford's history, and no street or alley is unfamiliar to me. As mayor, I have nodded in appreciative pride when others say Milford is like a Norman Rockwell painting or a Currier & Ives print. Three-quarters of the borough constitutes a National Historic District.

Milford's reputation as an attractive spot is longstanding, right from 1796 when John Biddis's, a circuit court judge and budding real estate developer, purchased a bucolic flat acreage sitting on a bluff 100 feet above the Delaware River.

He laid out Milford in an aesthetically pleasing perfect grid pattern. The two main streets—Broad and High—were designed with wider cartways, with the intent that government buildings would cluster where they intersect, similar to Philadelphia's central intersection at Market and Broad. Side streets in one direction are numbered; in the other they are named after Biddis' children. Behind each street is an alley, named for berries and fruit trees.

As early as the 1840s, a book on Pennsylvania's county seats described Milford as among the state's most attractive, crediting the town's tidy appearance to the influence of Milford's French settlers.

In 1961, Atlantic Magazine went further, calling Milford the "prettiest county seat in the nation."

Richard's photographs begin with this history and go a step further. They evocatively capture infinite permutations of light, lending mystery, mood and magic. Like a painter working *en plein air*, Richard worked with the light he saw, ever-changing day and night.

Moonlight bright and clear one minute, mysteriously lurking behind shifting clouds or gauzed through evening fog or morning mist the next. Soft-wattage porch lights and starkly bright security lights. Hearth light's golden glow warming the windows of Victorian homes.

Pedestrian and utility lights. Holiday lights. The proud "look at me" lighting of illuminated historic properties and even lightbox signs, with a touch of neon. Transitional light at nightfall and daybreak. They all fit.

Collectively they communicate a reassuring sense of calm and tranquility, a reminder that beyond the intrusive barrage of conflict, cable news, texts, and email that define our modern age, there is still beauty all around us. All we need to do is take the time to go for a walk and appreciate it.

Richard's family first came to Milford over a century ago, purchasing land adjacent to Arisbe, the home of philosopher Charles Sanders Peirce, who is sometimes referred to as the "American Aristotle." Peirce believed that the function of art was to make qualities of feelings intelligible.

In *Milford Moons*, Richard's photography and narrative bring into focus the feelings of love and affection Milford inspires in its residents and visitors alike. Richard's family's former neighbor would surely approve.

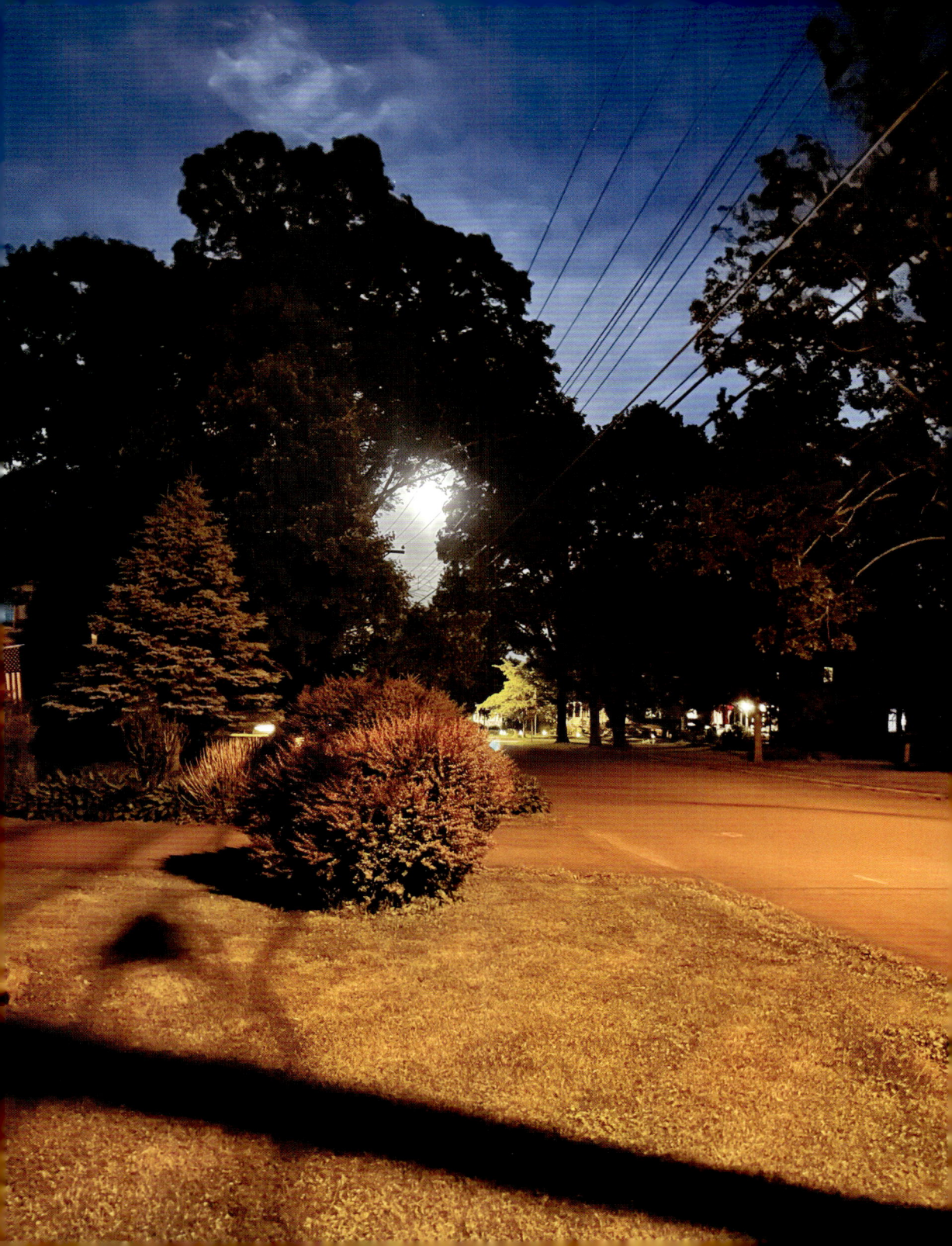

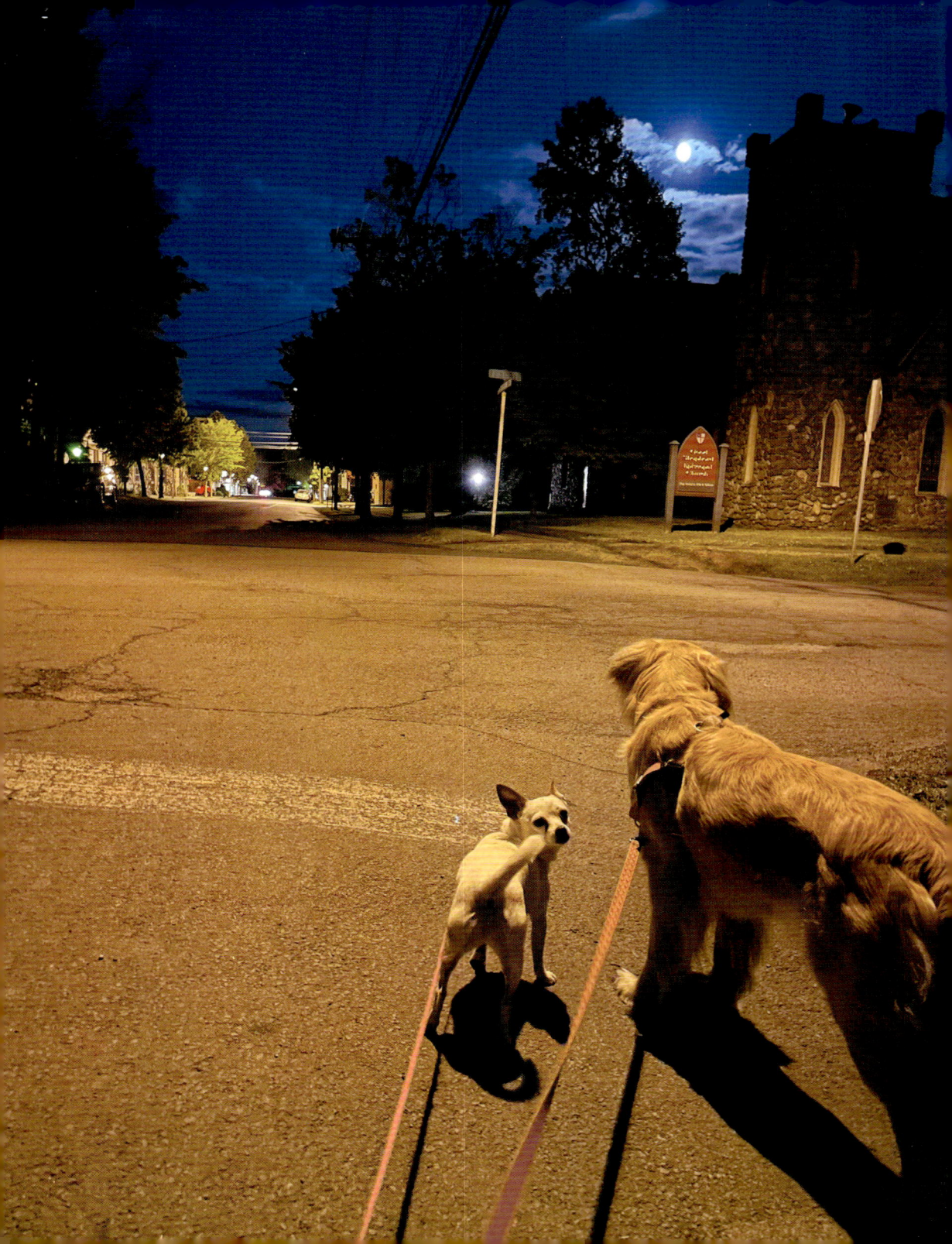

INTRODUCTION

I have, as they say about complicated relationships, "history with Milford."

At the dawn of the twentieth century, my maternal great-grand-mother (Luckings) used to take the train up to Port Jervis from New York City, where Great Aunt Elvira and whip-yielding Great Uncle Bill (Neidlinger) would pick her up in horse and buggy and drive her at a bonnet-clutching clop to the Hotel Fauchère.

My great aunt and uncle were devotees of the area, and in 1905 they built a stone house next door to the philosopher Charles S. Peirce, their Milford property stretching right down to the Delaware River. On the property's riverbank, they built a summer camp for the indigent parish children of St. Michael's, an Episcopal church on Manhattan's Upper West Side that my family essentially ran. Great Aunt Elvira was its choirmaster, my great-grandfather its sexton, and that Milford summer camp they owned and ran in service to the church stood roughly where the Kittatinny Canoes River Beach Campground now stands opposite Cummins Hill Road on Rt. 209.

Mid-century, a second wave of family arrived in the area. My grand-father Harold Sweet owned a seat on the New York Stock Exchange, lost everything in the 1929 Crash, and after that we were downwardly mobile WASPs, which despite the bad press is really not a bad fate. In the 1950s, the family sold for near nothing our Upper West Side brownstone on West Ninety-Fourth, after the neighborhood had turned *West Side Story*–rough, and that's when three more of my spinster great-aunts moved to bucolic Milford and Matamoras.

I grew up in Switzerland, where my ex-pat family lived, and I remember visiting my great aunts in the late 1960s as a wide-eyed boy from Europe. After Sunday service at the Good Shepherd Episcopal Church in Milford, my white-gloved and behatted great aunts would take us to the roast beef dinner at the Tom Quick Inn, or for soup-and-sandwiches at Flo-Jean, a doll-filled restaurant that once clung precariously to the Delaware River's cliff just above Matamoras's steel bridge.

That's also around the time the U.S. government seized our main Milford property to build Interstate 84, and in the late 1970s, when I was a teenager attending Sarah Lawrence College, my last surviving great aunt died and left us a modest house on Avenue L in Matamoras, to which I retreated periodically for alcohol-fueled weekends with my friends. Then, in 1990, my ex-pat parents in Europe retired, and after forty years abroad, they moved to the elegant 1850s white farmhouse on High Street that stands opposite Milford's old Catholic church and can be found in the pages of this book. My 90-year-old grandmother followed them to Milford, and my parents are now, along with my uncle, Richard Sweet, buried in the local cemetery.

It was, inevitably, my turn to return from my wanderings around the globe. I was once *Forbes'* European Bureau Chief and its longest serving foreign correspondent. In 2014, my former wife, Susan, and I bought an odd little house on Milford's Mott Street—with the mad money I earned from *The Hundred-Foot Journey* film made from my novel of the same name—and today I live on the grander Catharine Street with my partner, Robert Radley, and our dog, Sherry. So, I am the fourth generation of my family to have found respite in Milford, and one day, maybe my daughter, Kate, will become its fifth generation inhabitant.

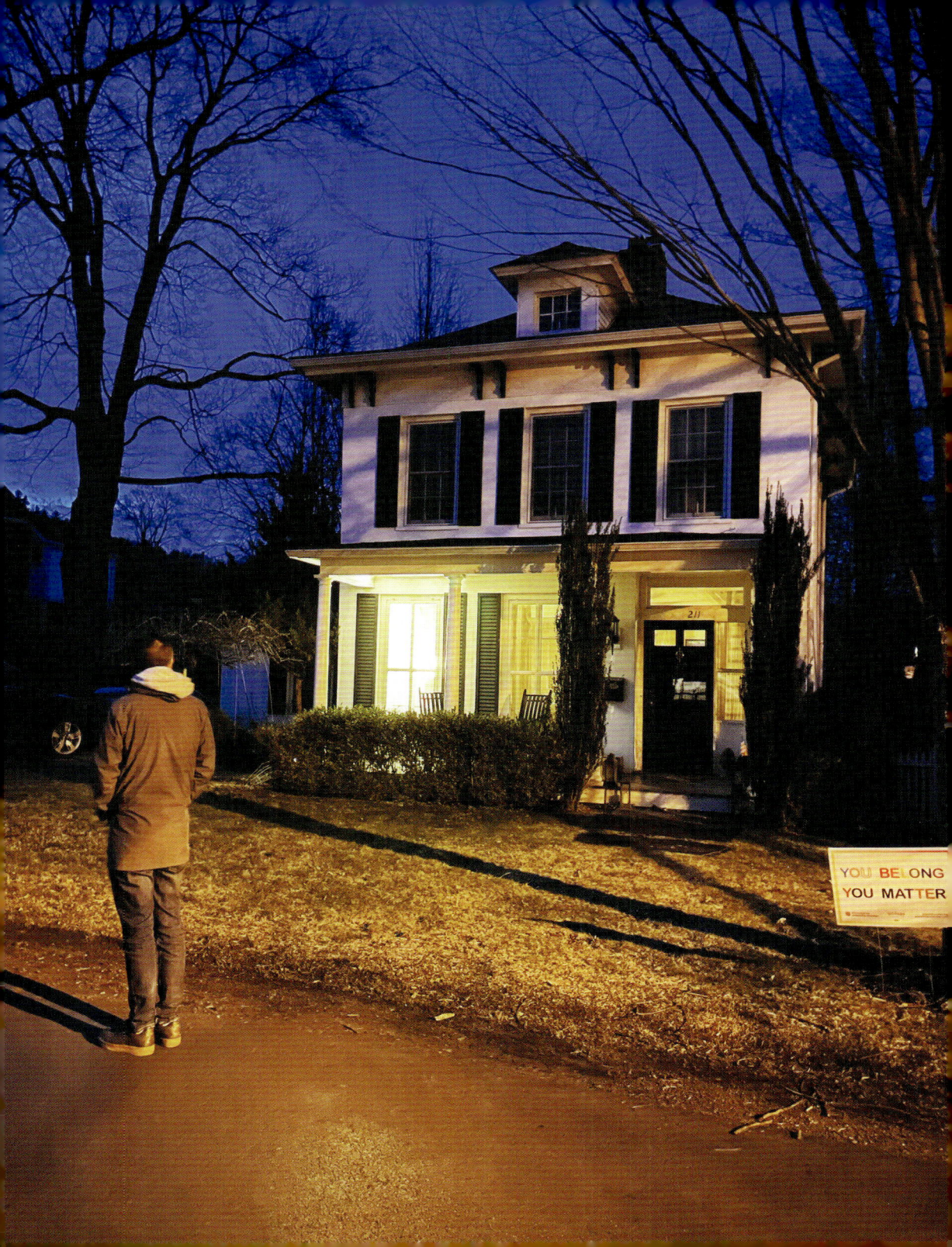

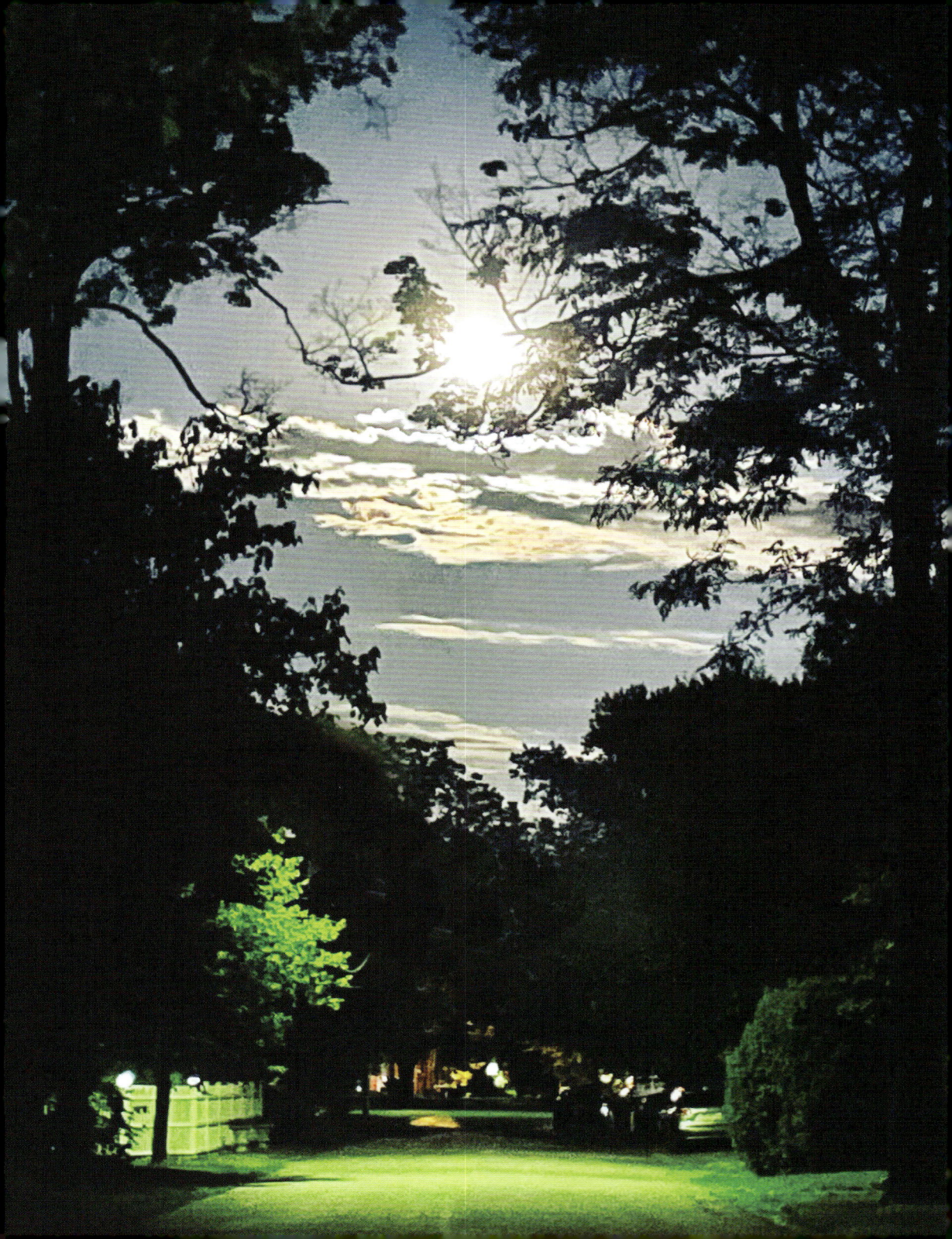

Which brings me to this book. I heard many stories about my family's local history over the years, and most of them I did not believe, simply because the Luckings-Sweet side of my family never let facts interrupt a good story. They were notorious exaggerators. But when I told some of my family lore to Matt Osterberg, Pike County's Commissioner and my grandmother's former landlord, he generously had some historical research conducted about my family and we discovered that much of what I had been told was true.

In fact, a 1928 article in the *Pike County Dispatch* that Matt uncovered had a profound effect on me. That year Ethel Busse, a fourteen-year-old girl from the Bronx and a member of St. Michael's Episcopal Church, was attending my family's summer camp in Milford. She was picking berries by the side of road when she abruptly stepped out and was struck by a doctor driving along Rt 209 in his car.

"The wheels passed over her chest, breaking four ribs and causing internal injuries, besides lacerating her scalp," the paper duly reported. The poor girl died from her injuries a few hours later and her mother, who came up from the Bronx to retrieve her body, "was prostrated by shock and was under Dr. Barckley's care for nearly five hours Saturday night before she became calm."

For some reason this story seized my imagination, I couldn't shake it, and during COVID, it sparked a literary wildfire. I began writing a murder mystery, something I had never done before. My point for recounting all this: I am a sensory-driven writer, and during pensive late-night walks with my dogs Sherry and Maya, I began searching for an image that would best capture the mood and feel of the novel that was slowly coming to life on the page.

One evening, the full moon, standing over a back alley in the village, cast deep shadows and luminous light across my path. The scene was beautiful and mysterious and dark.

It was the perfect image for my novel. I took out my iPhone and took a snap.

That one picture led to more, which led to this book.

As you will shortly discover, this work ended the way it began, with a car again passing over a much-loved being. The karmic ripples of my Milford story continue.

But that is life.

No person, nor any one place, is all good or all bad, and that's what I hope I have captured in this book.

My Milford, my ancestral village, light and darkness, all.

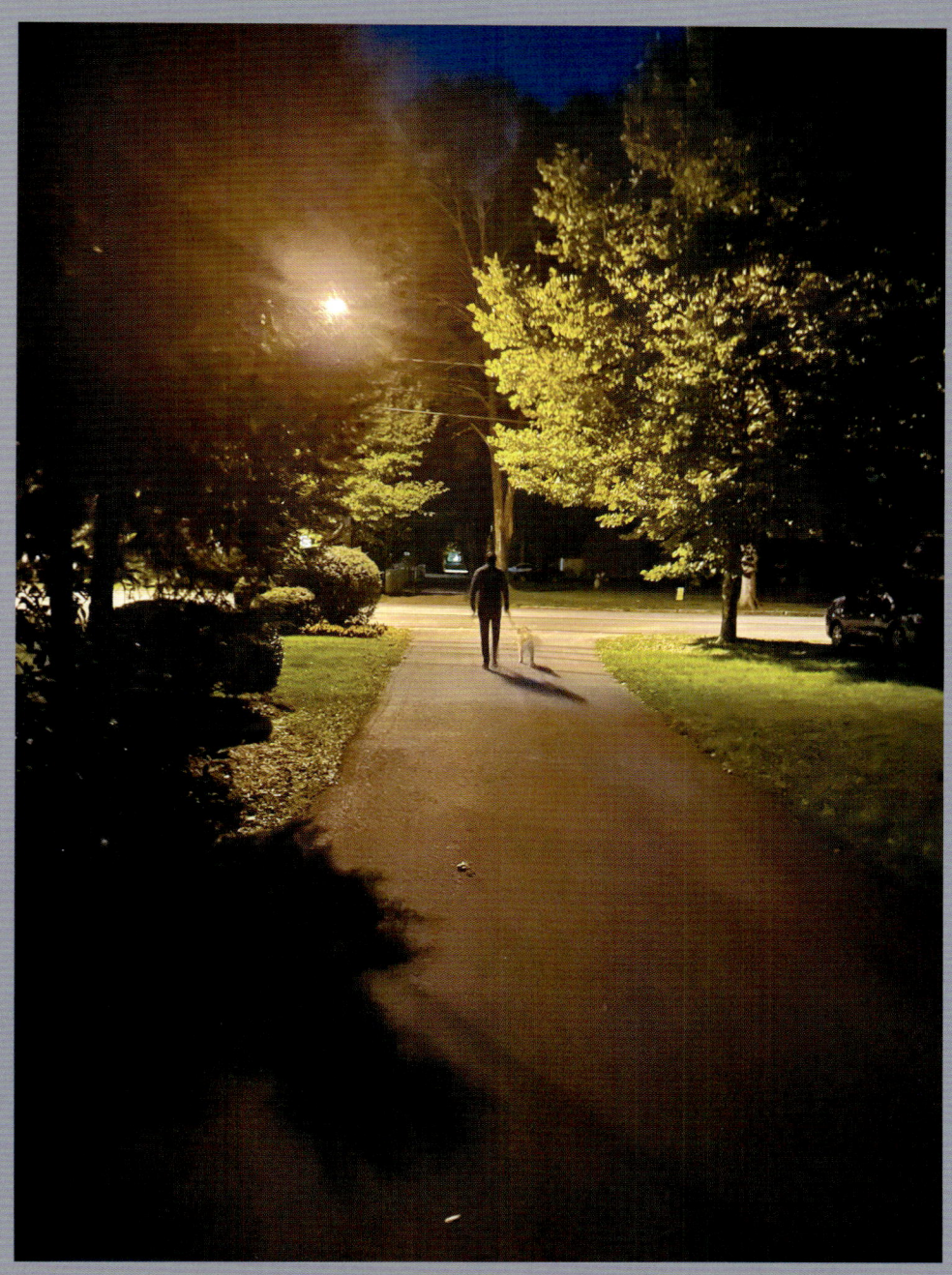

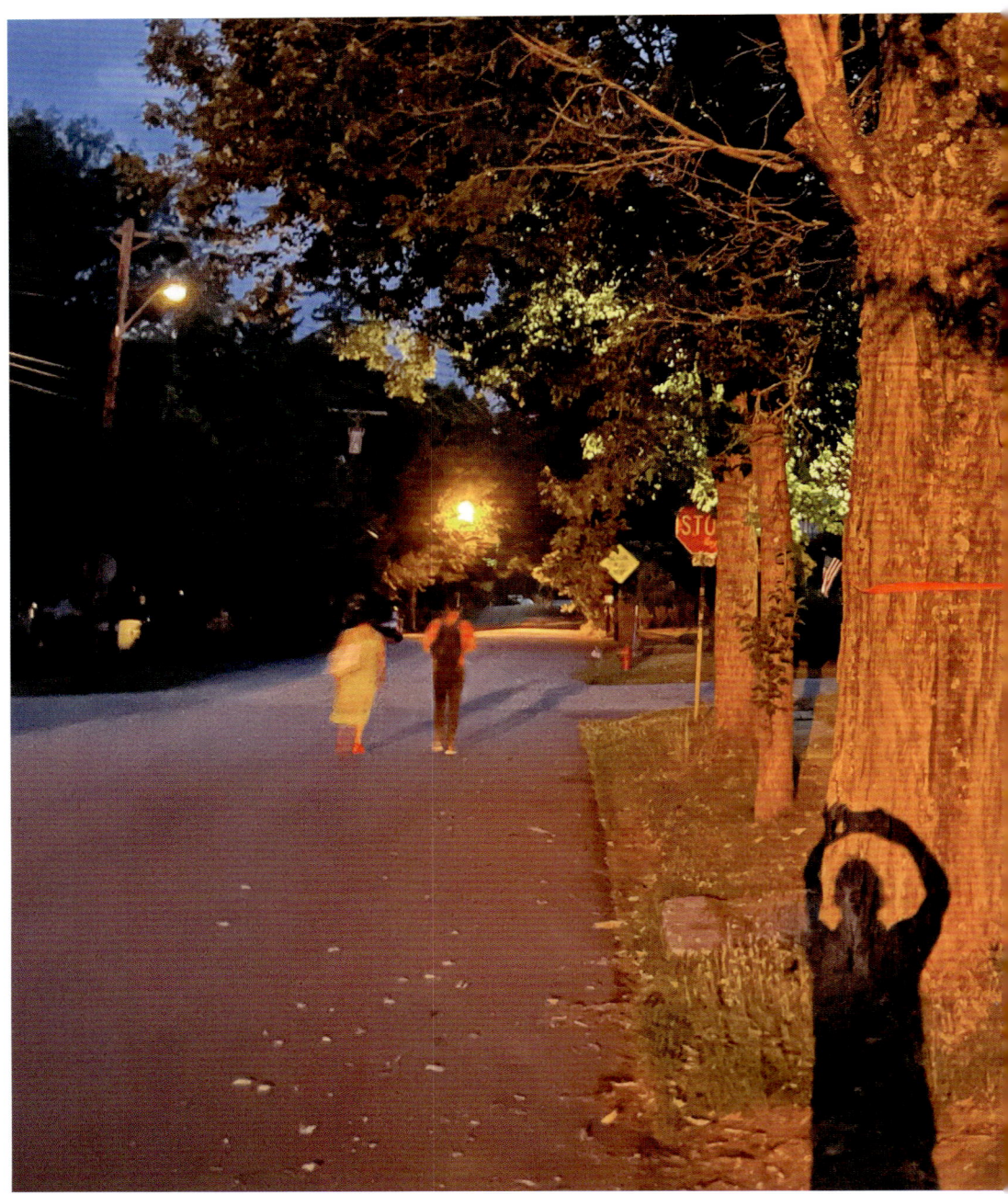

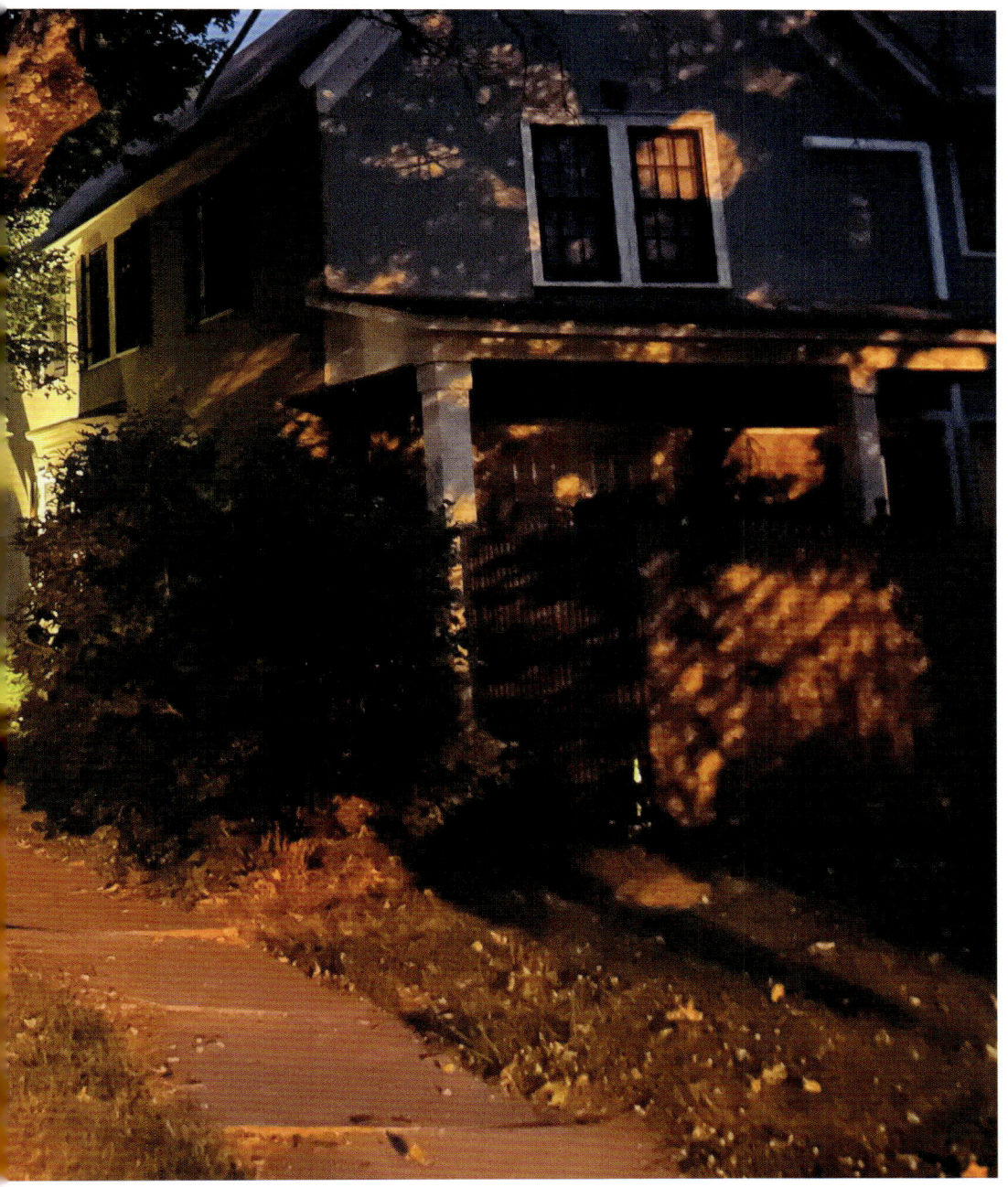

PATHS

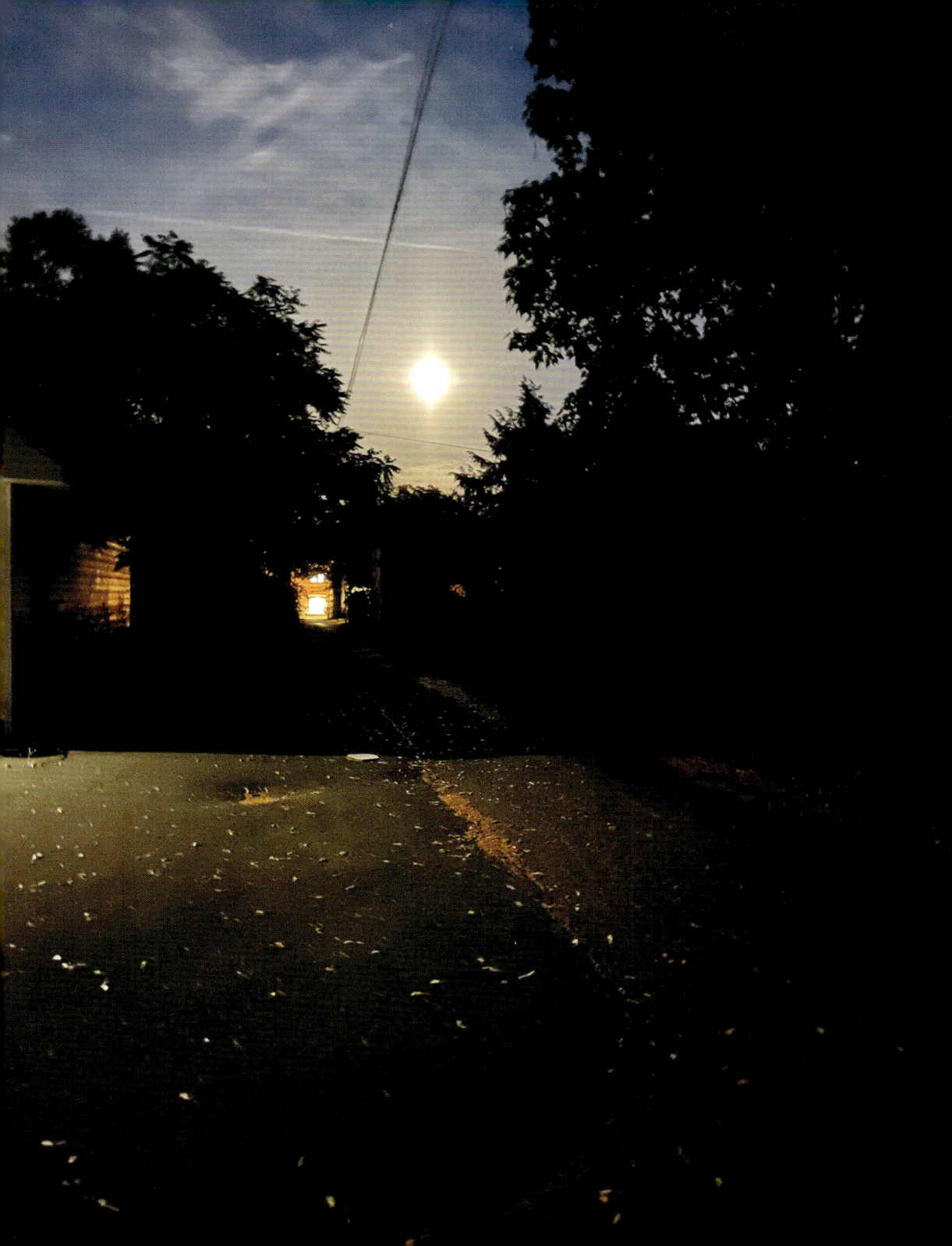

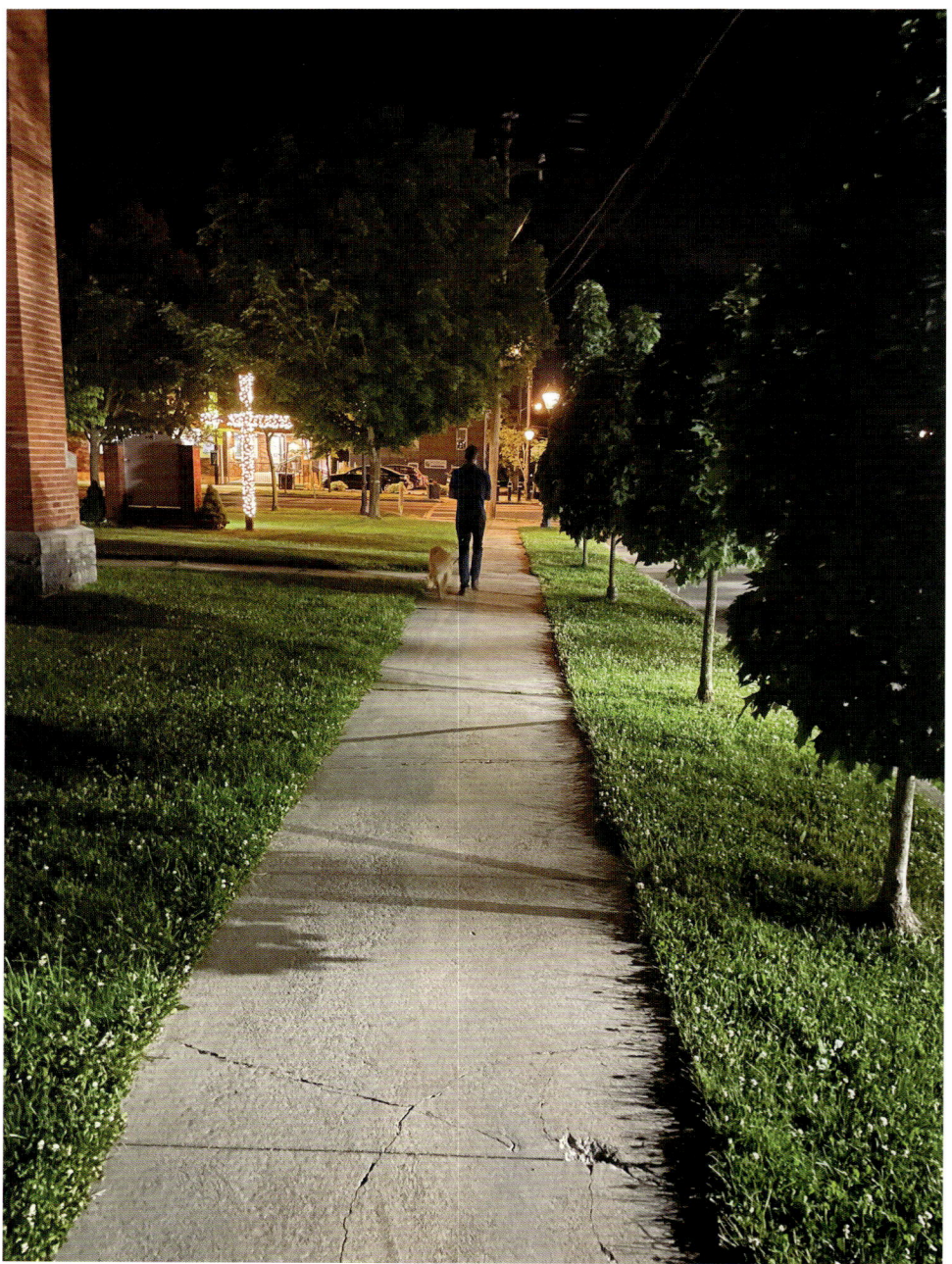

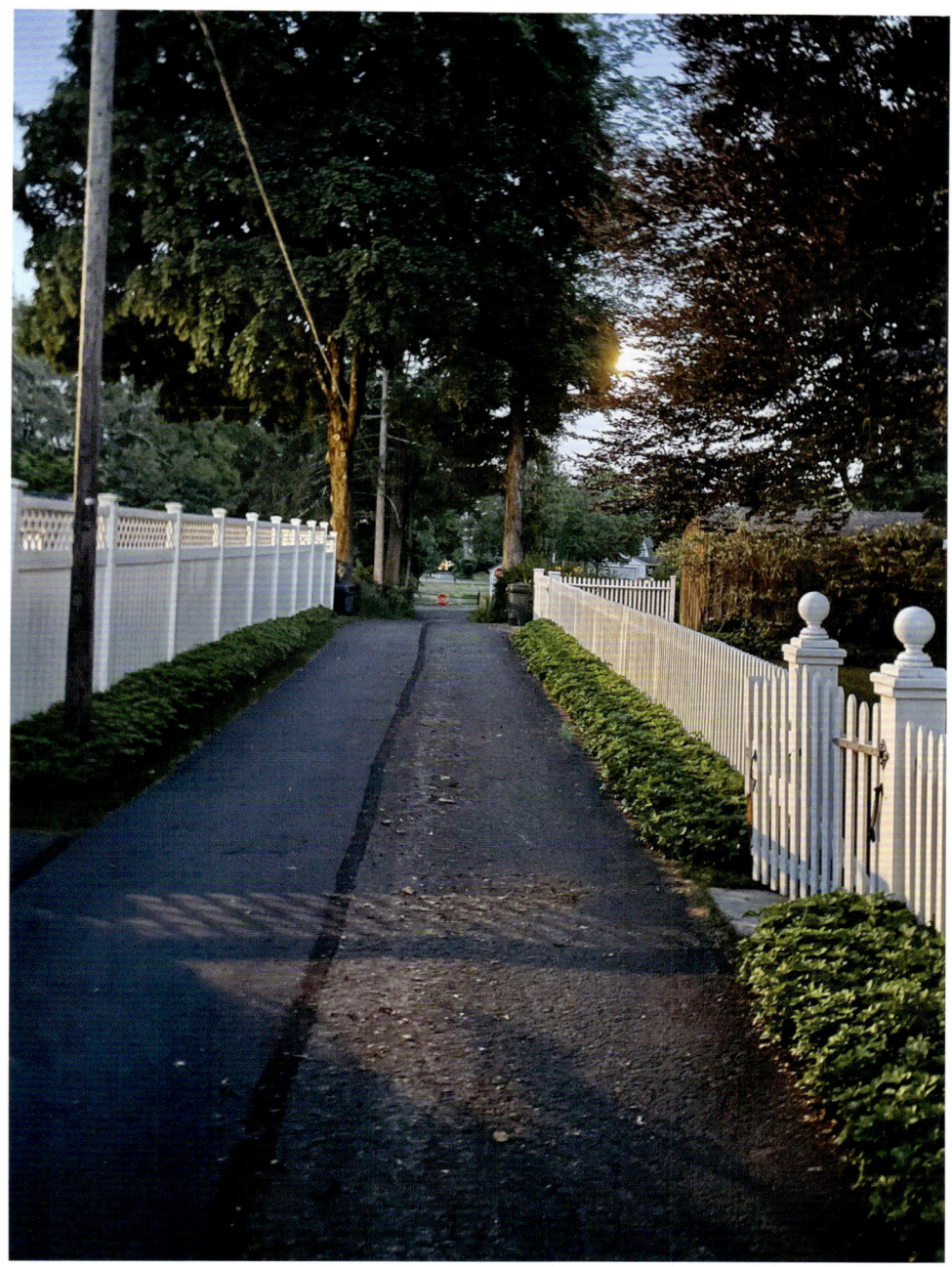

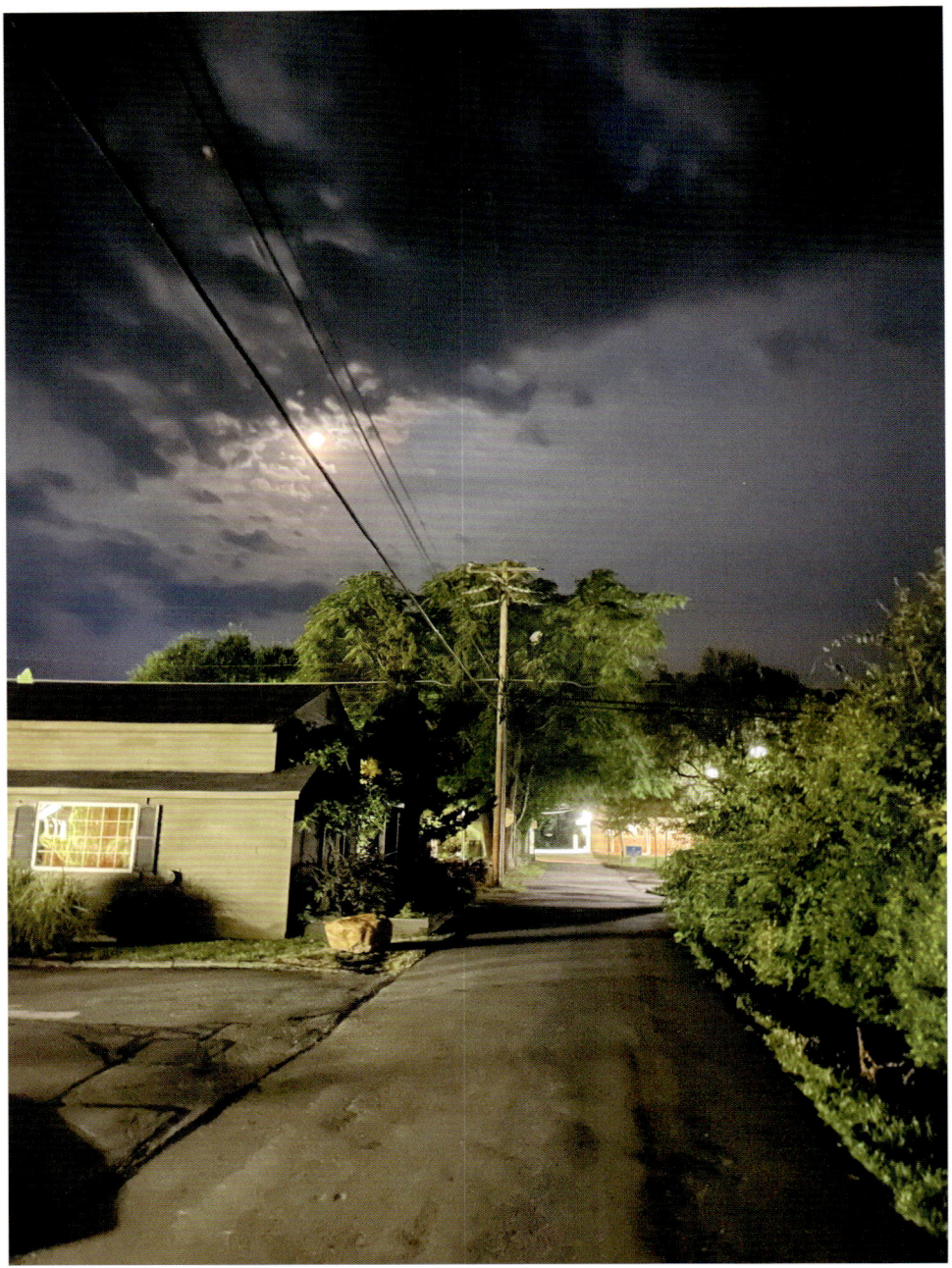

If you pick up a copy of *Grimms' Fairy Tales*, you will be struck by how many boys and girls, princes and princesses, are trying to find their path through a dark forest or are forced to choose their way forward when they come across a fork in the road.

There is good reason for that.

The path—as an image—is the perfect symbol for our journey into life and the unknown. It has always been a meaningful image for me. When I was a junior at Sarah Lawrence College, I didn't have the funds to go home over the Christmas break. I instead apartment-sat a 1920s Bronxville walkup, watering plants and taking in mail, all while working the graveyard shift at the central security desk of the closed and abandoned college admissions office.

I was nineteen and it was a difficult and lonely time. I yearned for a better future. But I consoled myself by doing what I always do: I relied on my imagination to transport me somewhere else, somewhere better. Whenever possible, I took out an artist pad and some colored chalk and scribbled furiously across the page.

Oddly, I kept on sketching the same image again and again.

A monotonous path stretched diagonally across a barren landscape, vanishing in the distance. The path or road was always heading toward lush mountains on the far horizon, which seemed to promise something better, or at least had signs of life and vitality. Now, look-ing back, I realize the mountains had an uncanny resemblance to the Knob, the ridge that overlooks Milford. High up and slightly to the right of my path-transversed drawings, a massive cross stood atop the mountain ridge, and depending on what mood I was in, the cross either stood tall, a beacon seemingly calling me forward toward something majestic, or it was in flames, signaling distress.

Well, I am in my sixties now, not a man-child anymore, but as you will see in these photographs of Milford, I am still searching for my path into the future—this time, of course, into my final years on earth. The images I have captured in these pages, showing me my path forward, do not strike me as particularly distressed or unpleasant.

They seem peaceful.

Maybe somewhat uncertain.

At times they might hint at the mystery of what is yet to come.

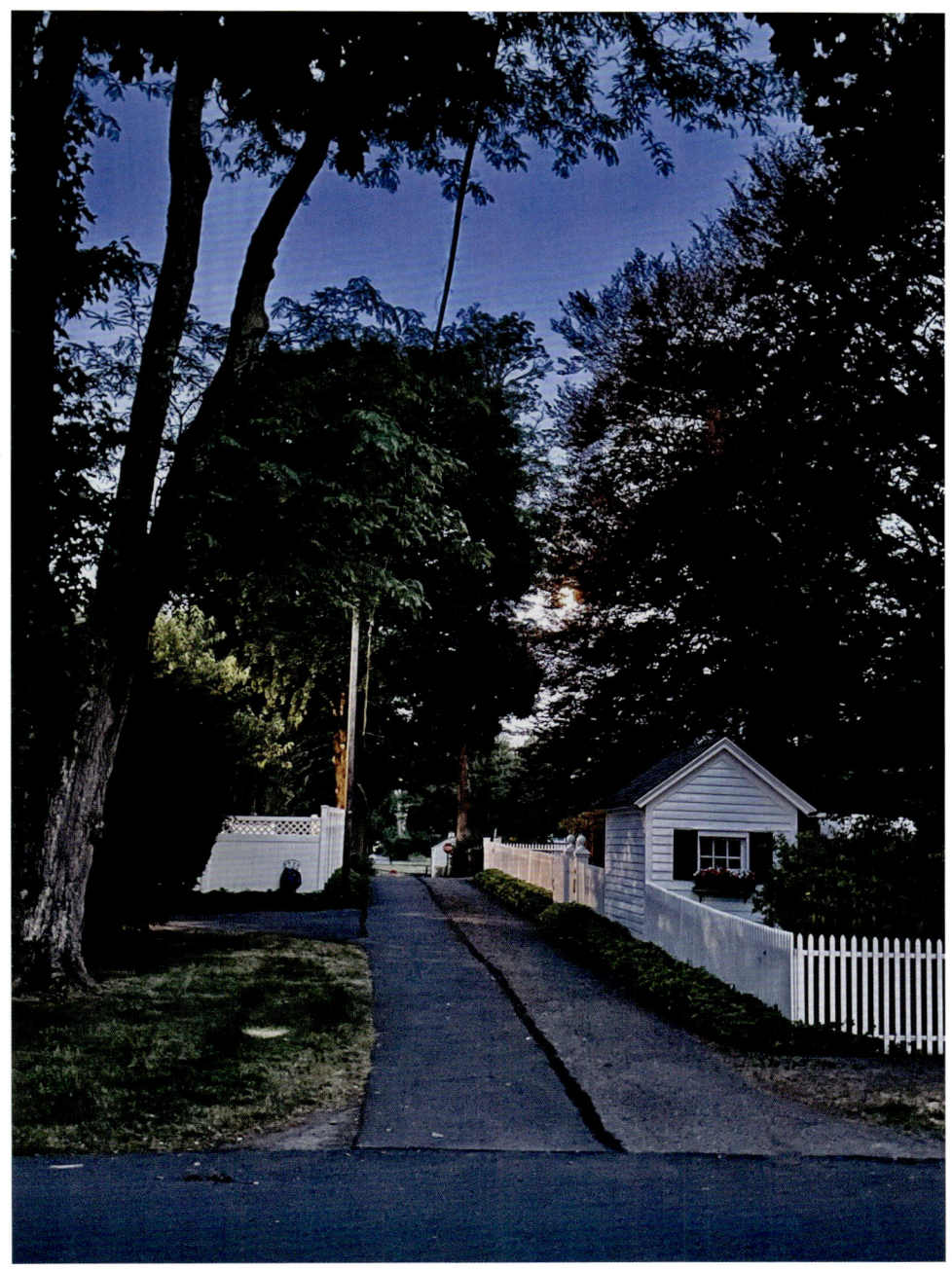

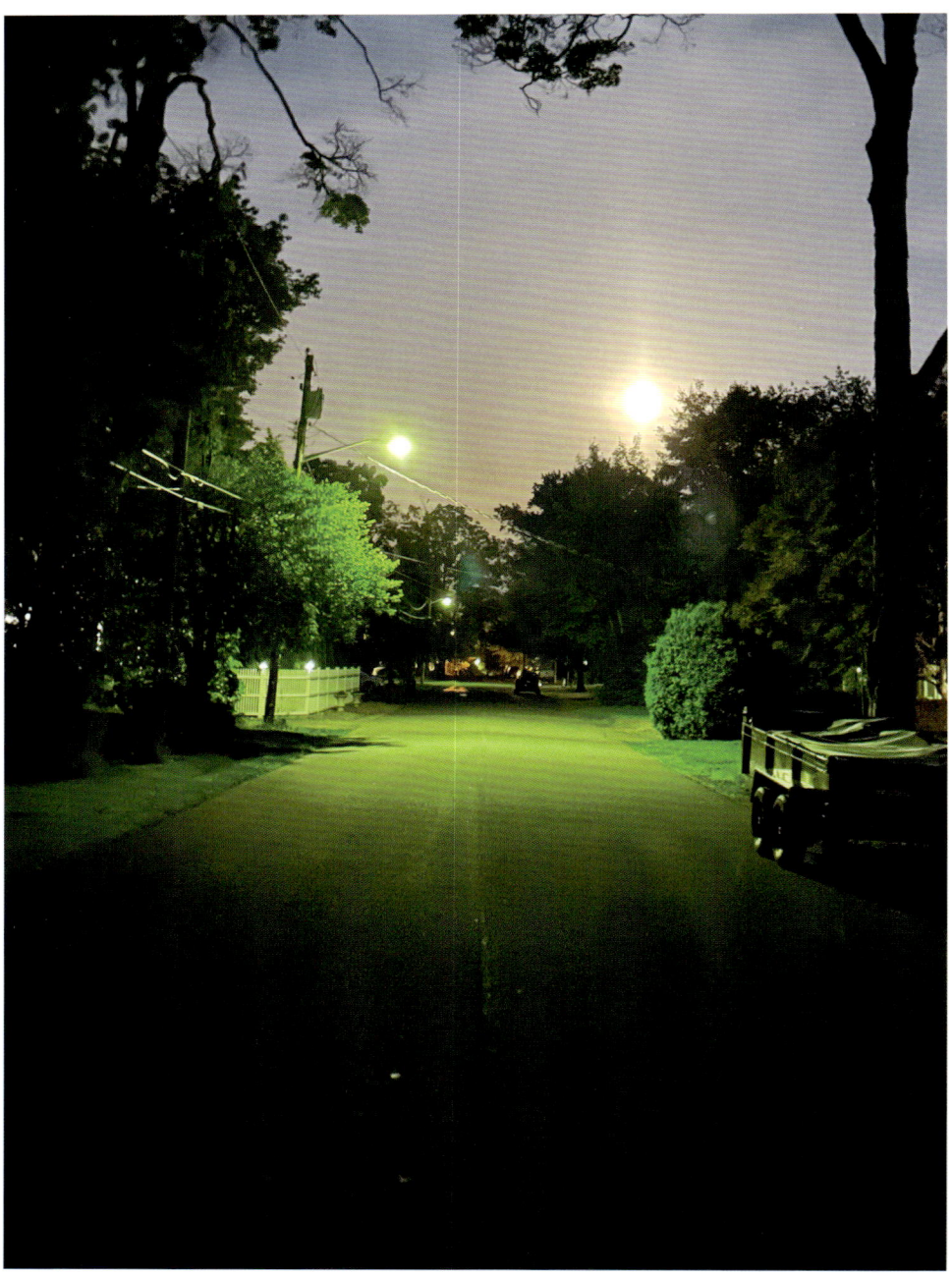

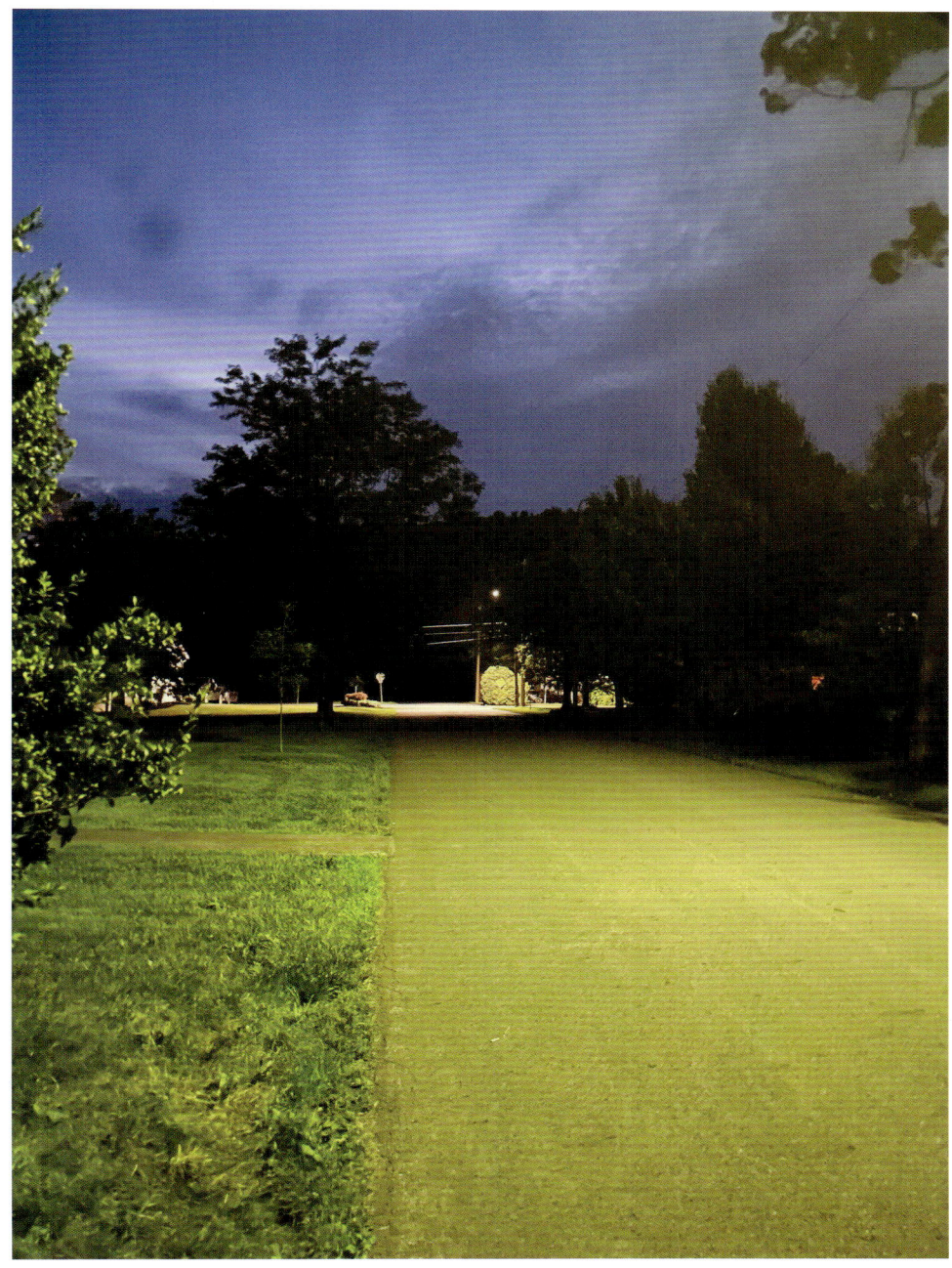

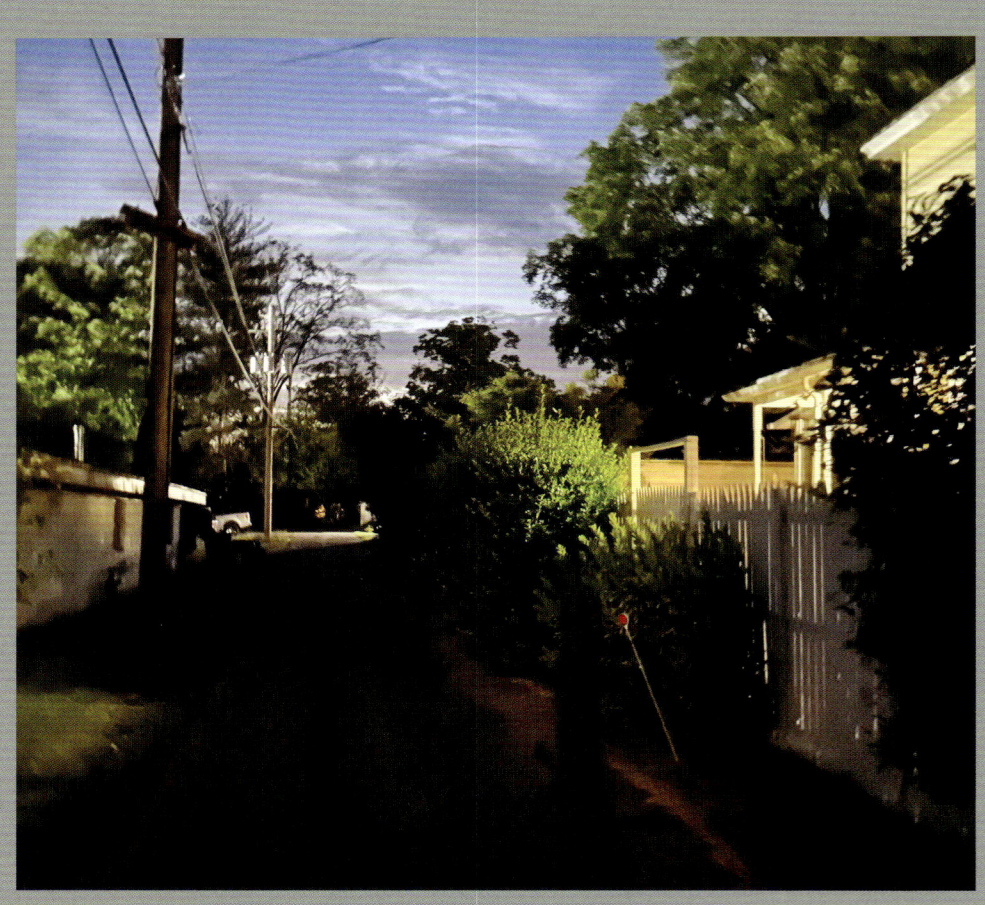

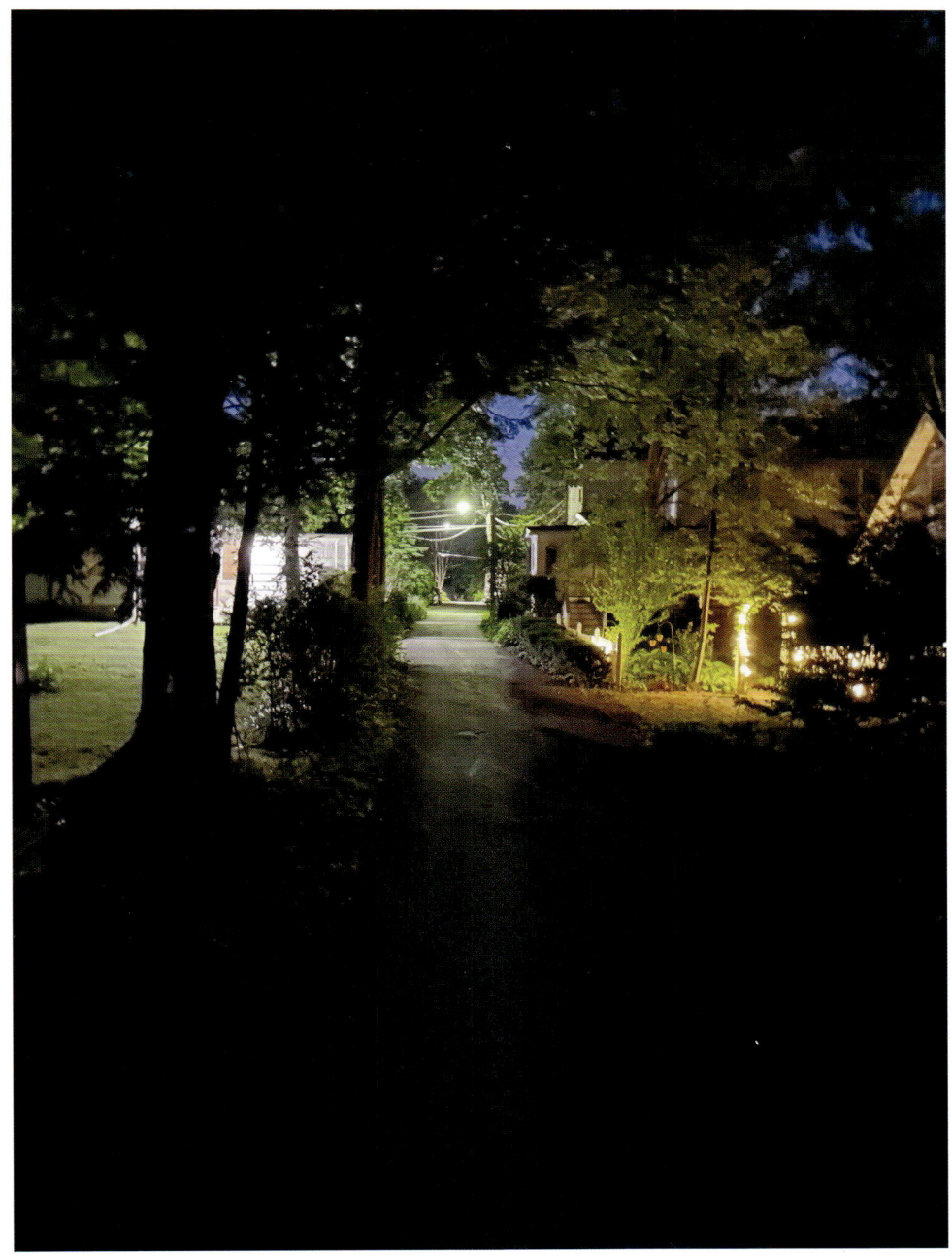

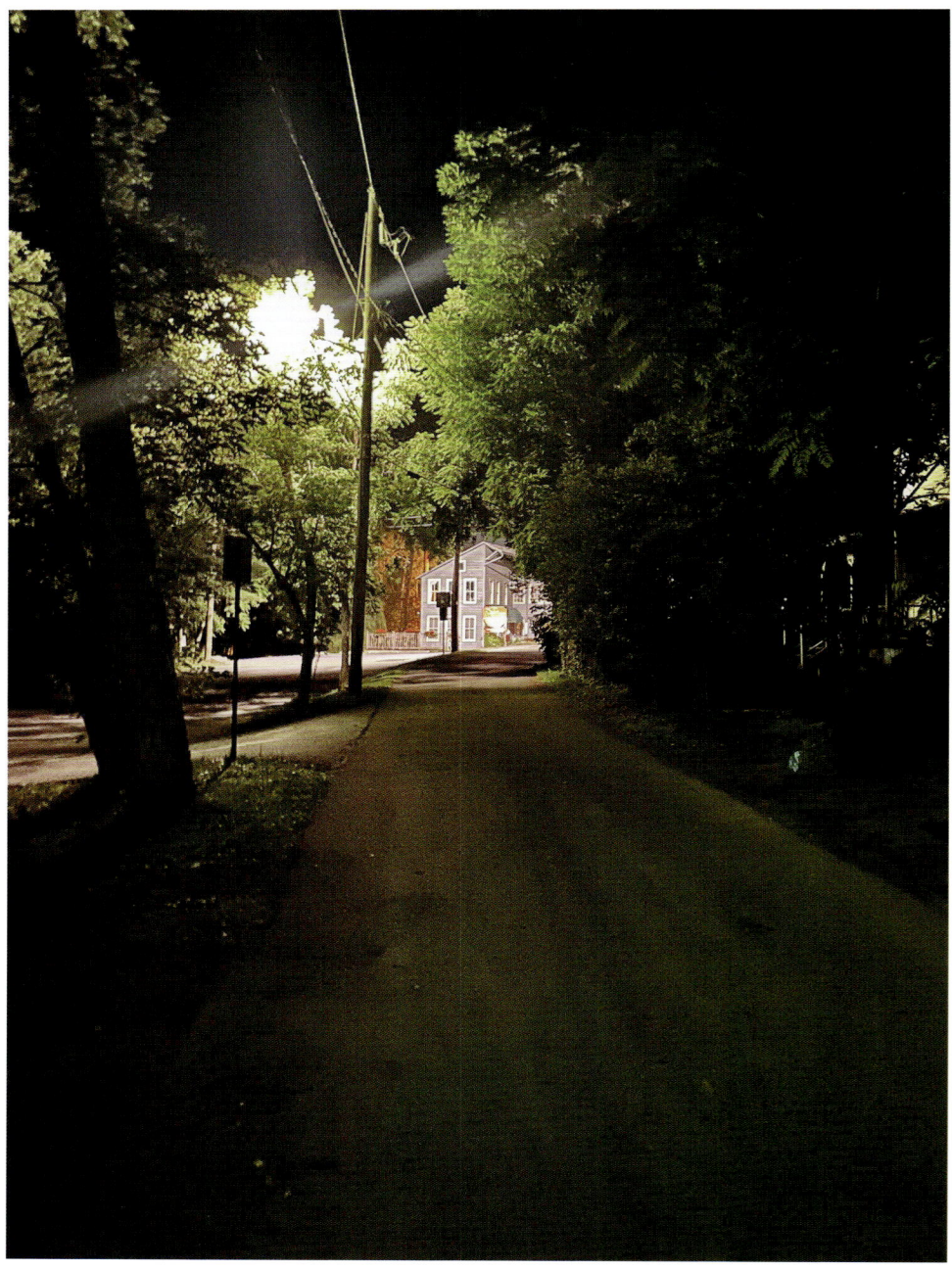

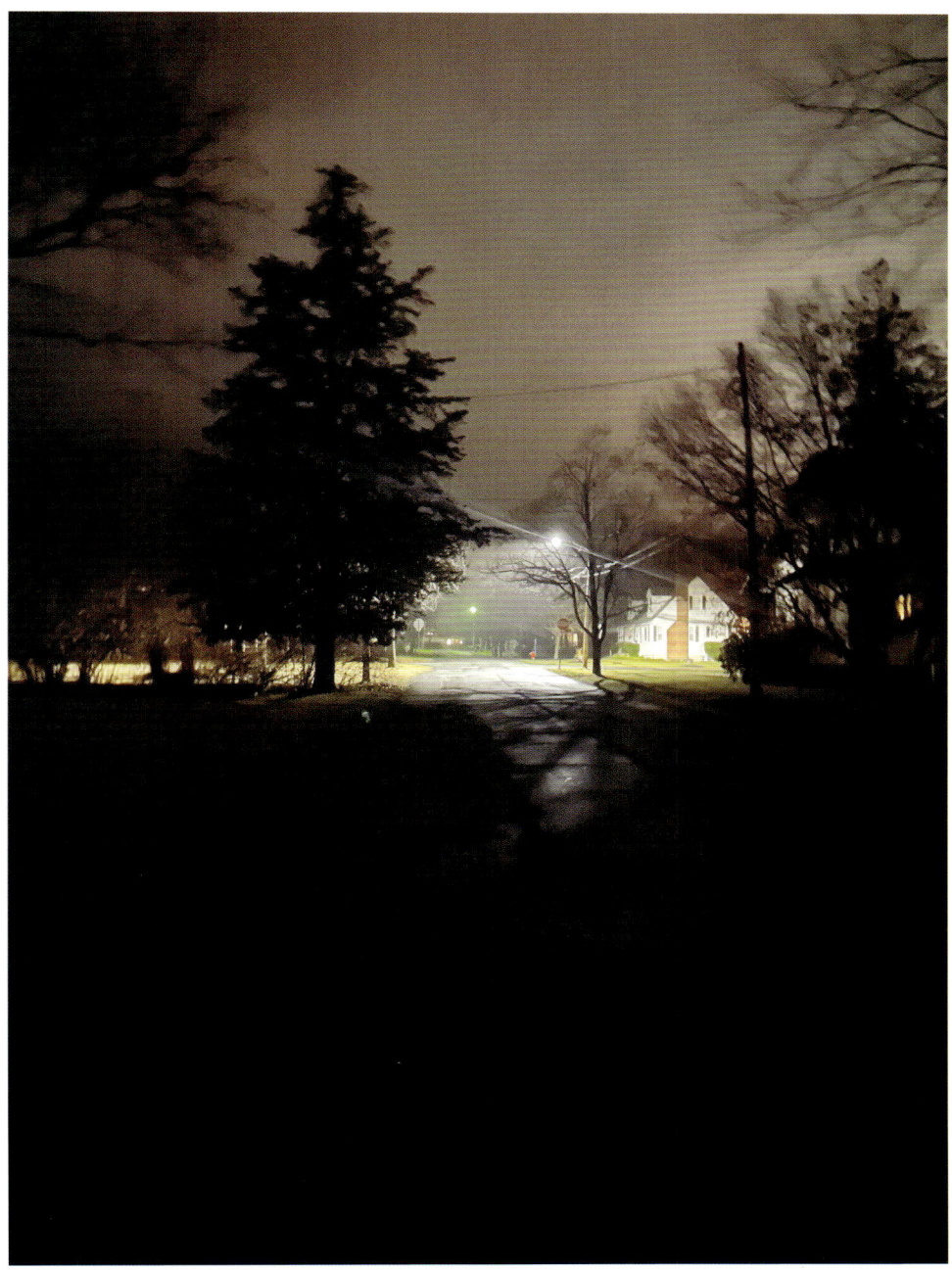

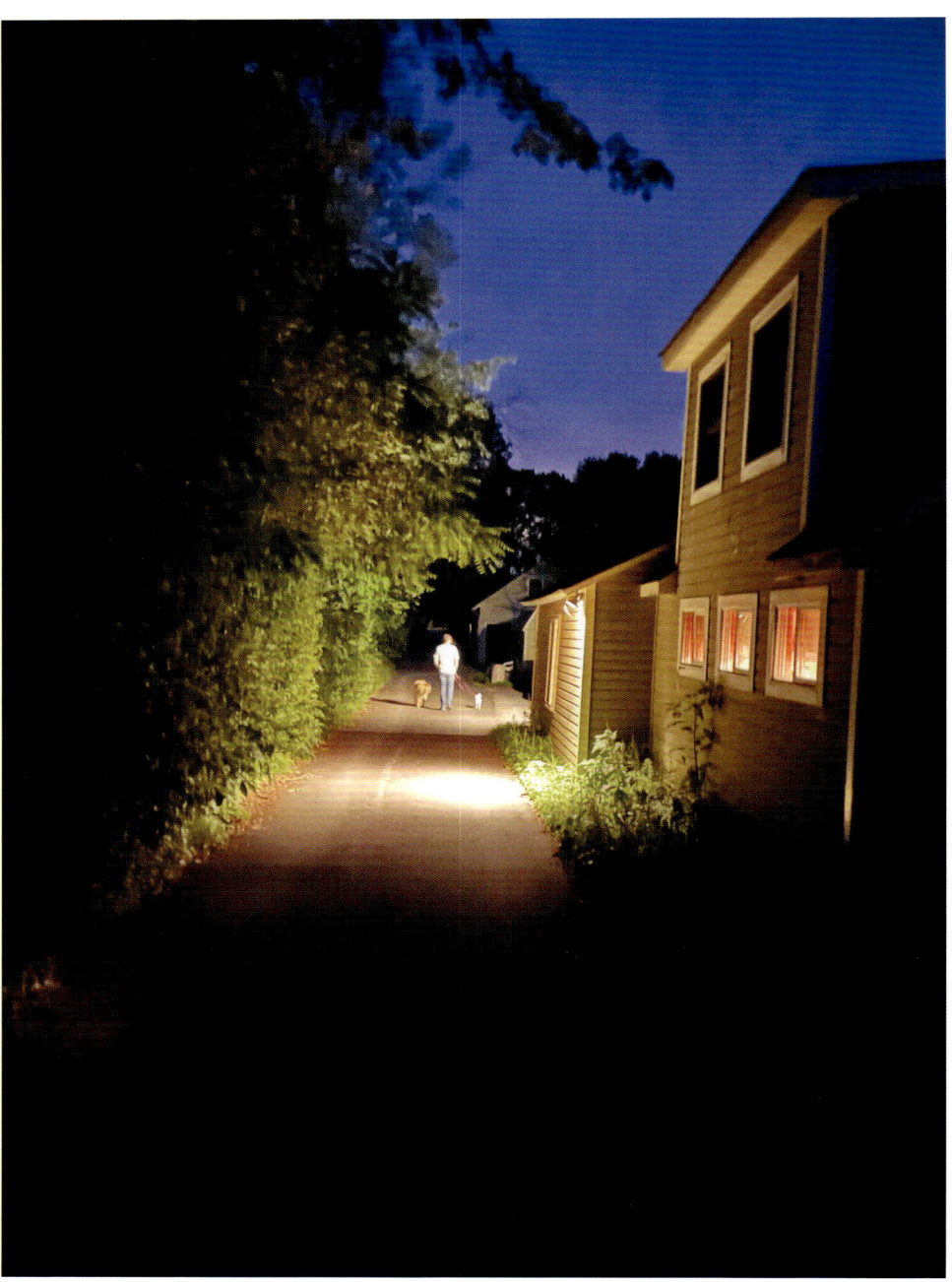

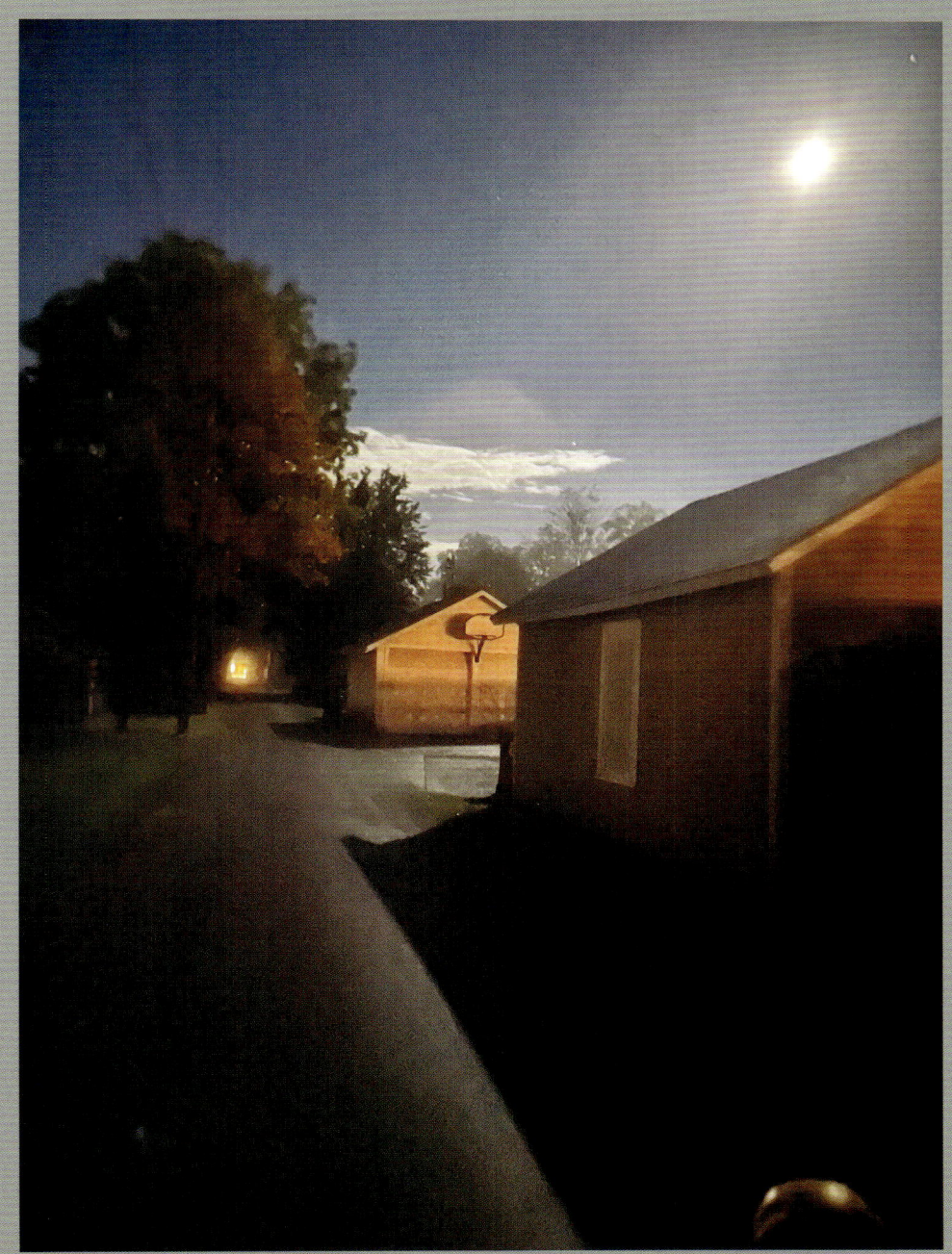

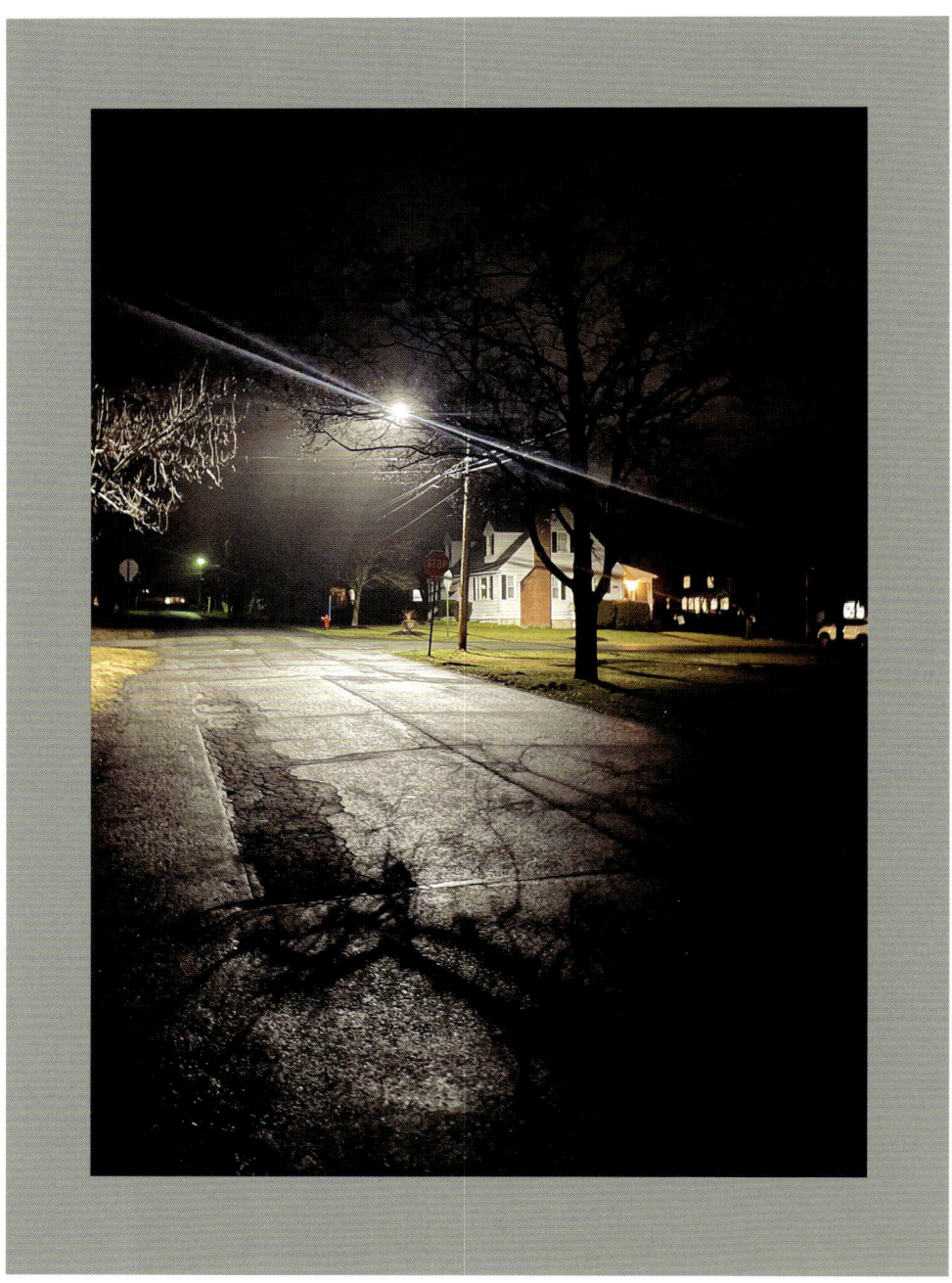

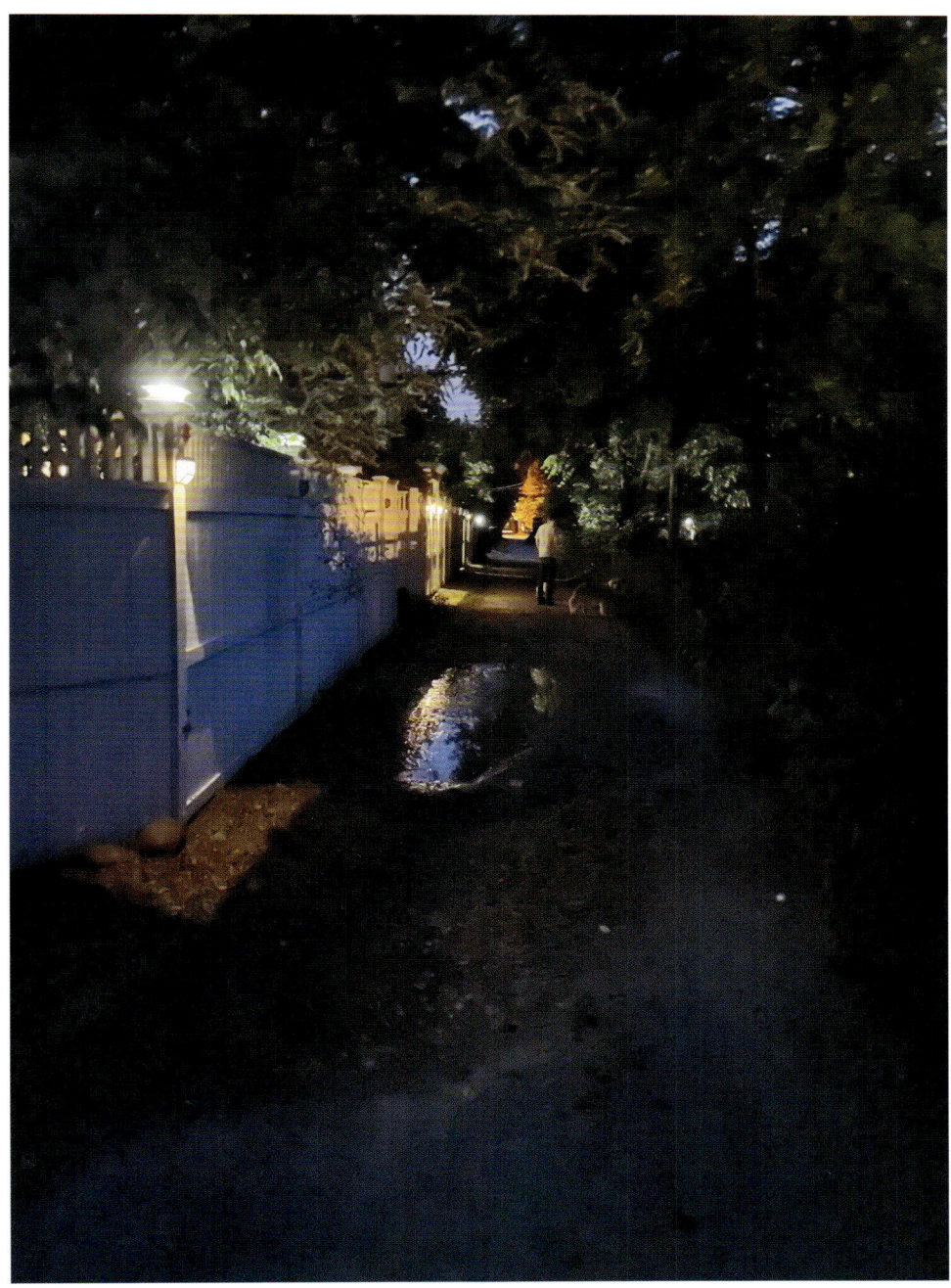

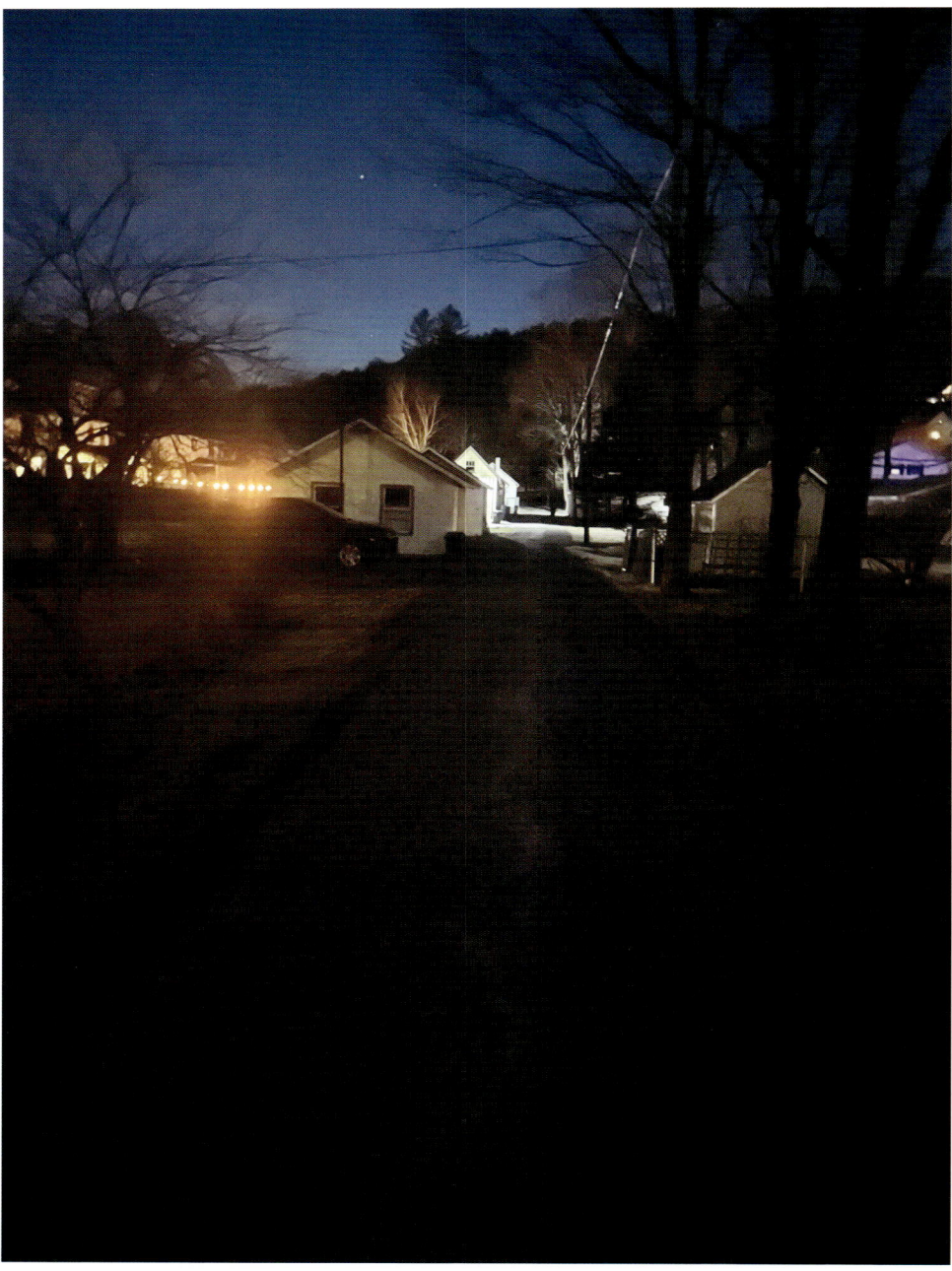

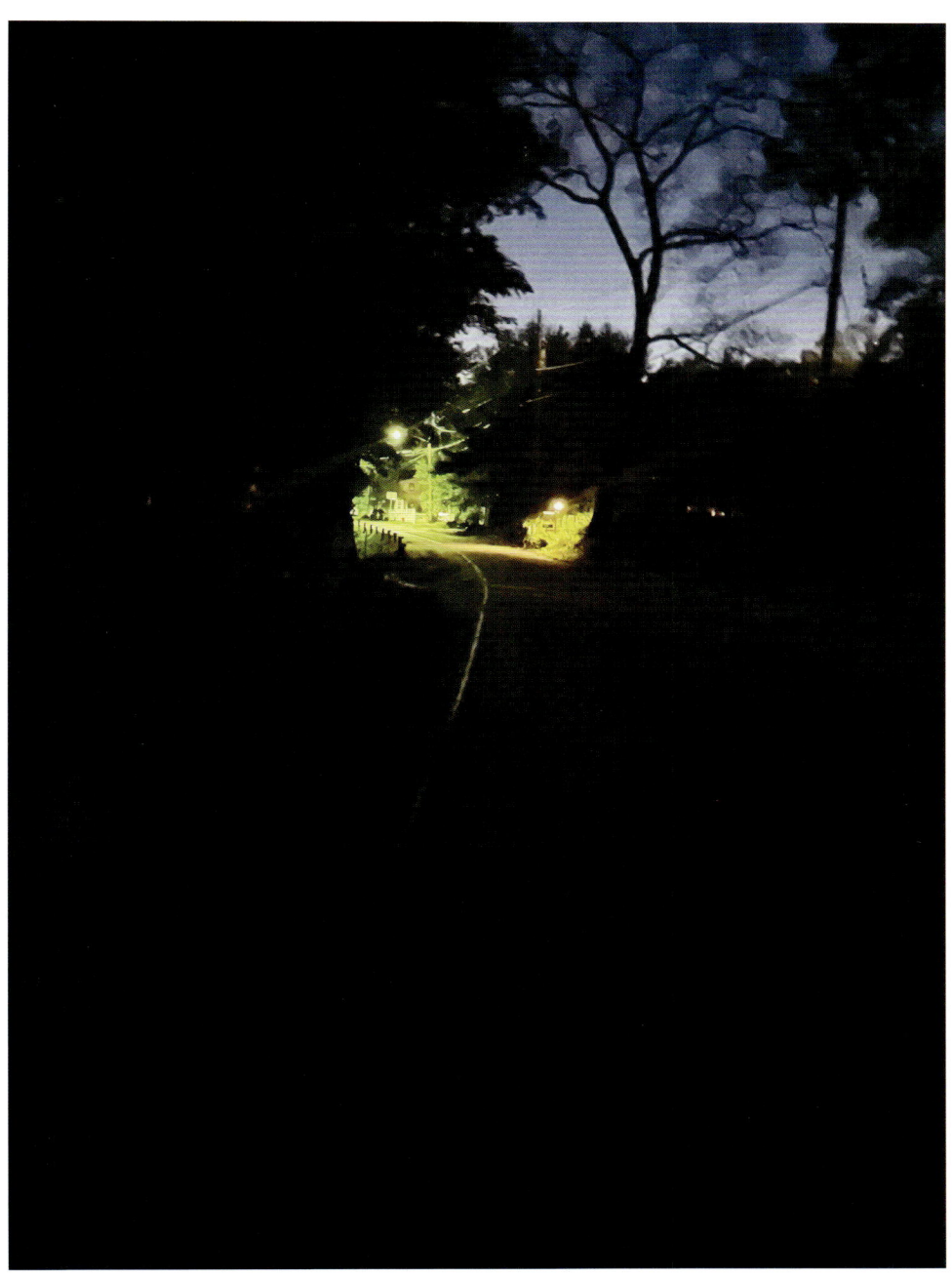

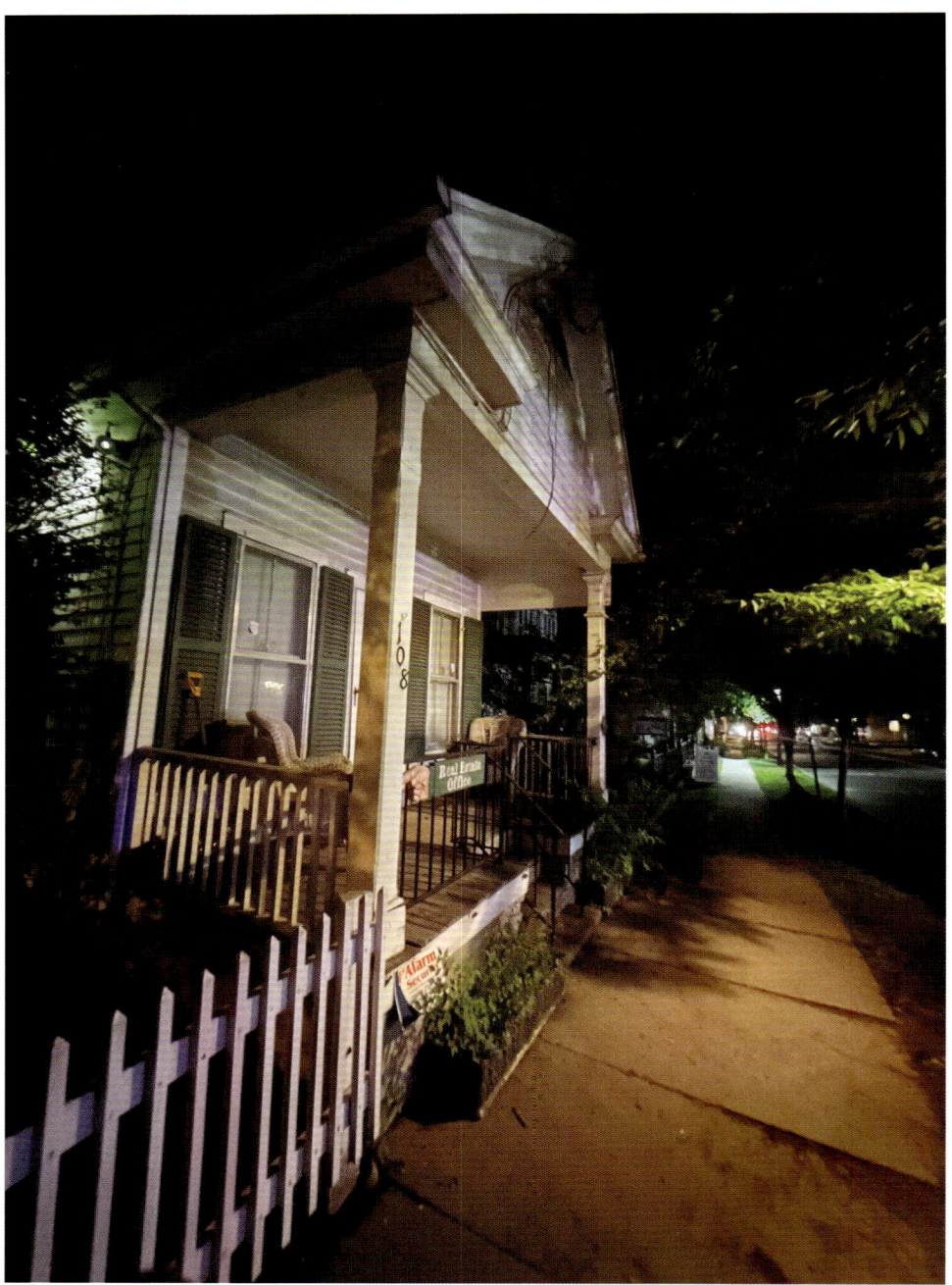

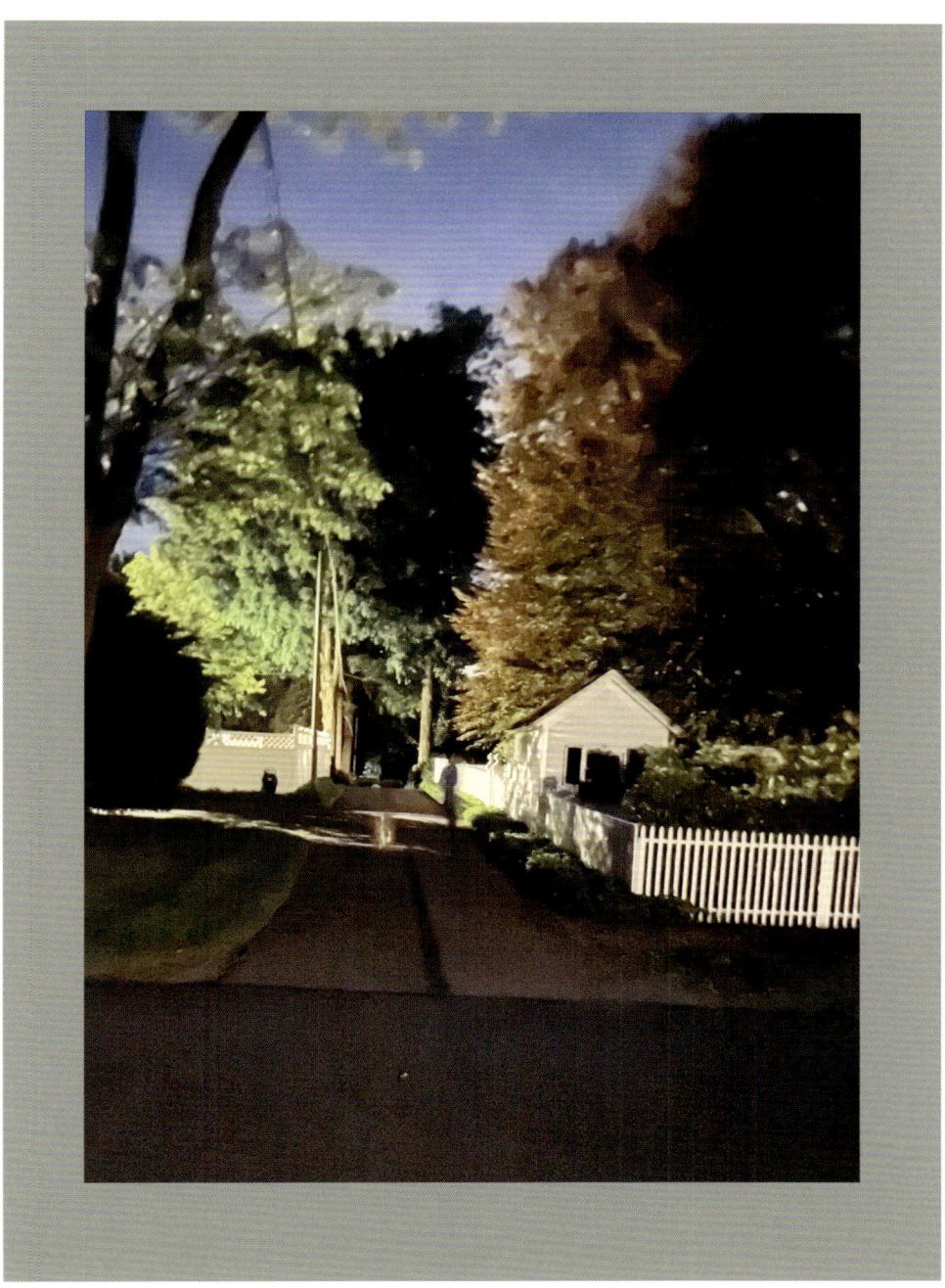

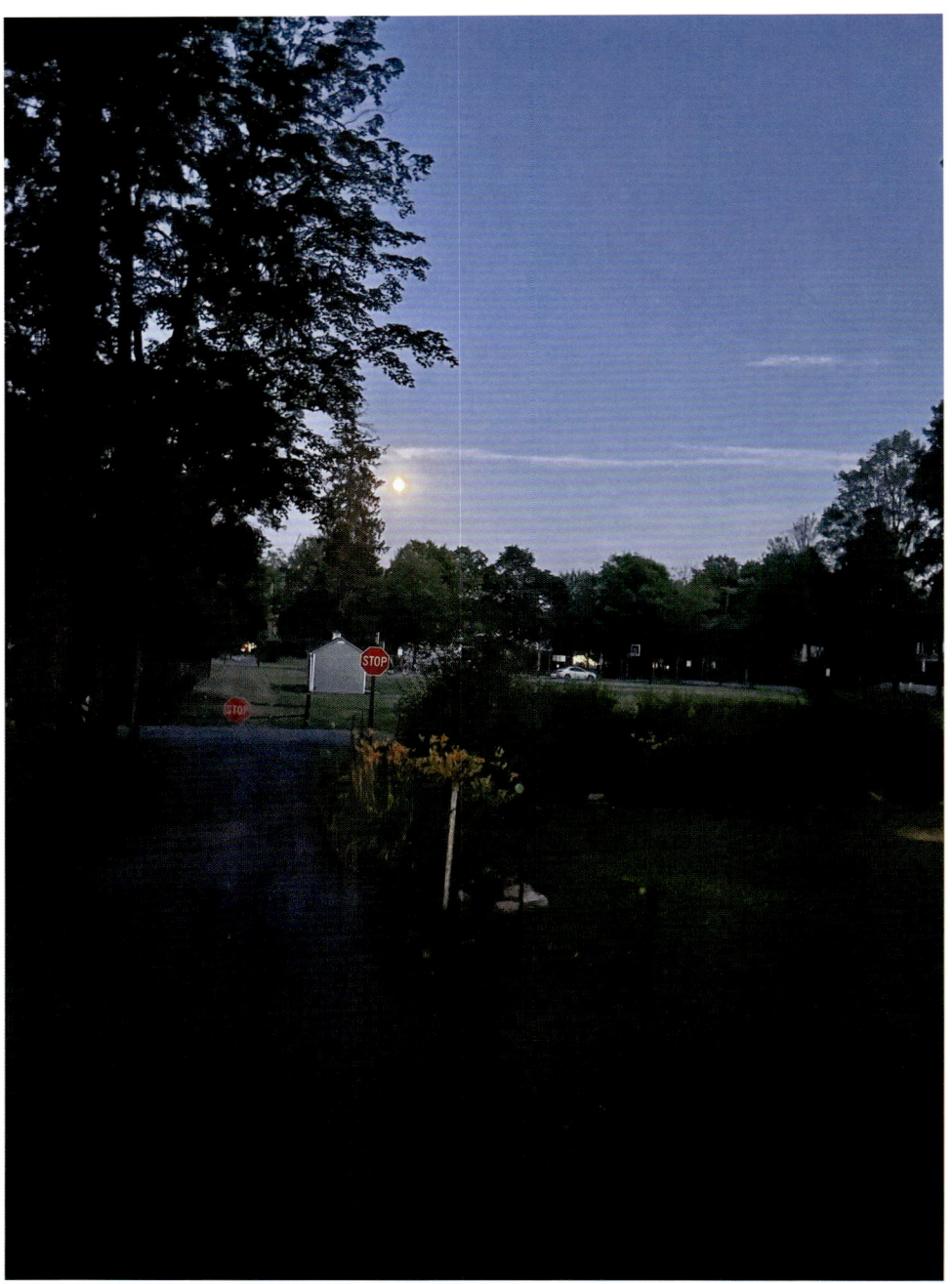

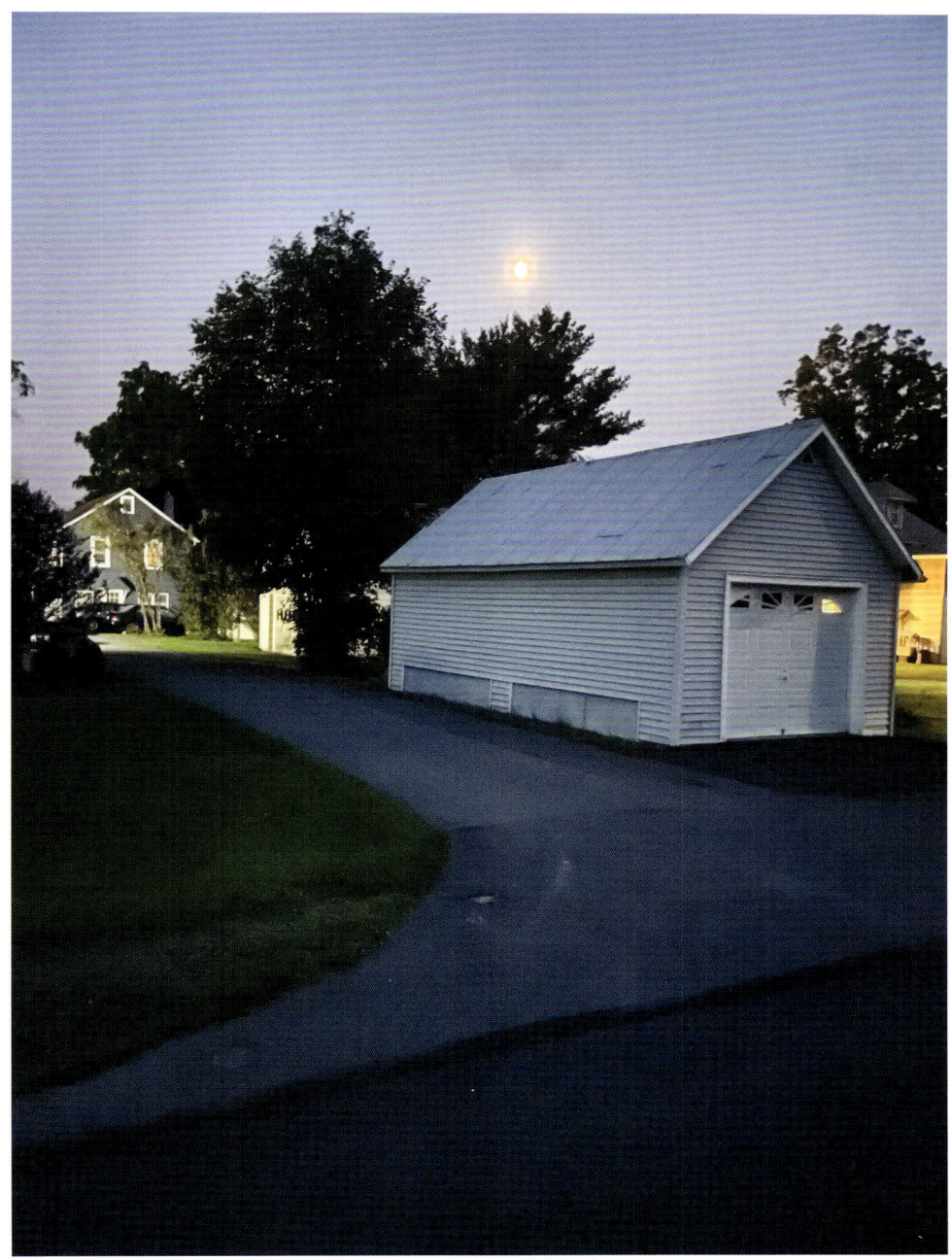

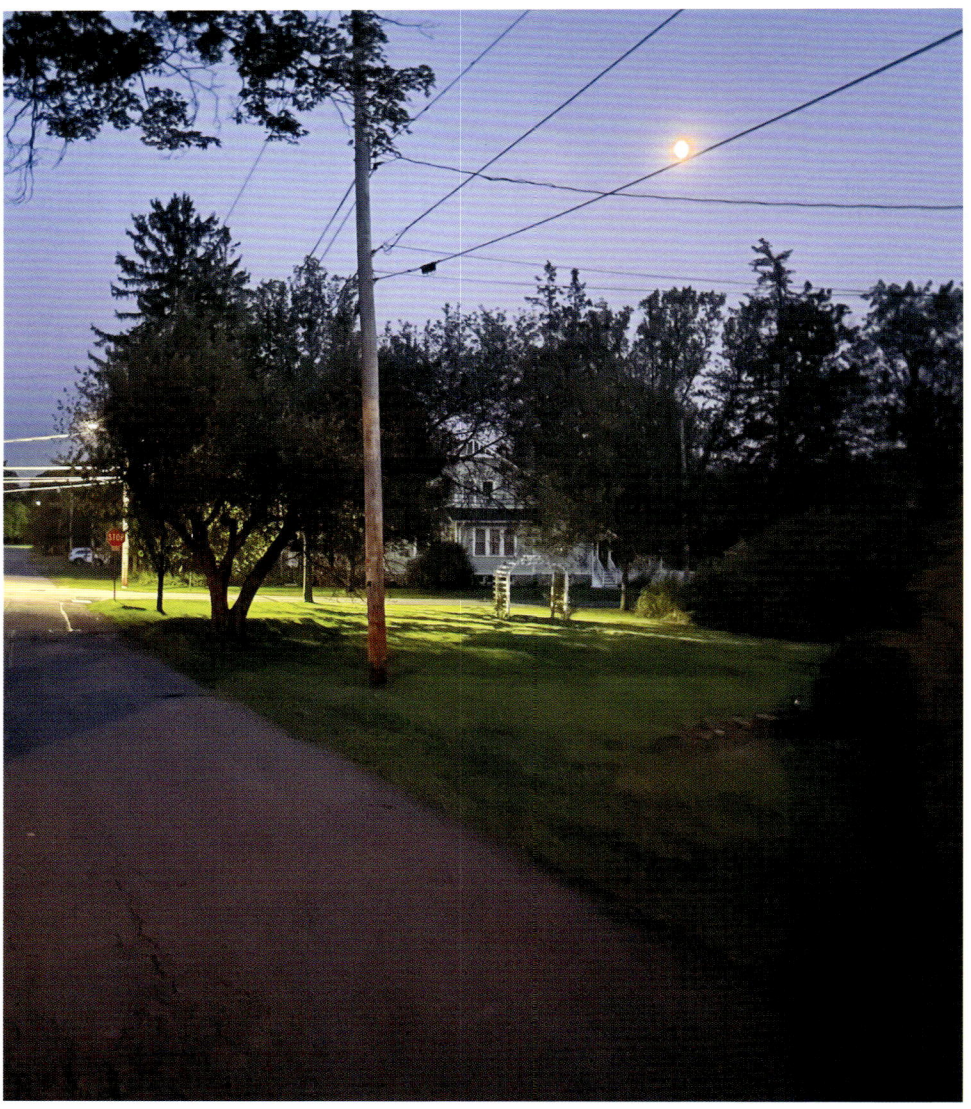

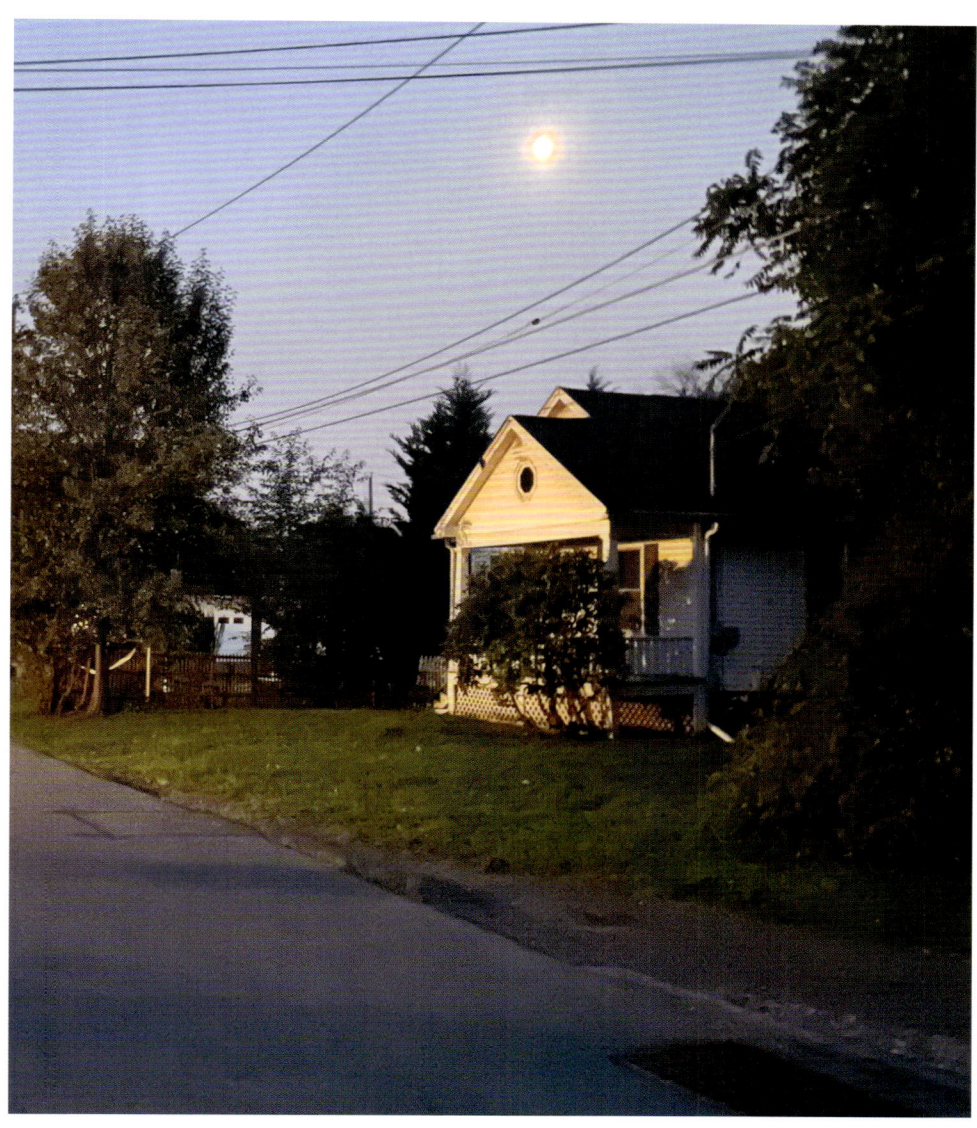

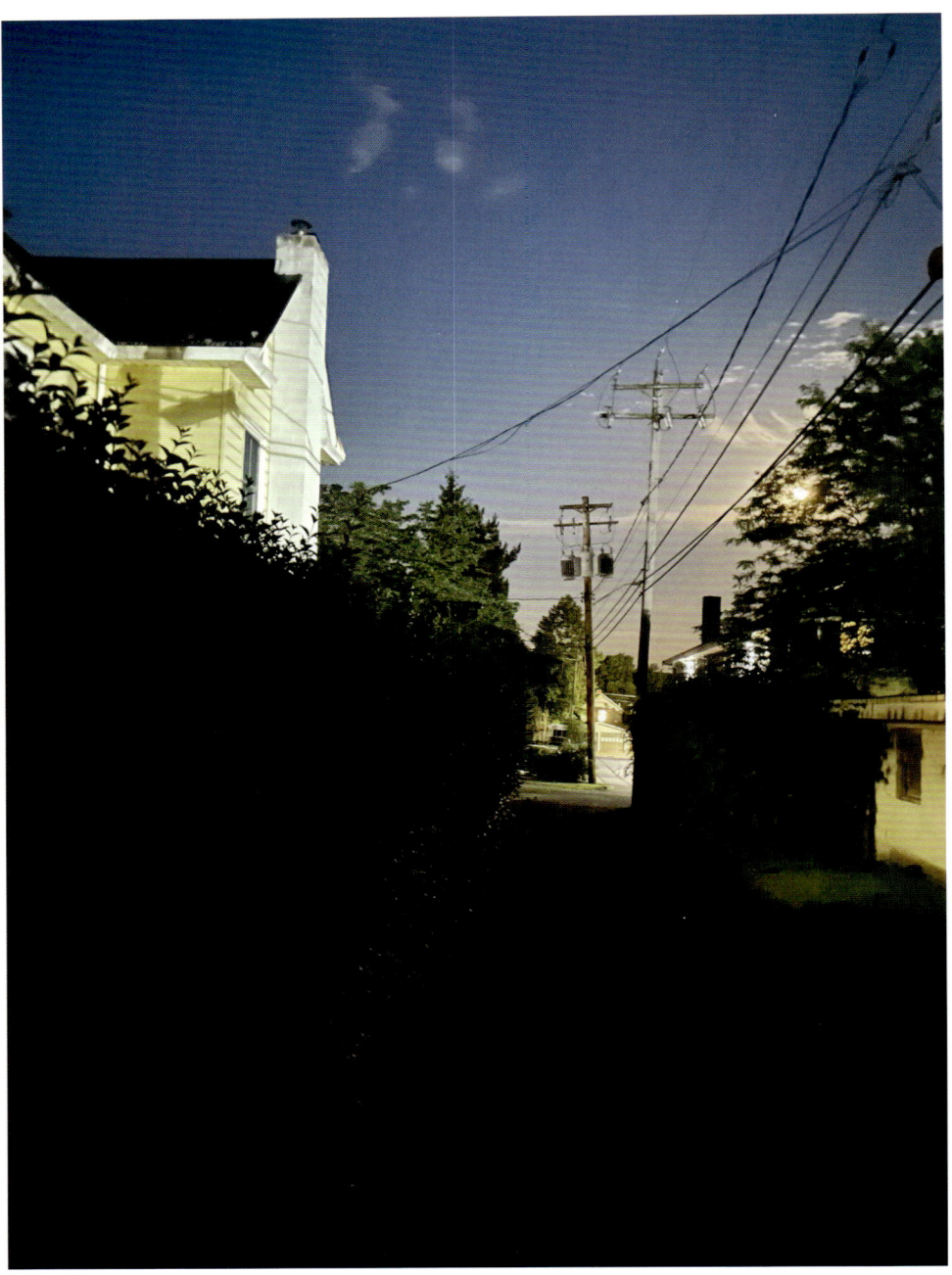

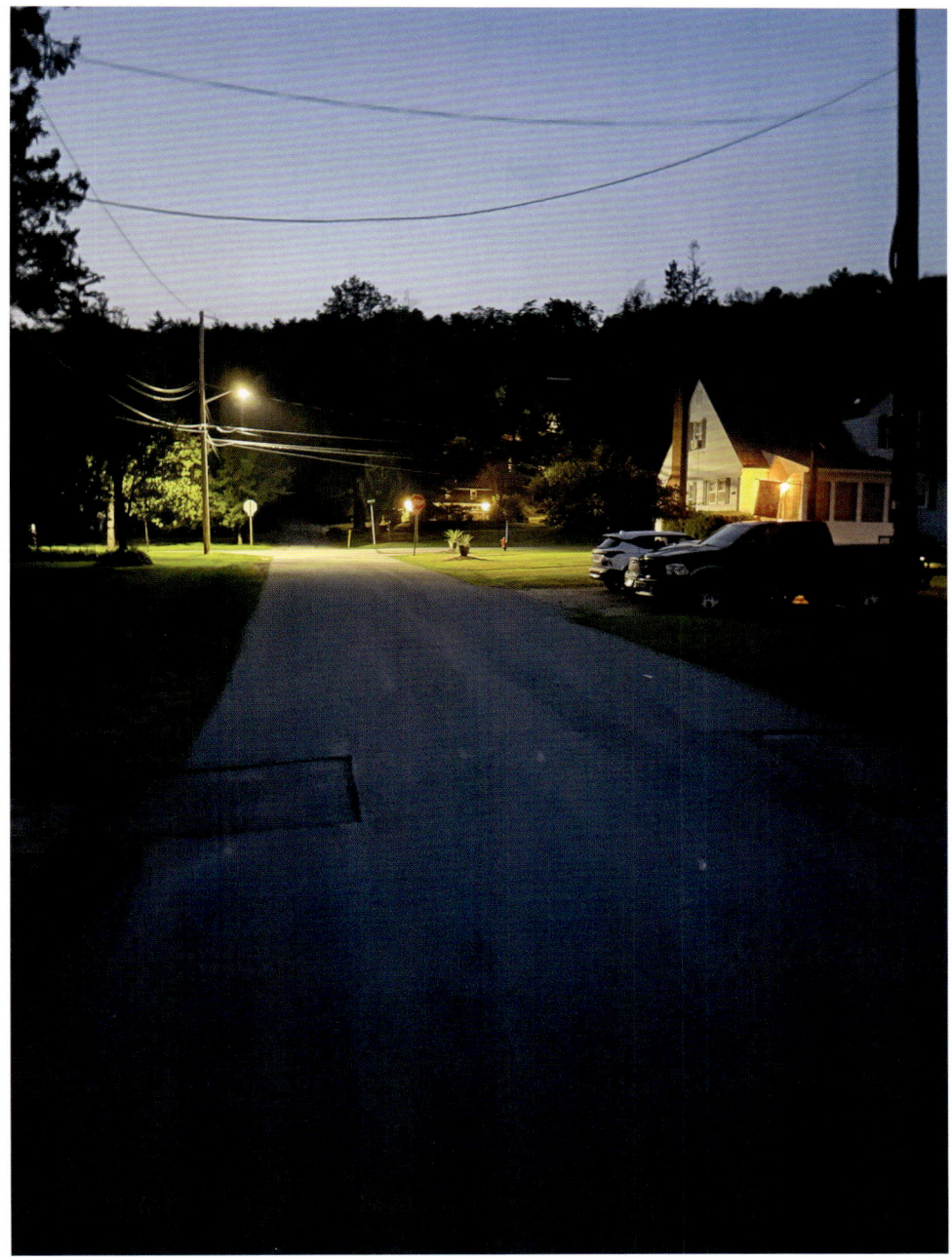

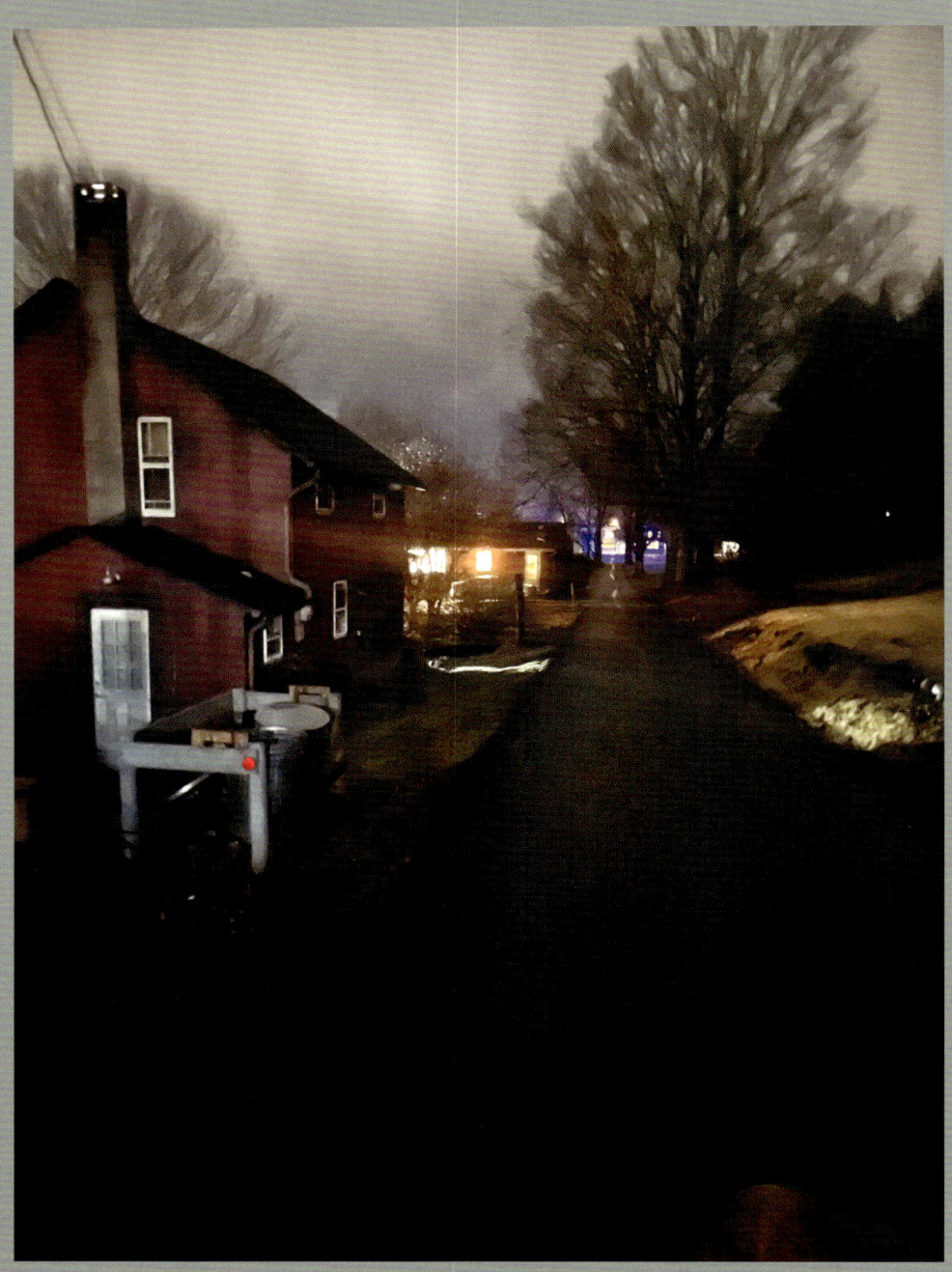

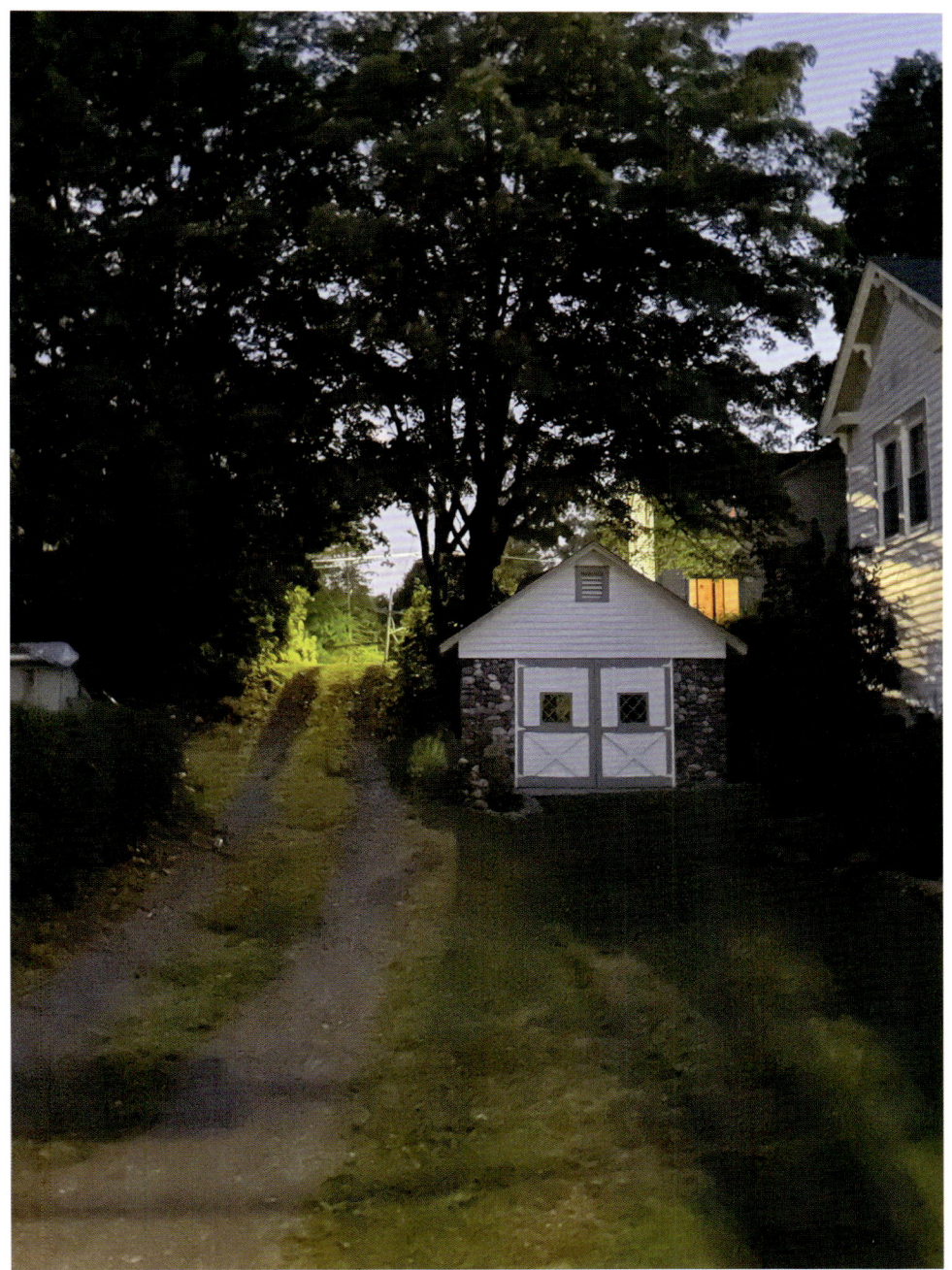

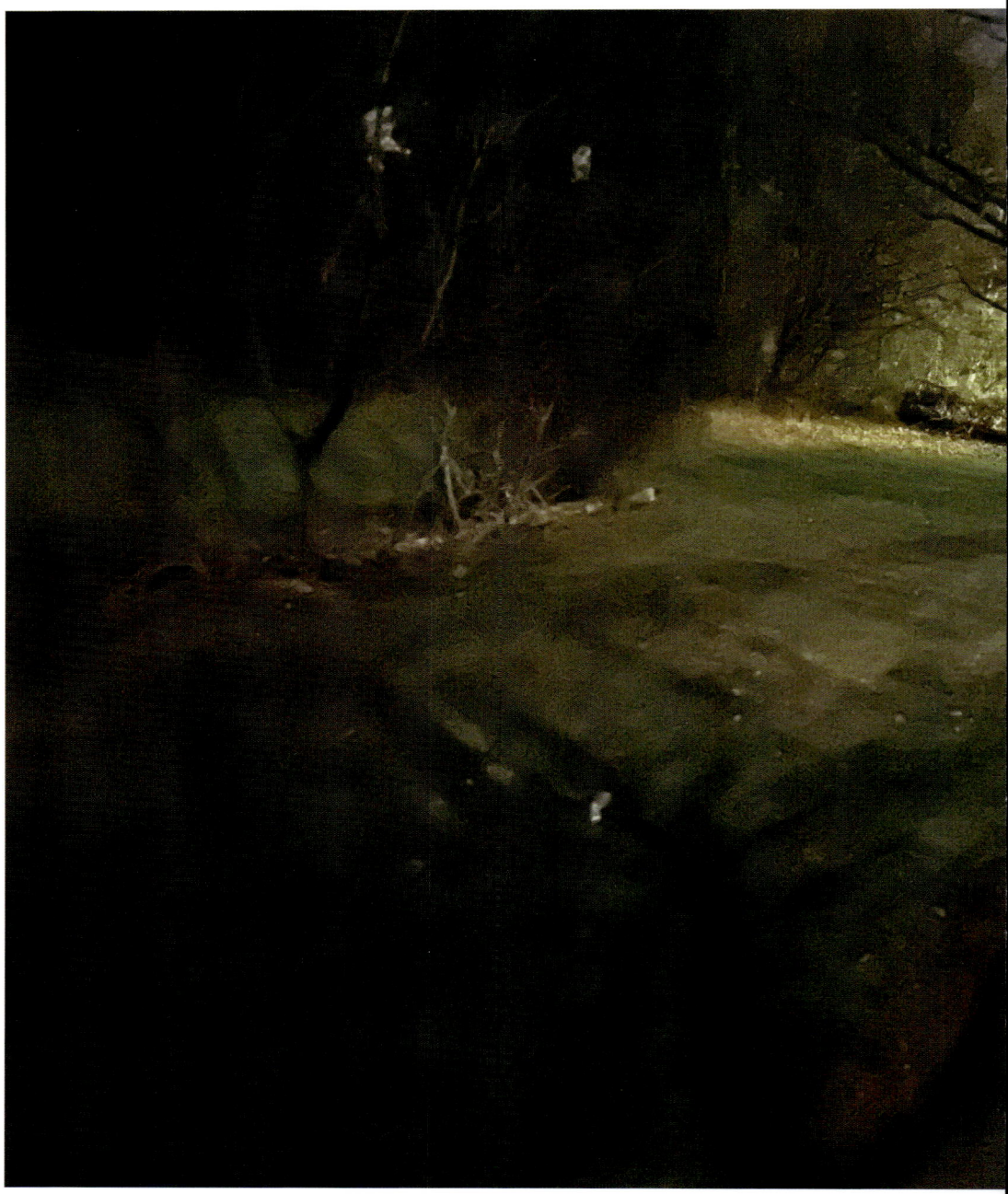

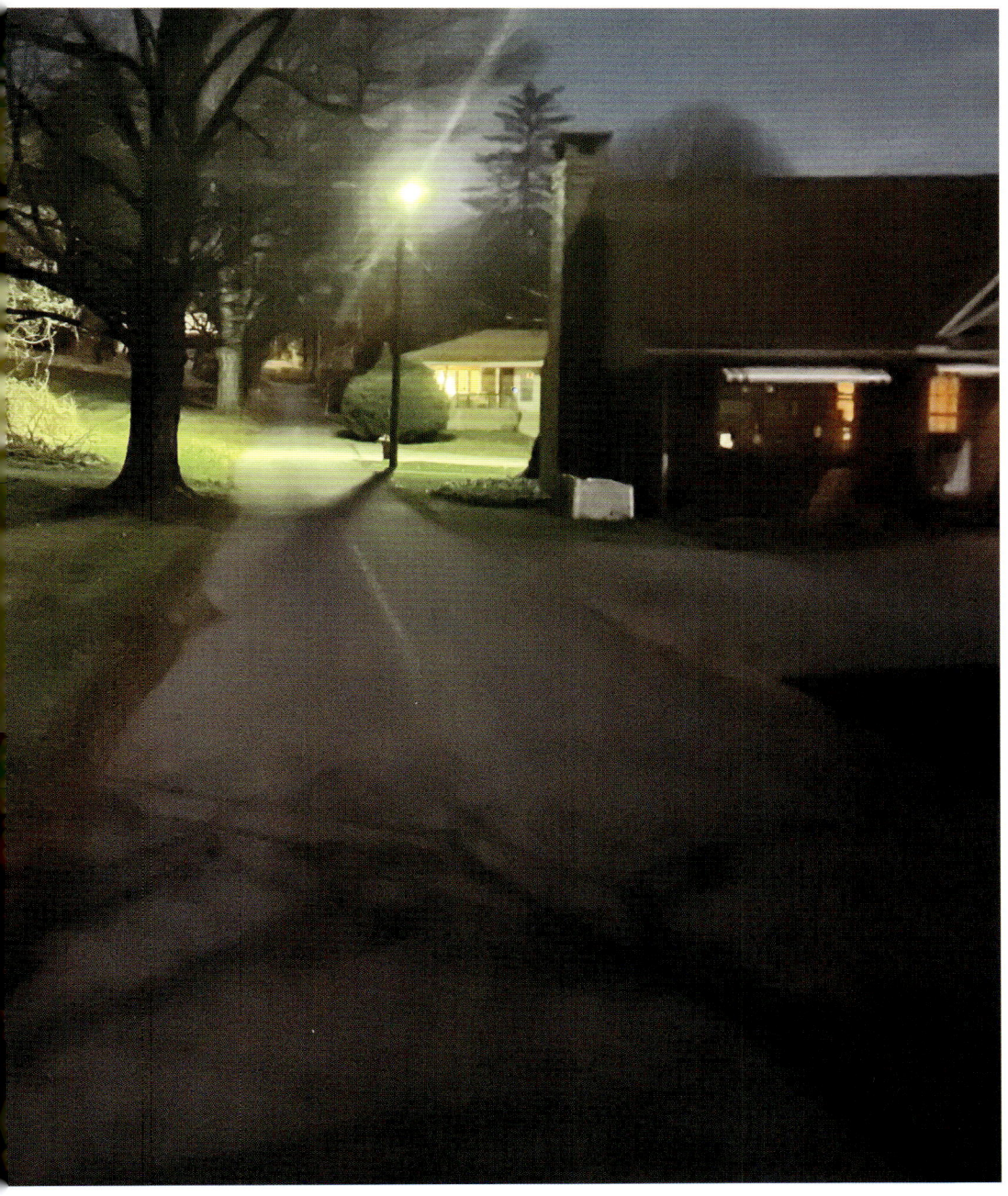

AFTERHOURS

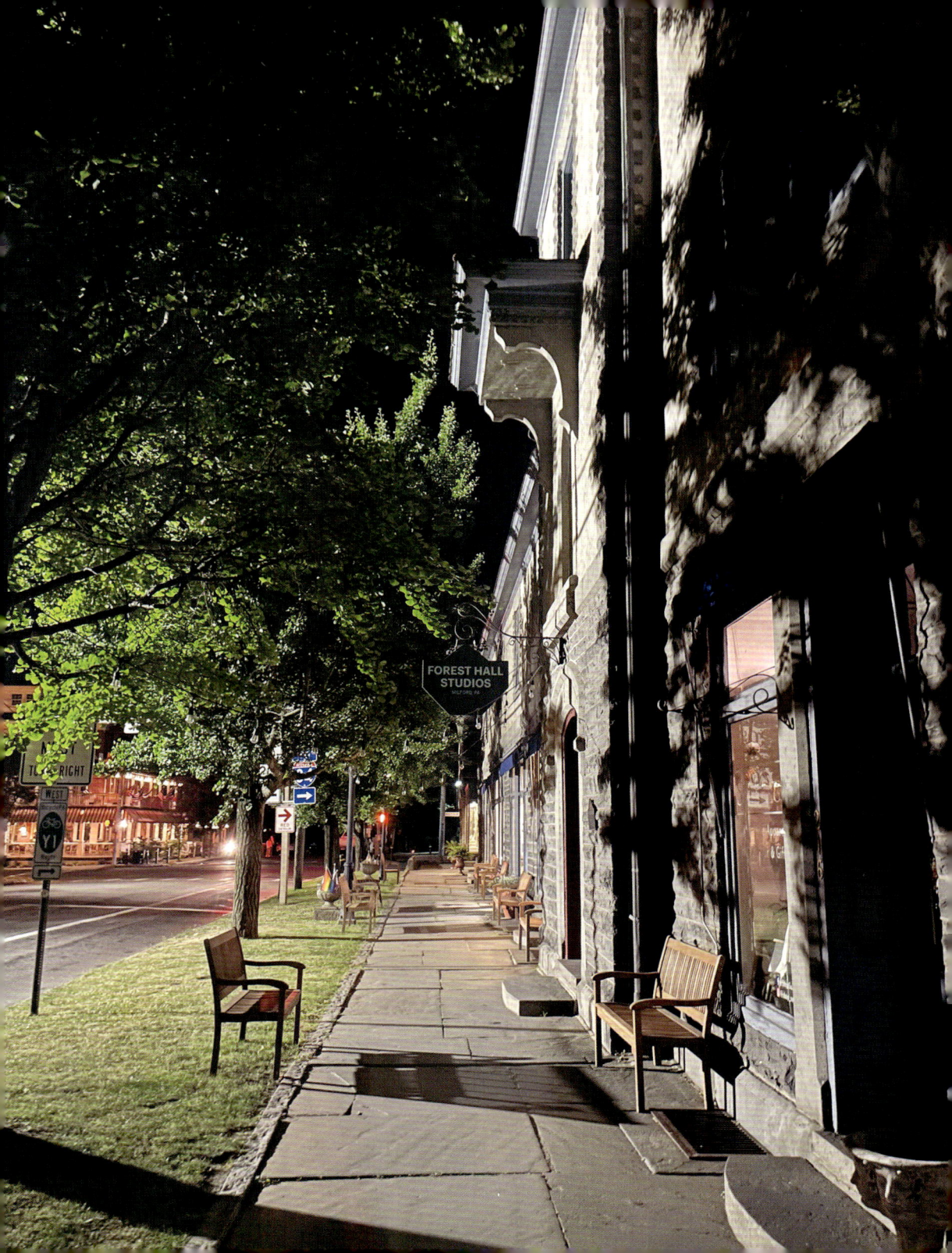

The early hours of the night, like the early years of adulthood, always produce in me a sense of excitement and promise. They make my pulse quicken. It is that time when, work complete, we are most social, full of bonhomie for our fellow man, drawn to good food, entertainment, wine—and the eternal promise of love and romance.

There is a 1954-published poem by Wallace Stevens called "Re-Statement of Romance," and it perfectly captures the possibility of love that the night can invoke in us. Stevens re-creates a time of the evening where we distinctly feel our separateness, feel our unique loneliness, but also this wonderous promise that we can, if lucky, also become one with someone we love.

Particularly when under a bright moon.

As Stevens writes—

> *Only we two are one, that I best perceive myself*
>
> *Not night and I, but you and I, alone*
>
> *So much alone, so deeply by ourselves,*
>
> *So far beyond the casual solitudes*

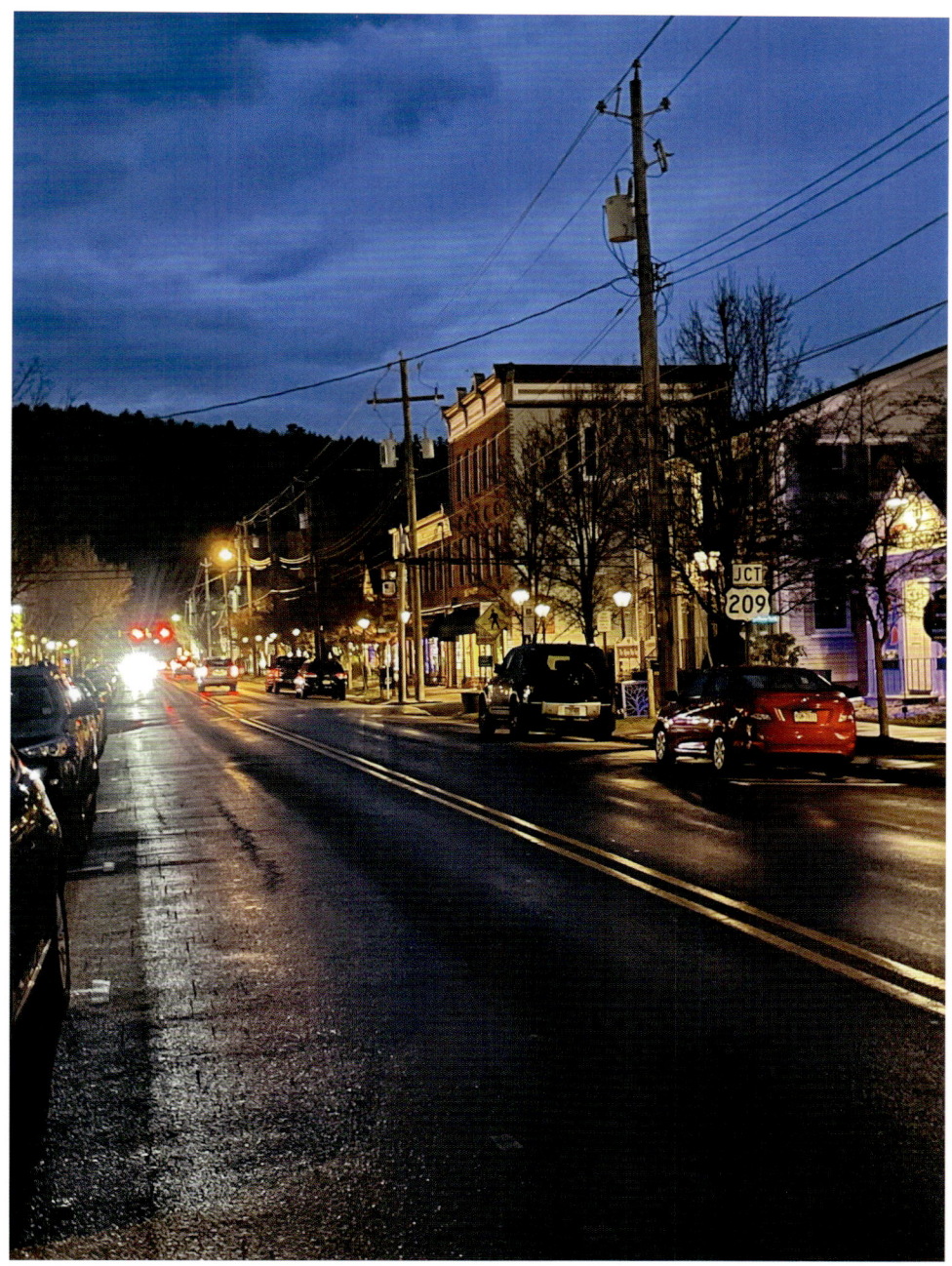

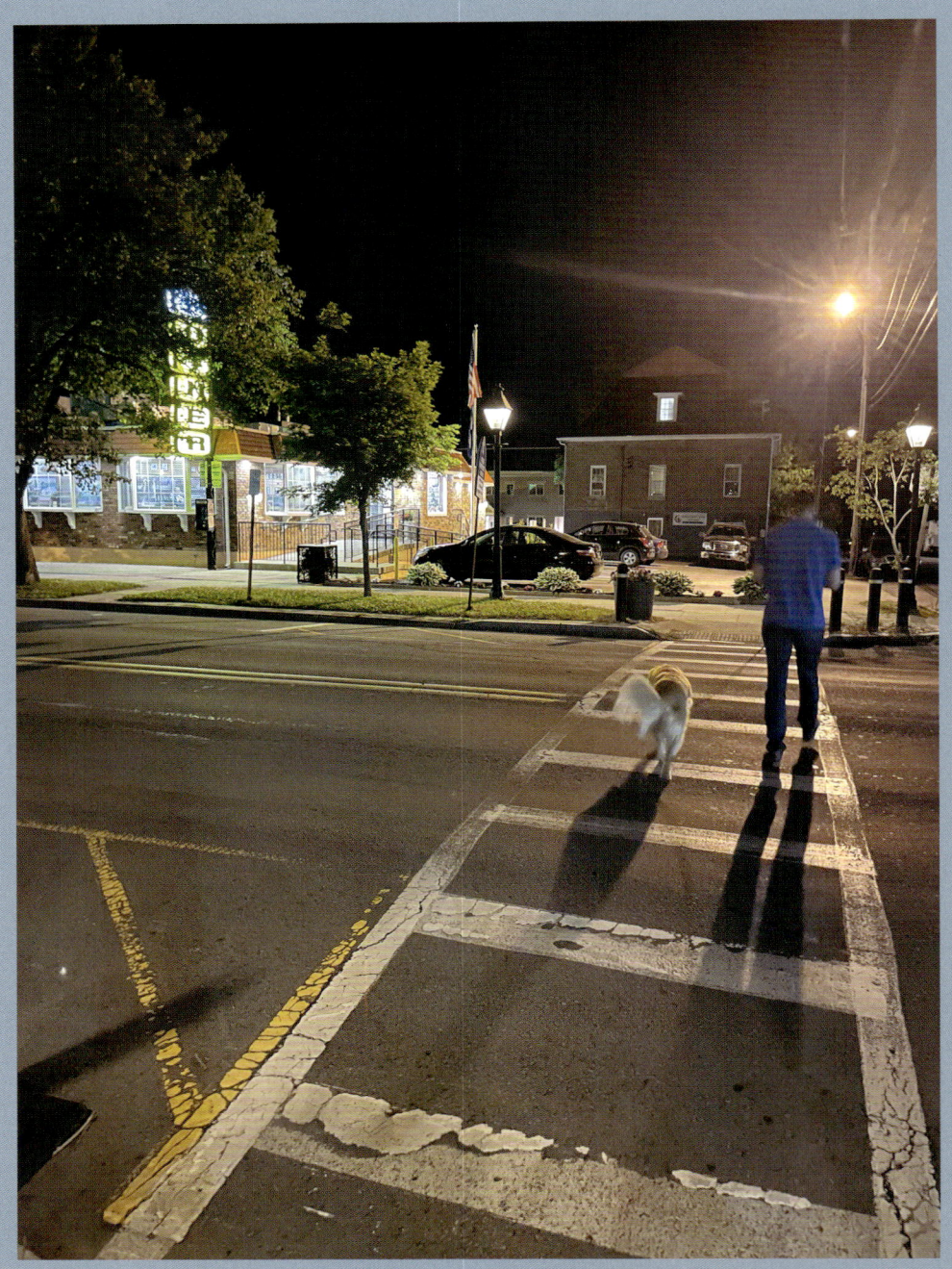

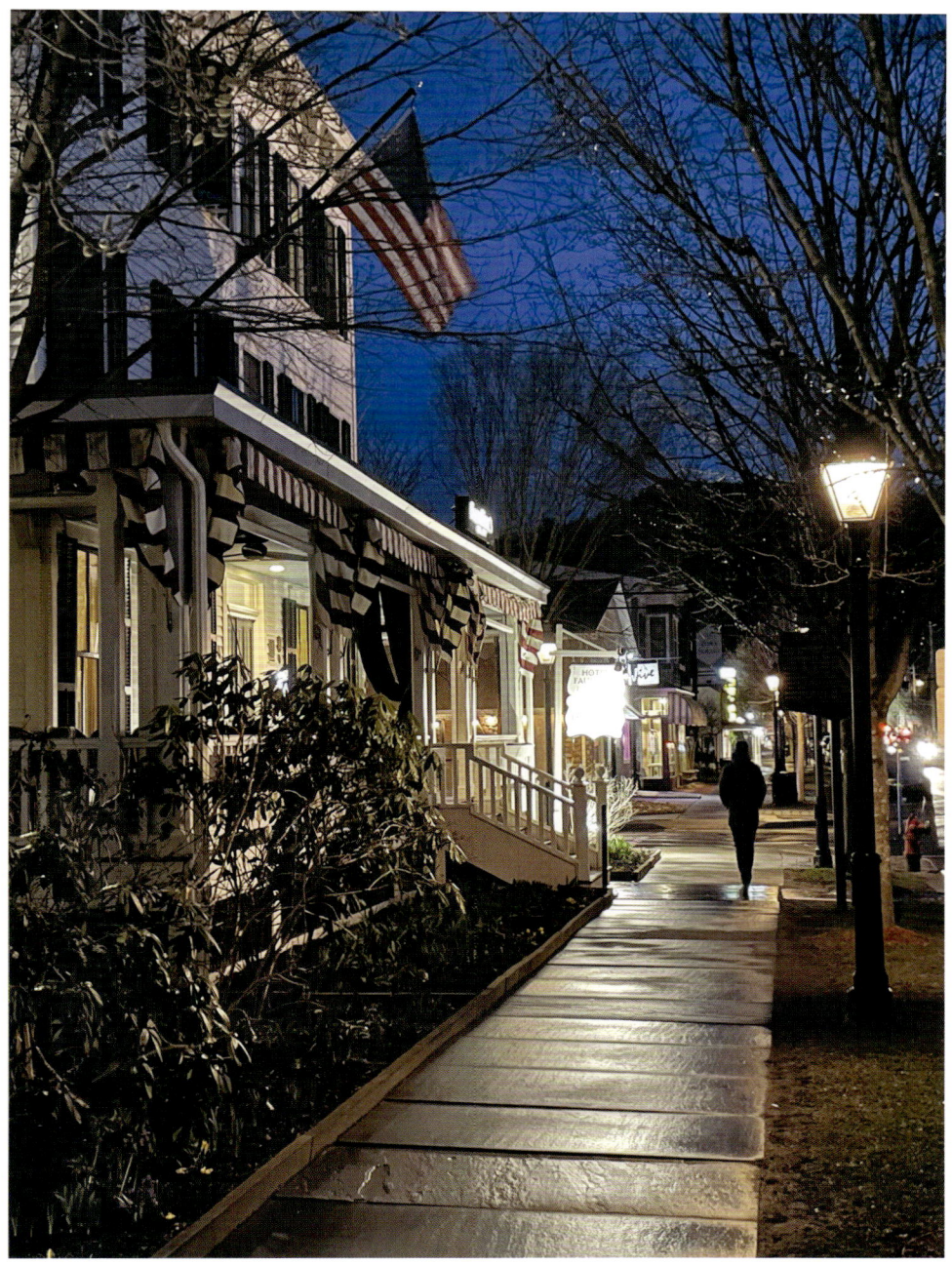

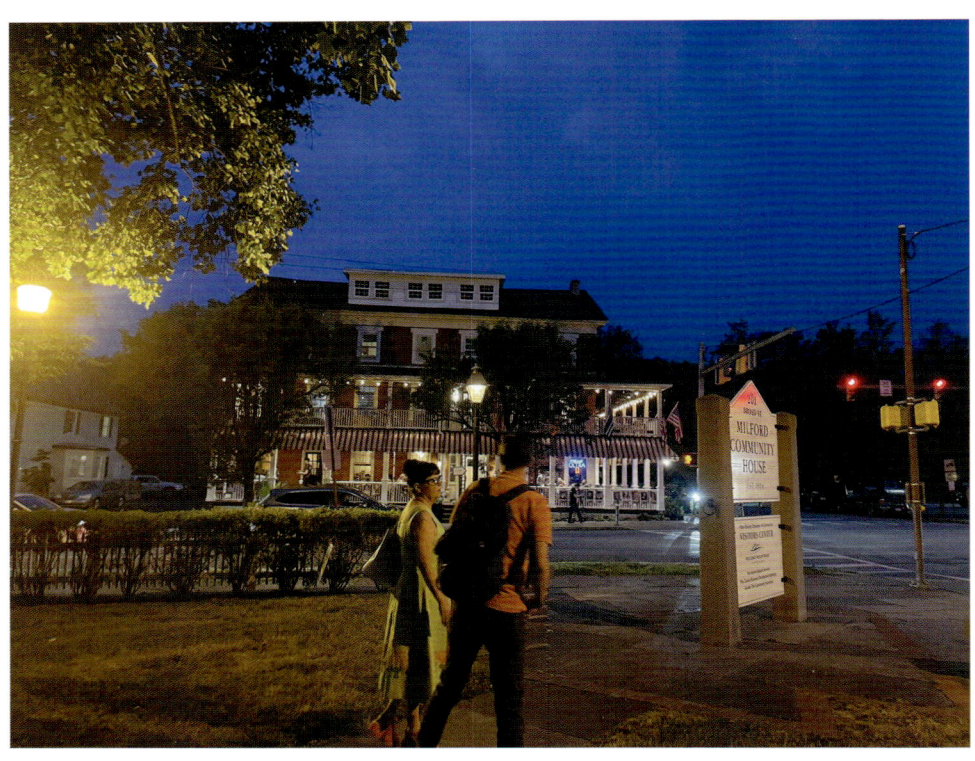

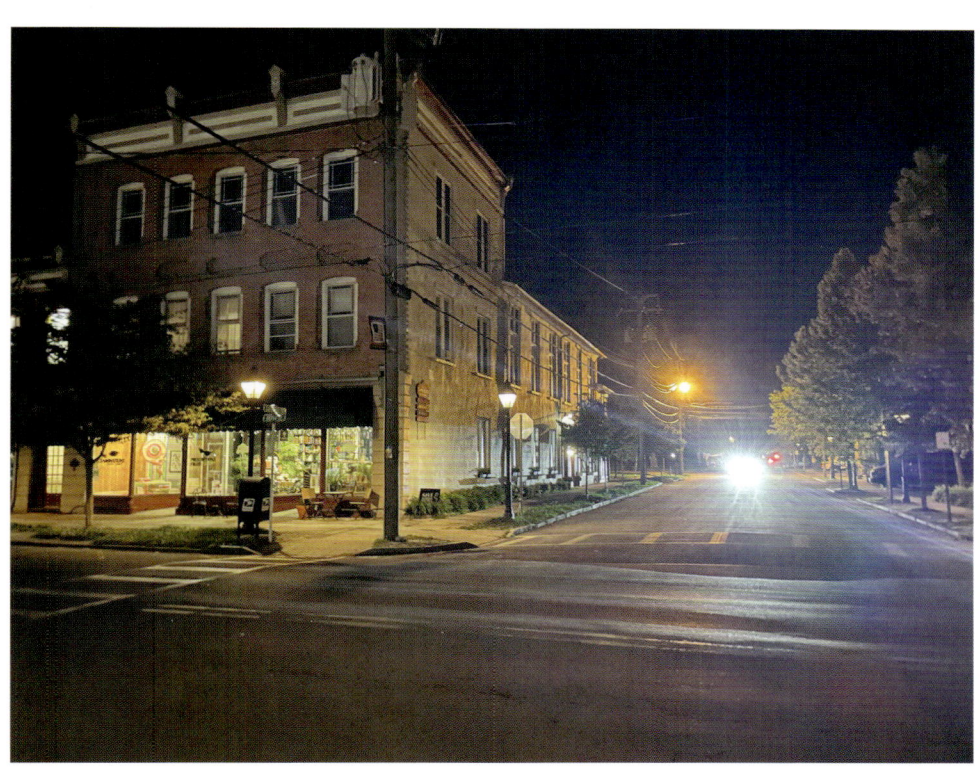

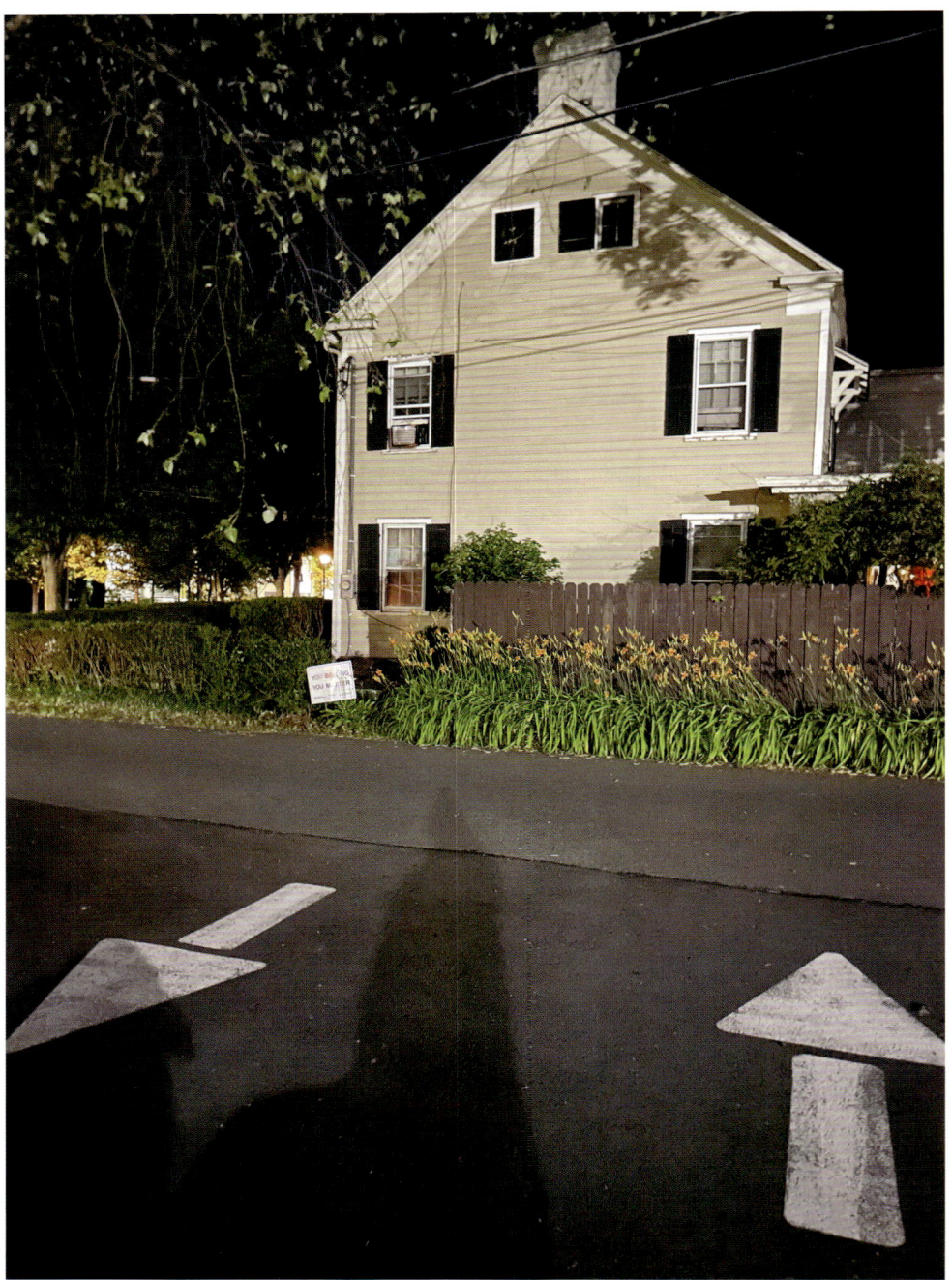

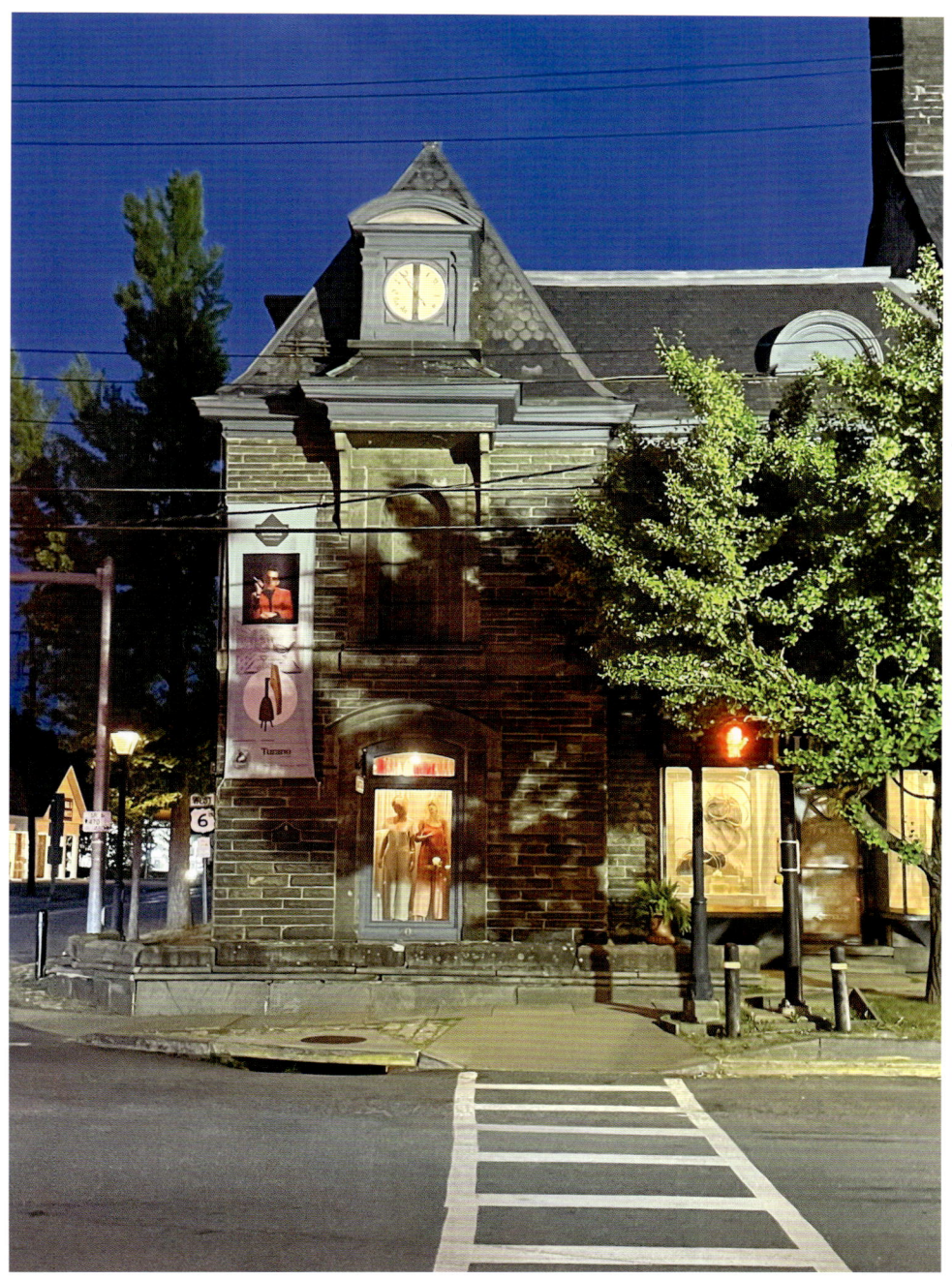

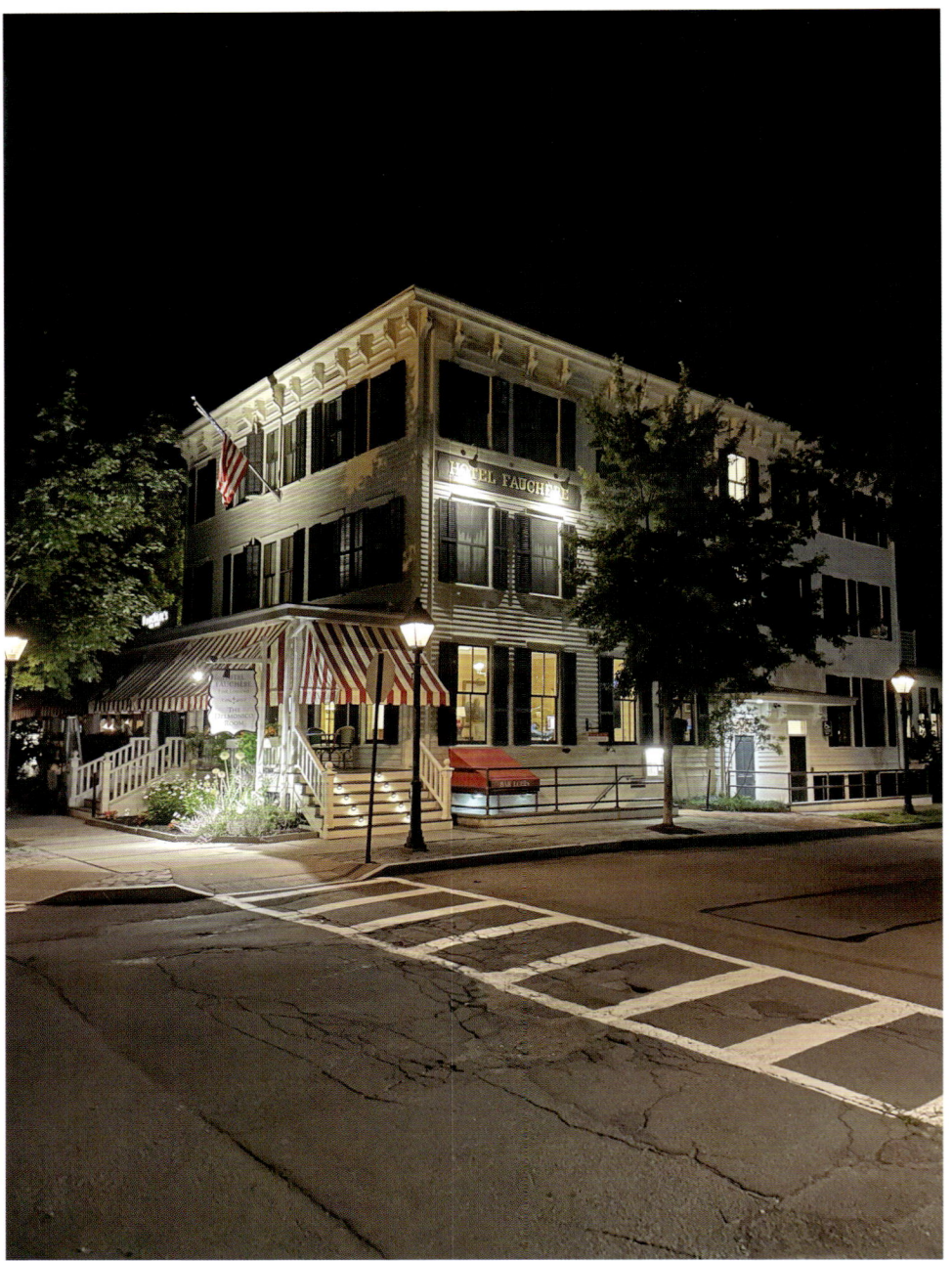

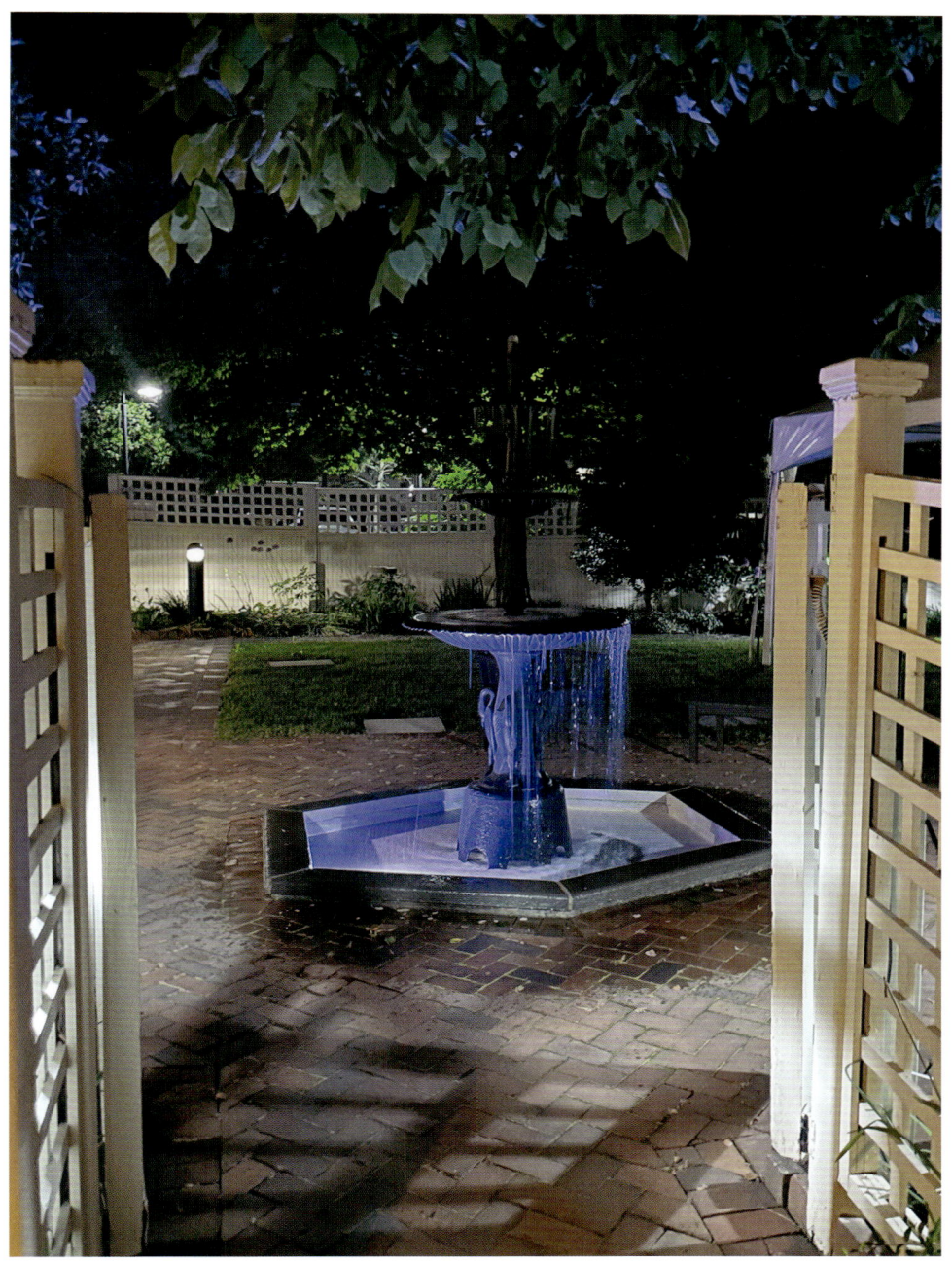

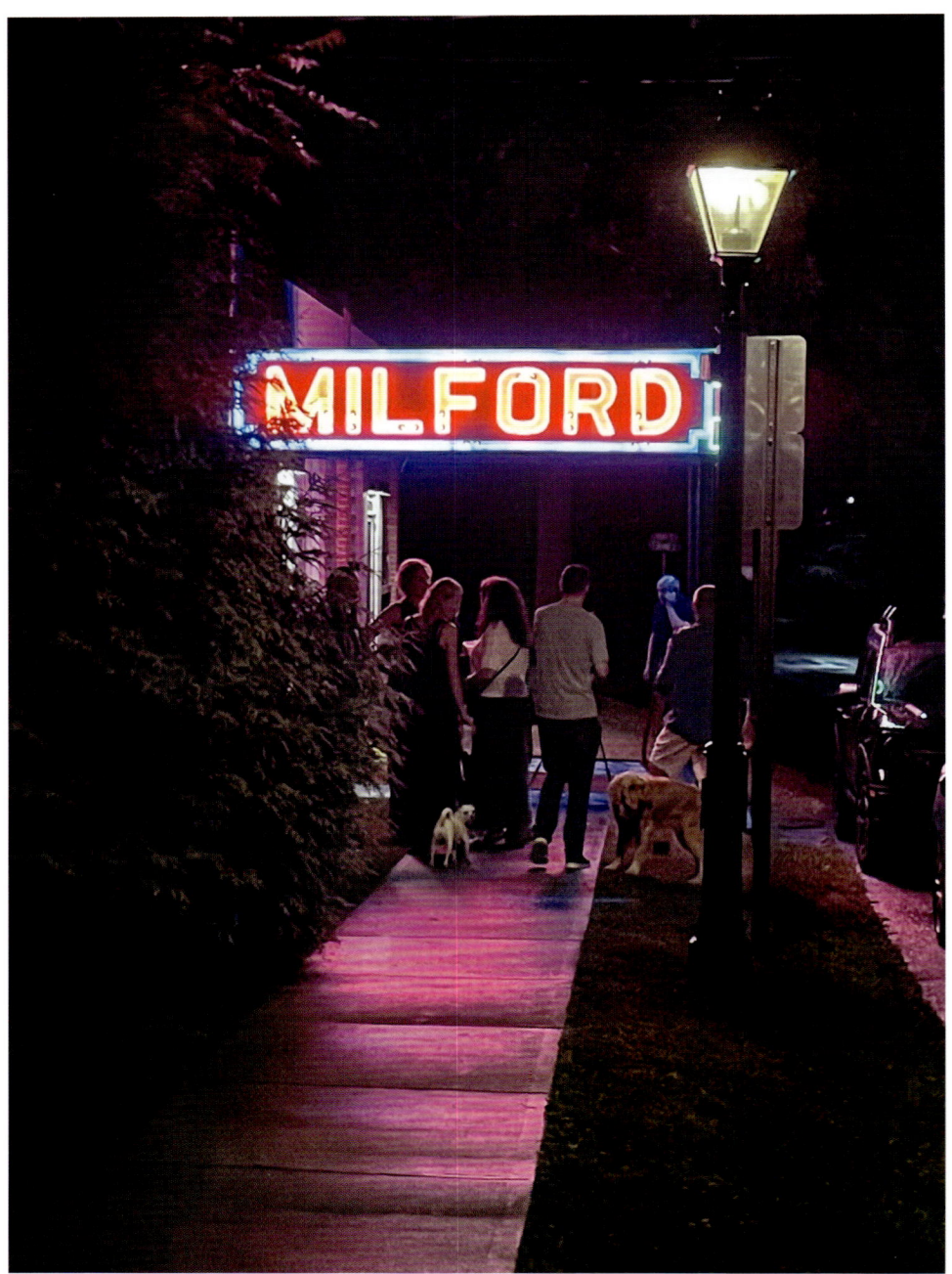

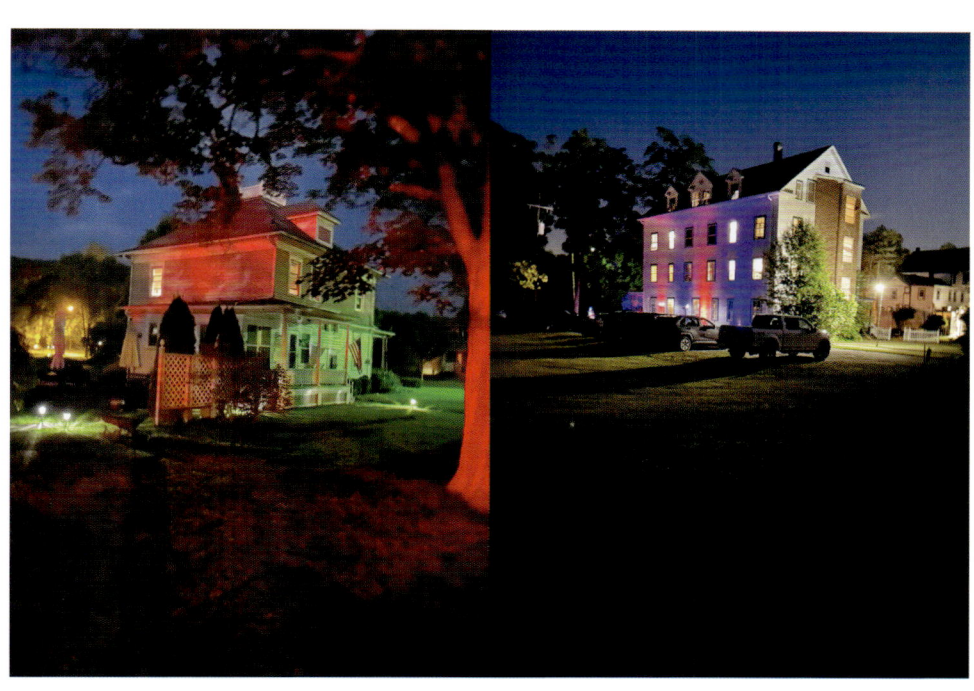

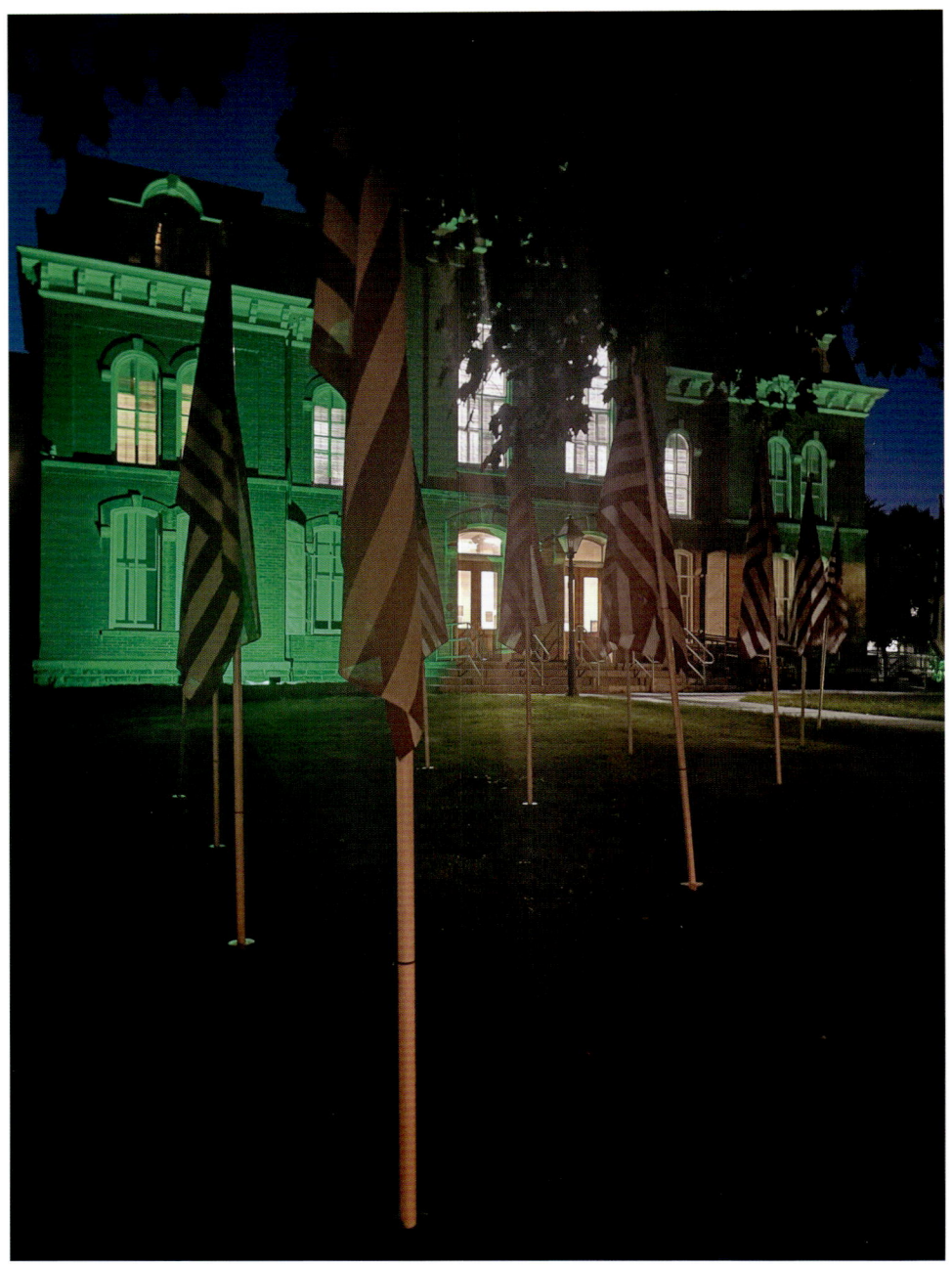

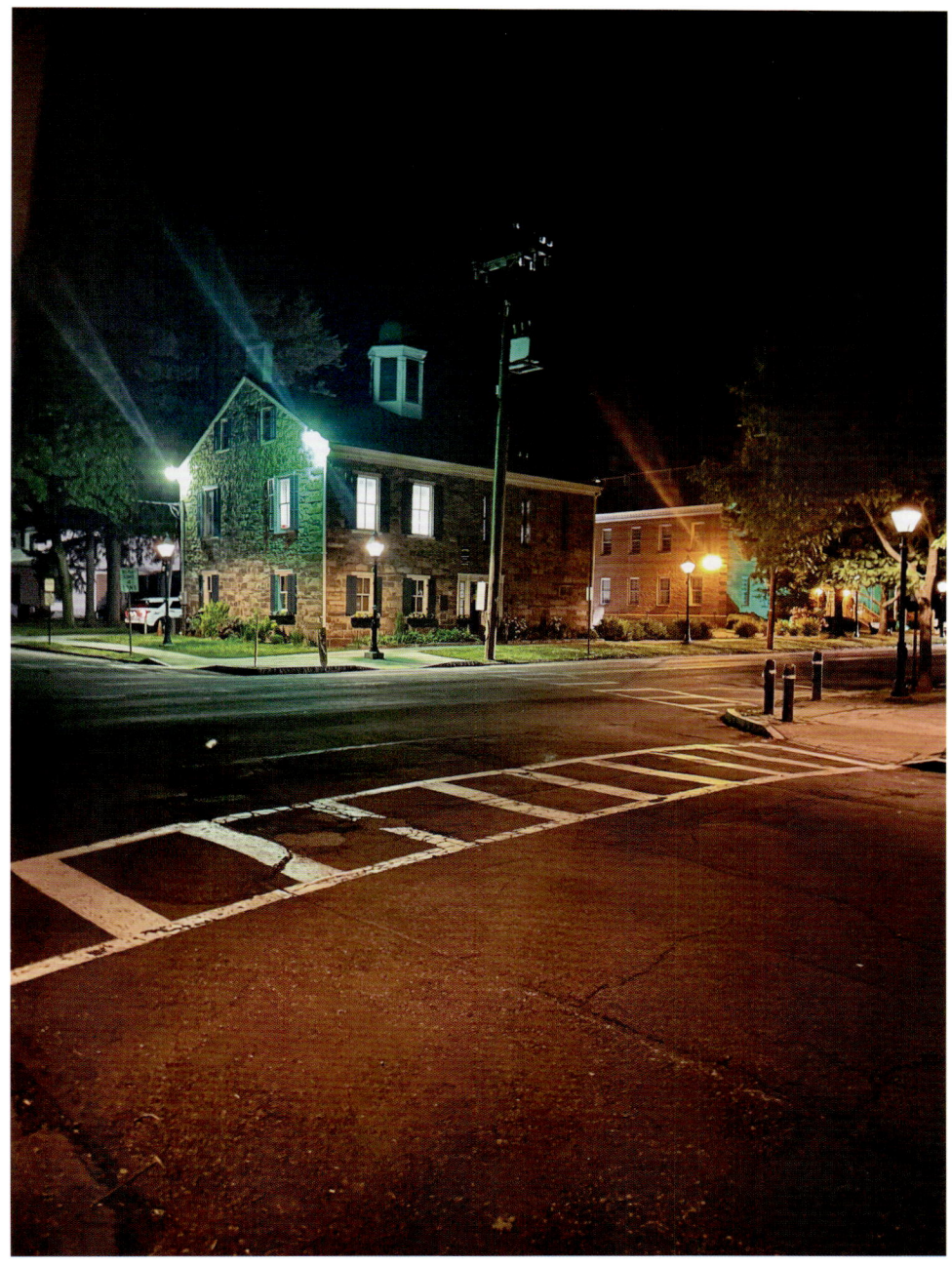

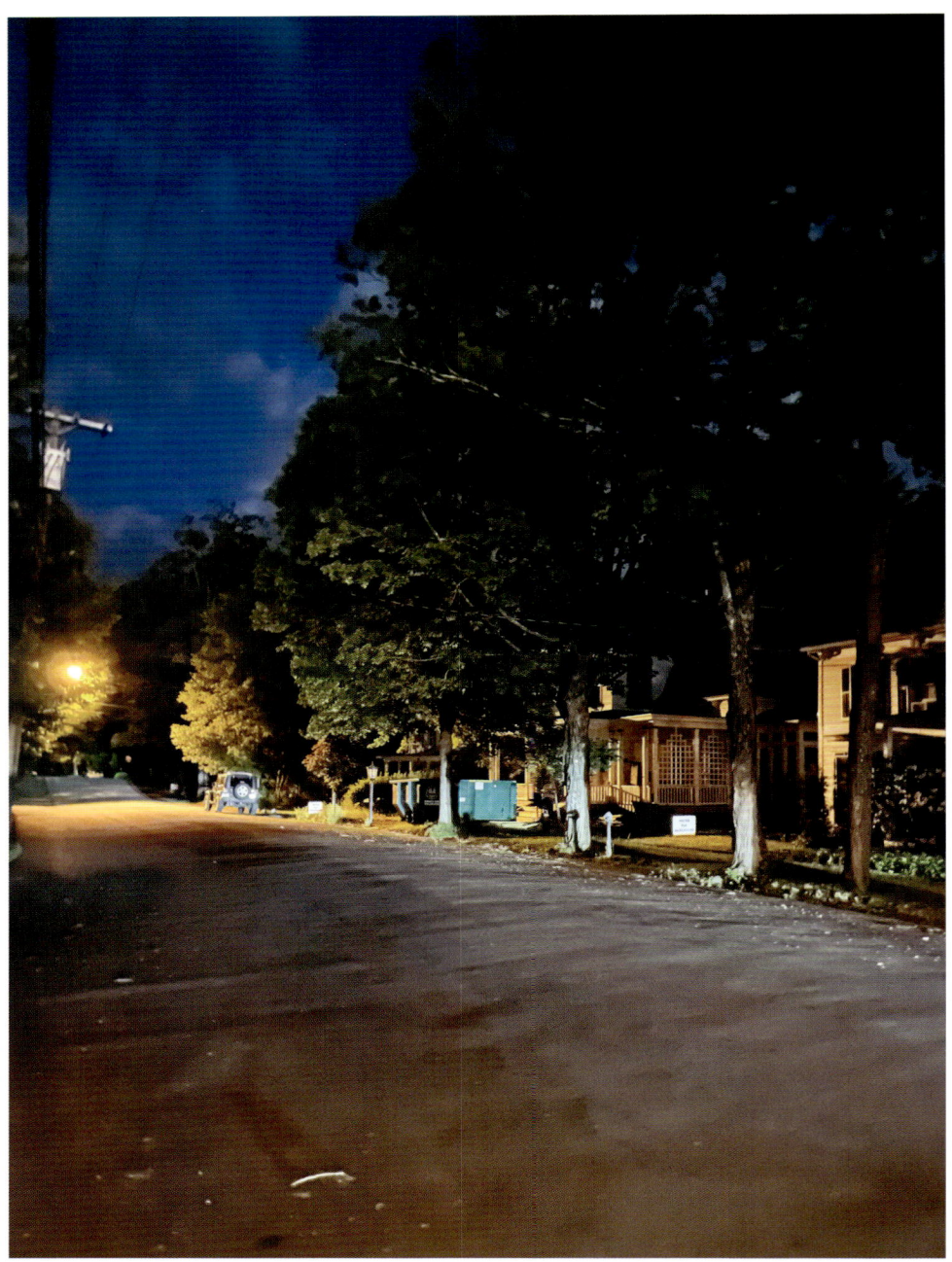

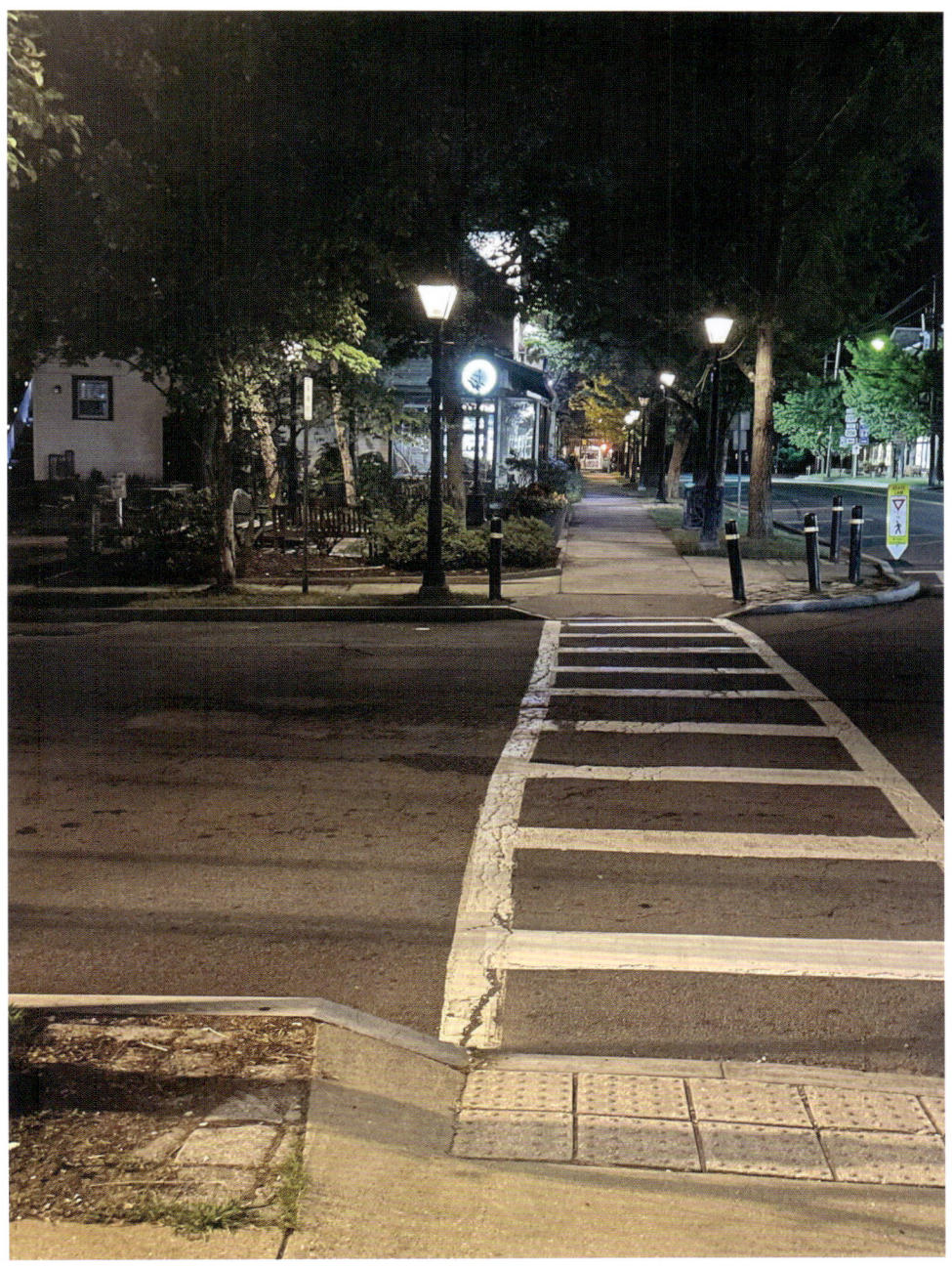

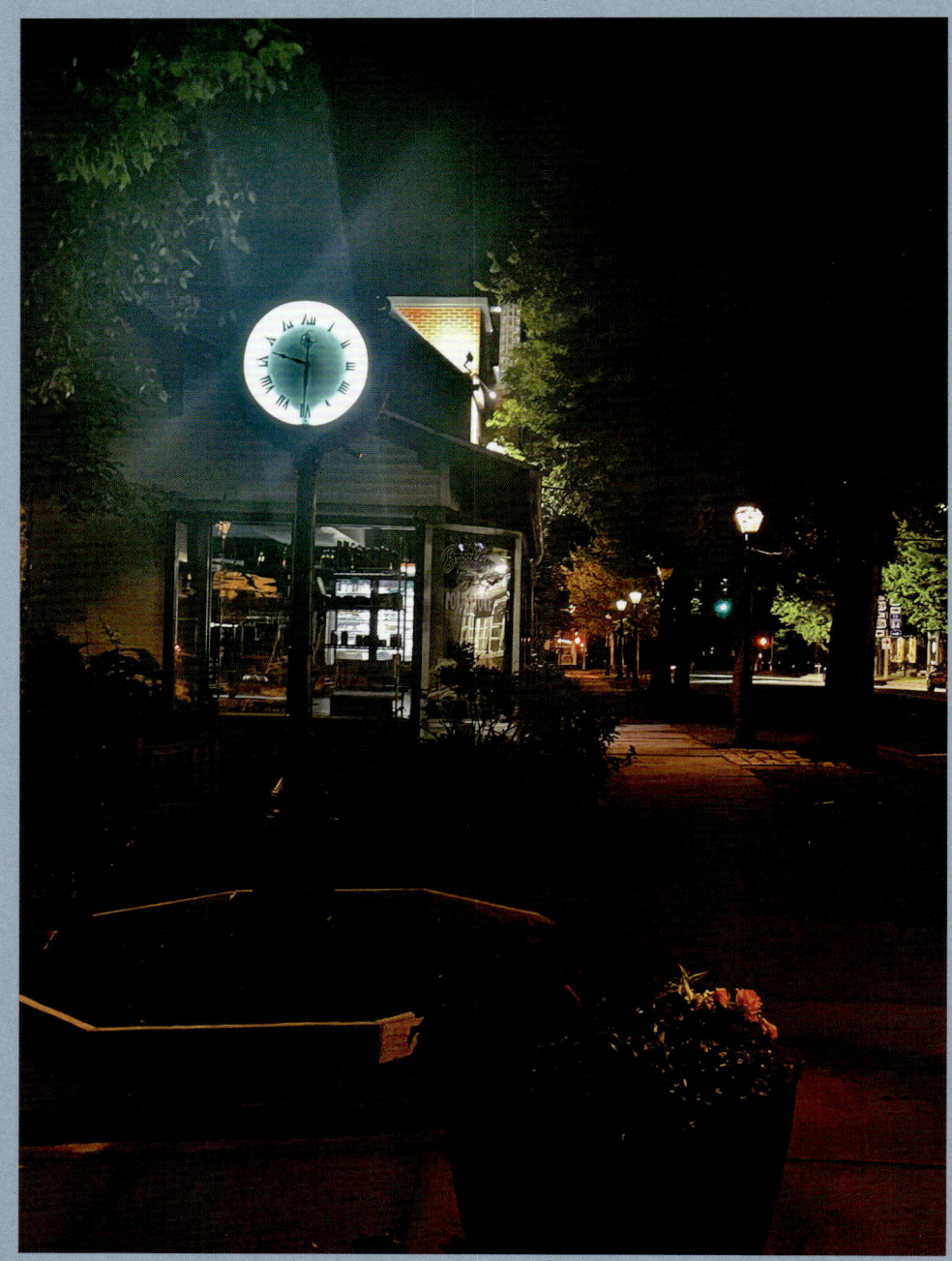

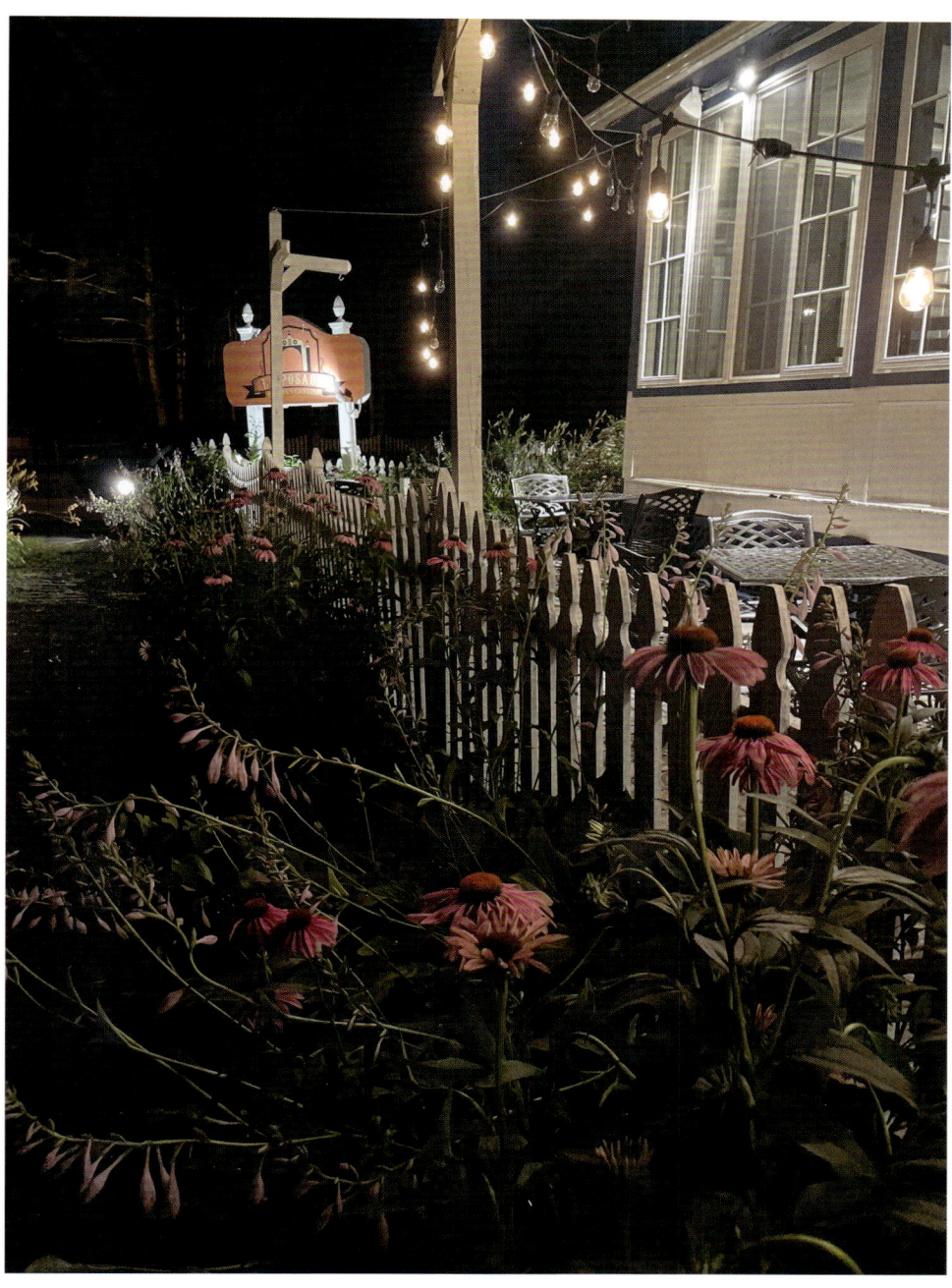

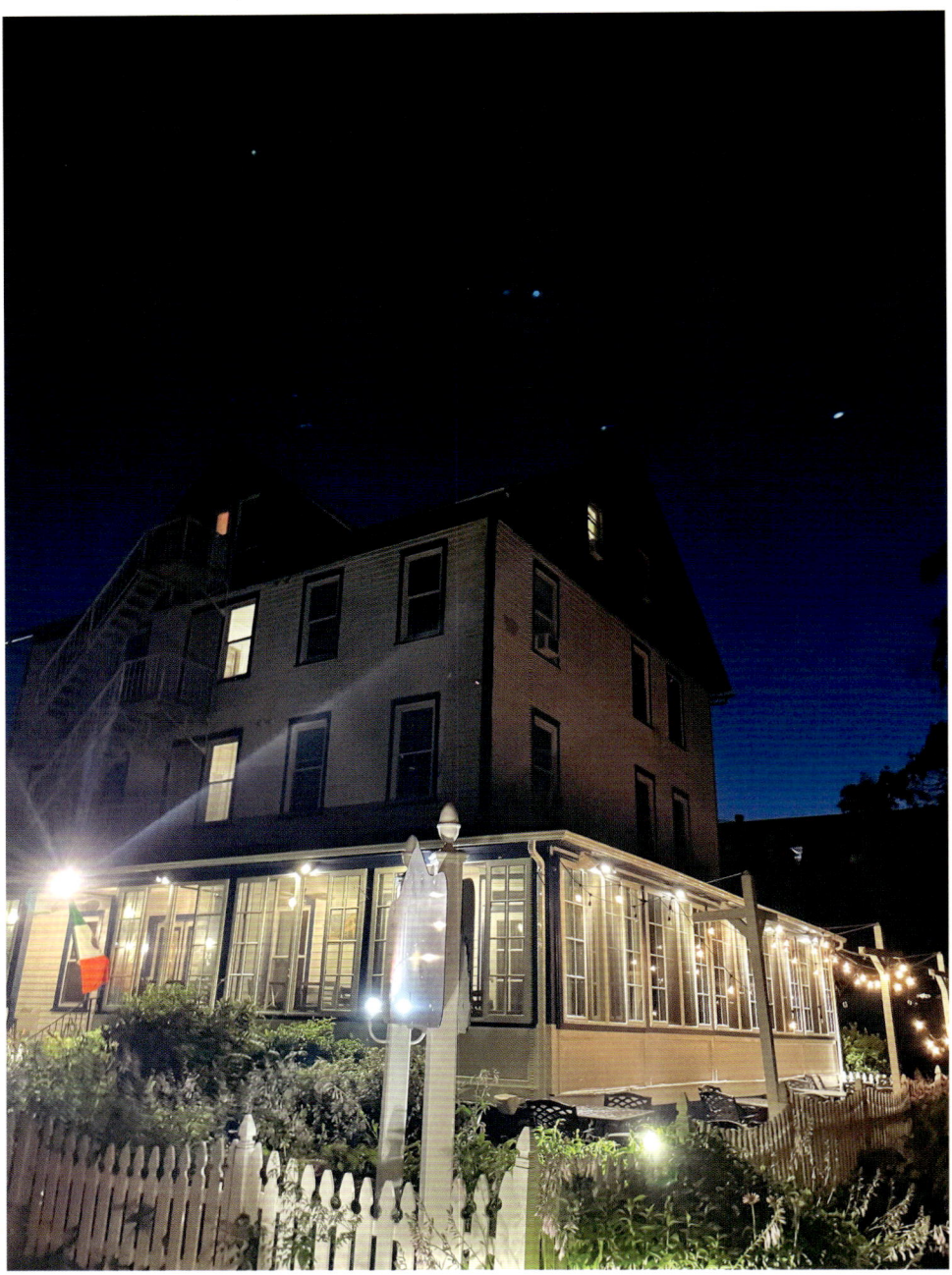

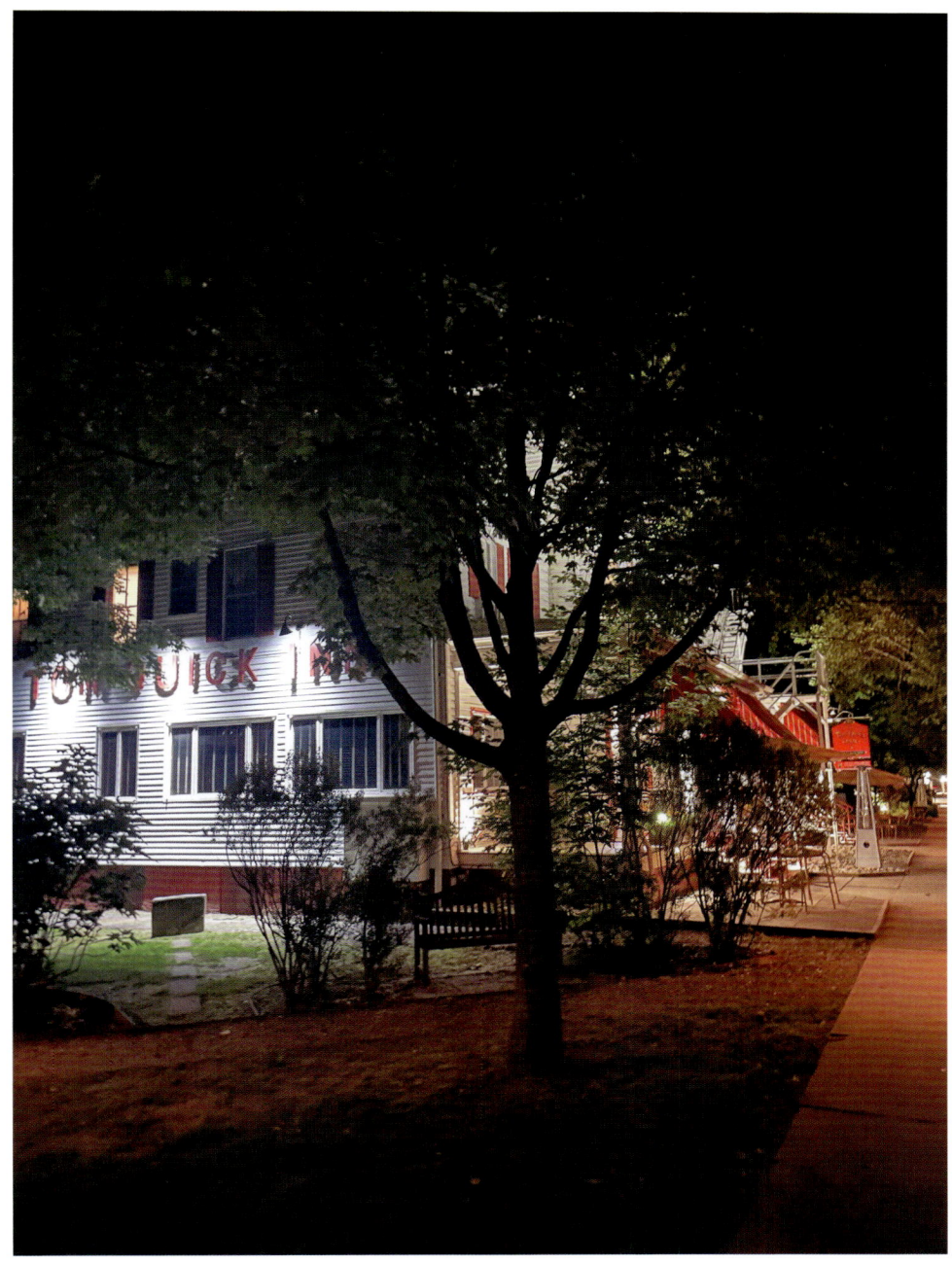

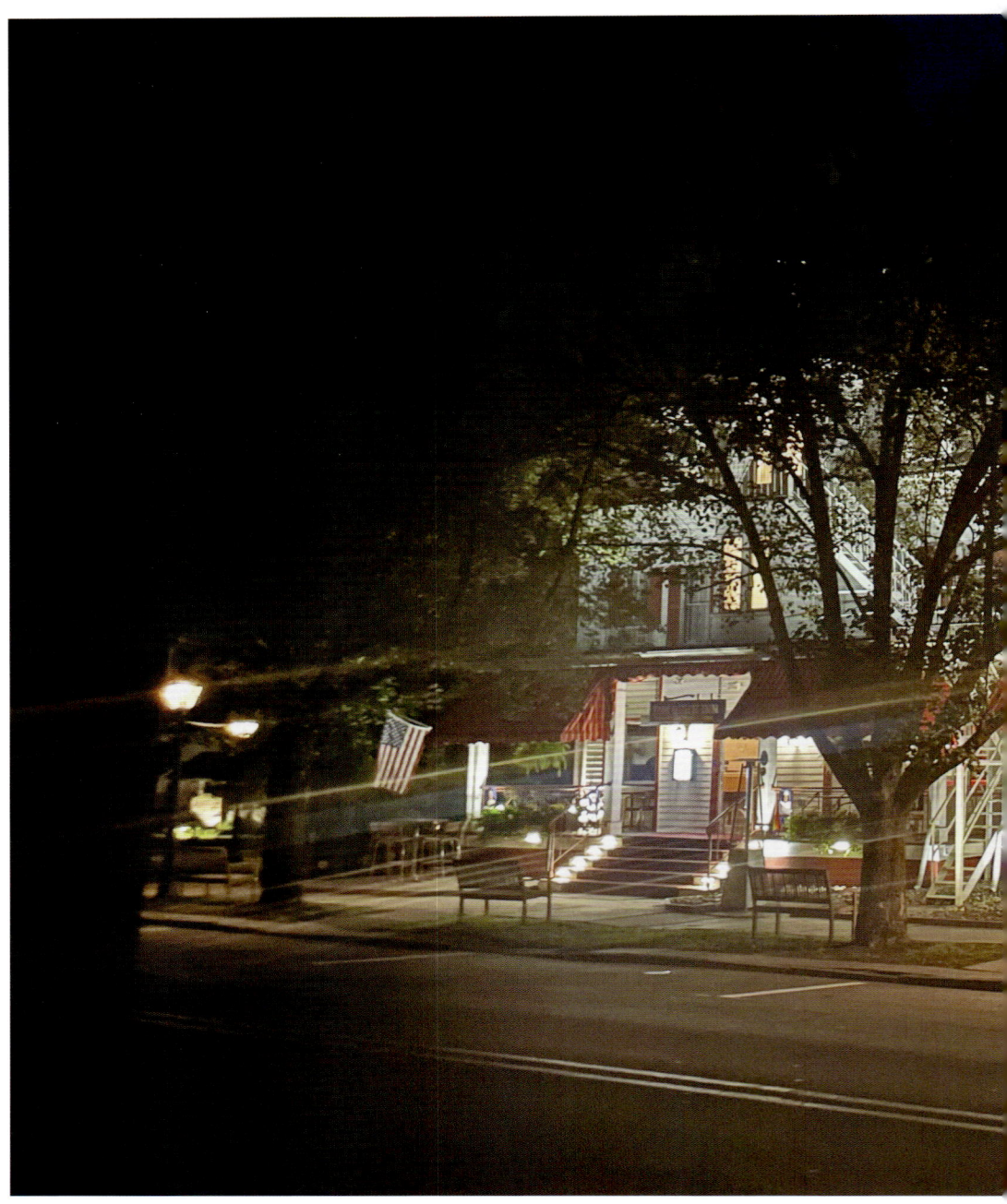

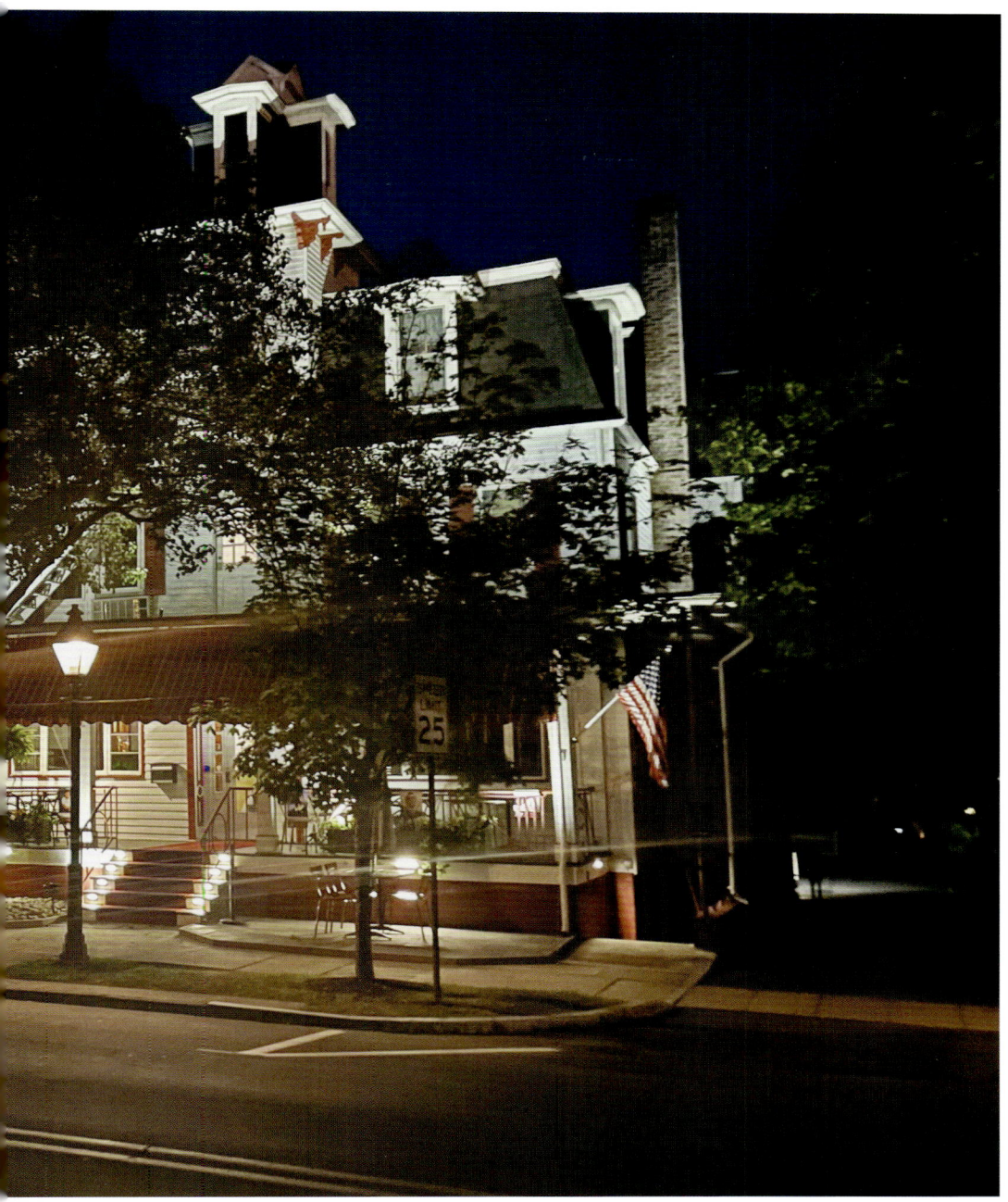

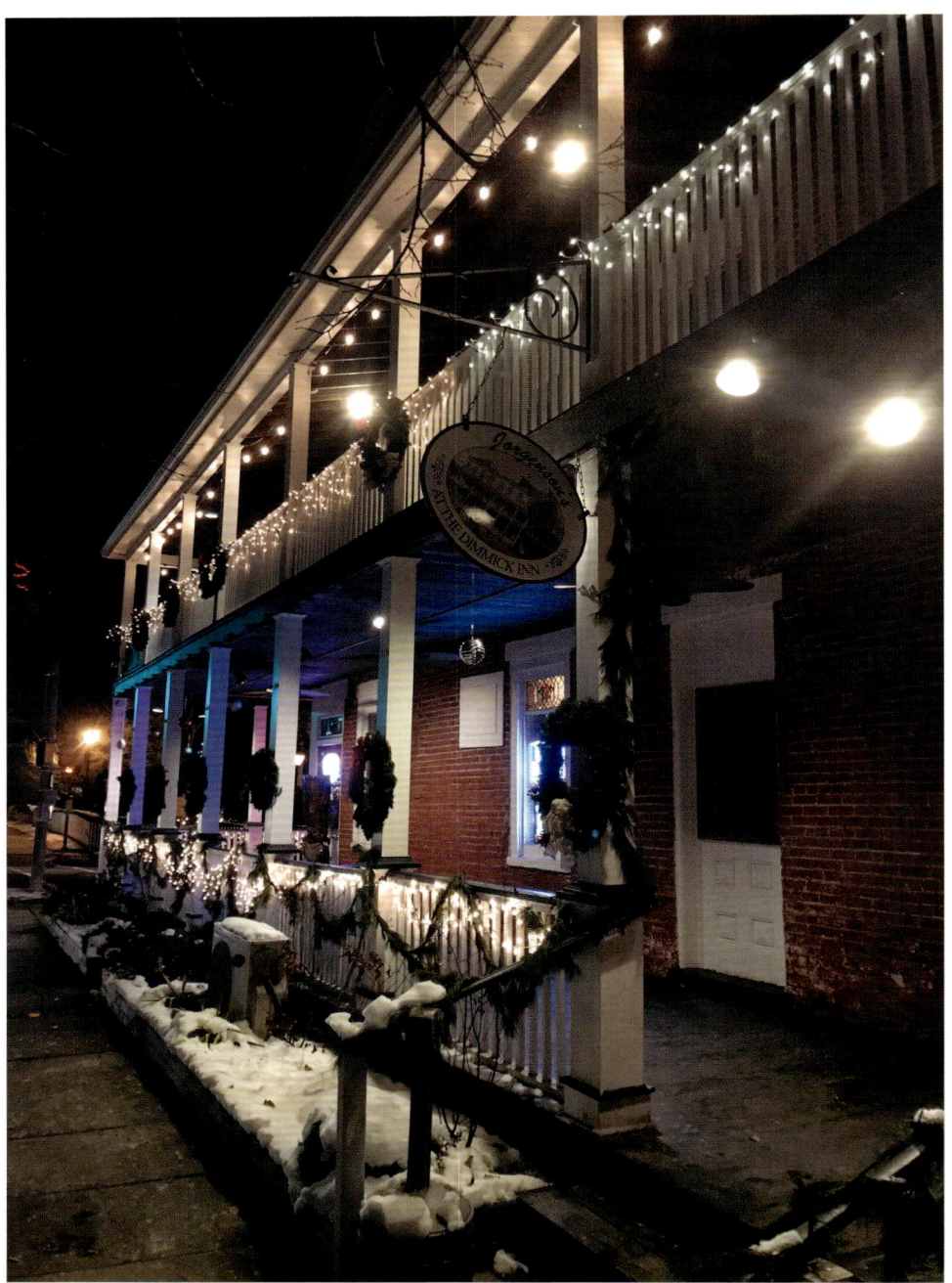

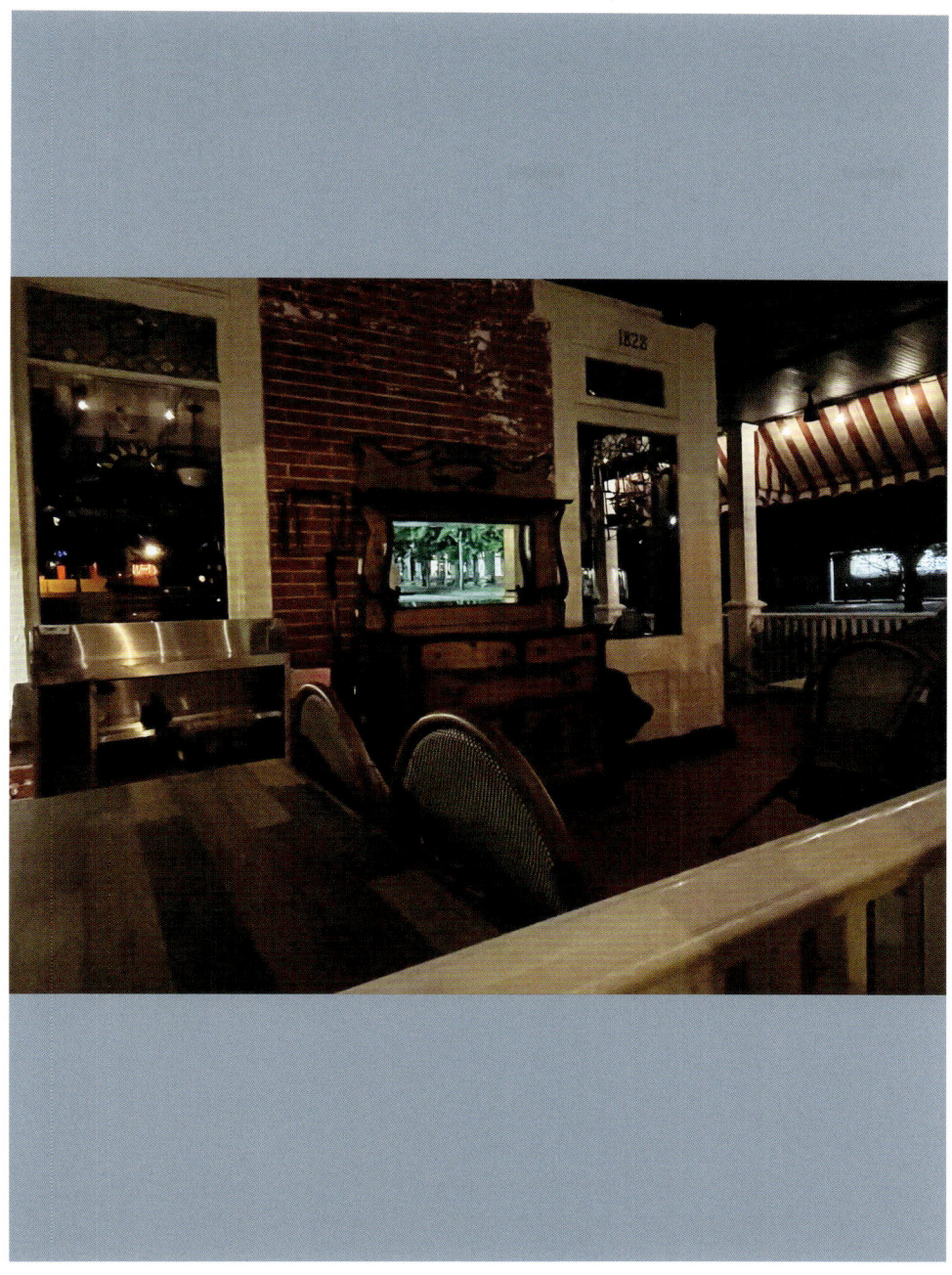

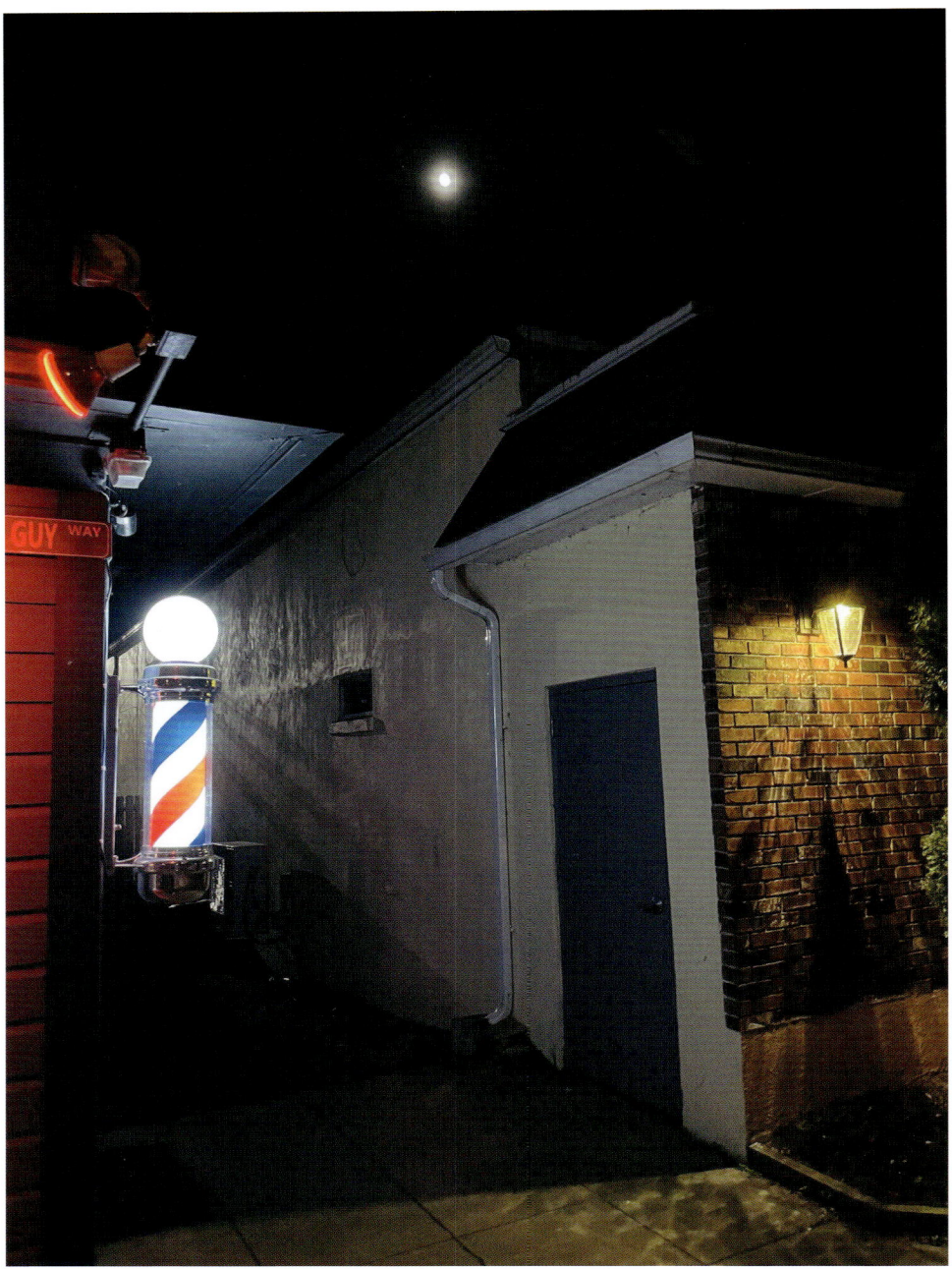

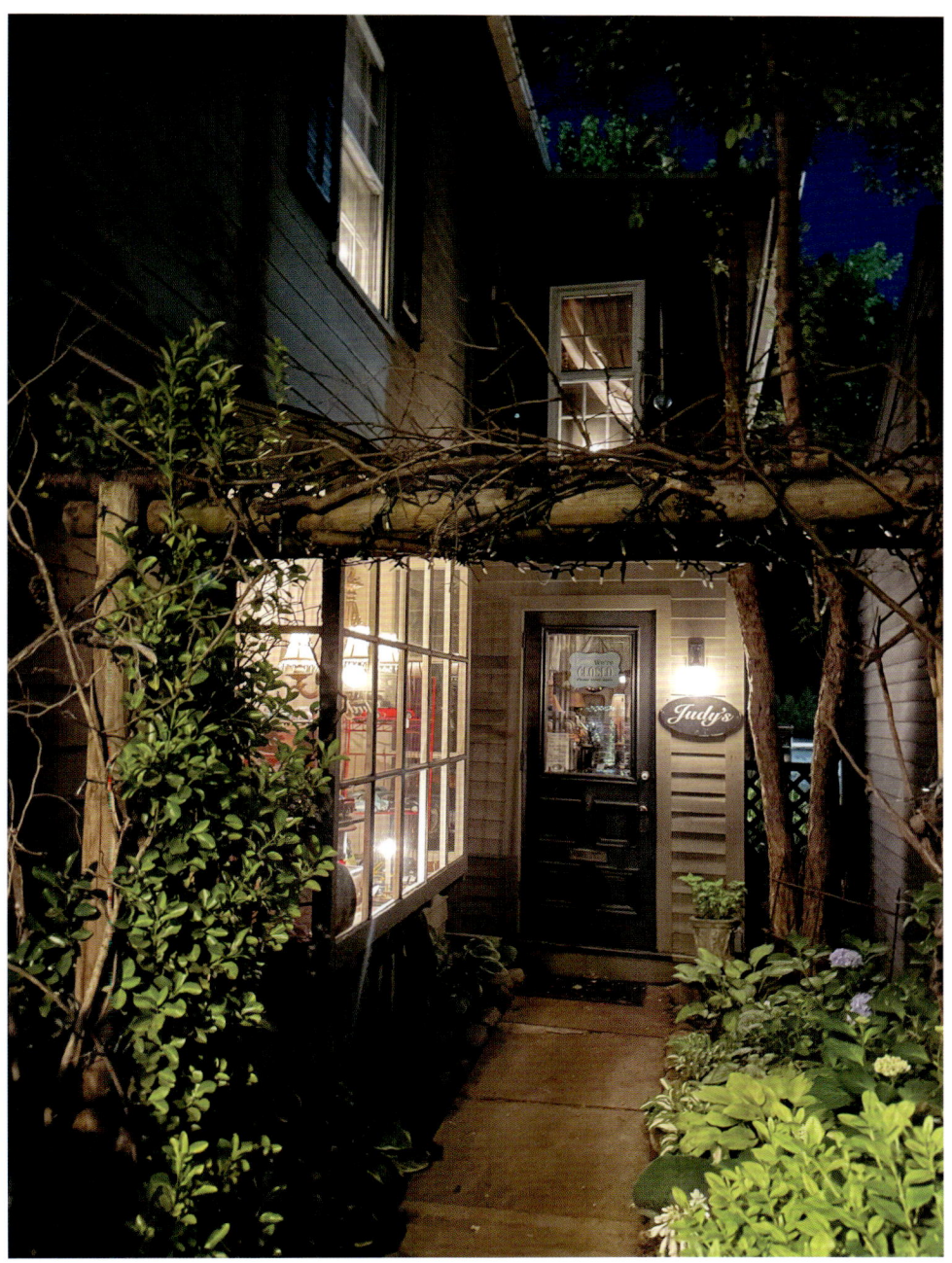

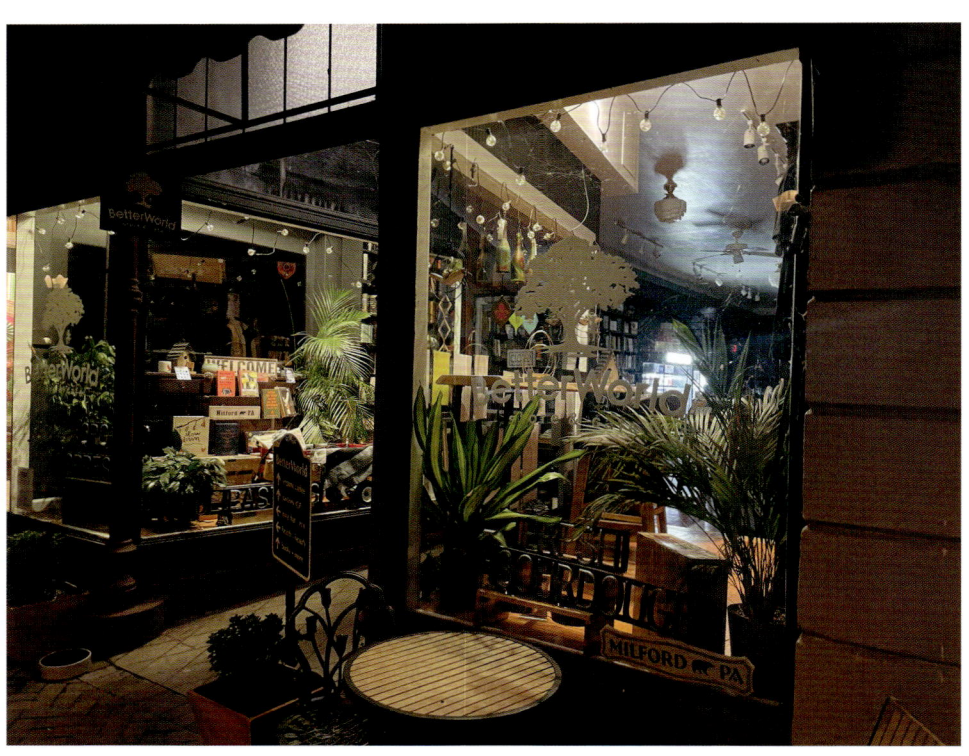

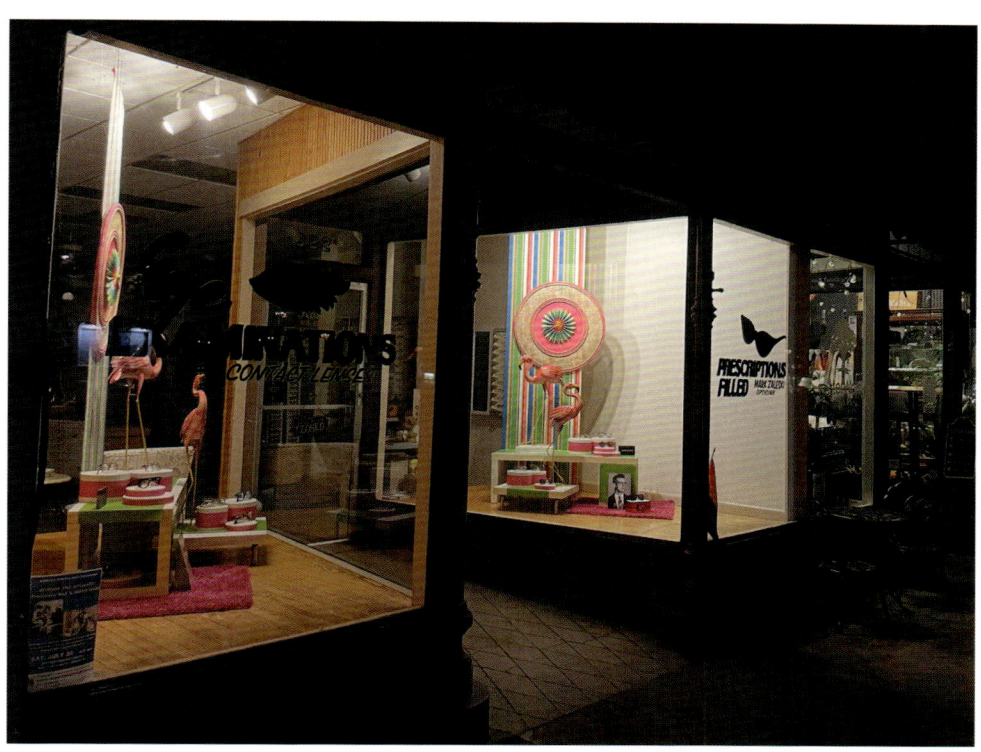

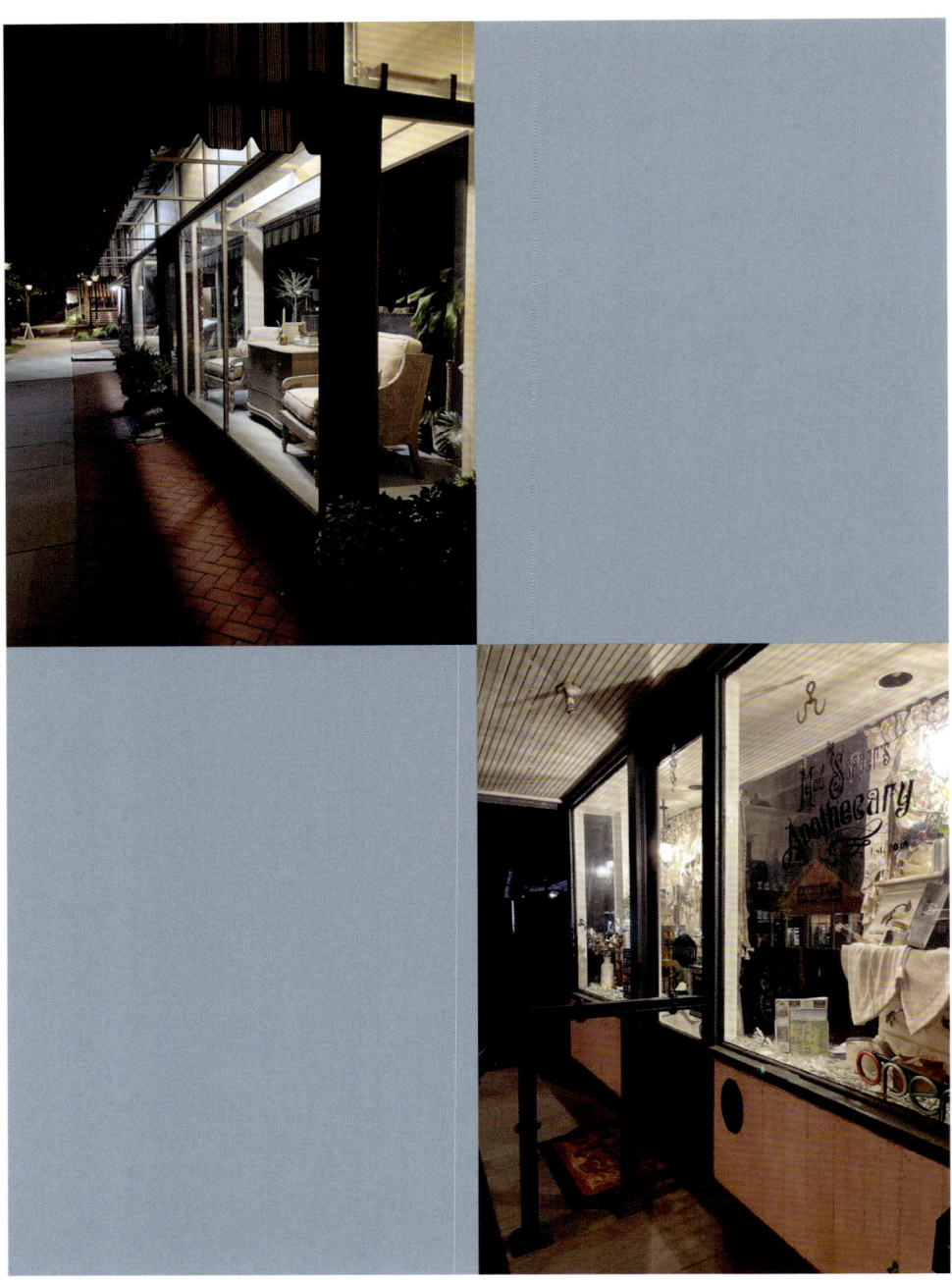

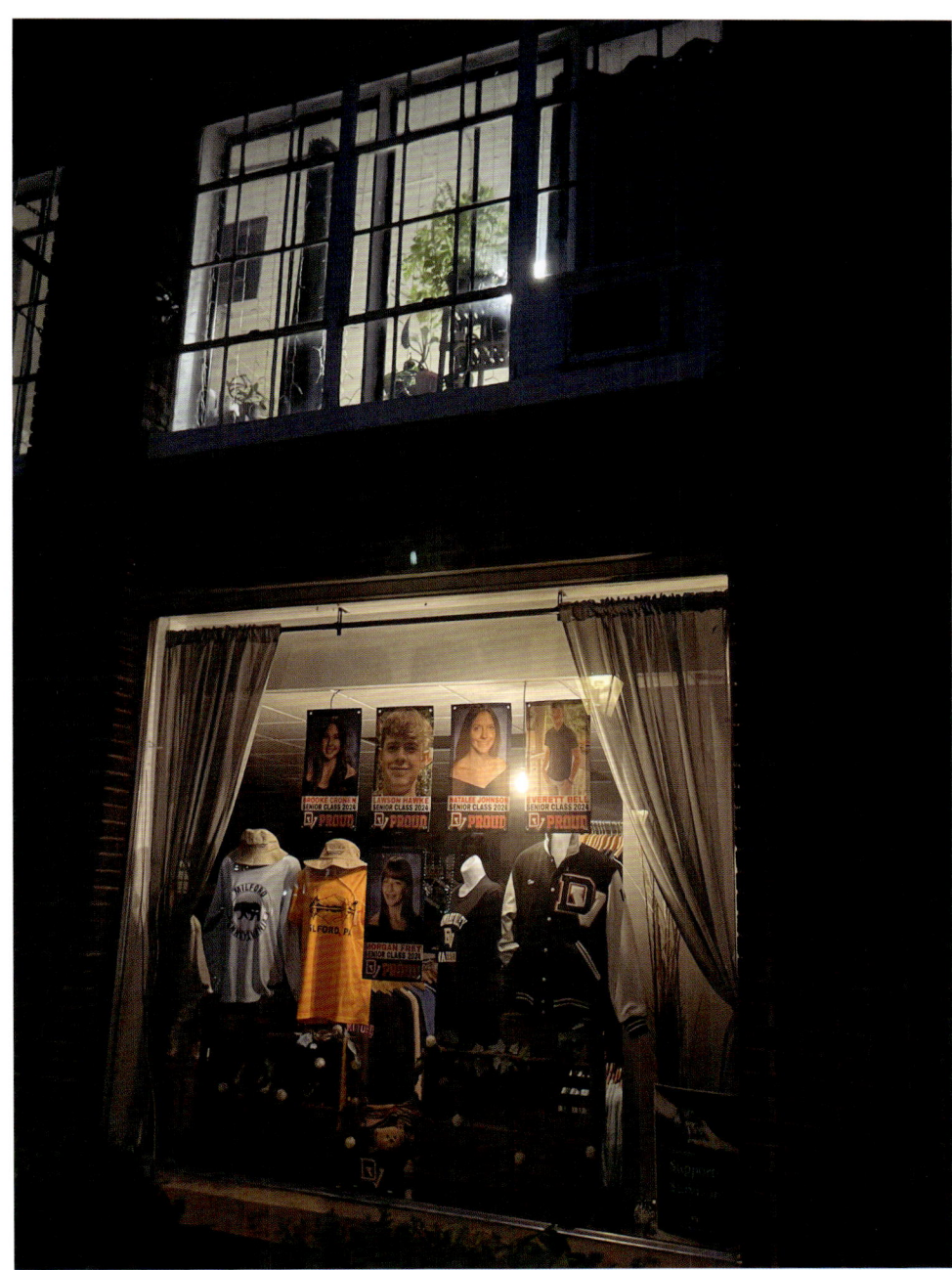

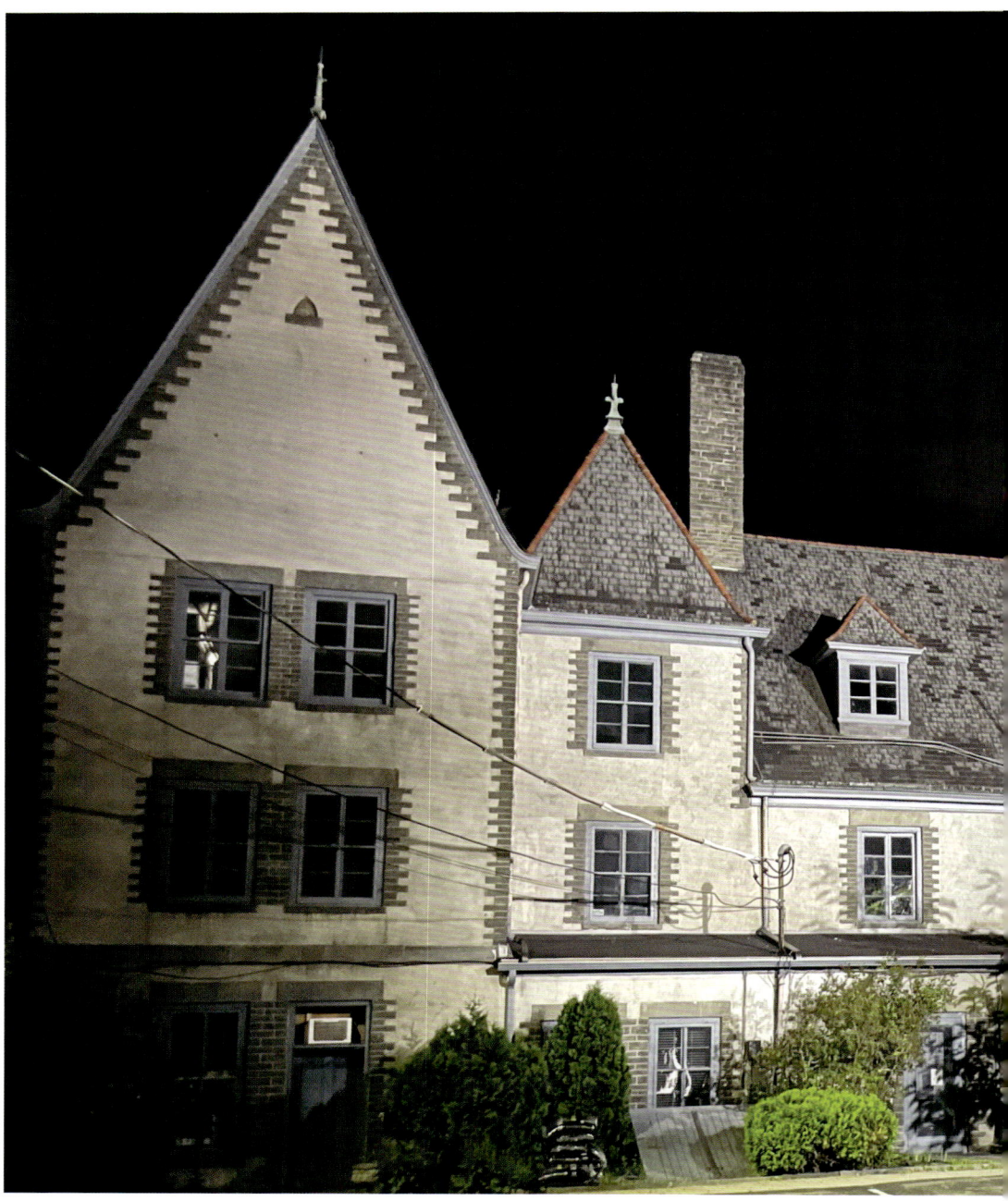

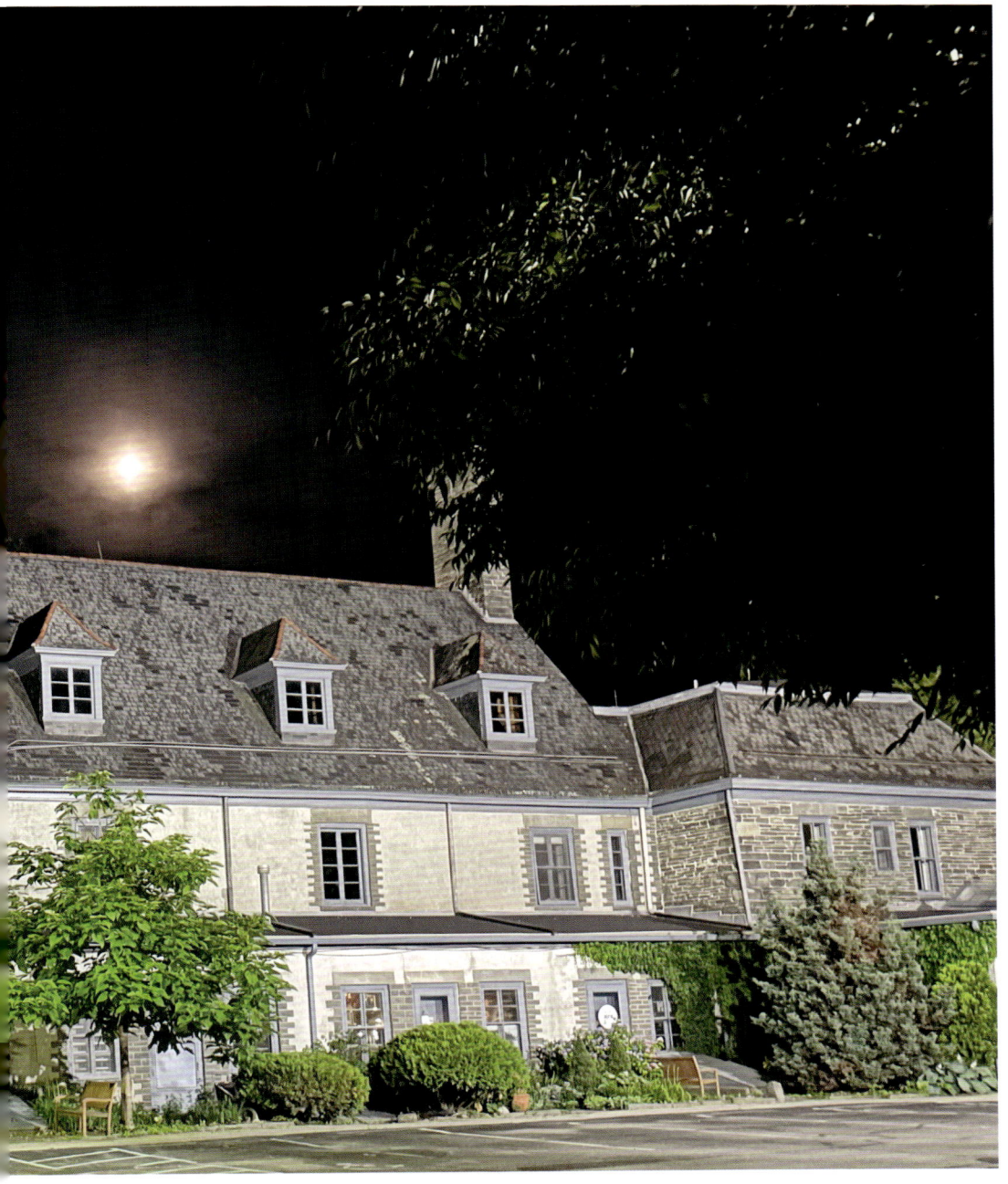

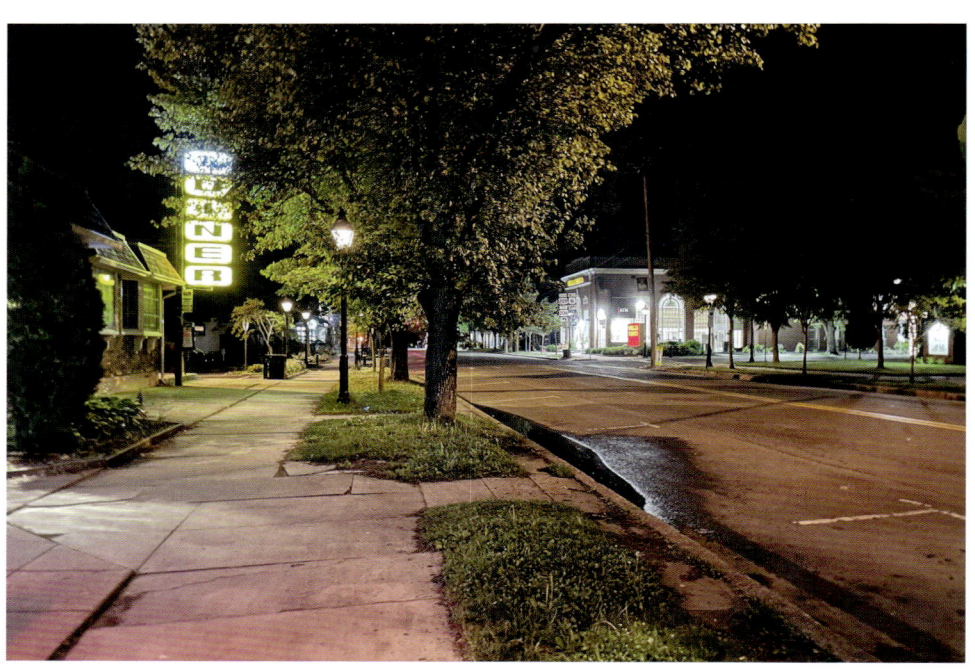

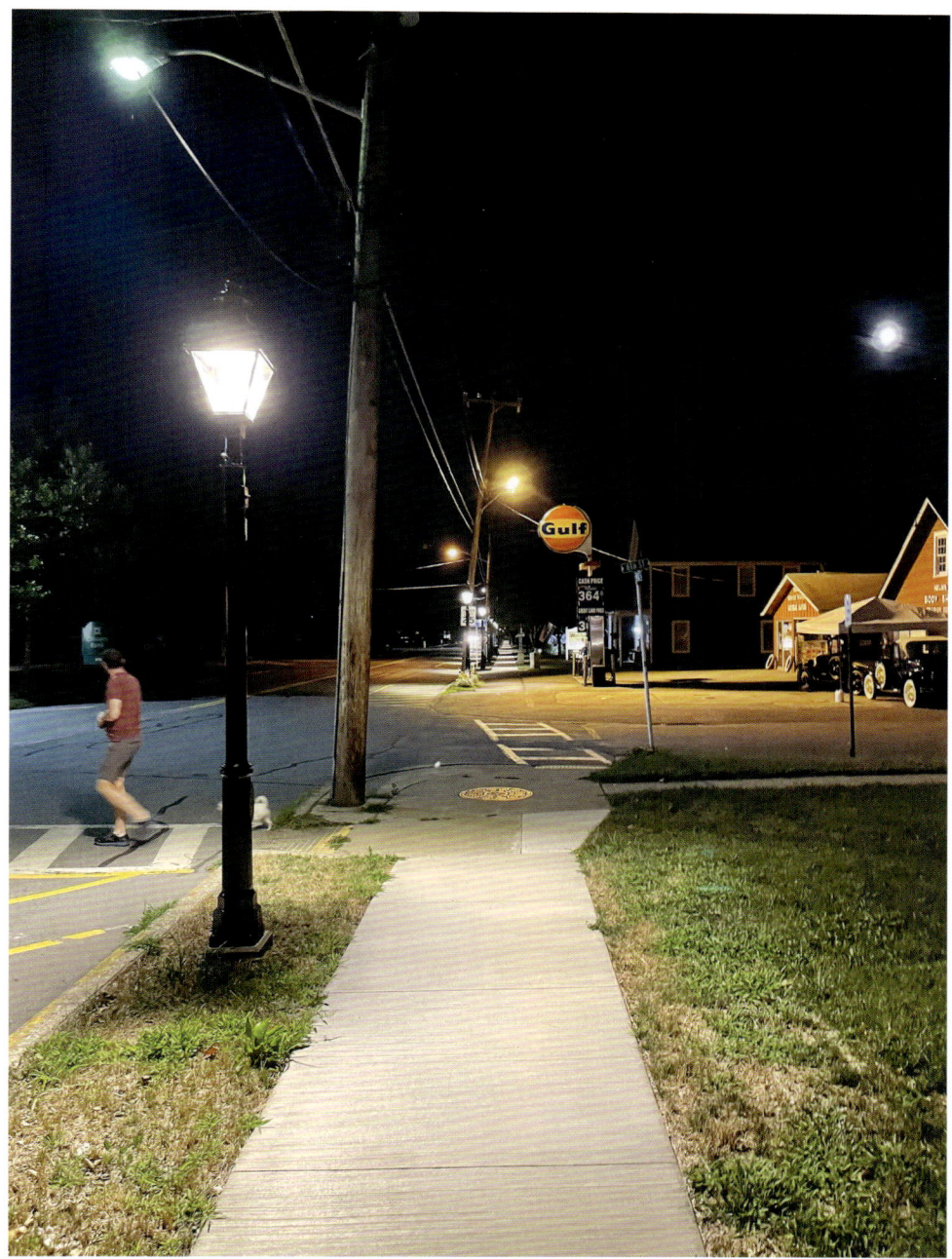

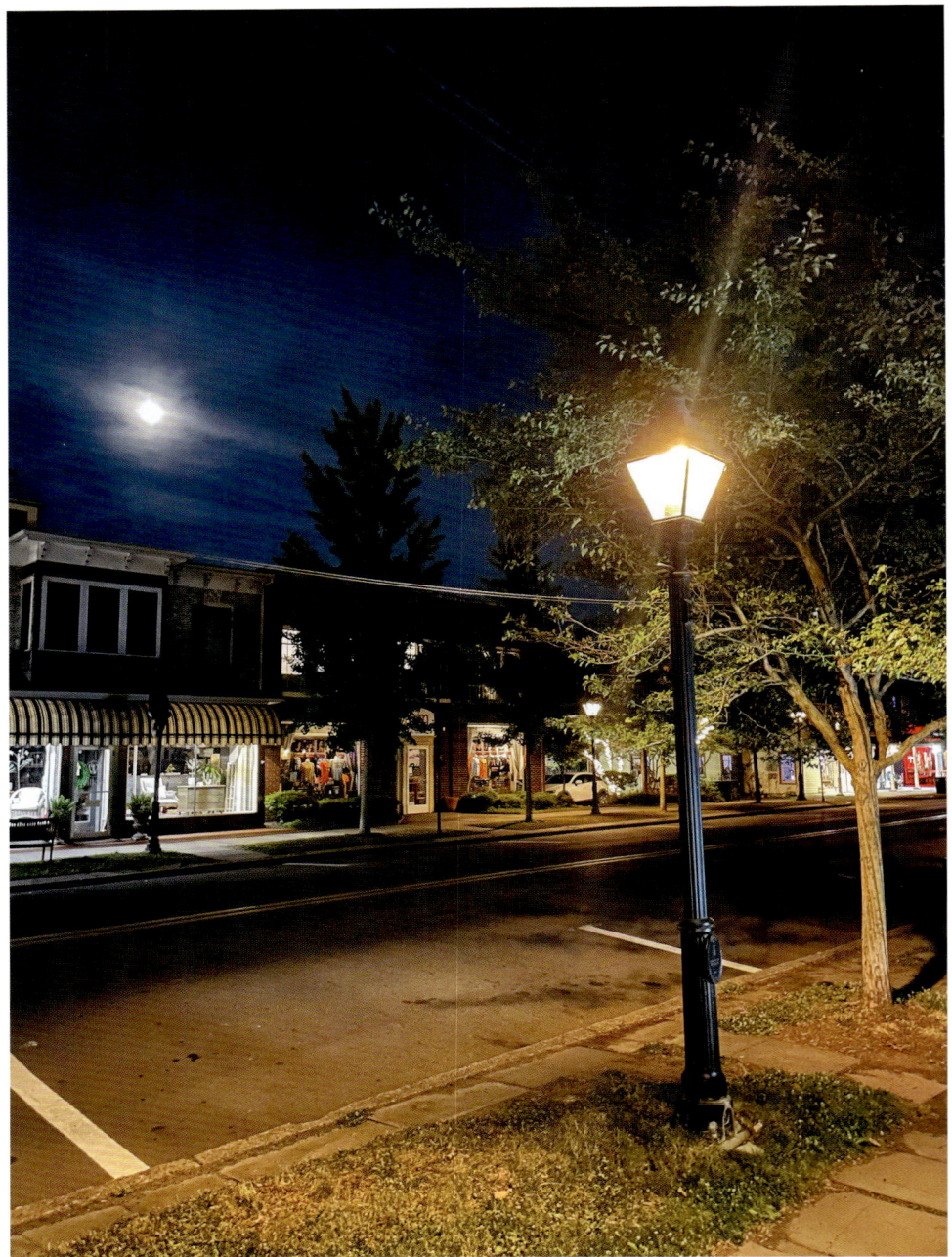

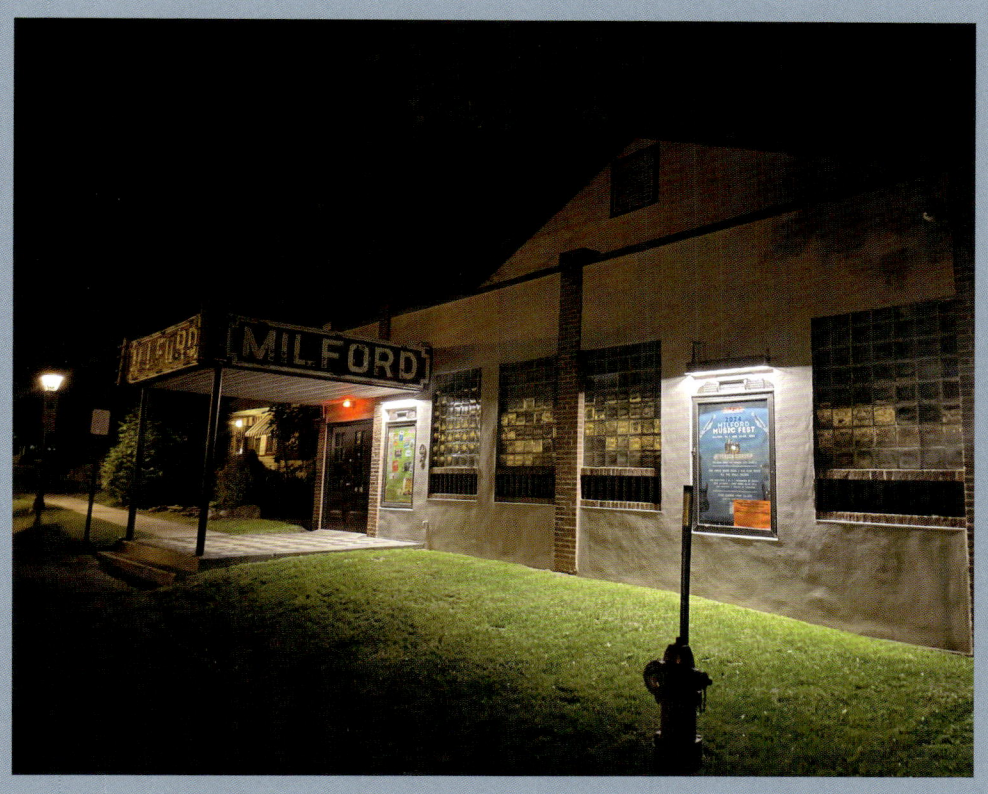

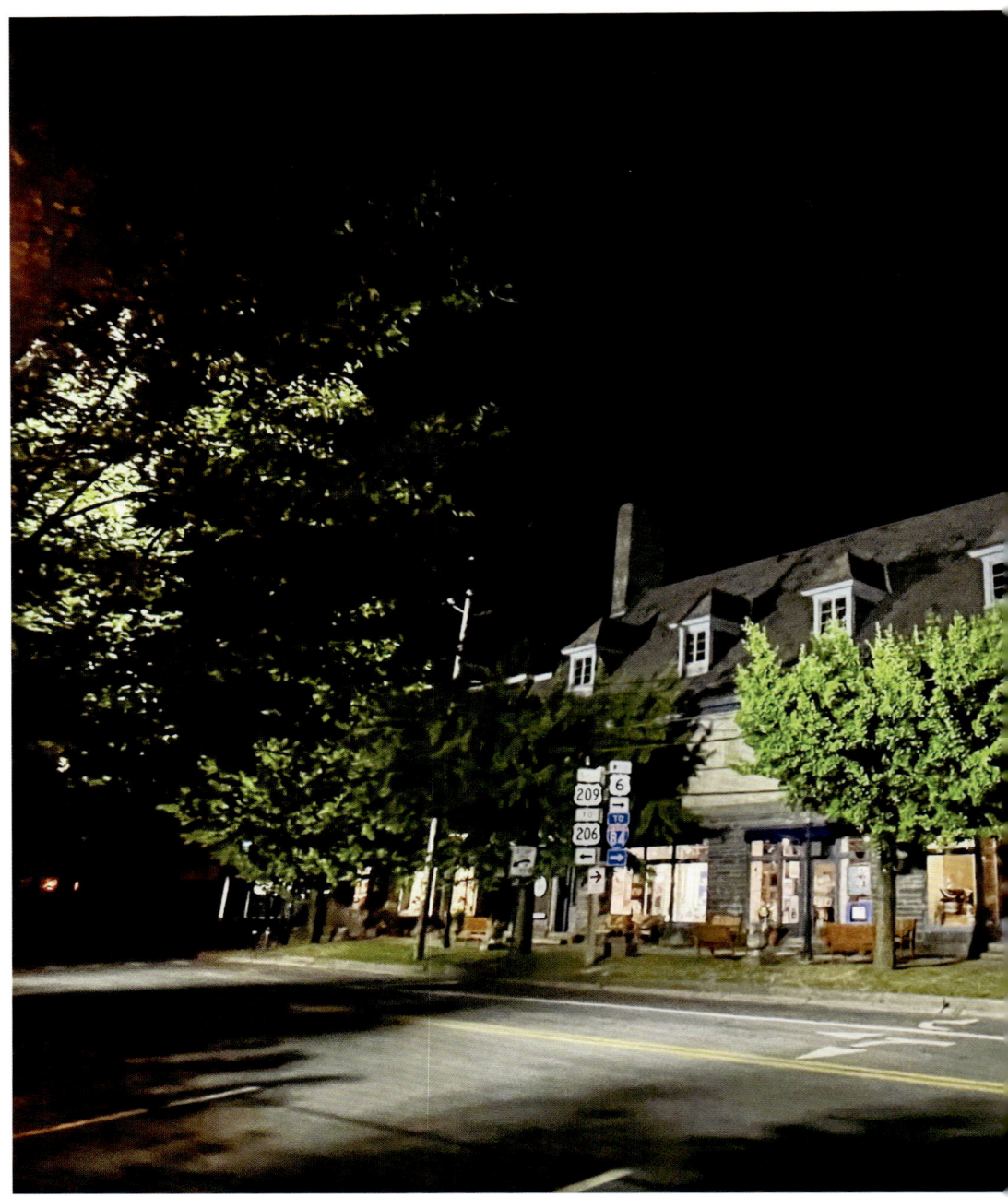

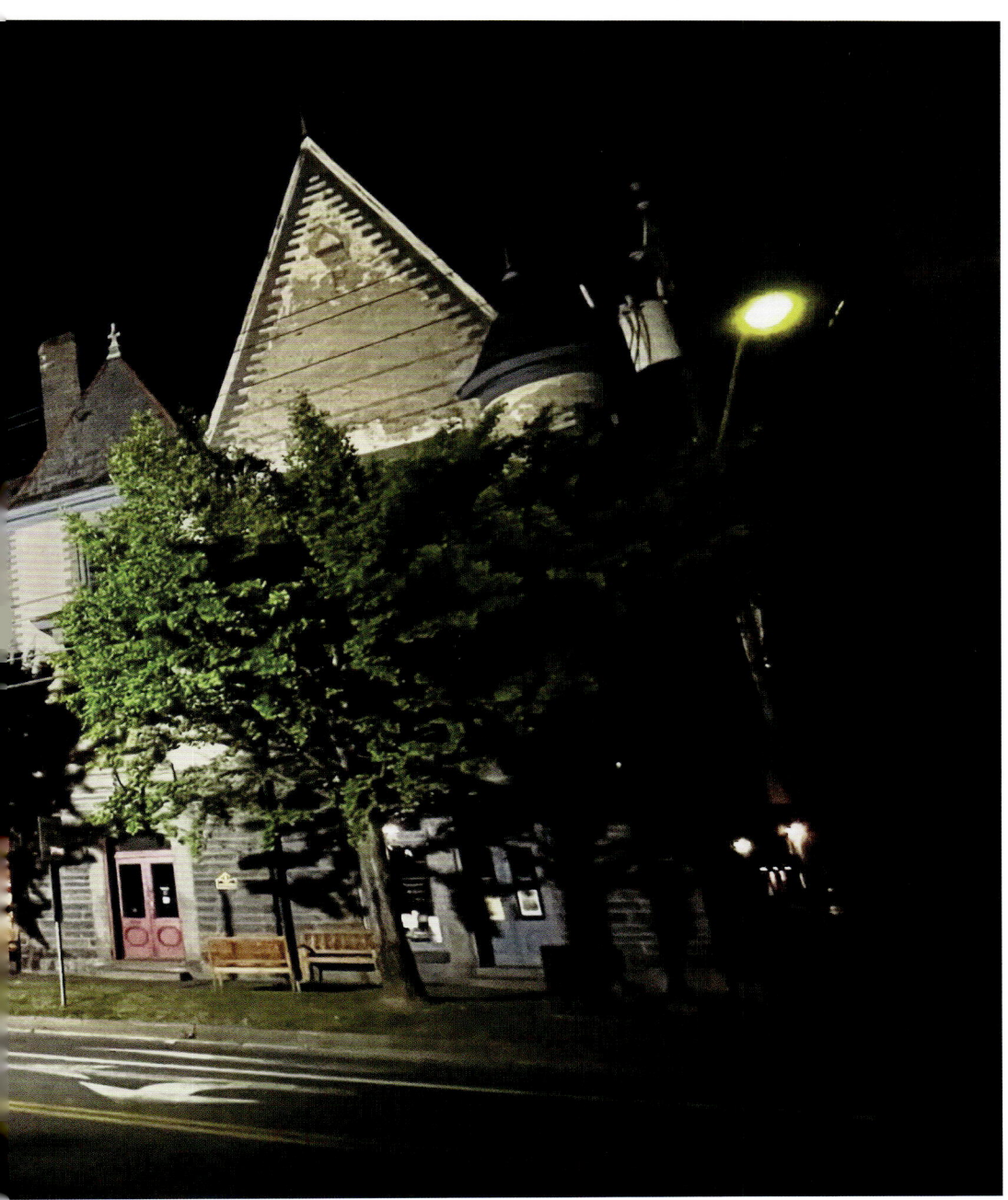

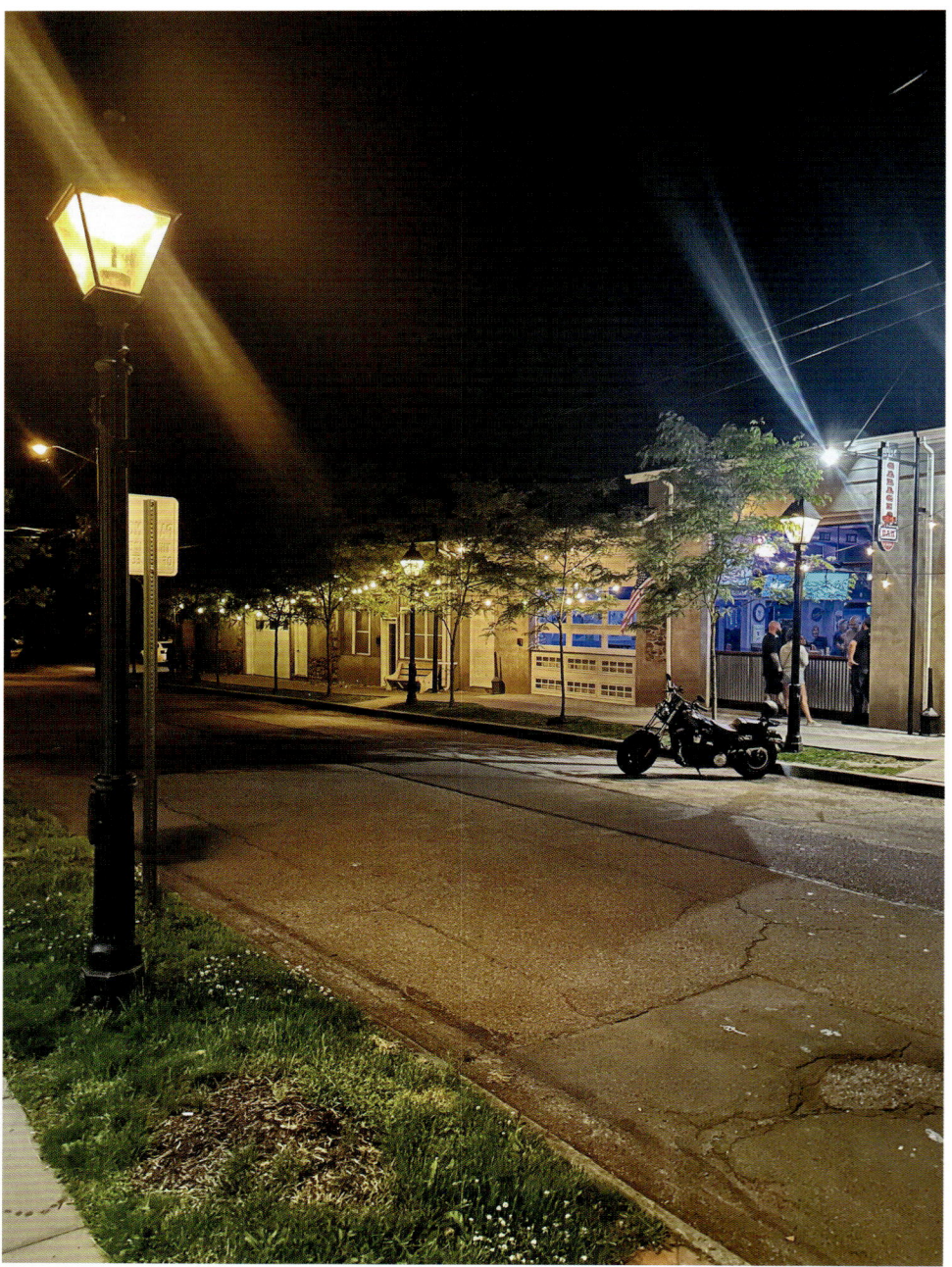

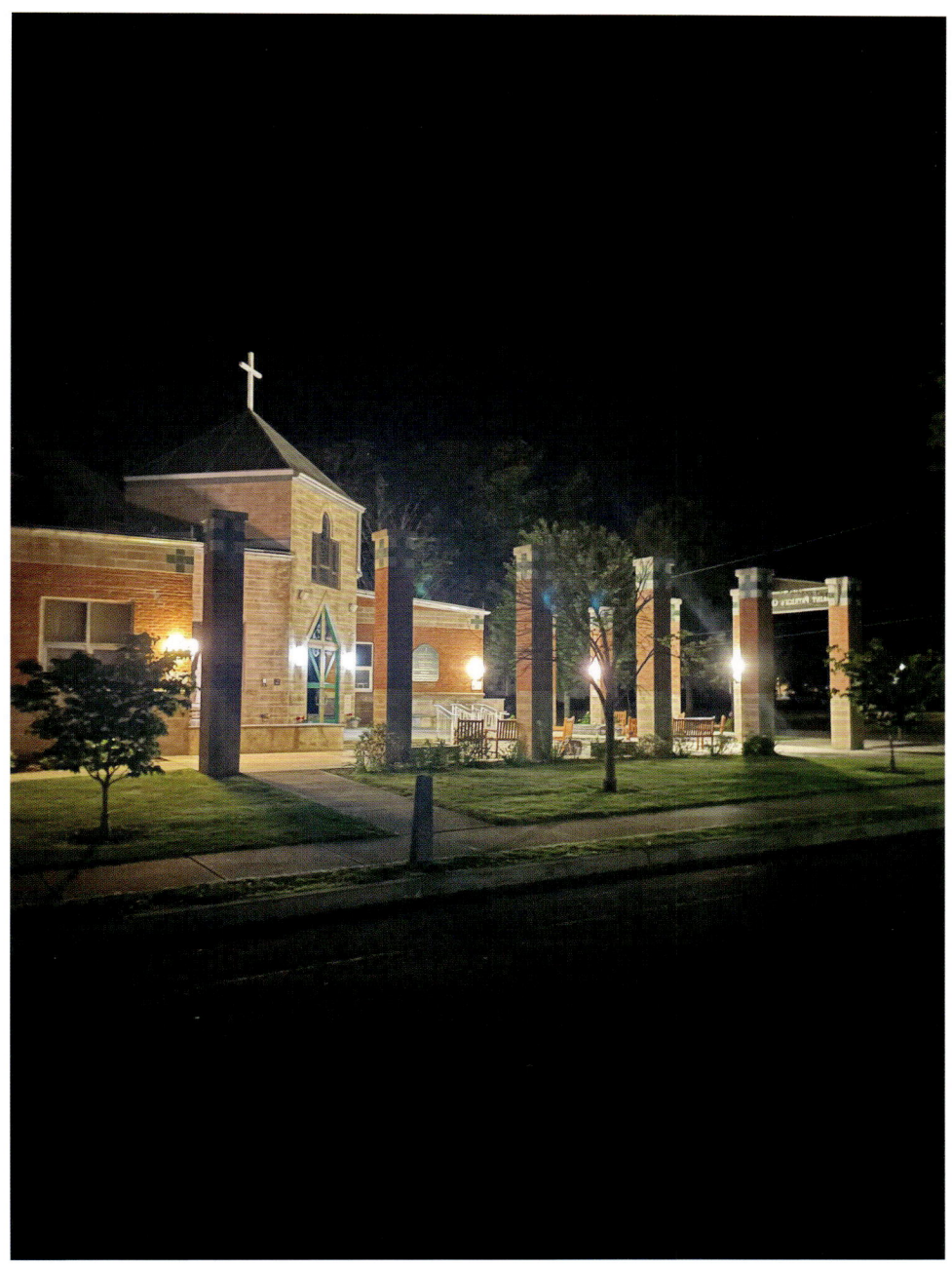

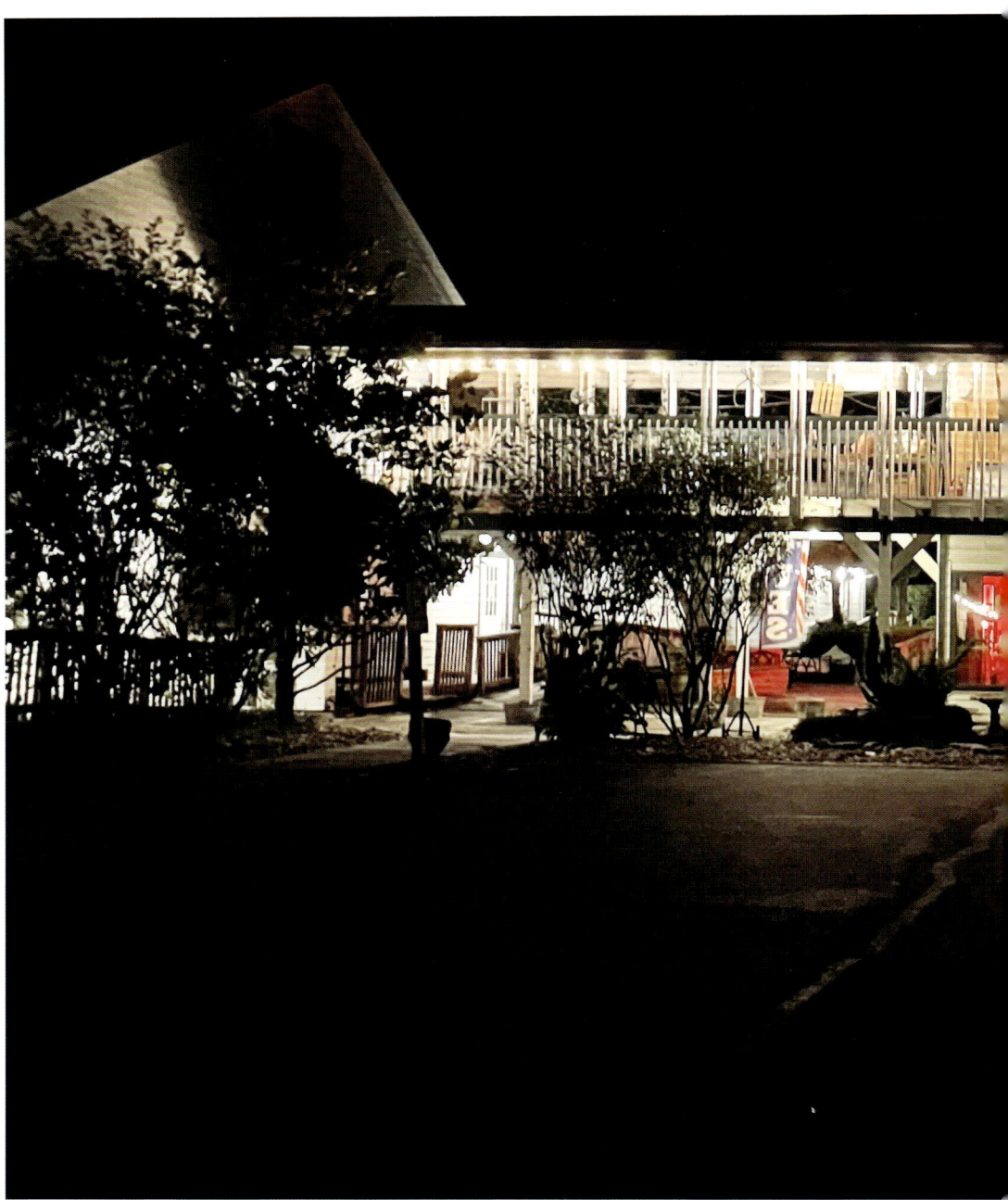

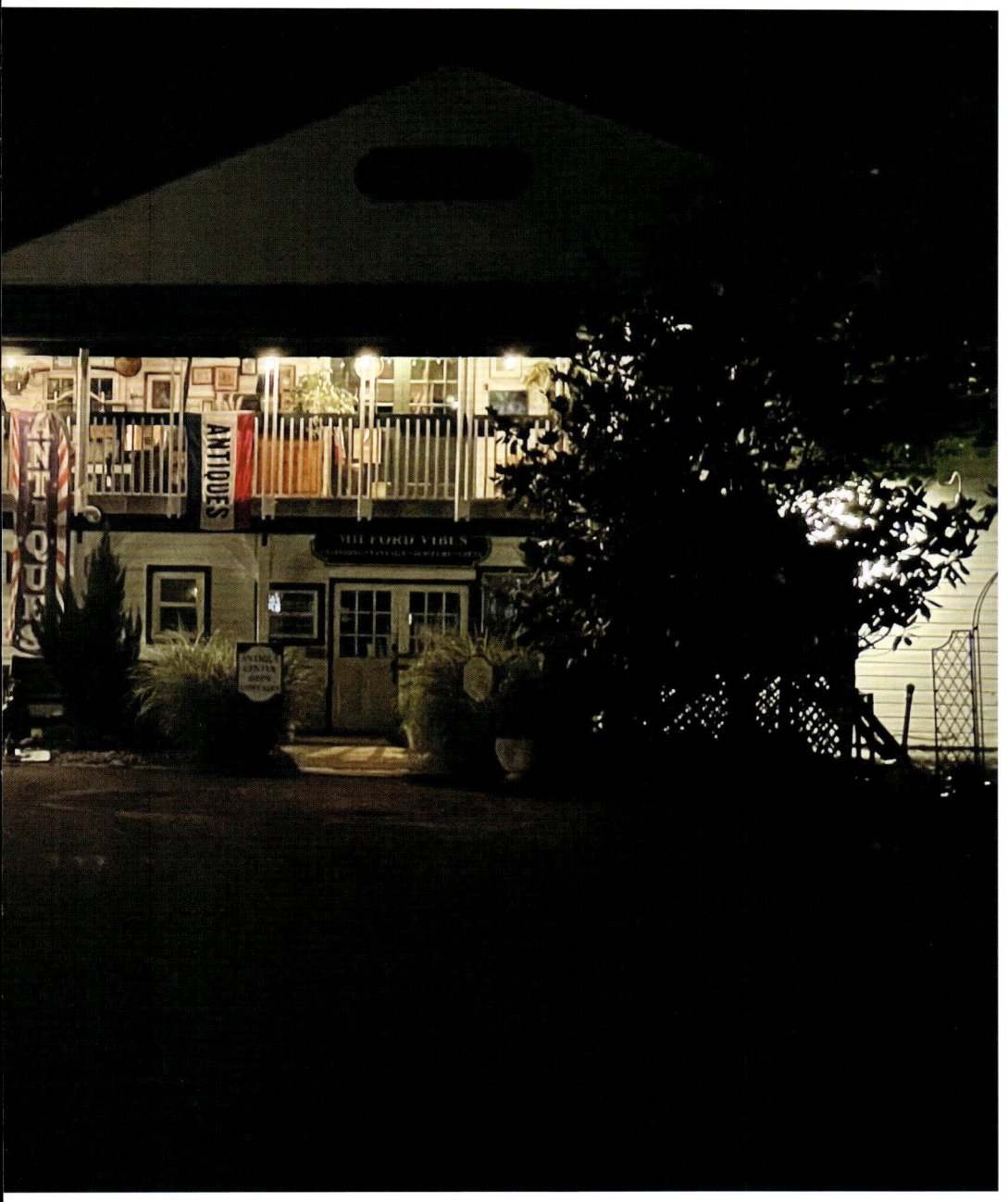

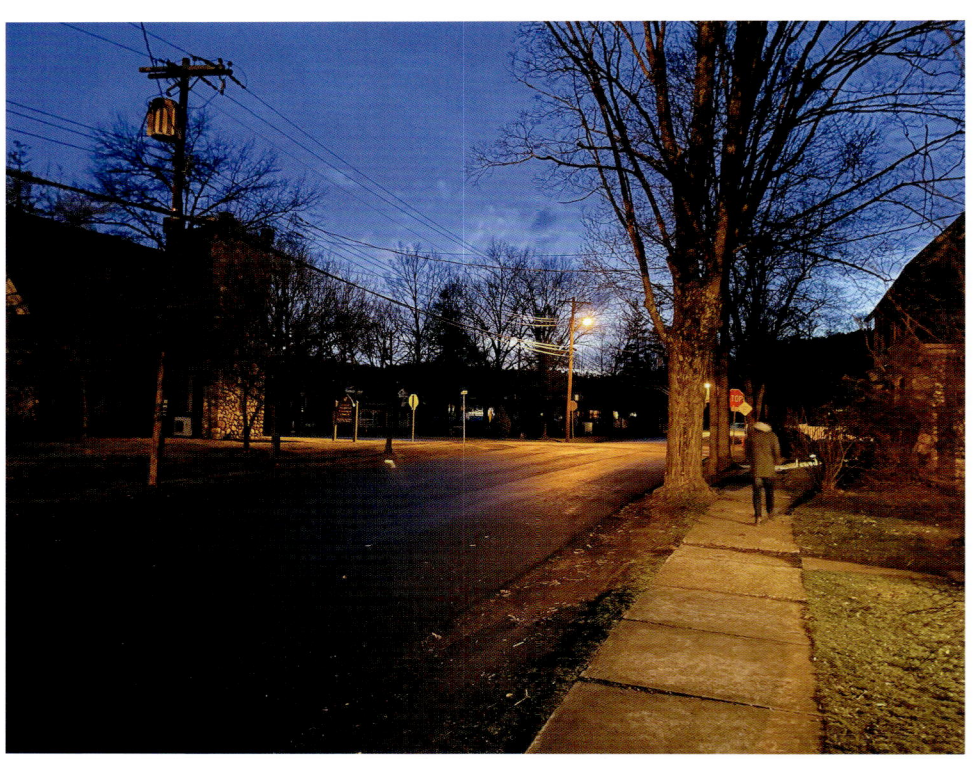

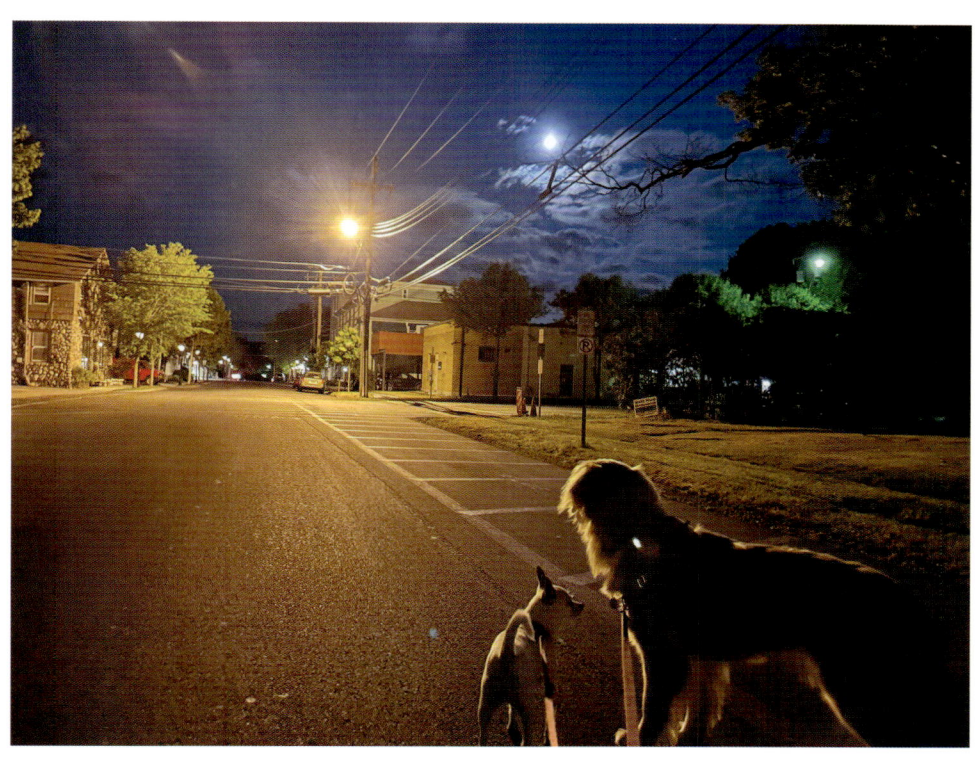

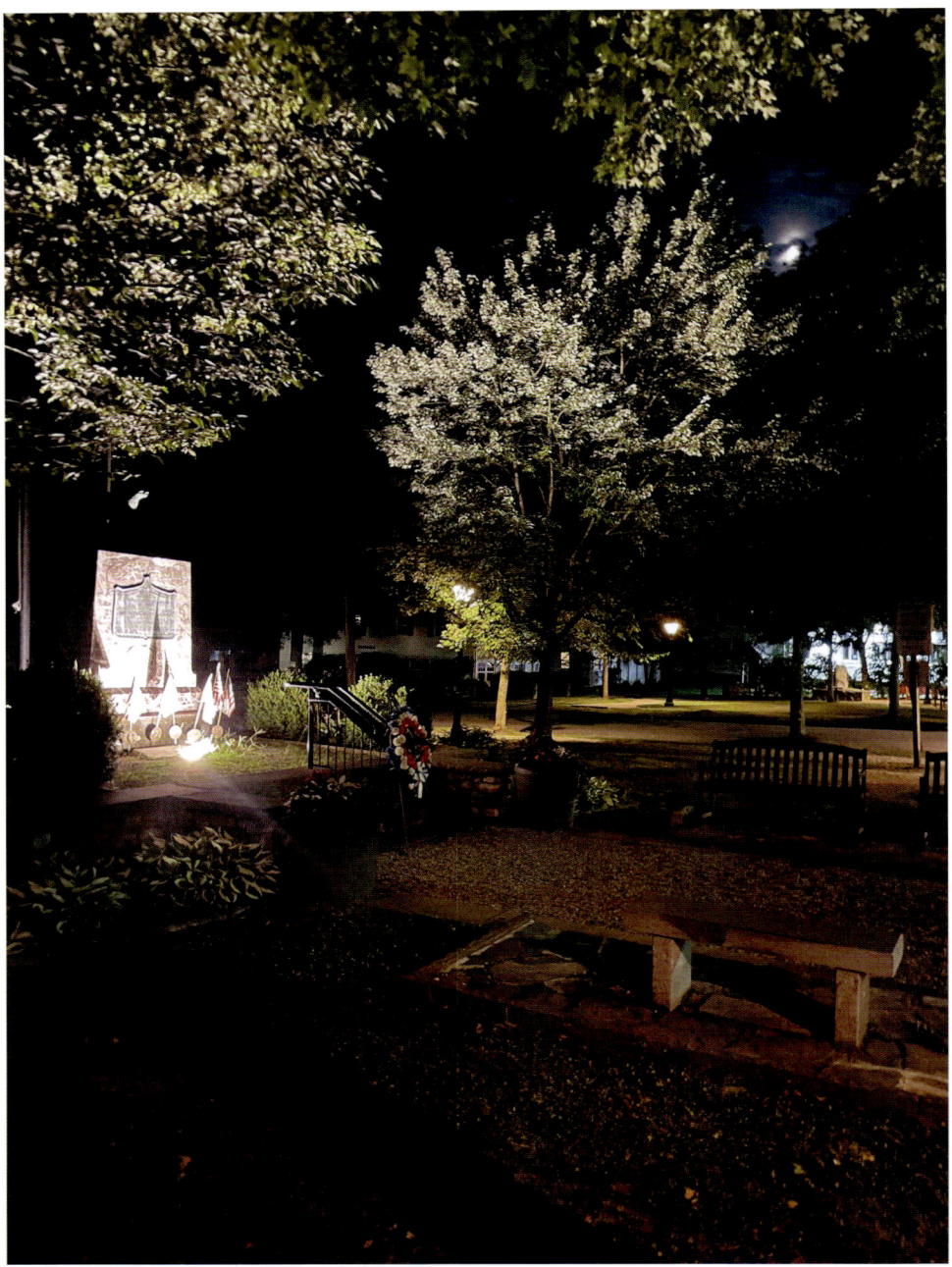

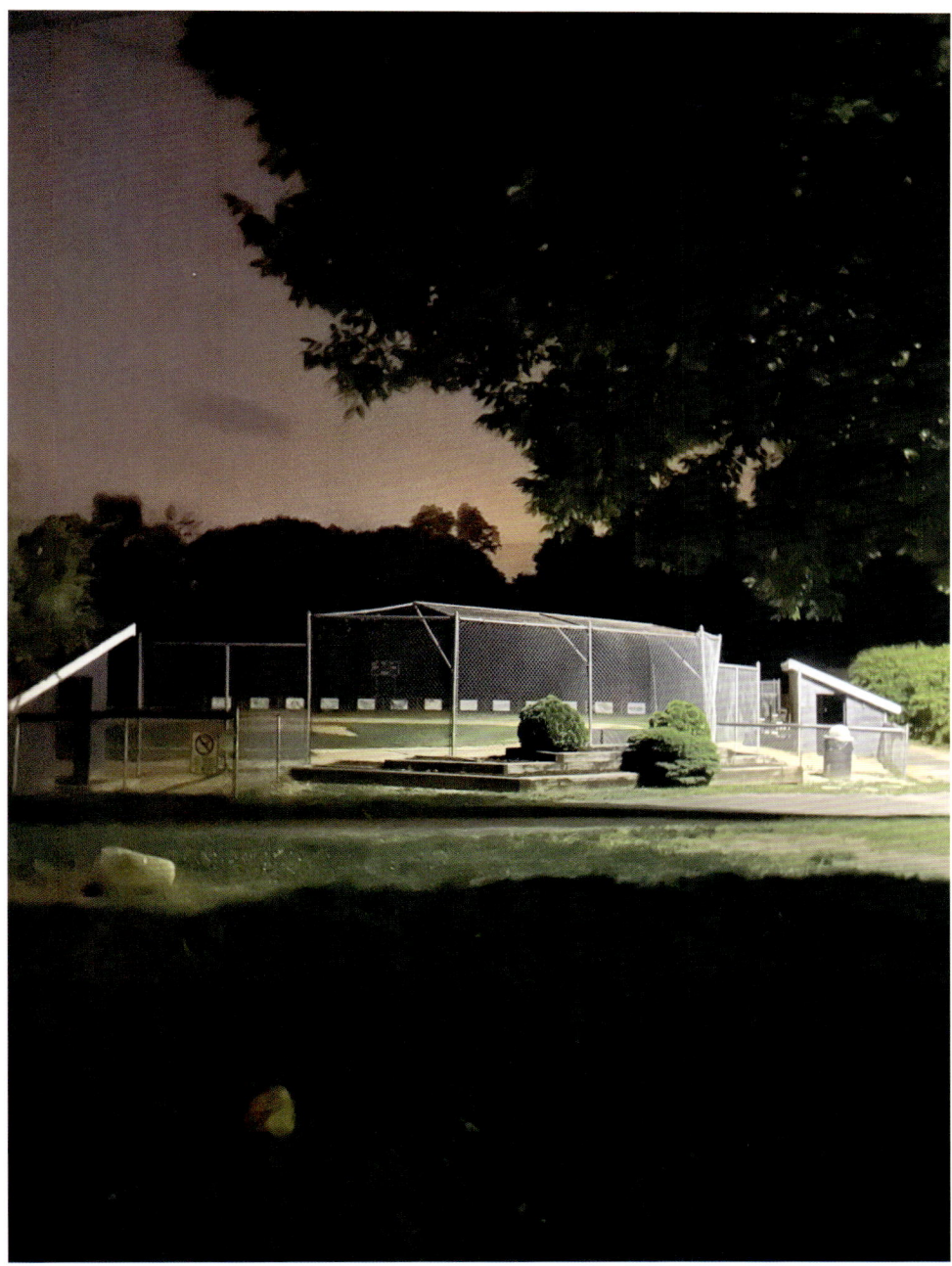

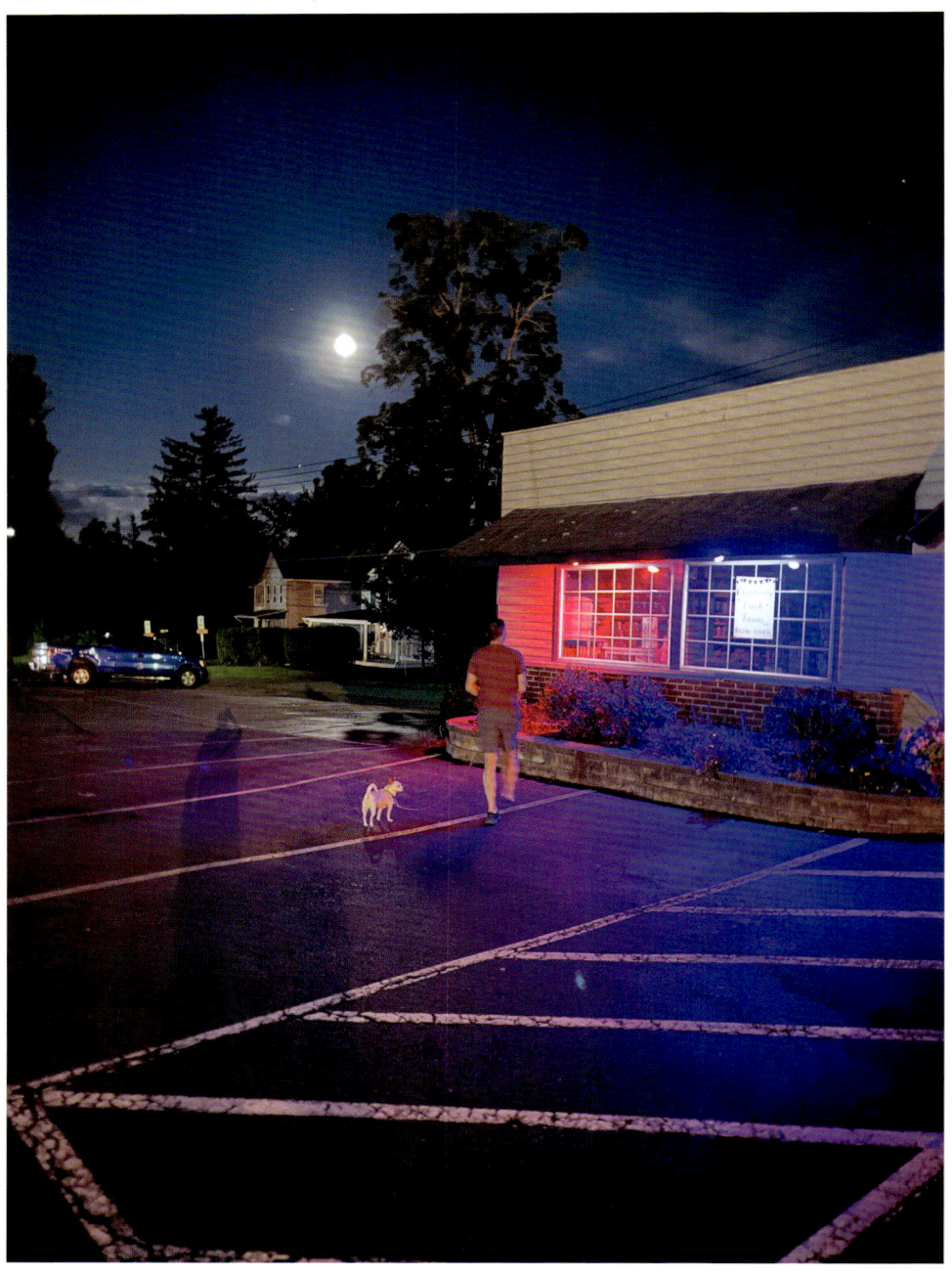

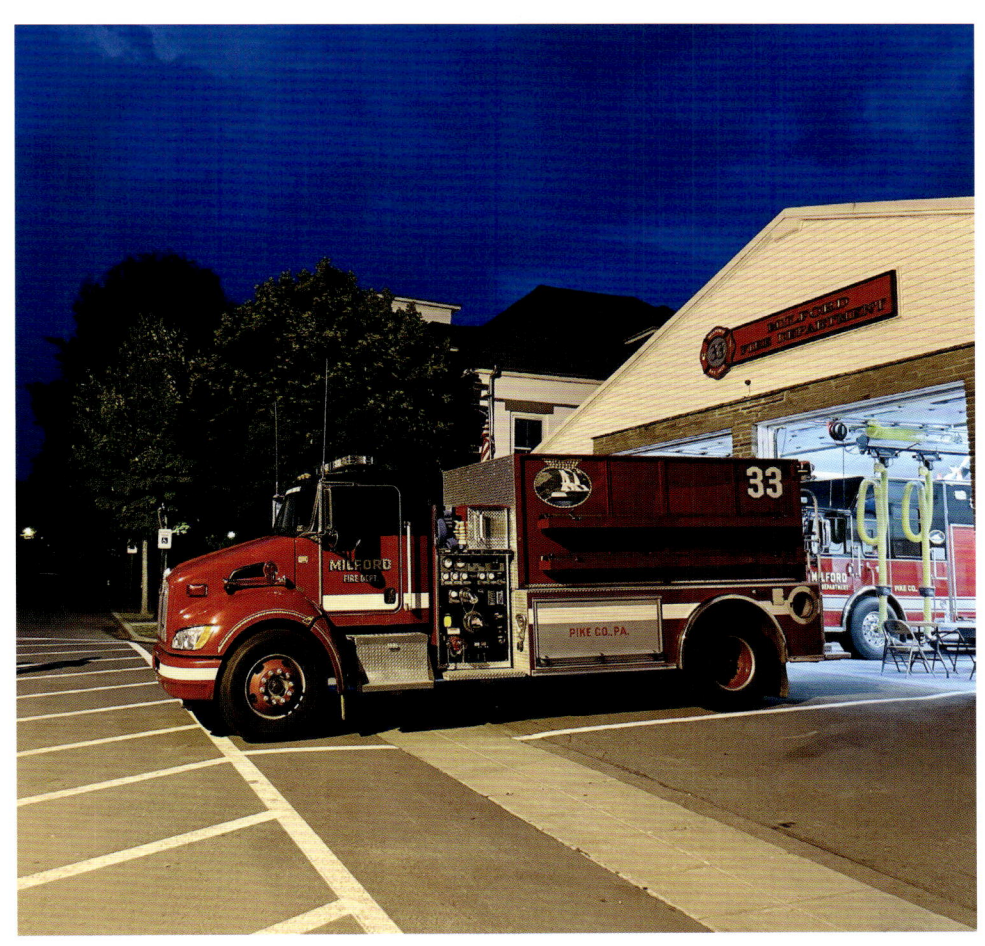

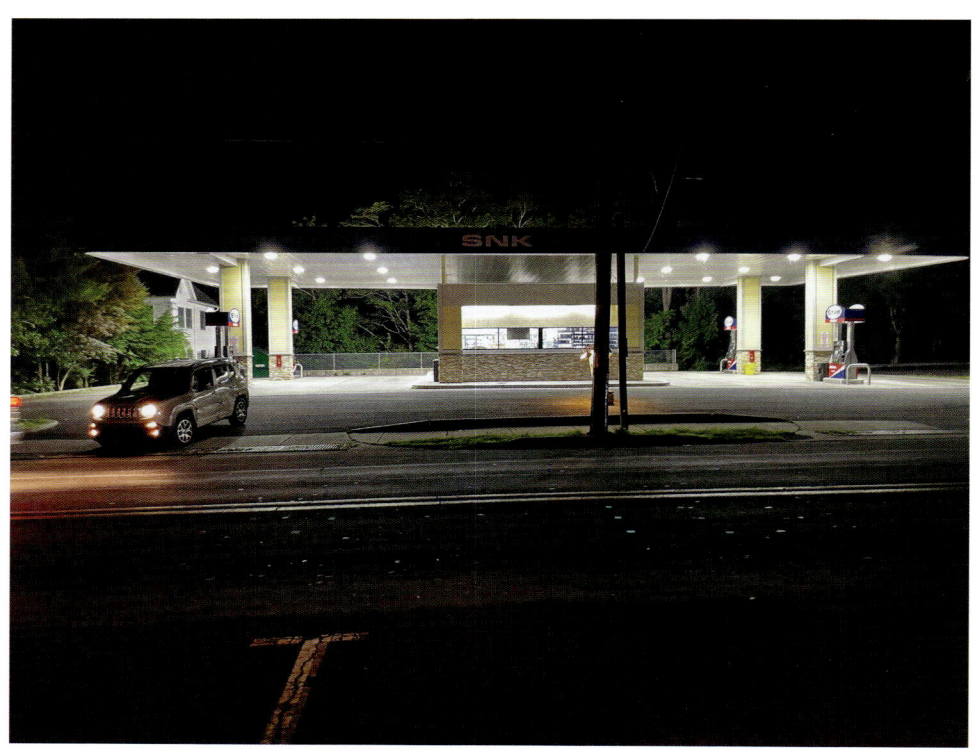

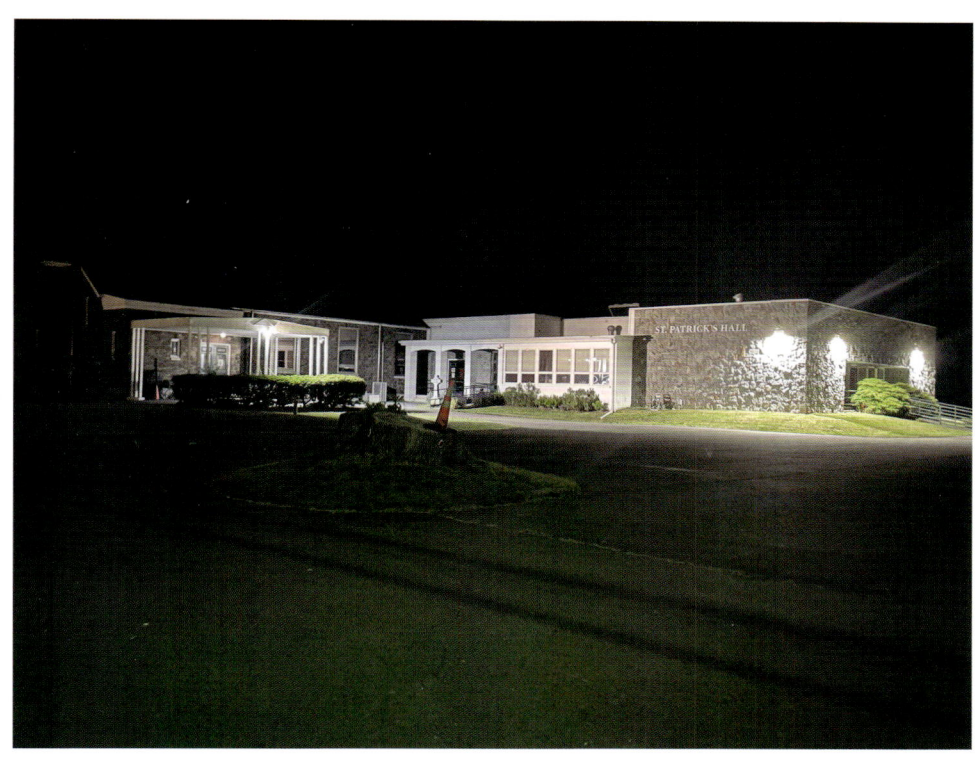

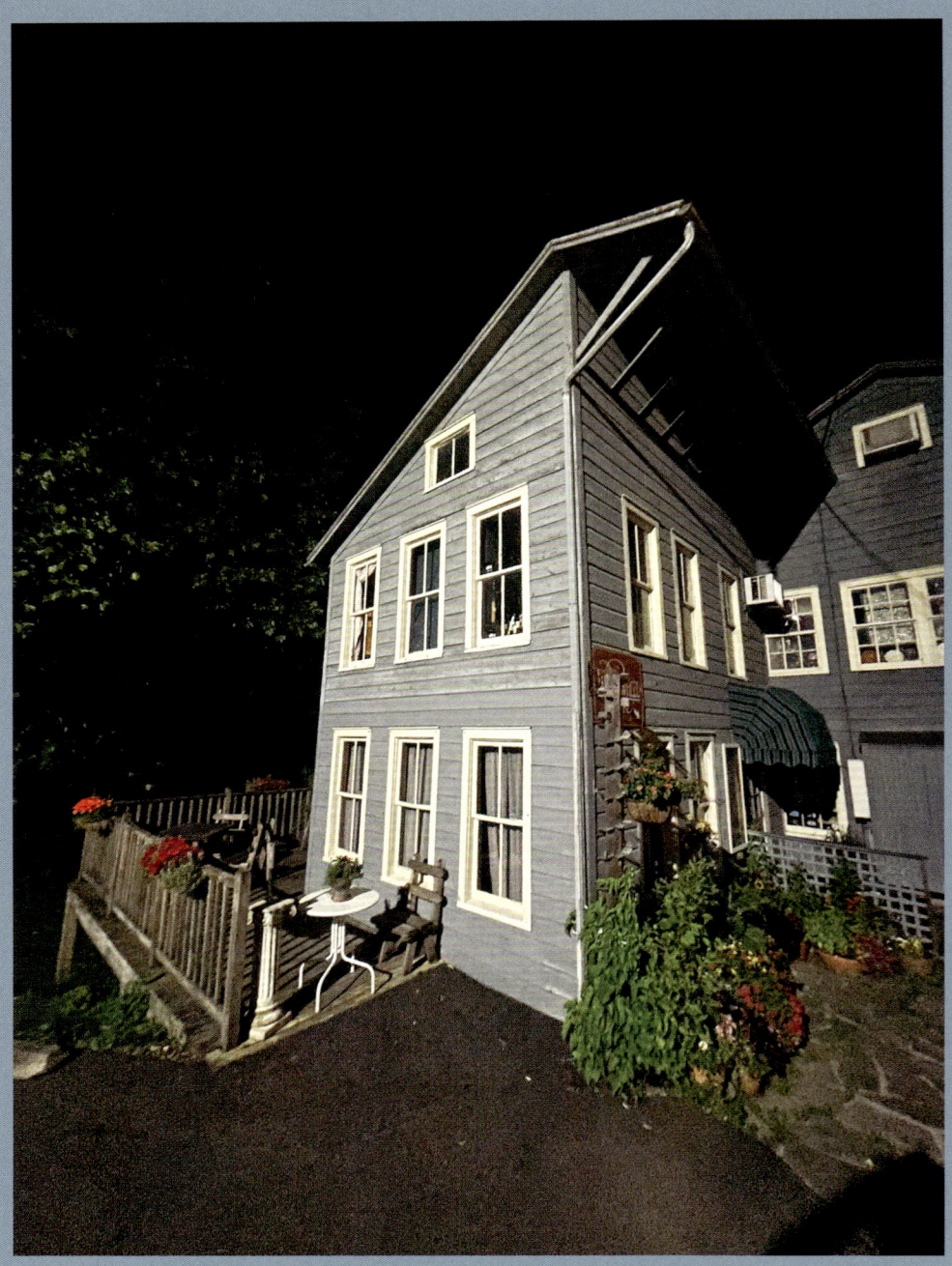

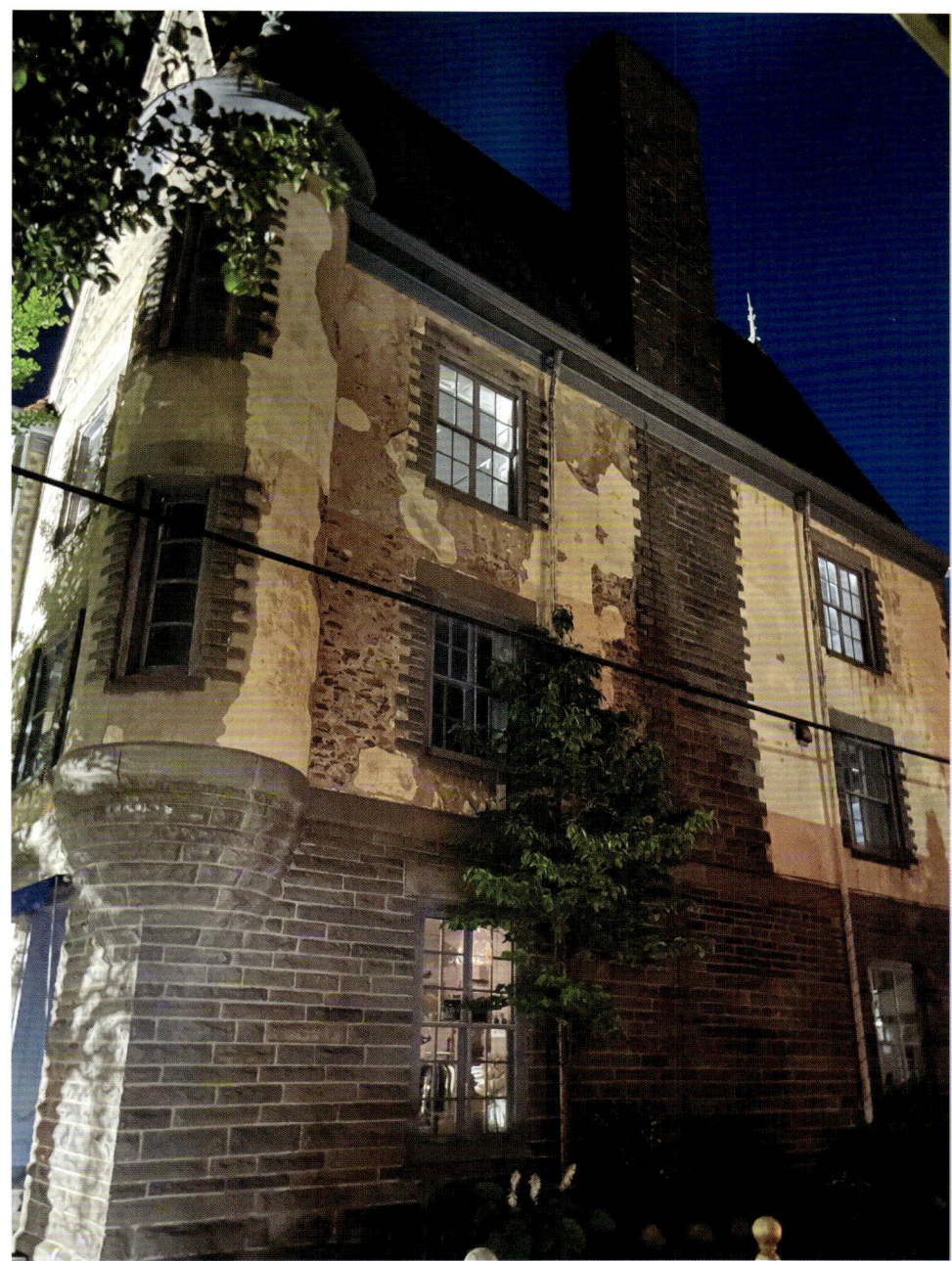

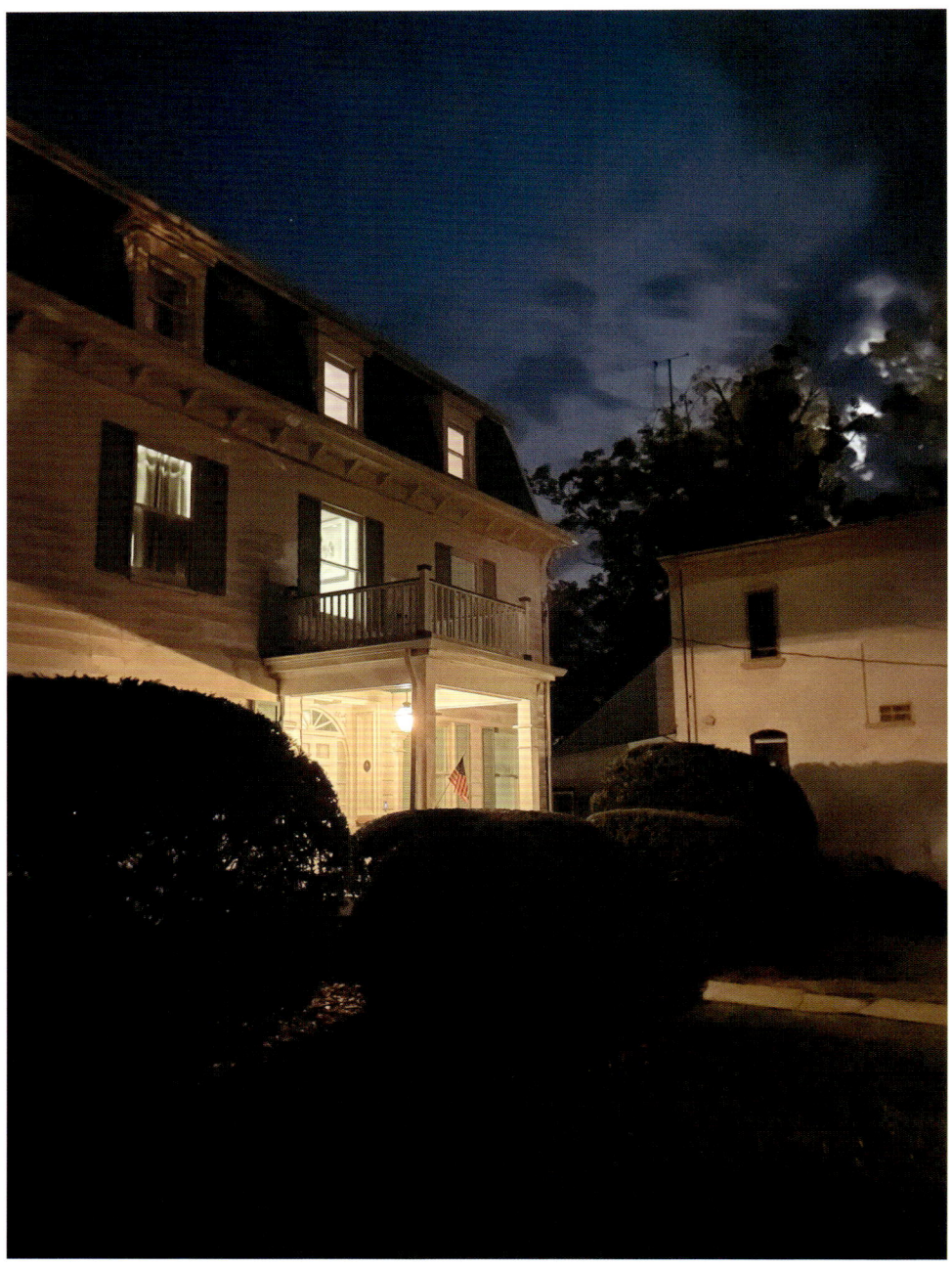

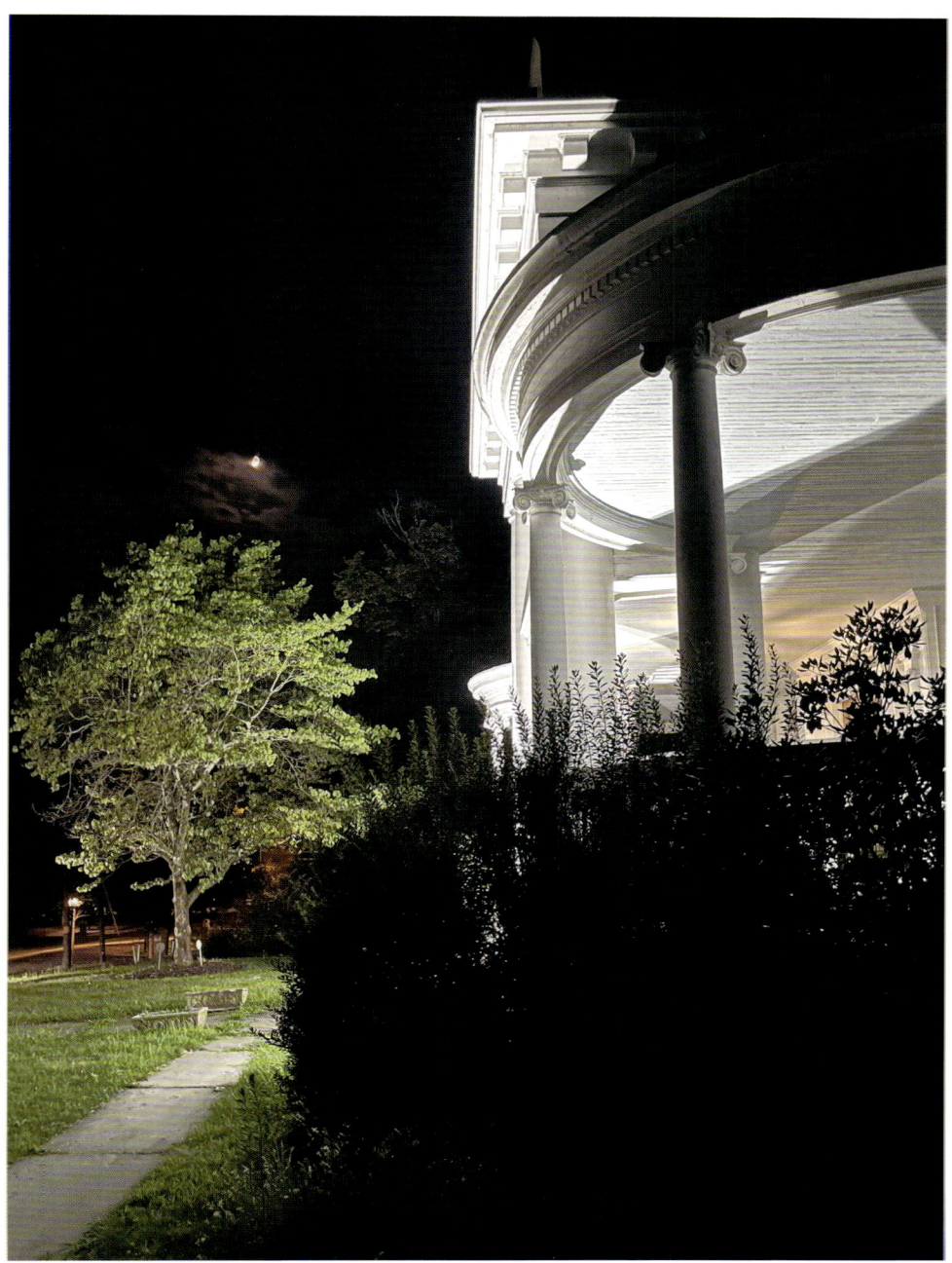

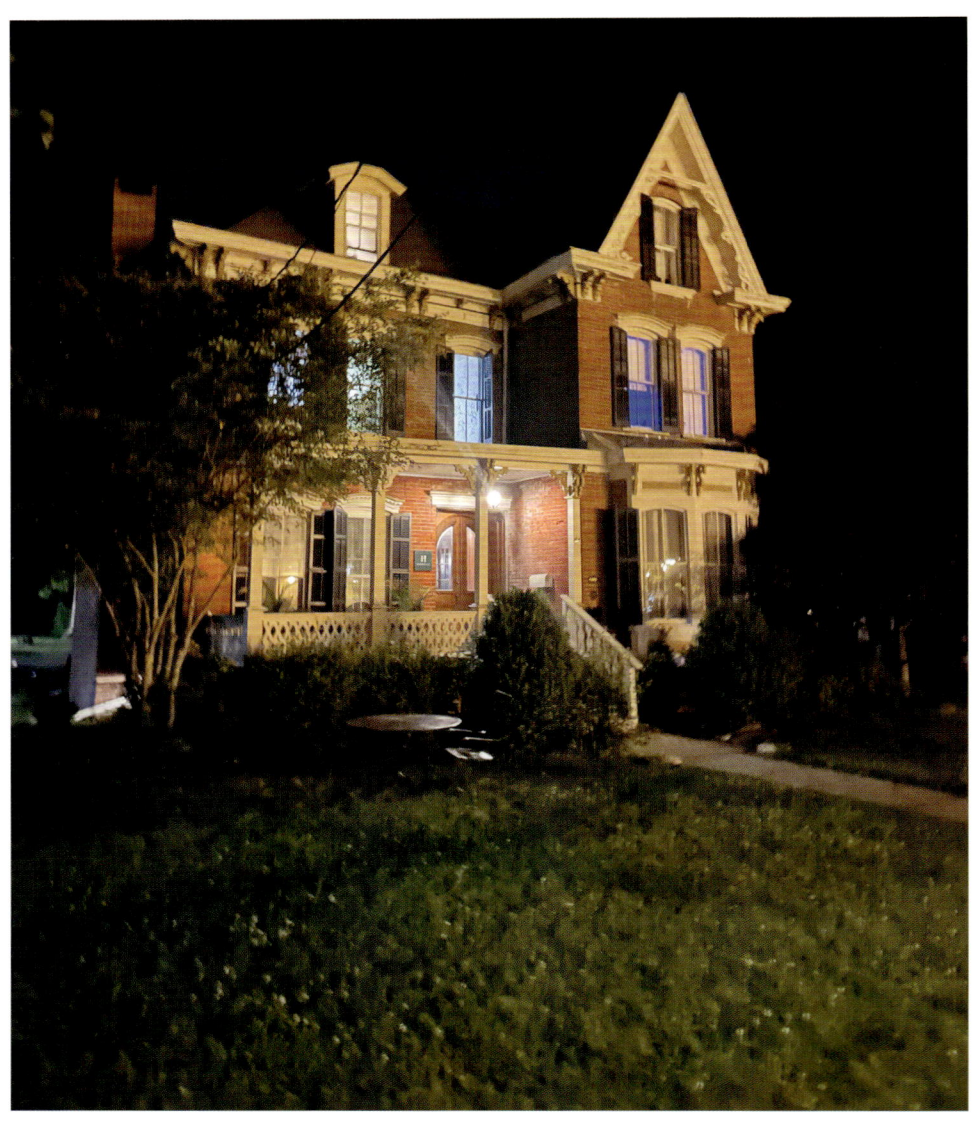

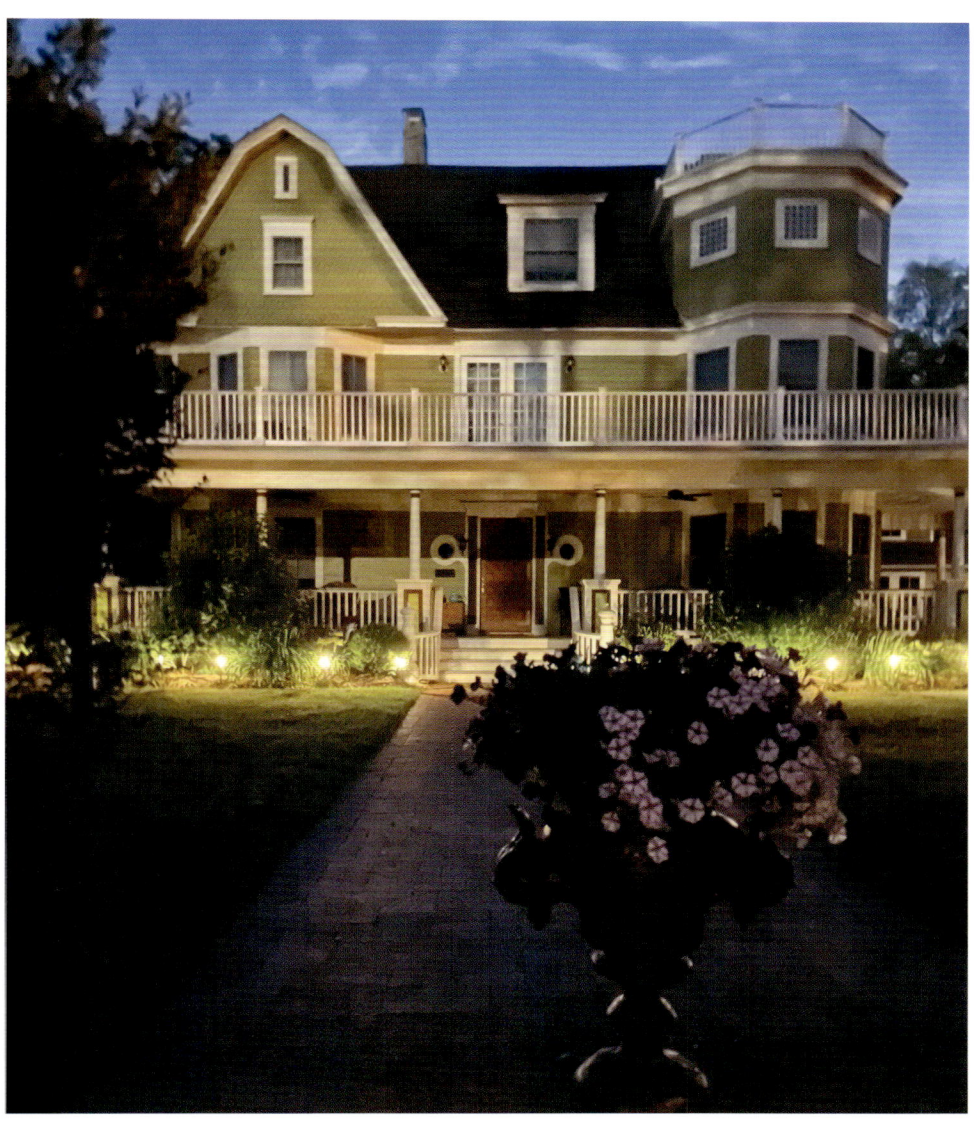

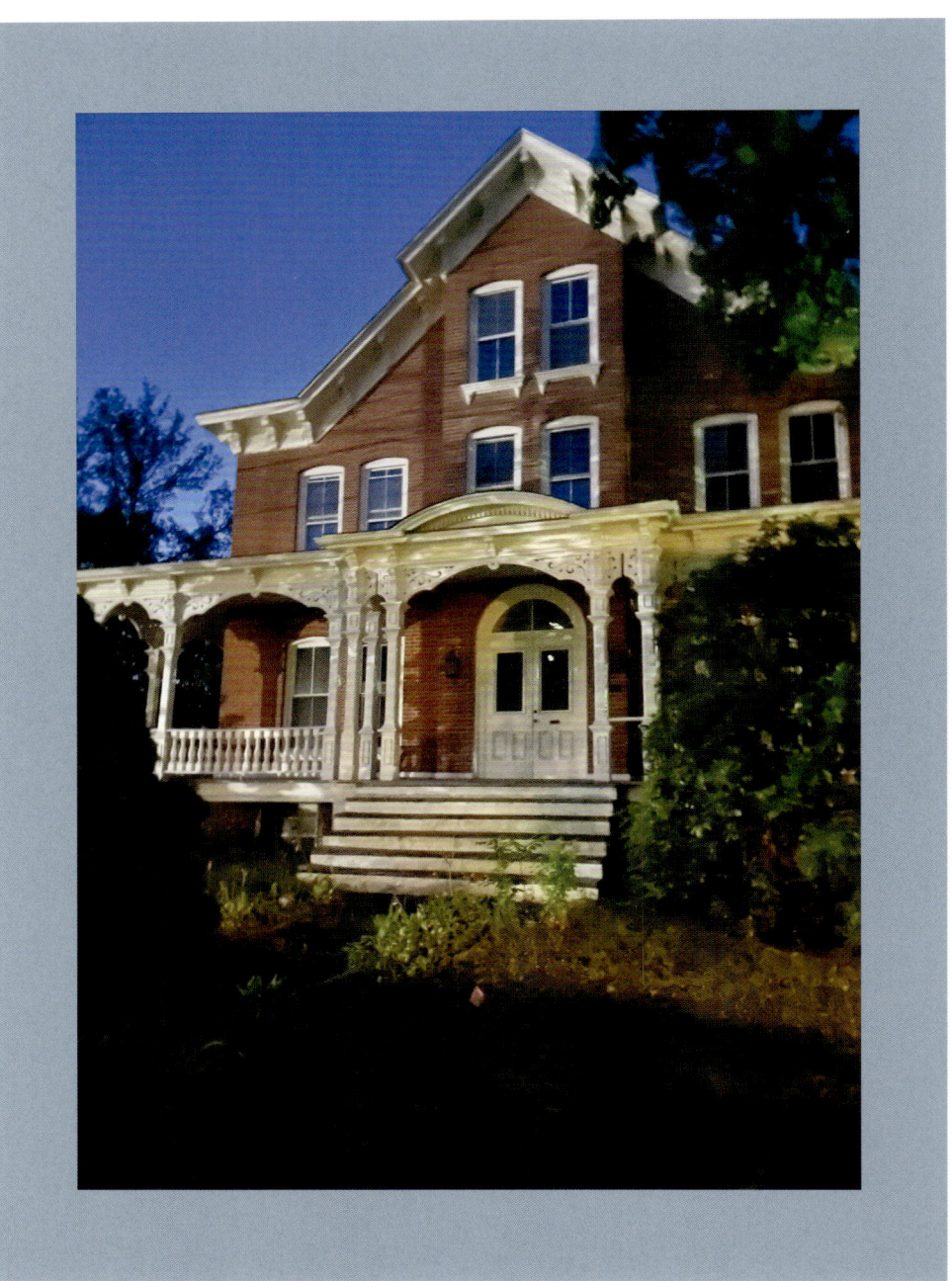

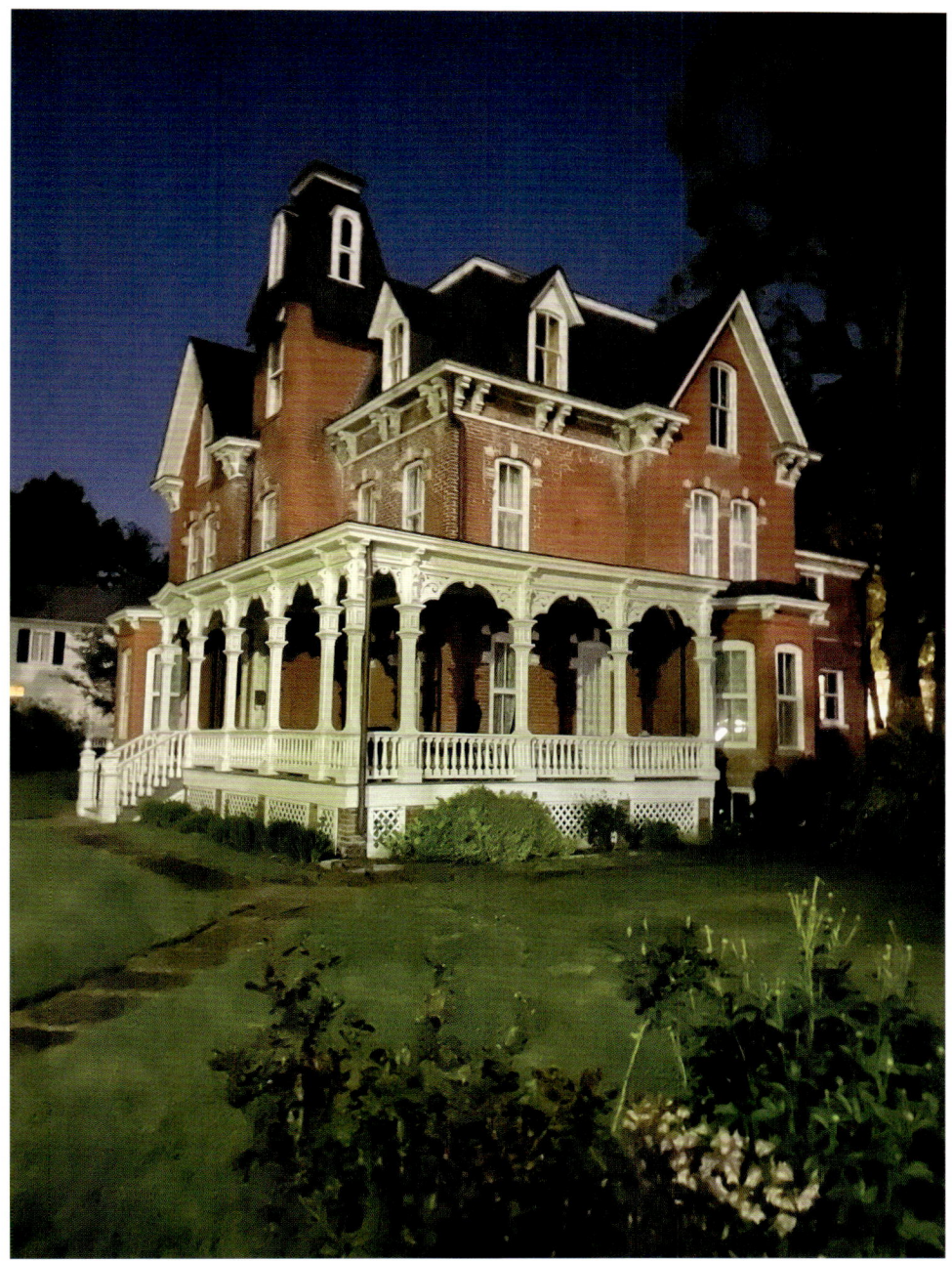

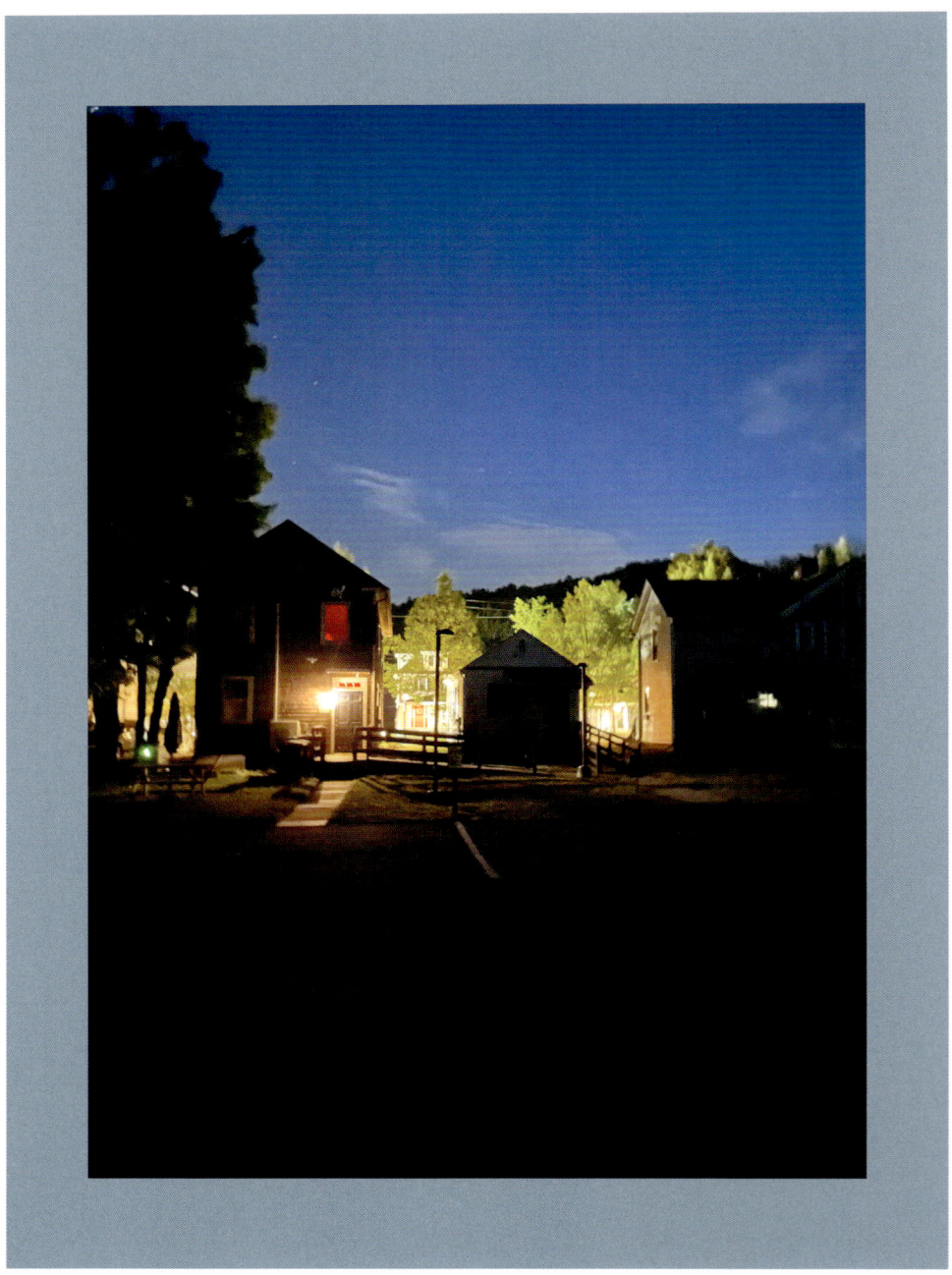

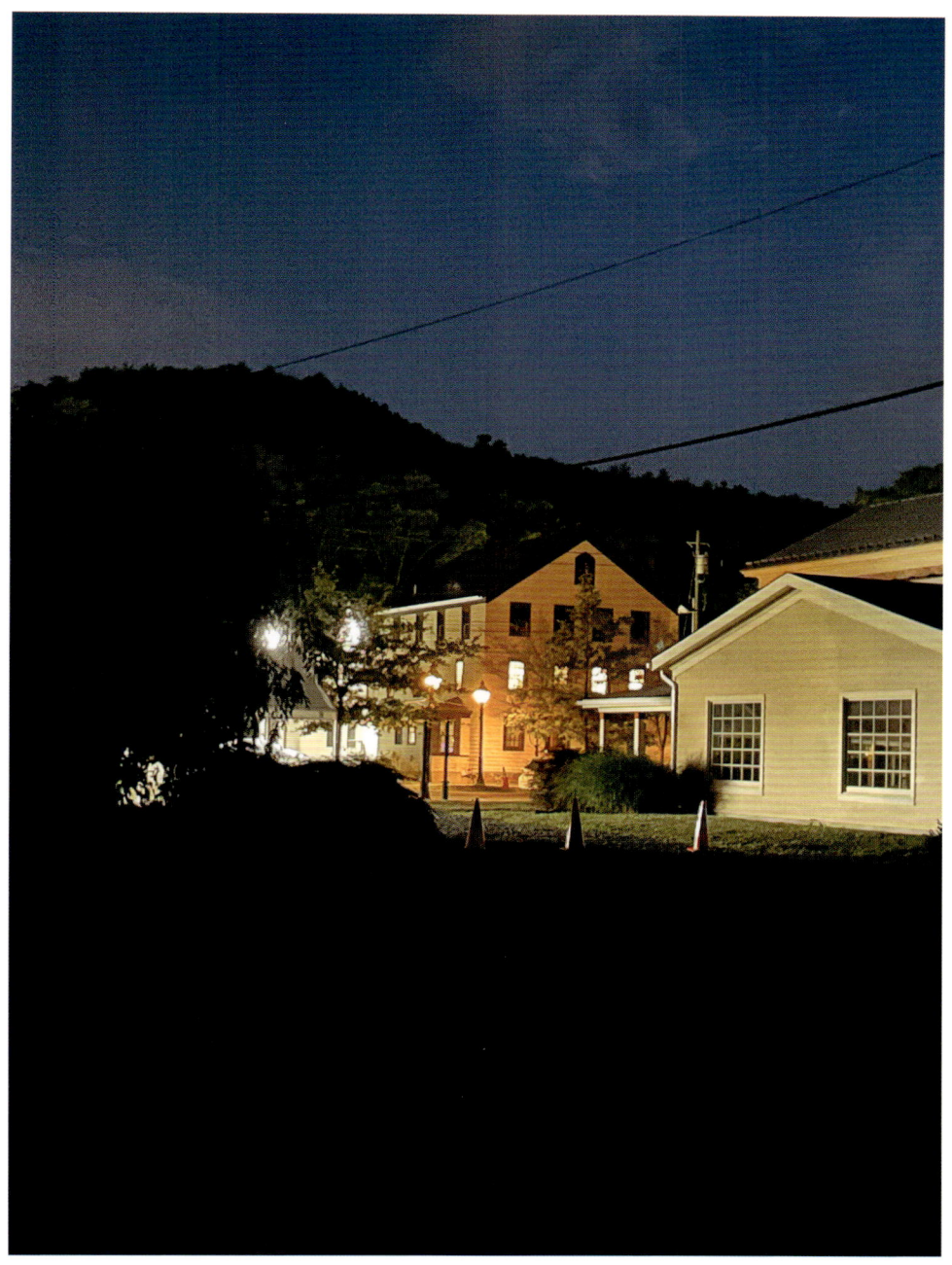

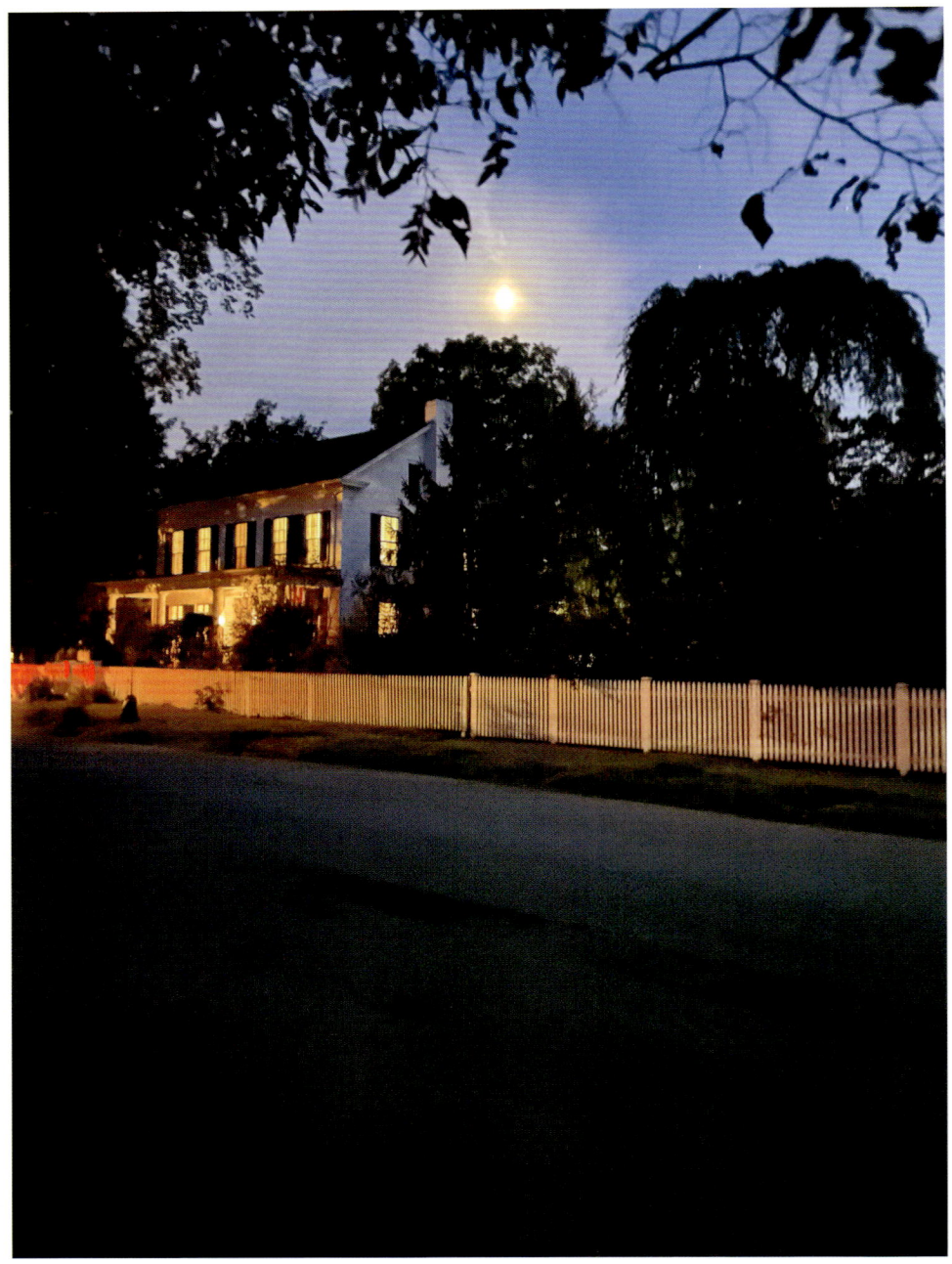

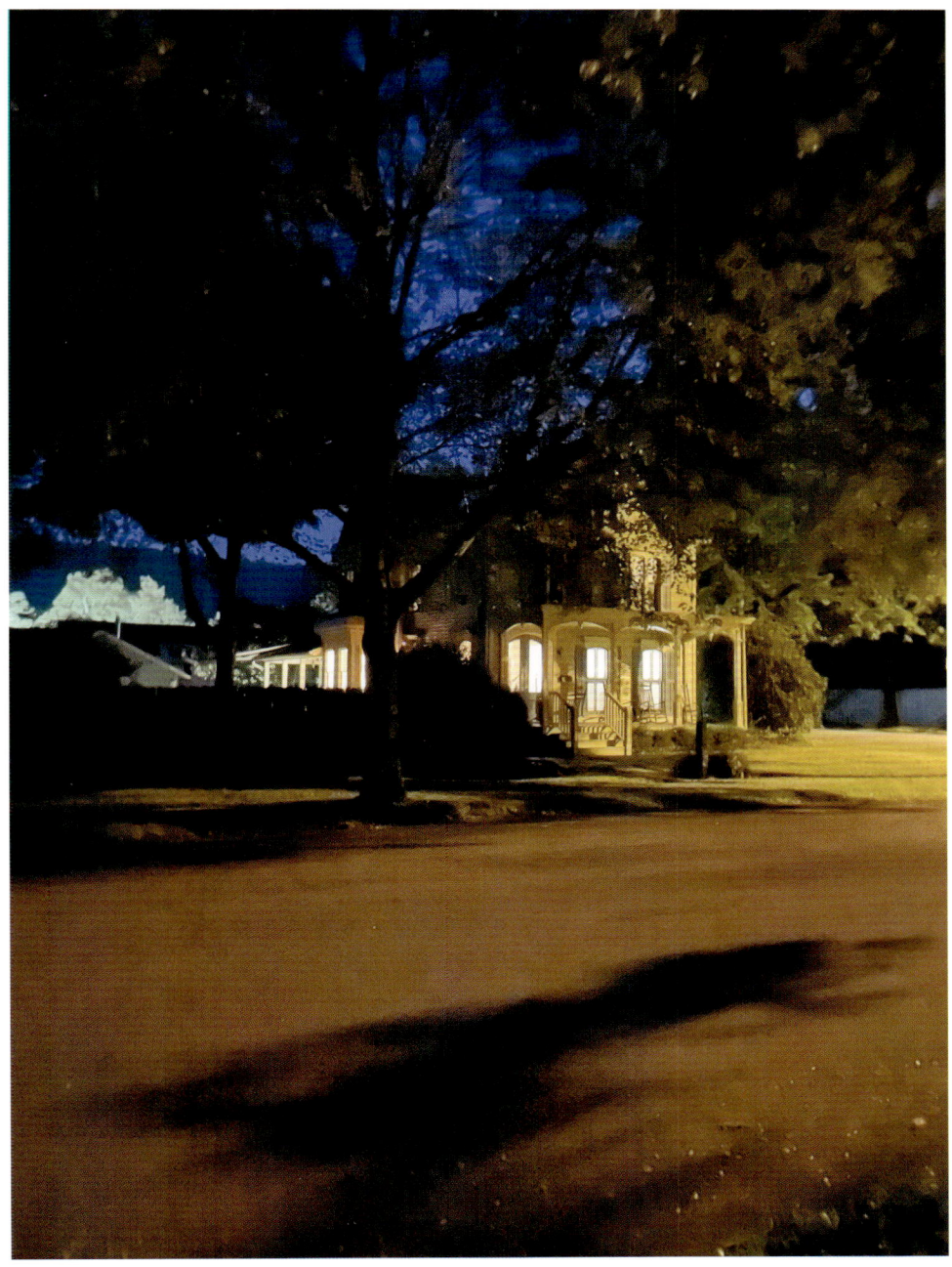

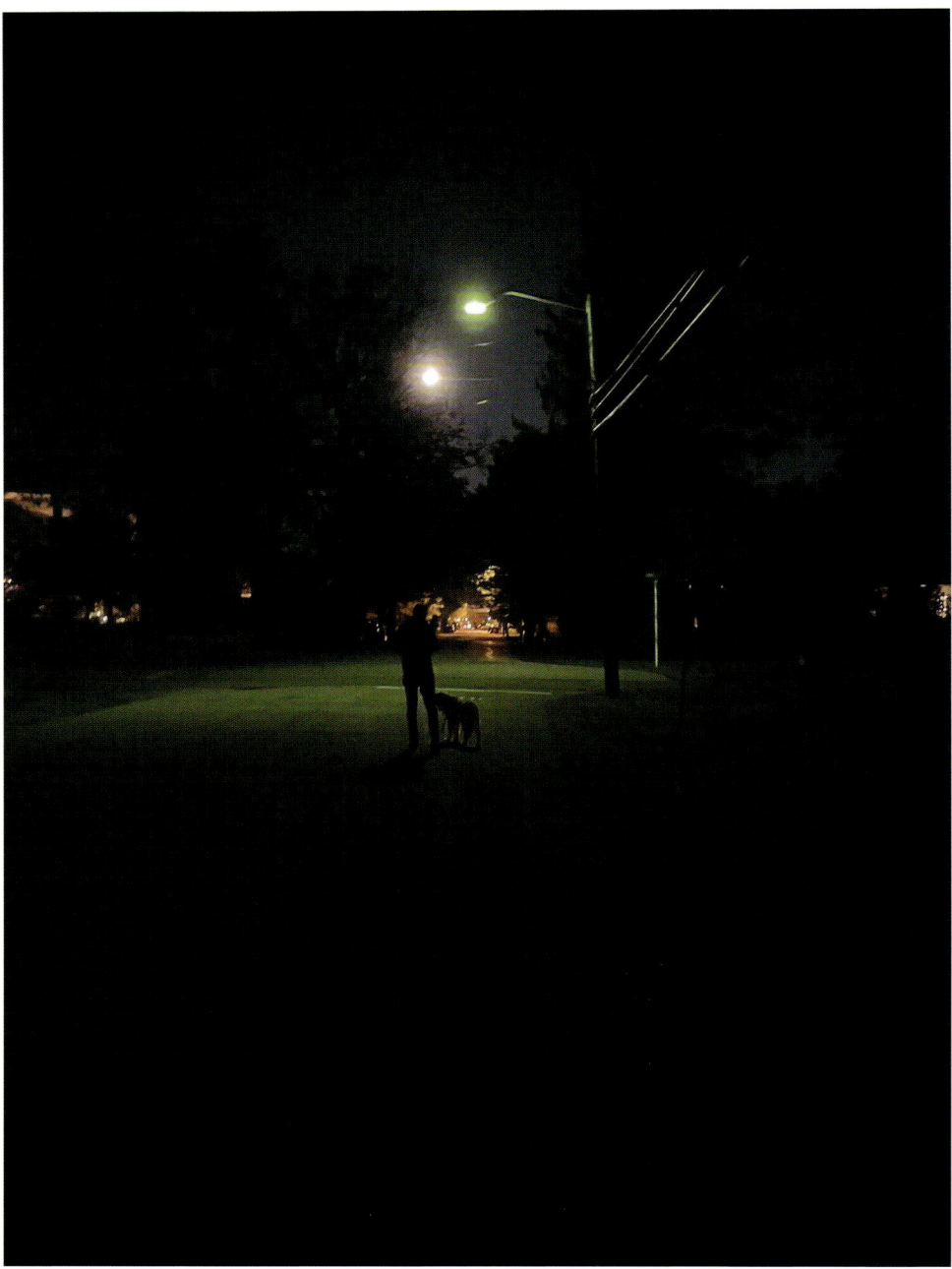

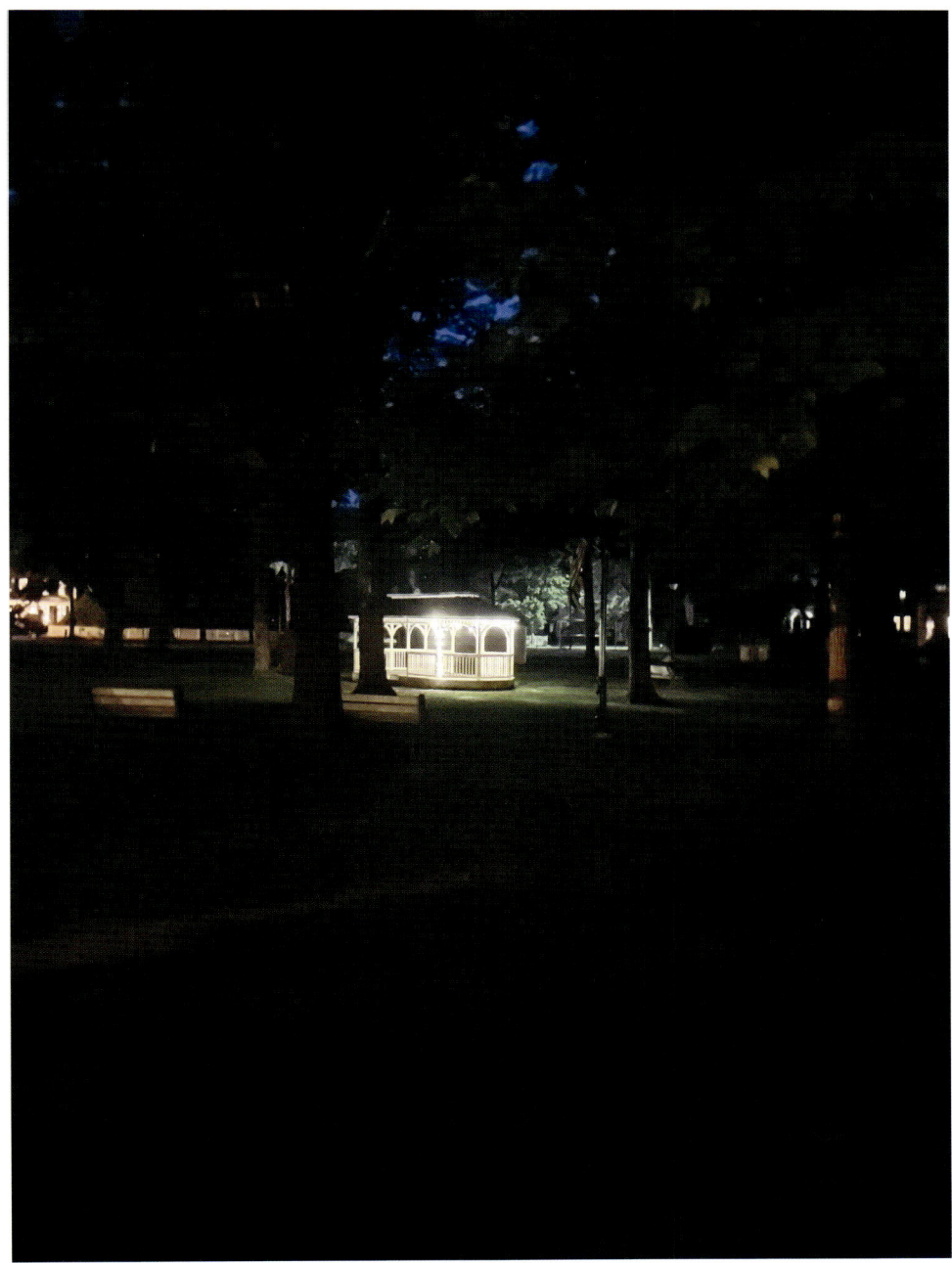

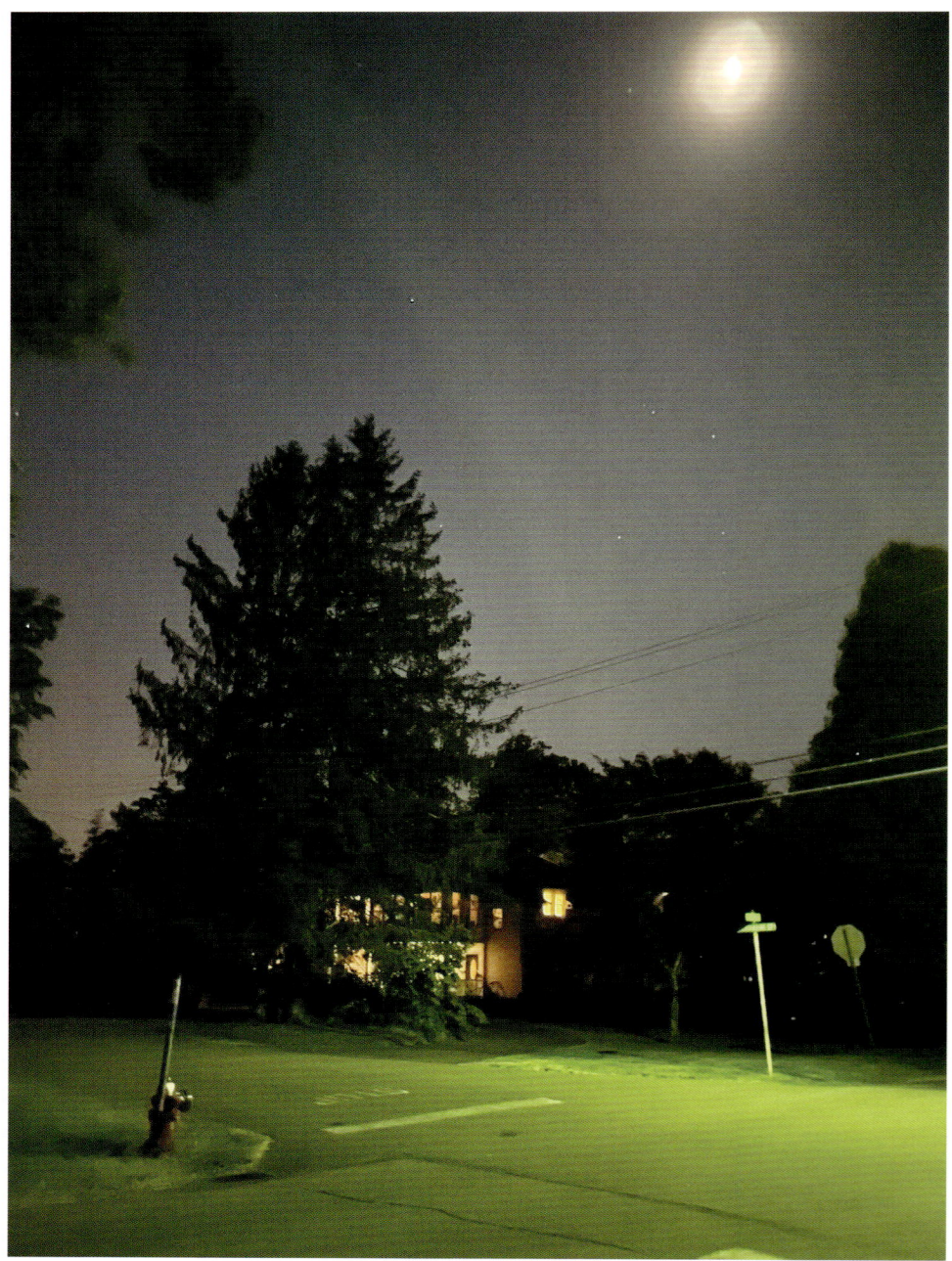

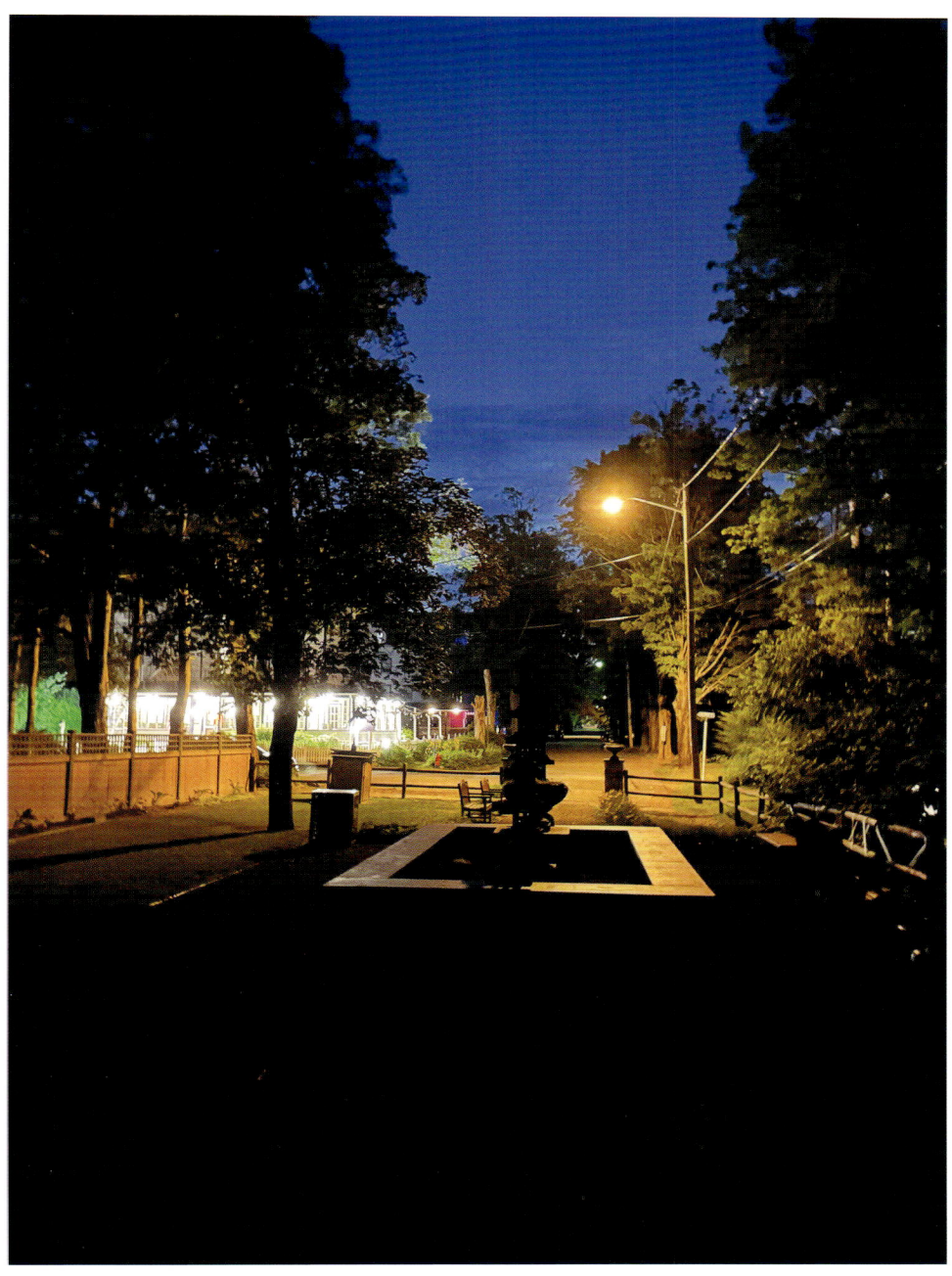

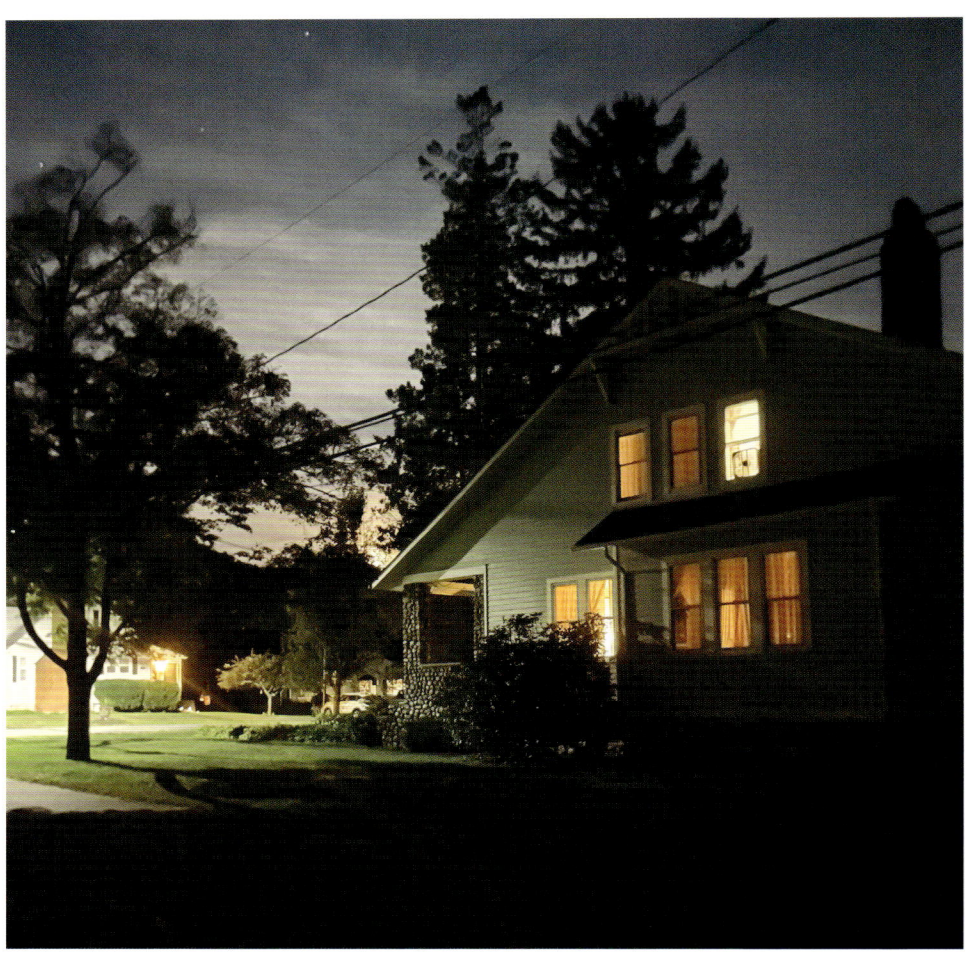

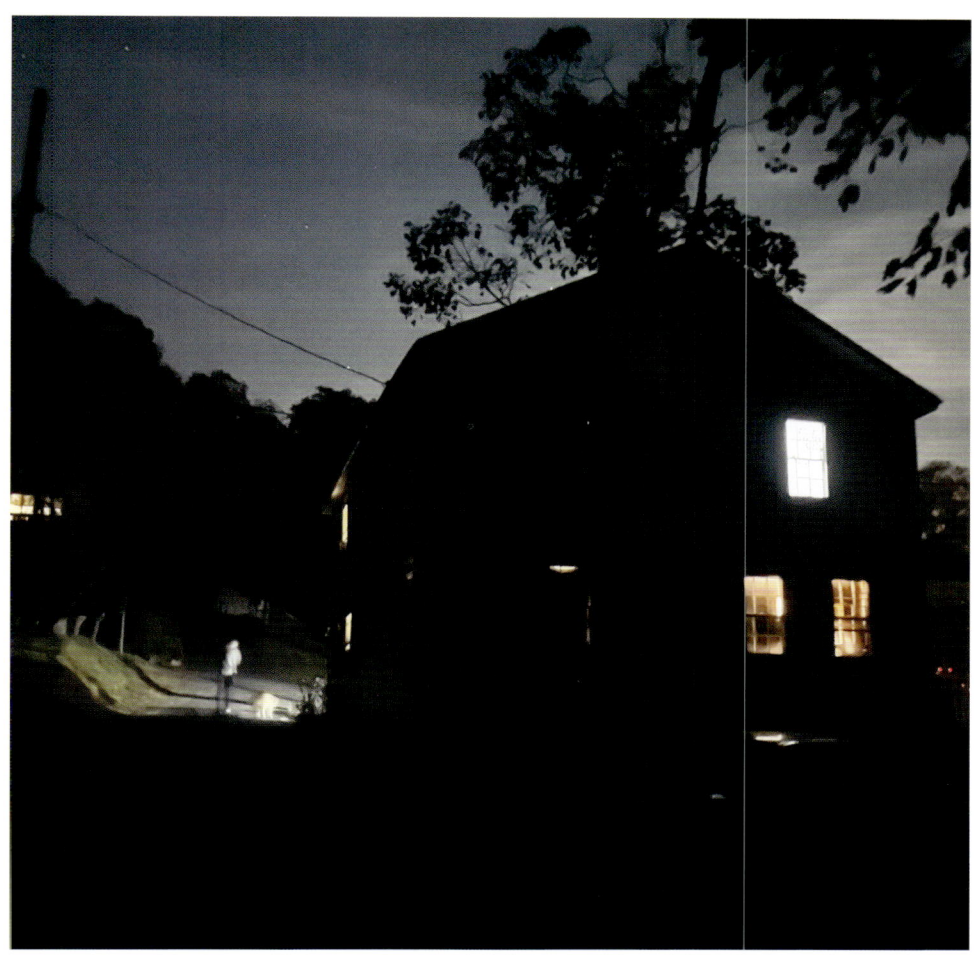

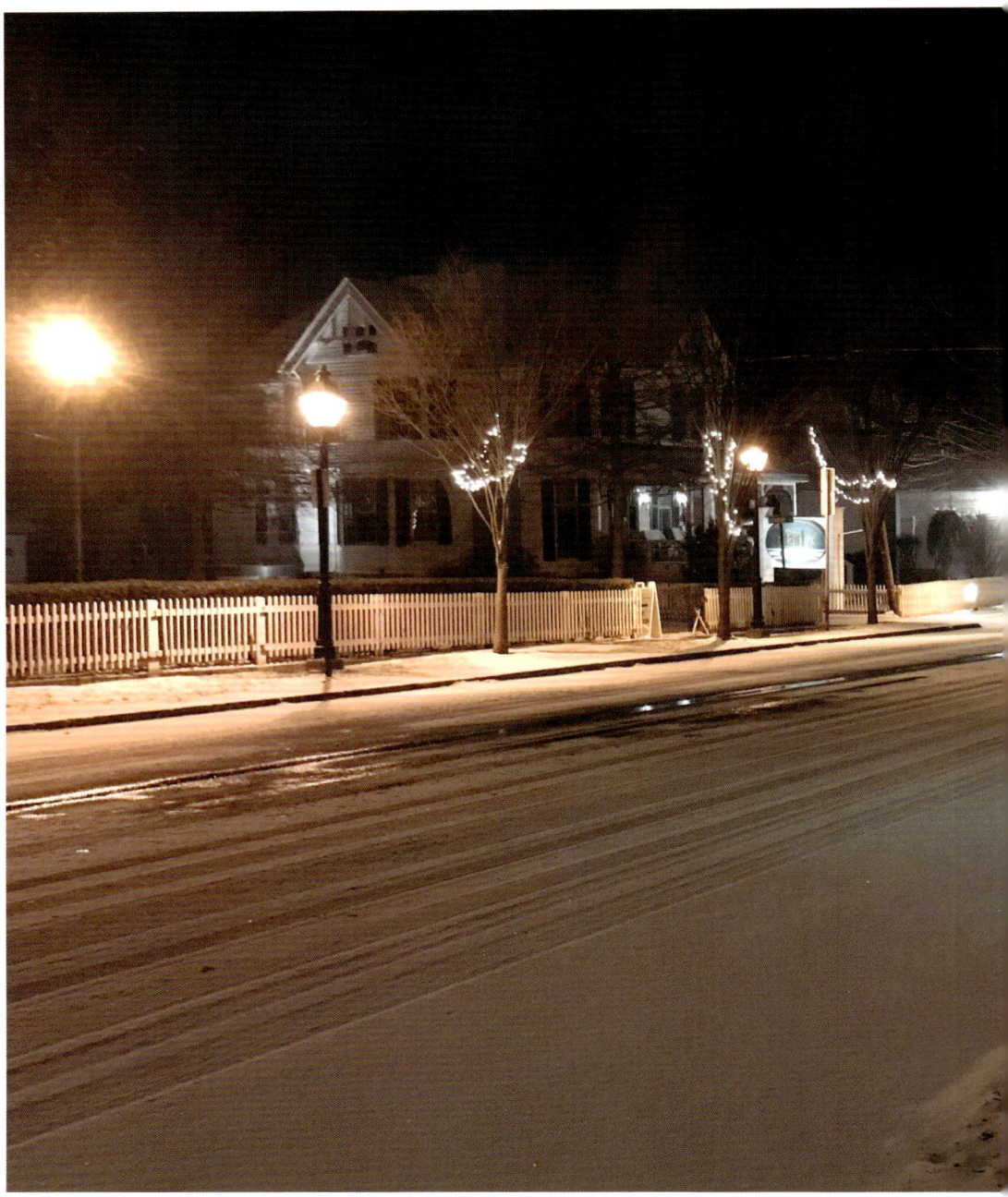

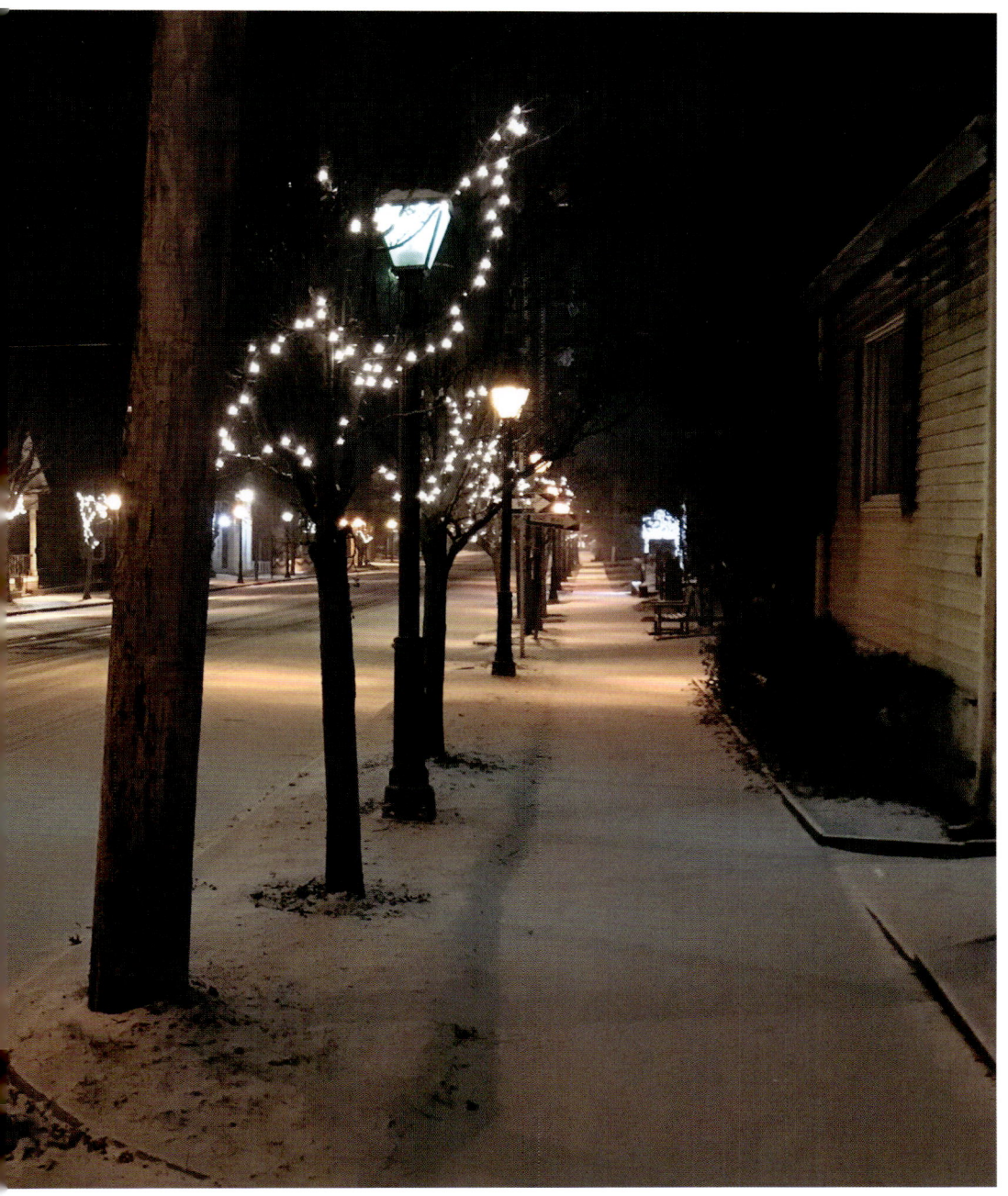

SHADOWS

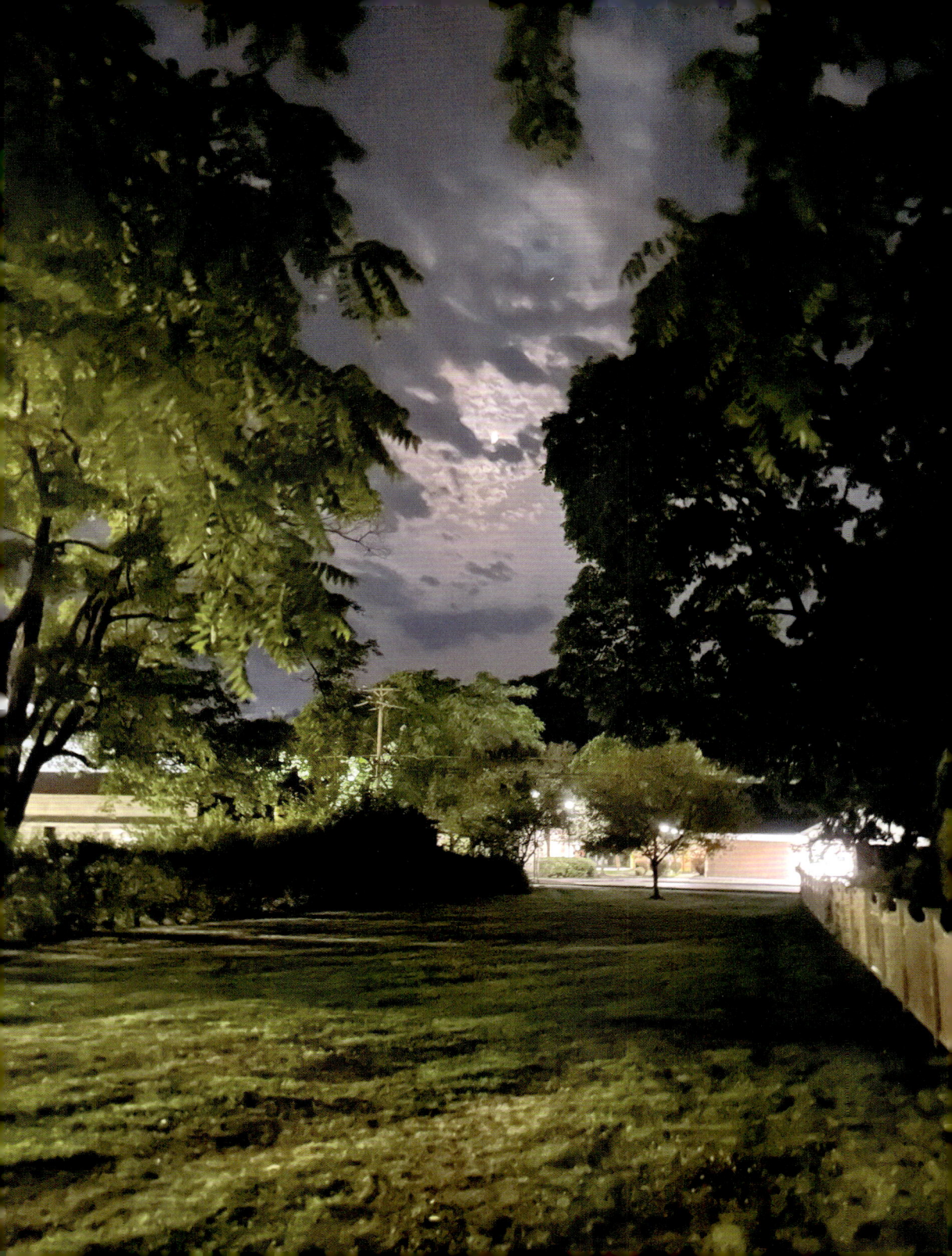

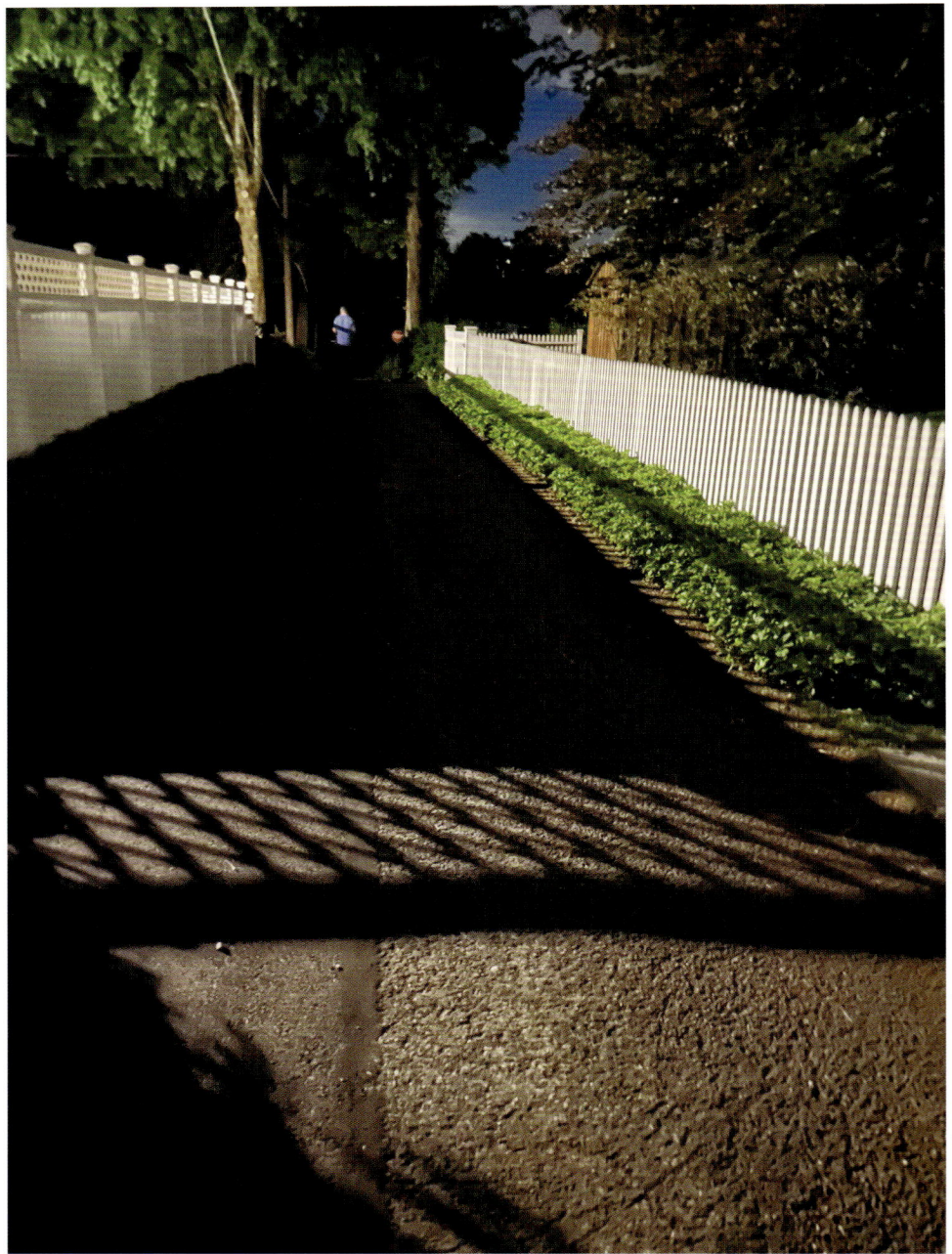

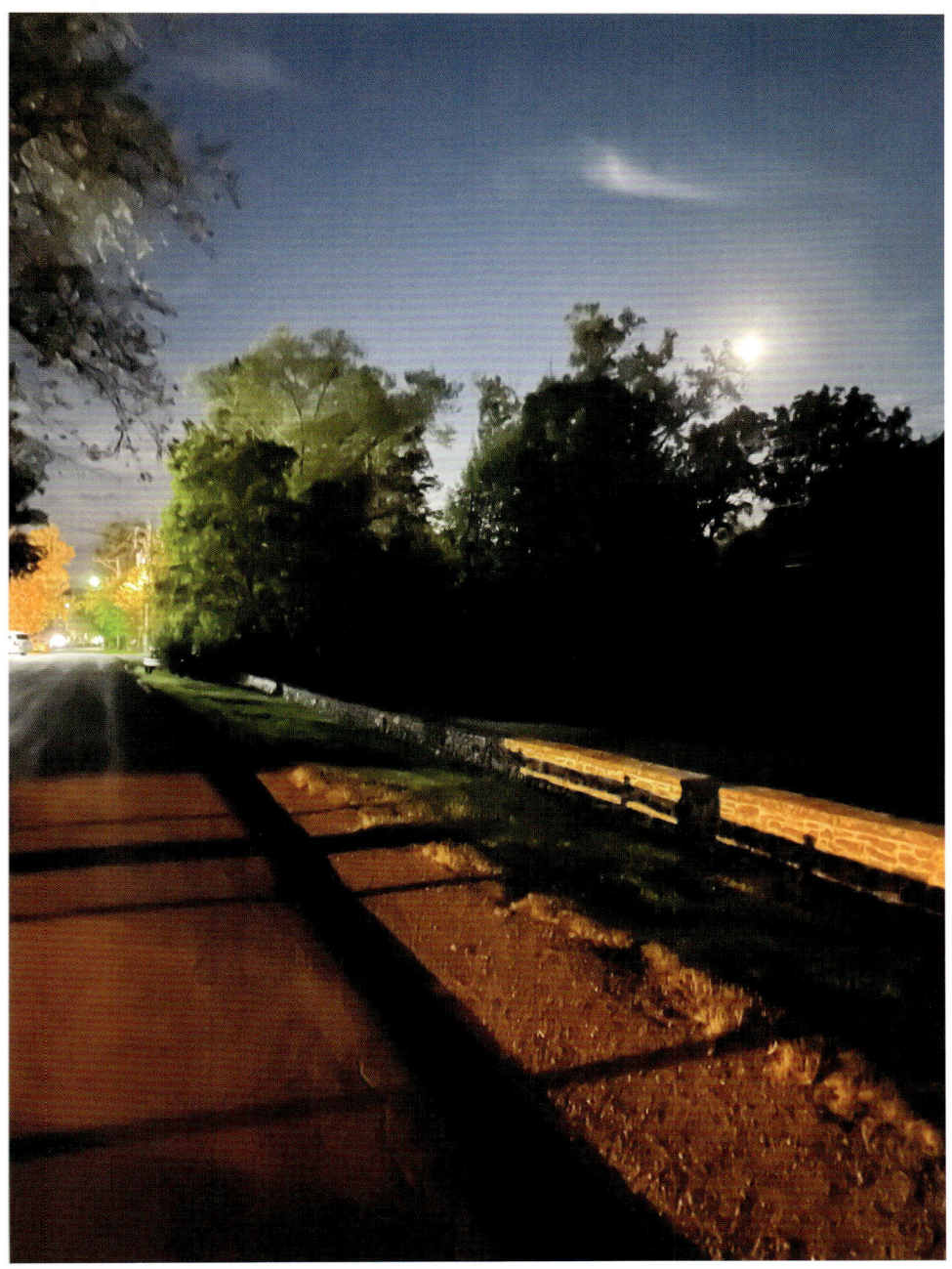

Carl Gustav Jung, the great Swiss psychiatrist, identified a human characteristic that he called "the shadow," which is that base and unpleasant part of us that we hide from our conscious self, are singularly unaware of, and are always projecting on to others— as their faults.

I have discovered, through taking these photographs and creating this book, a town or a village can also have a "shadow," as Milford does.

On September 4, 2024, at 9:20 p.m., I was crossing Broad Street with my dogs, Sherry and Maya. A hit-and-run driver plowed into us. I saved Sherry and myself, but little Maya, my loving companion, went under the wheel and was killed.

We must face the shadows that exist in life. It is the only way to be fully here. That is why this series of images, which starts out innocent enough, evolves into pictures of Maya standing alone and before our village funeral parlor, and even includes a photo of one of Milford's most dangerous crosswalks. It ends, finally, with the an image of an extinguished lightbulb and the shadows of night closing in on me, but for the grace of the moon, which, again, is reliably breaking through the dark, shedding light, even in the darkest hours.

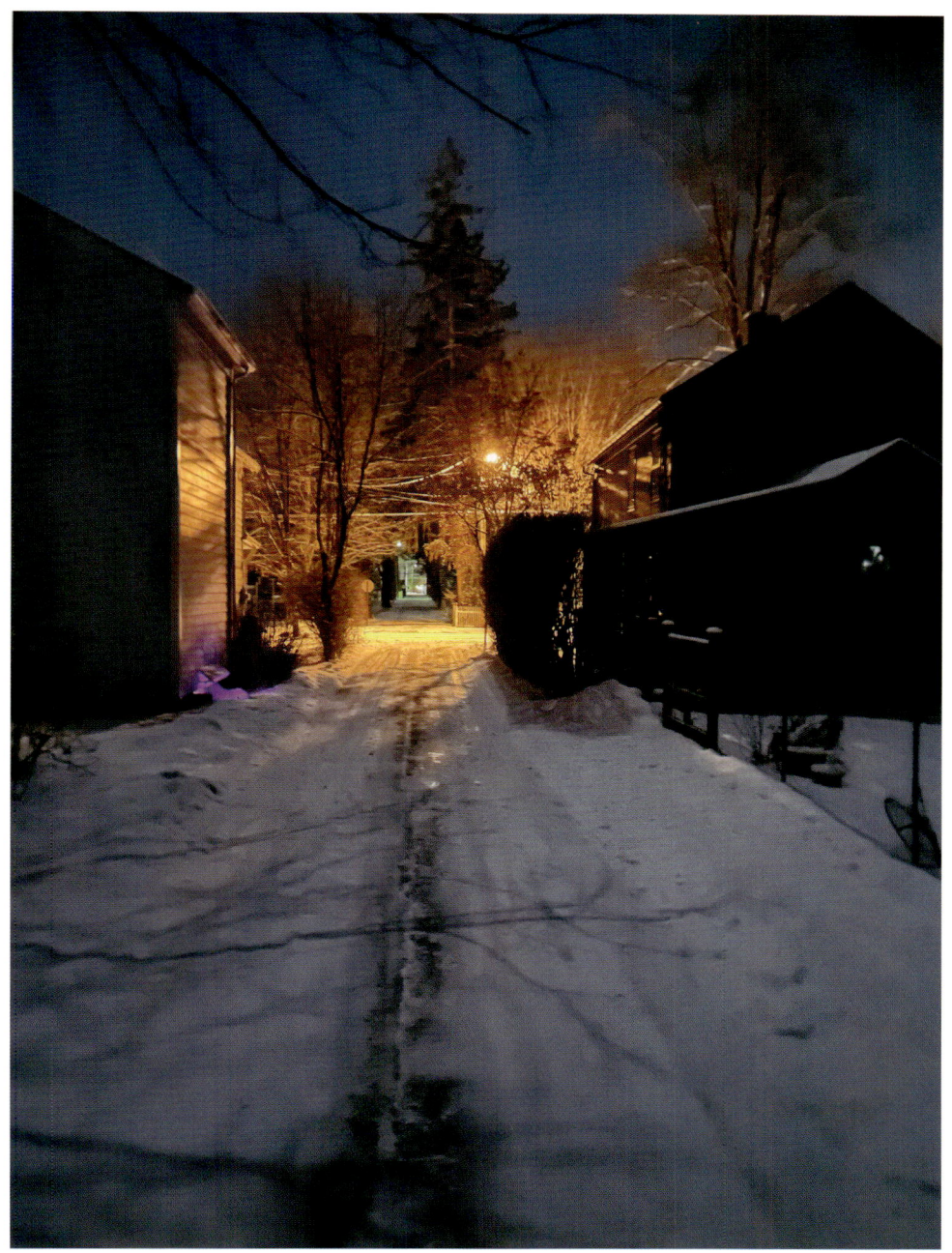

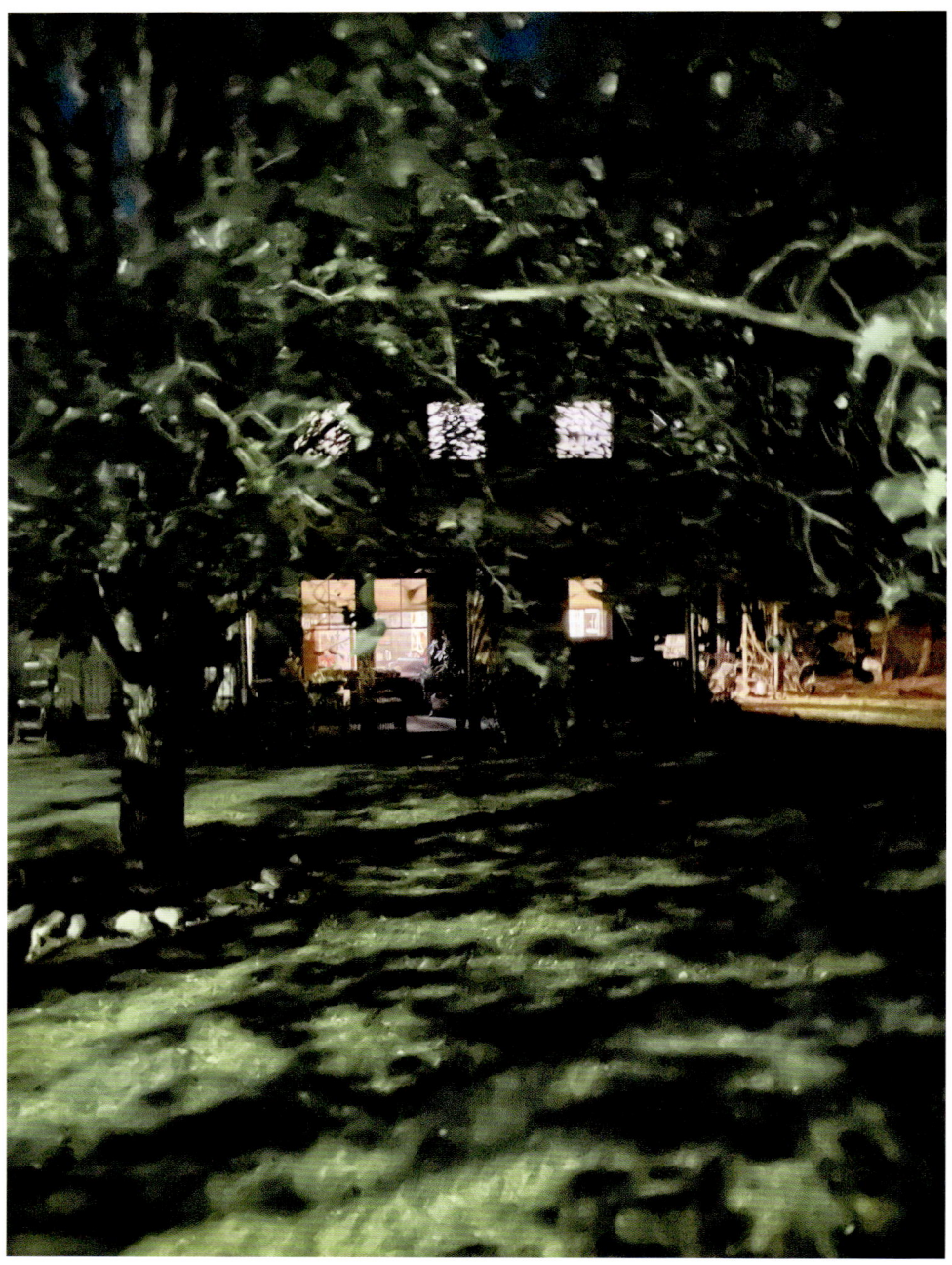

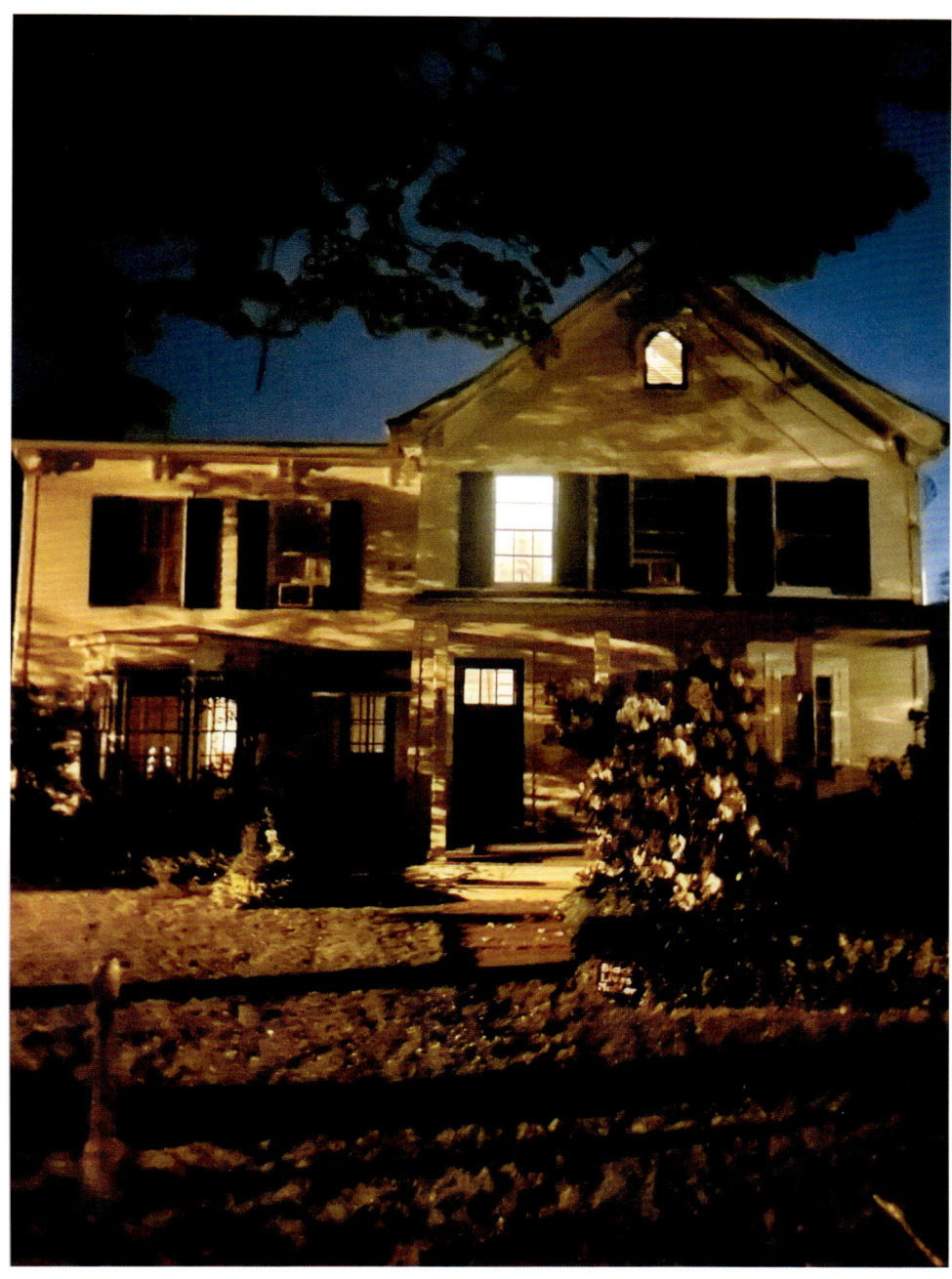

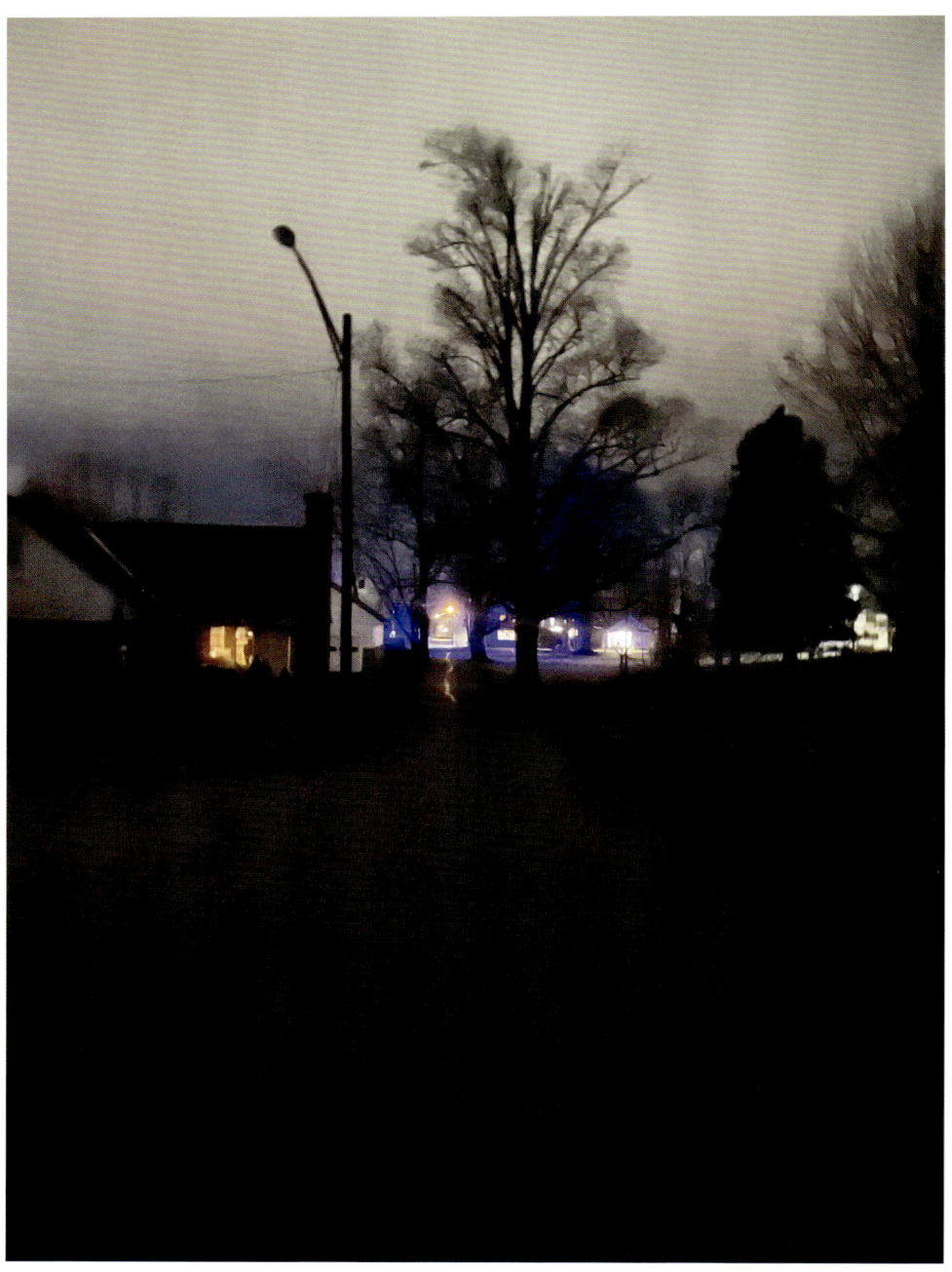

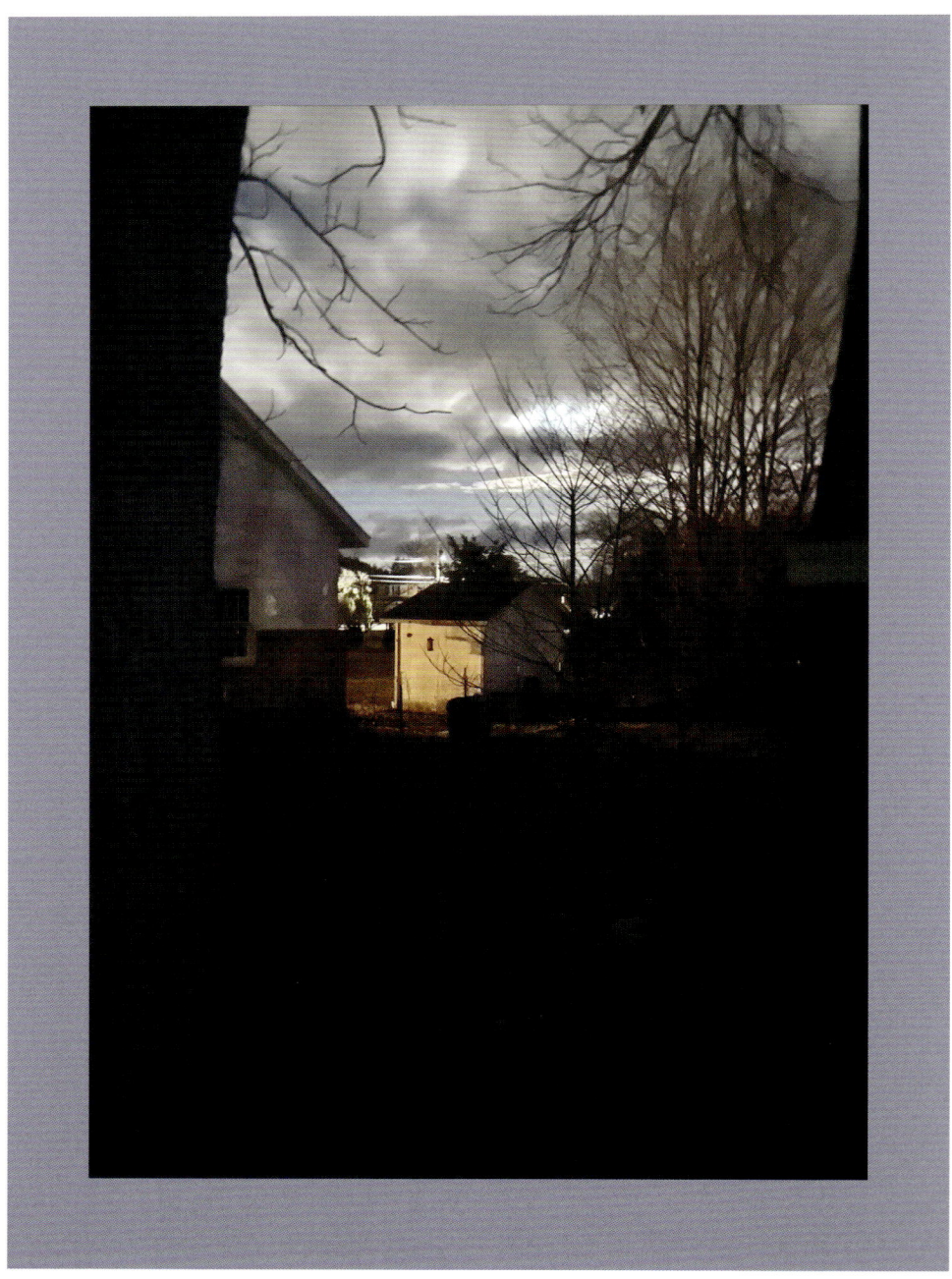

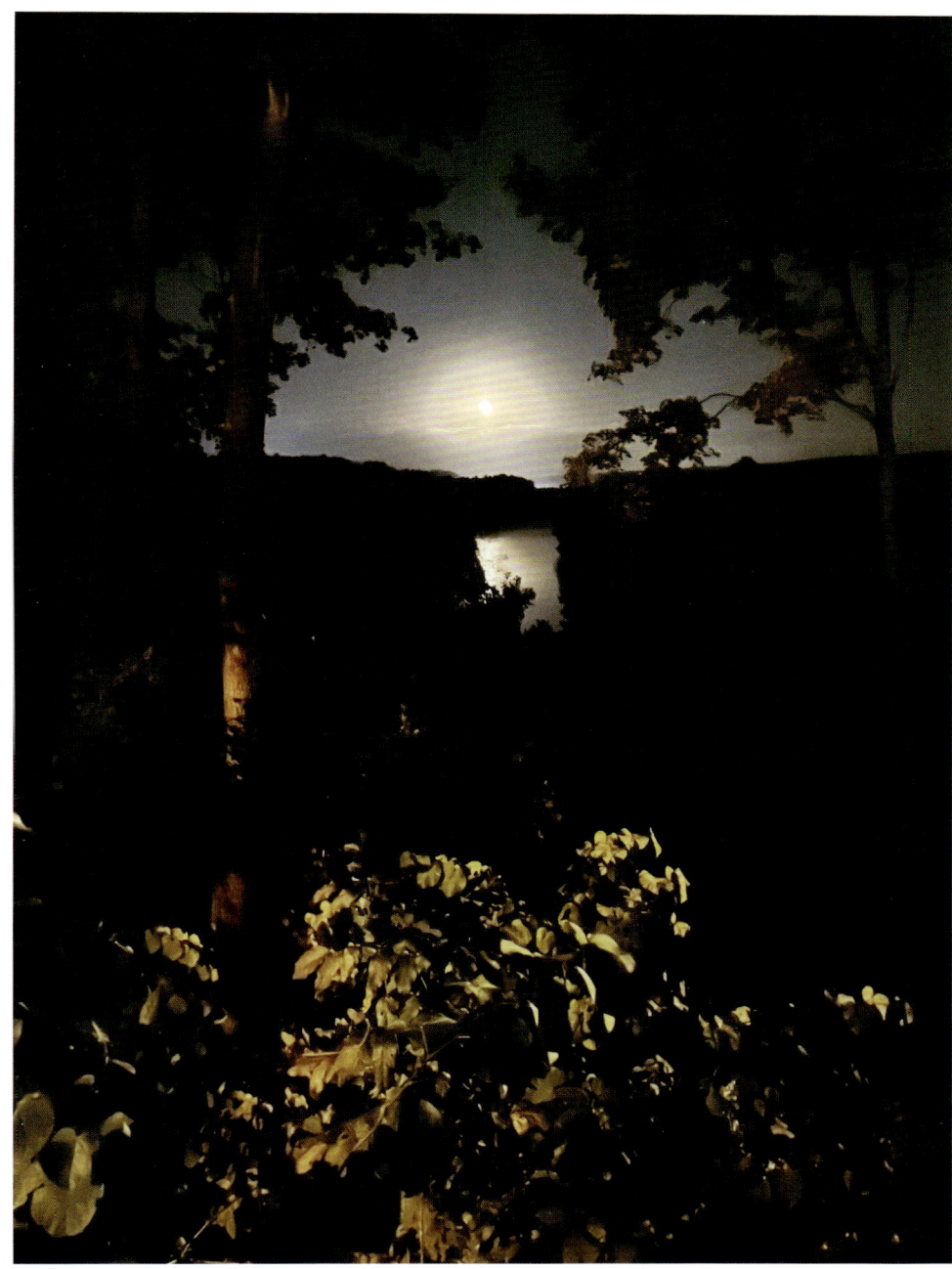

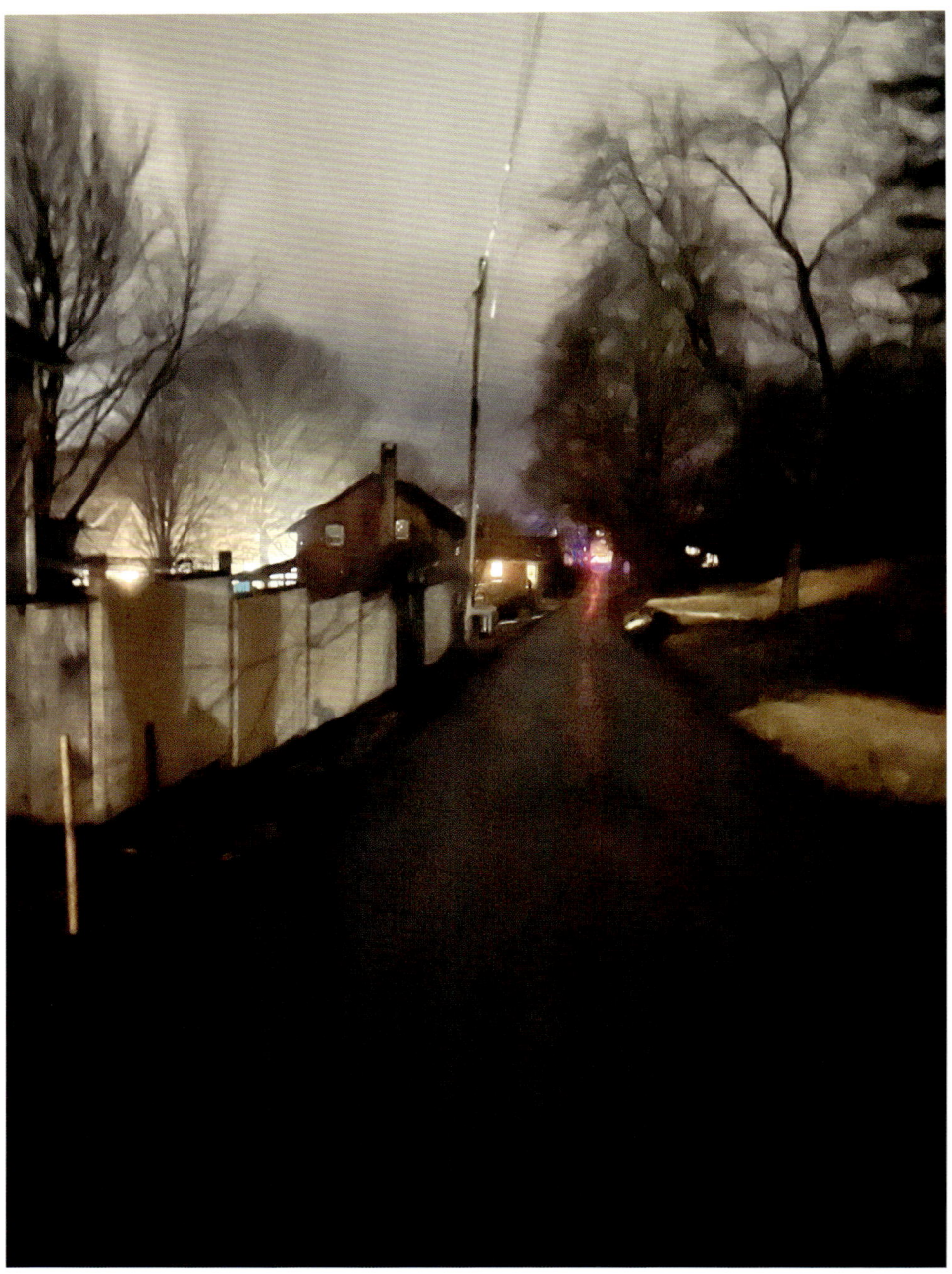

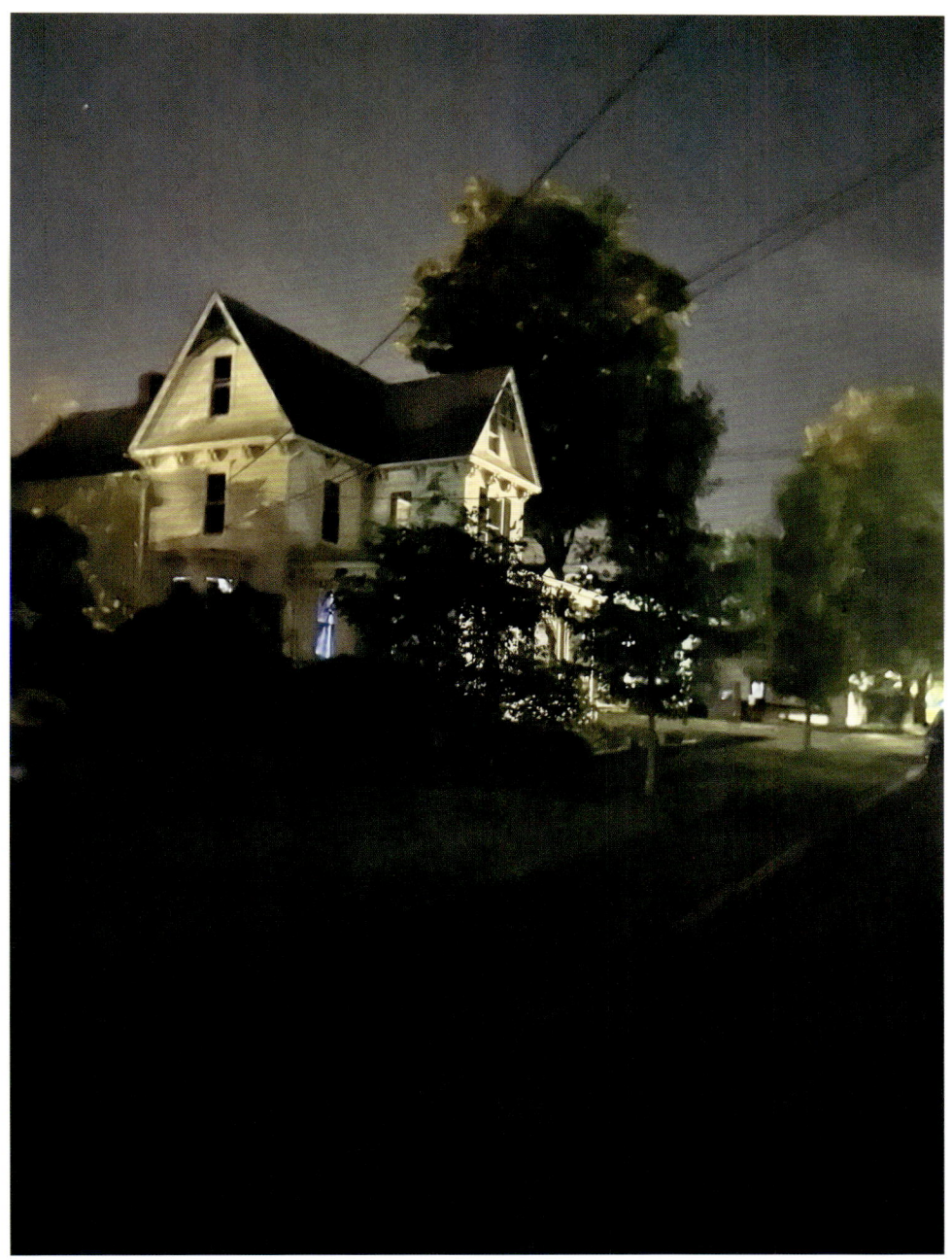

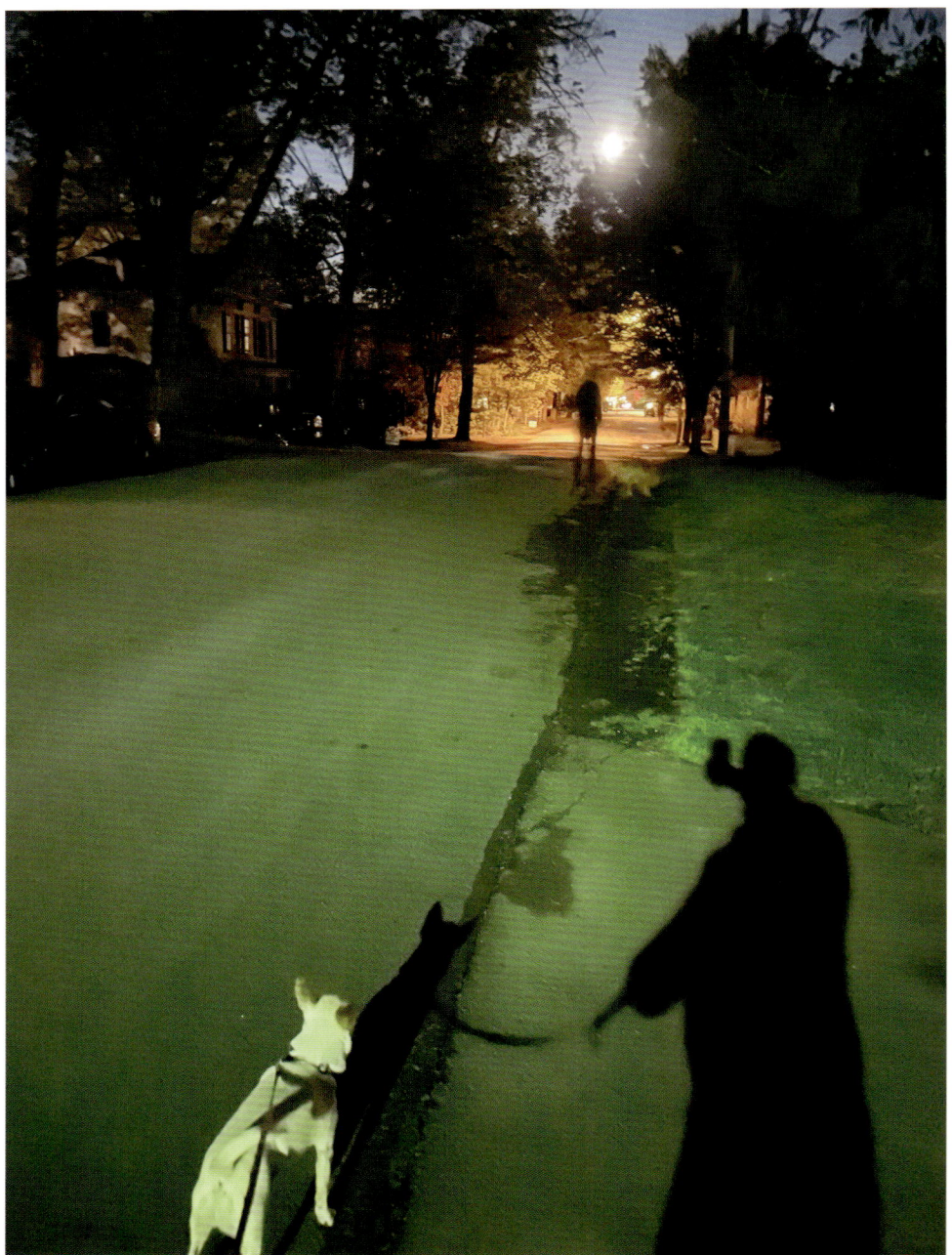

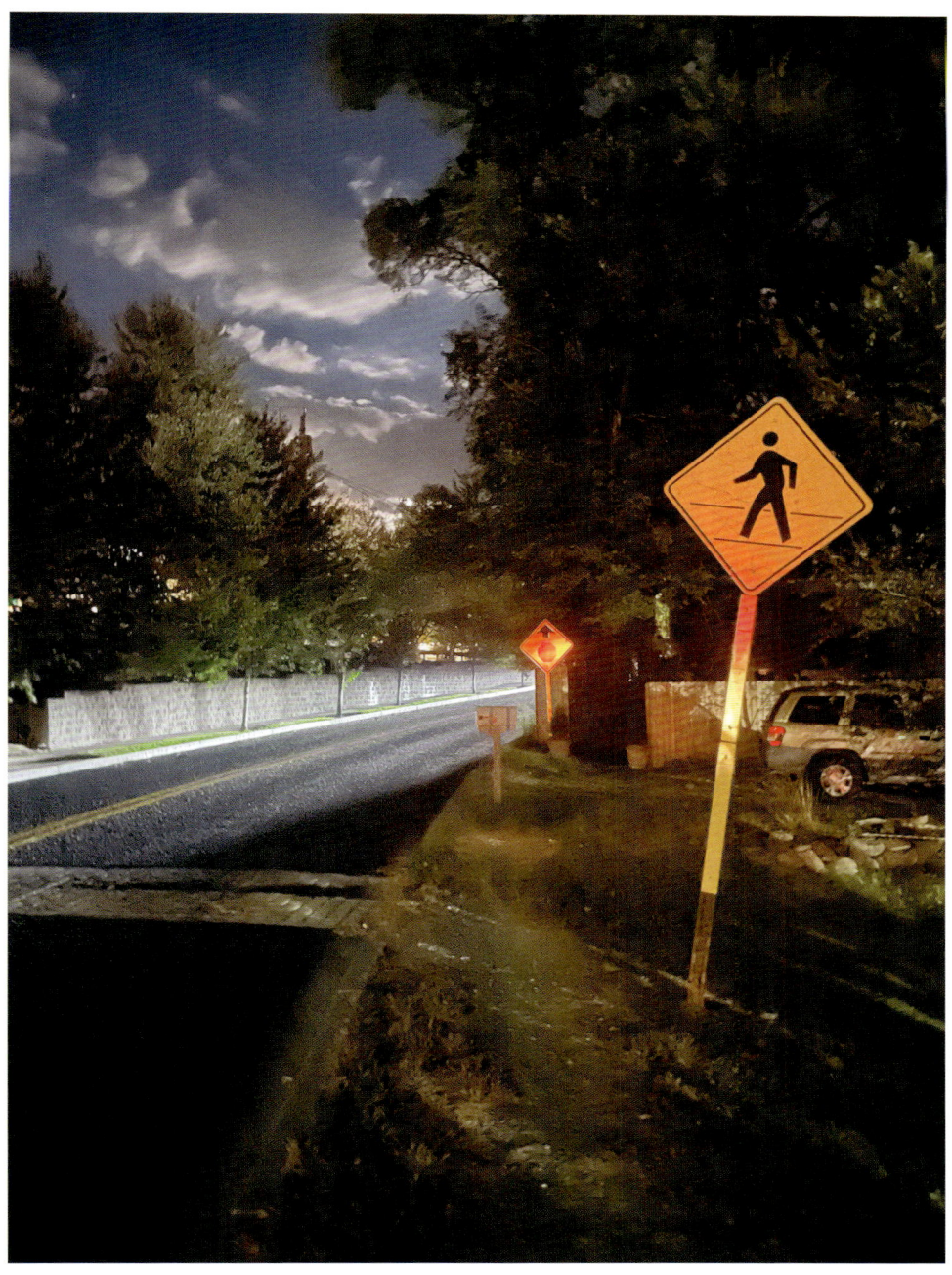

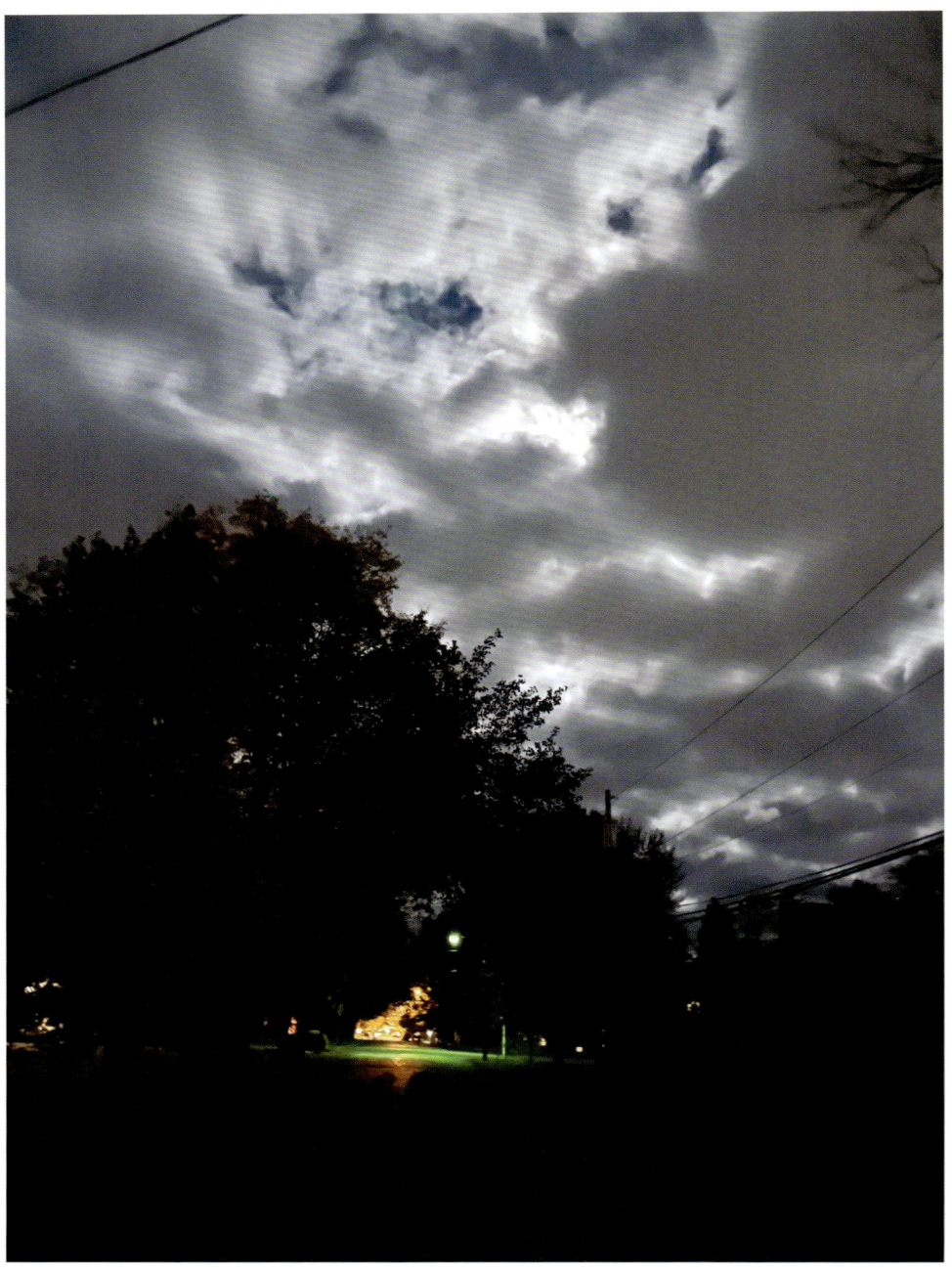

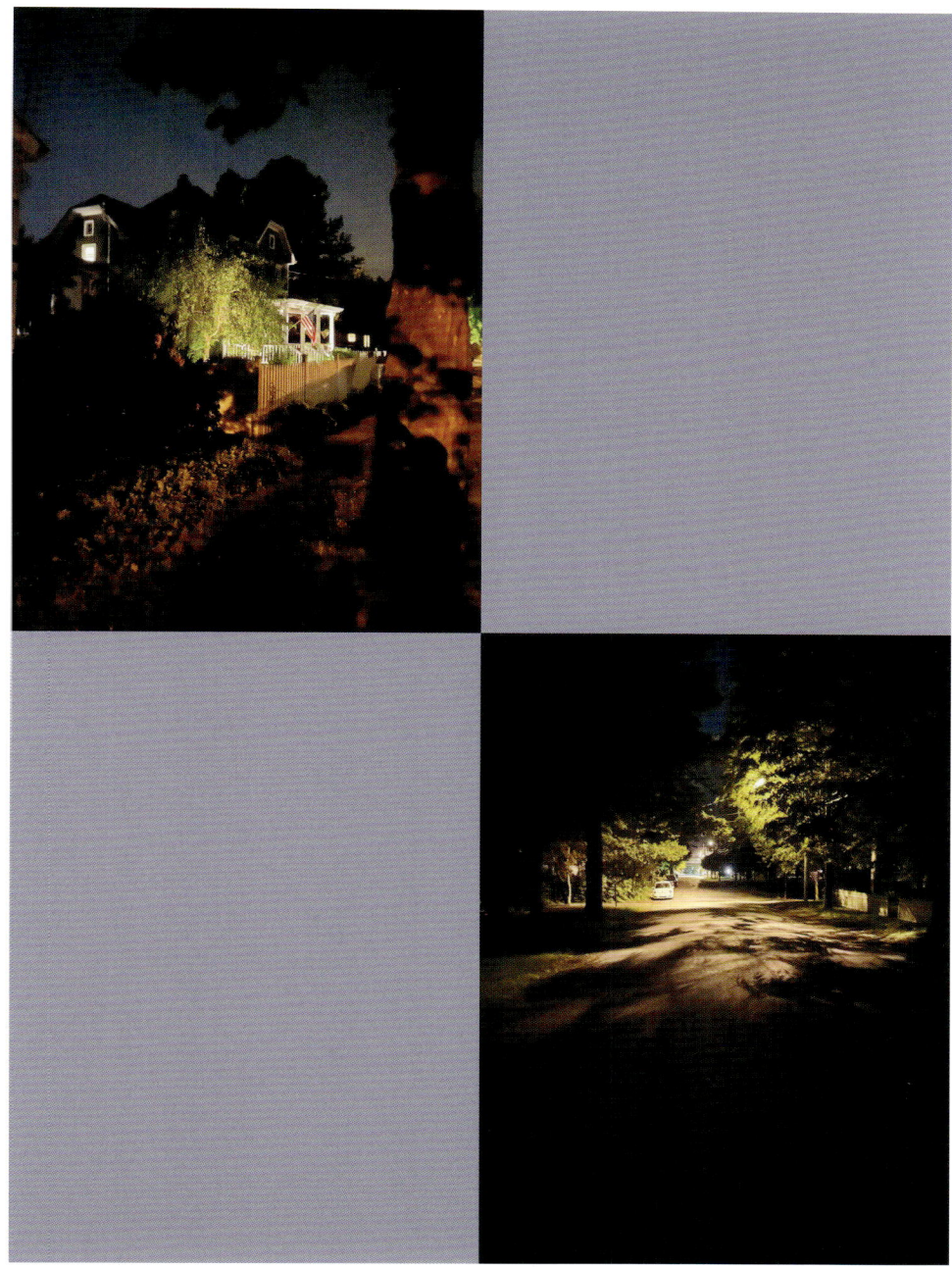

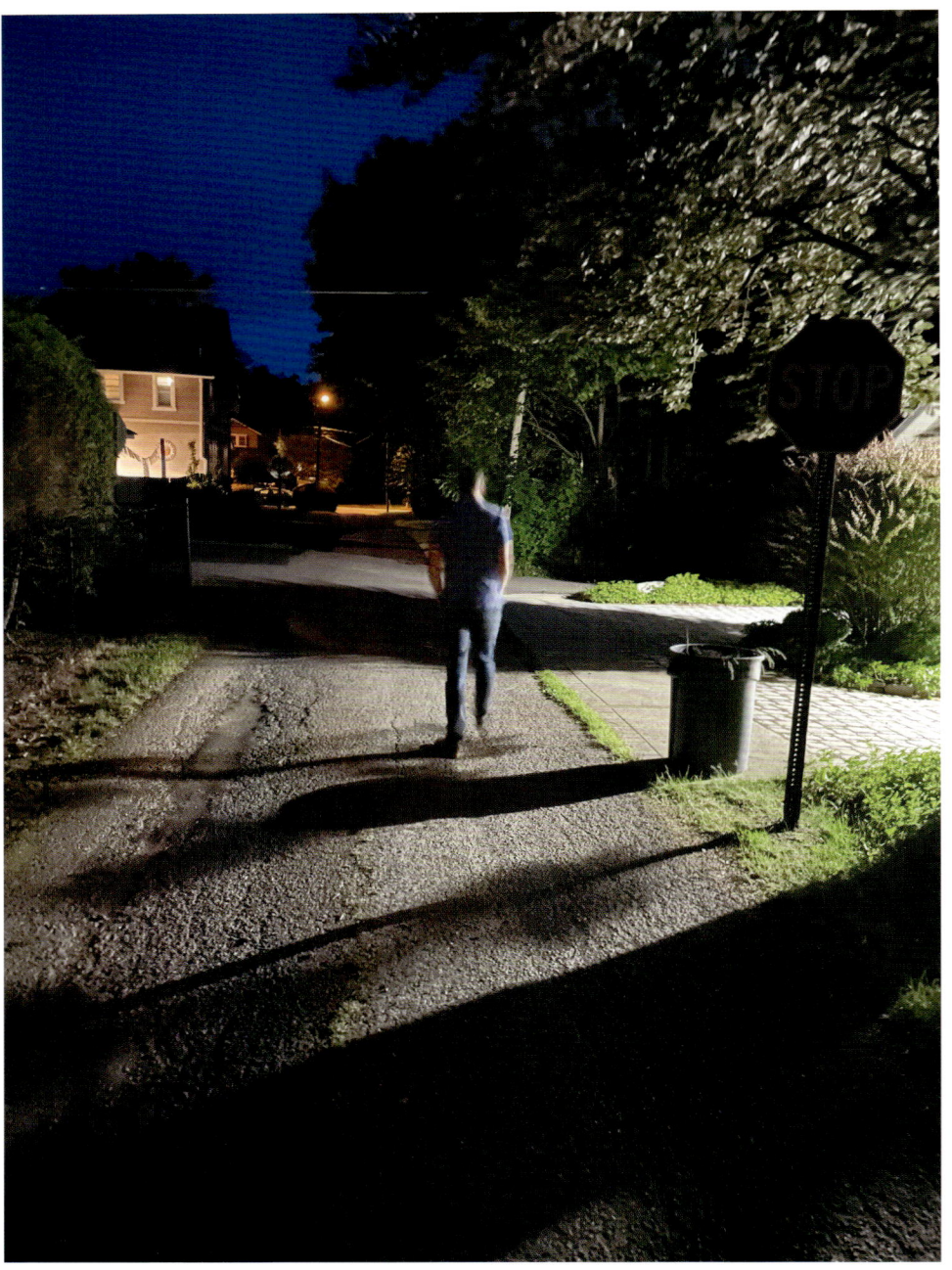

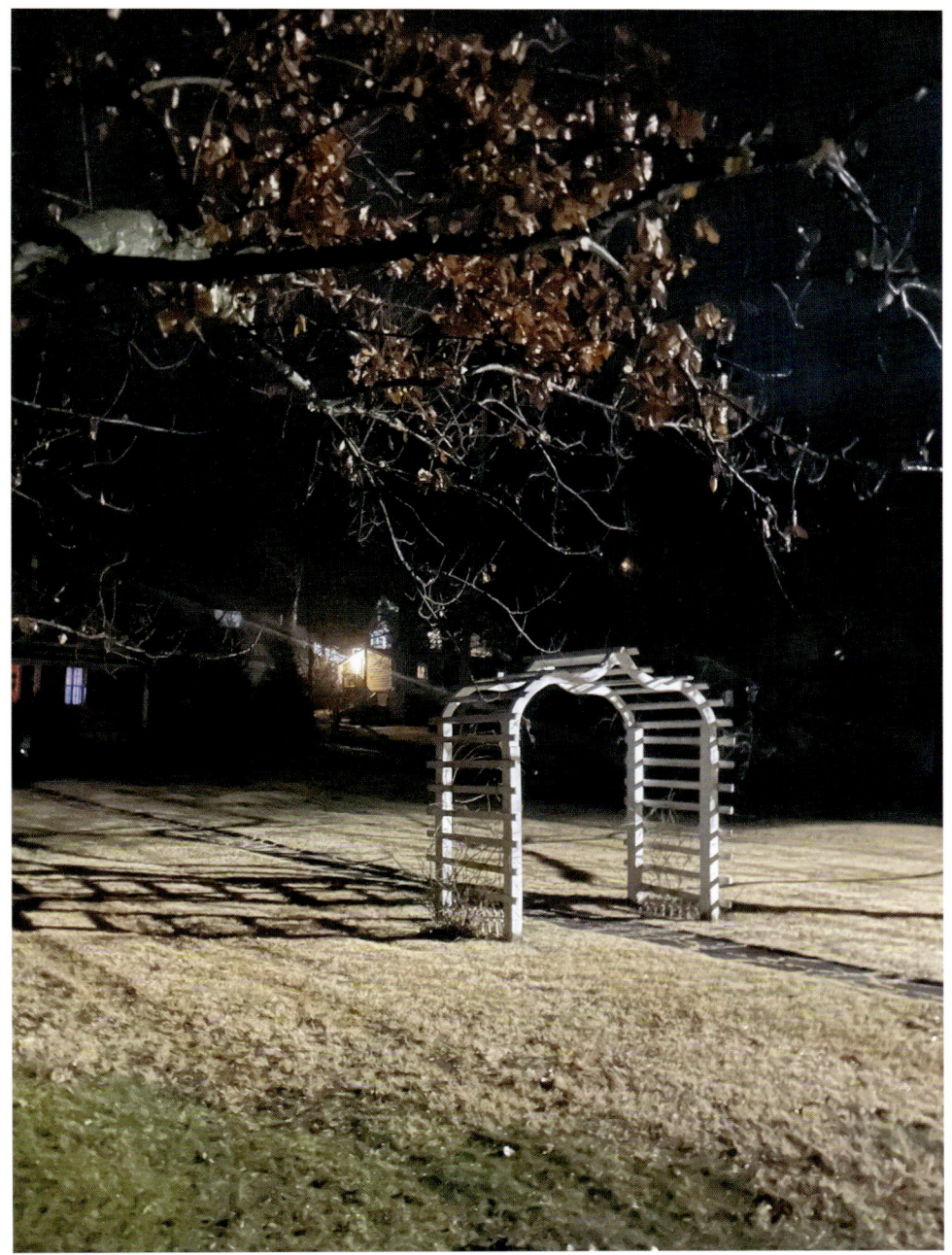

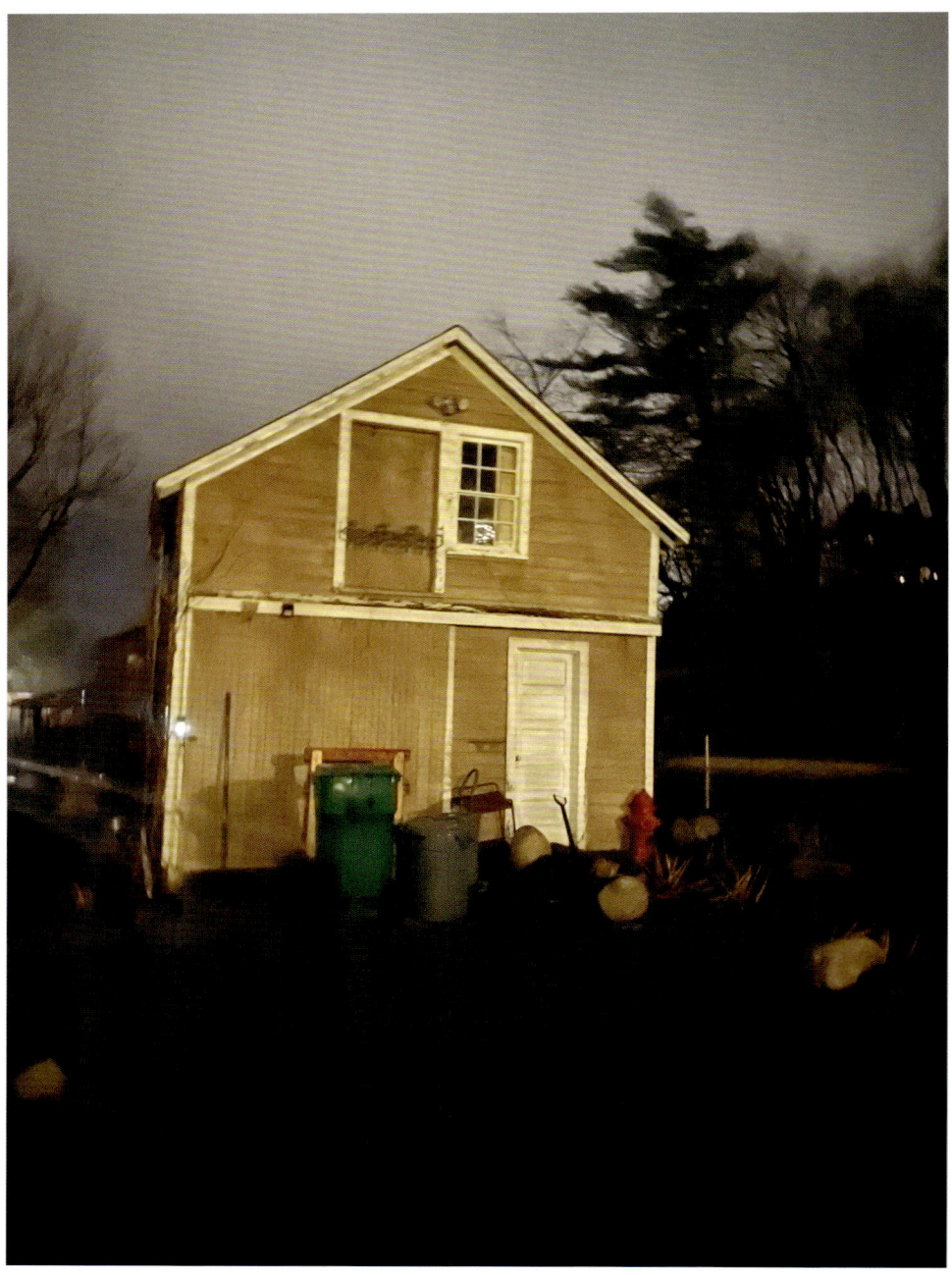

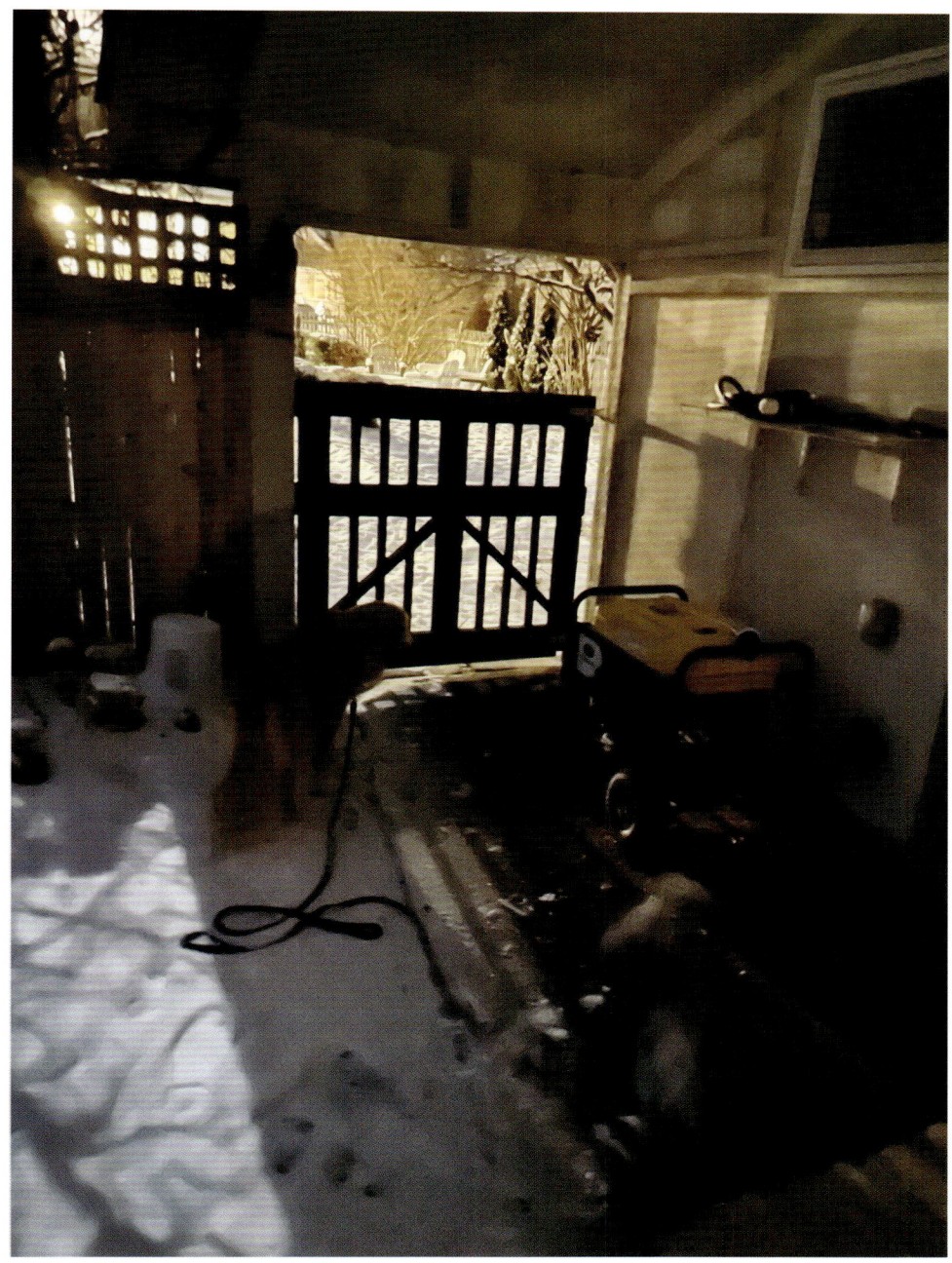

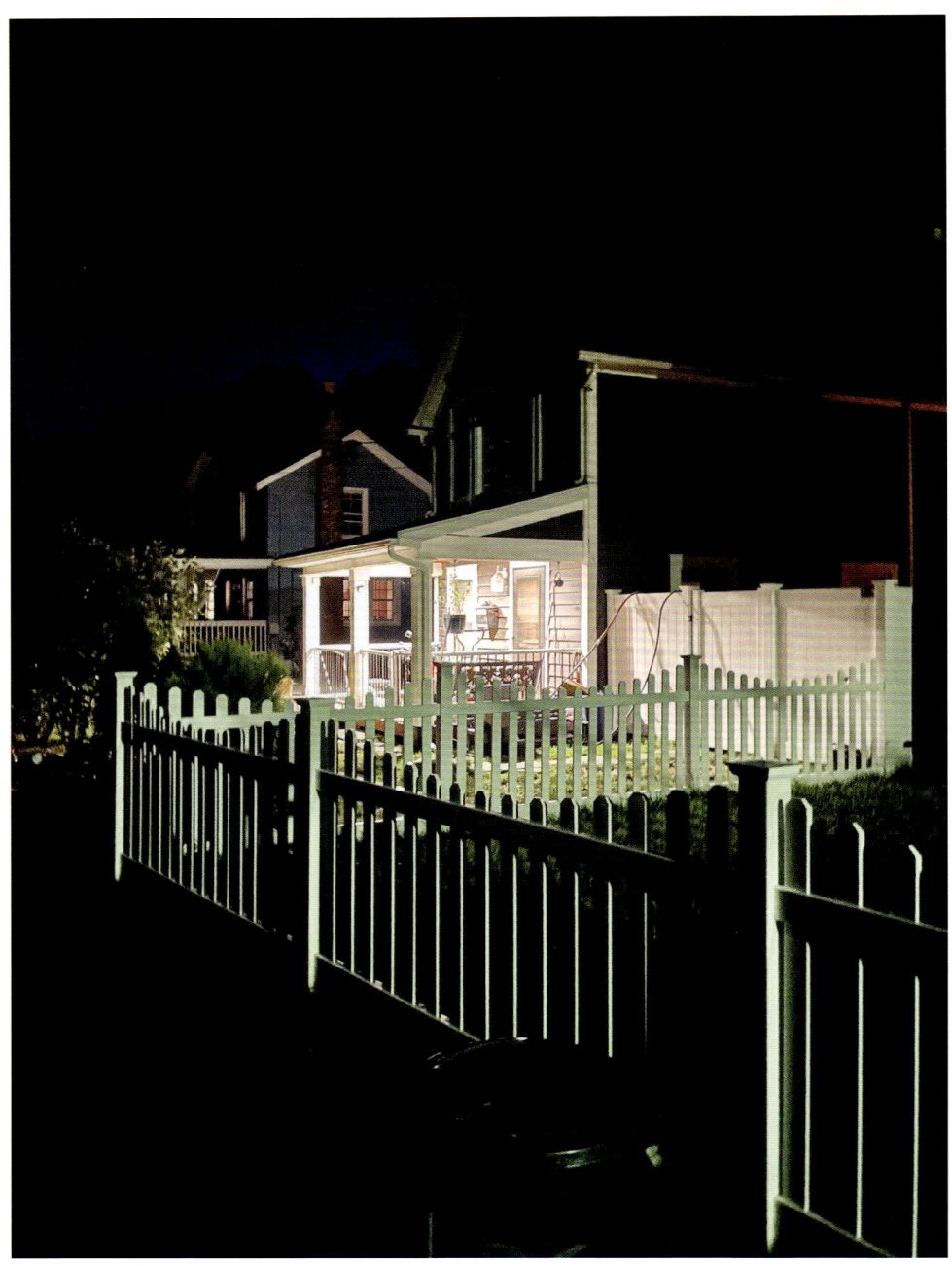

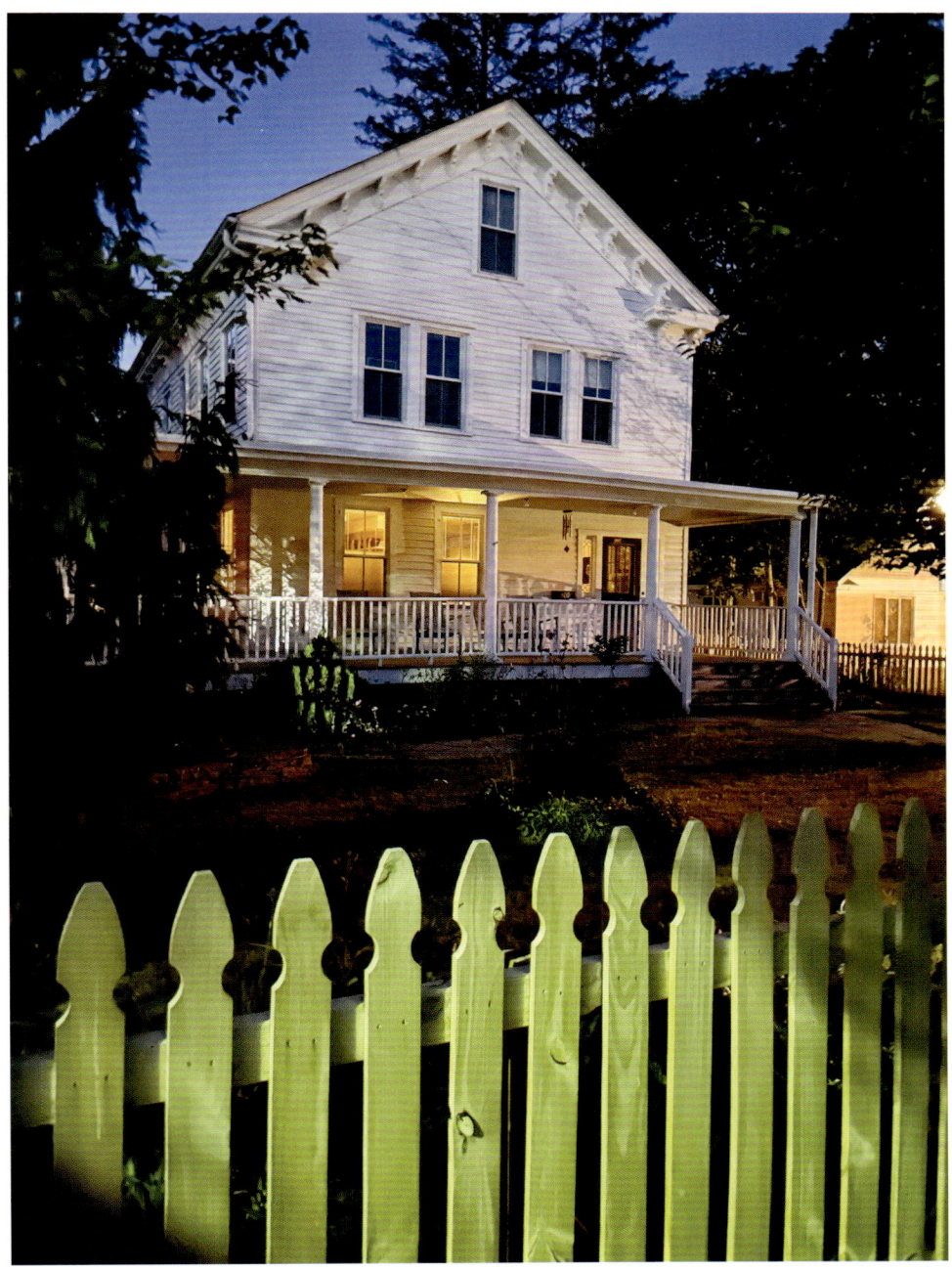

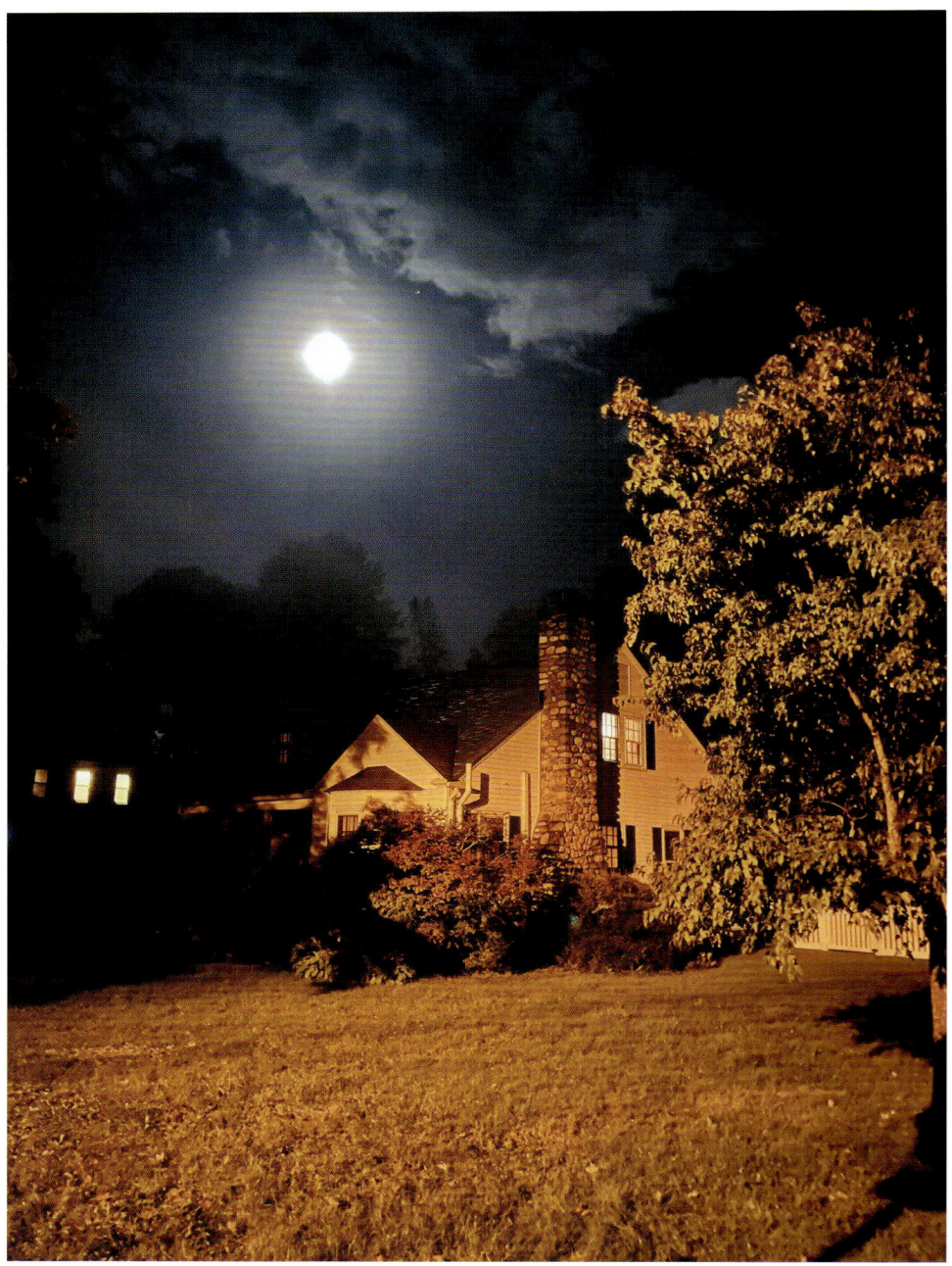

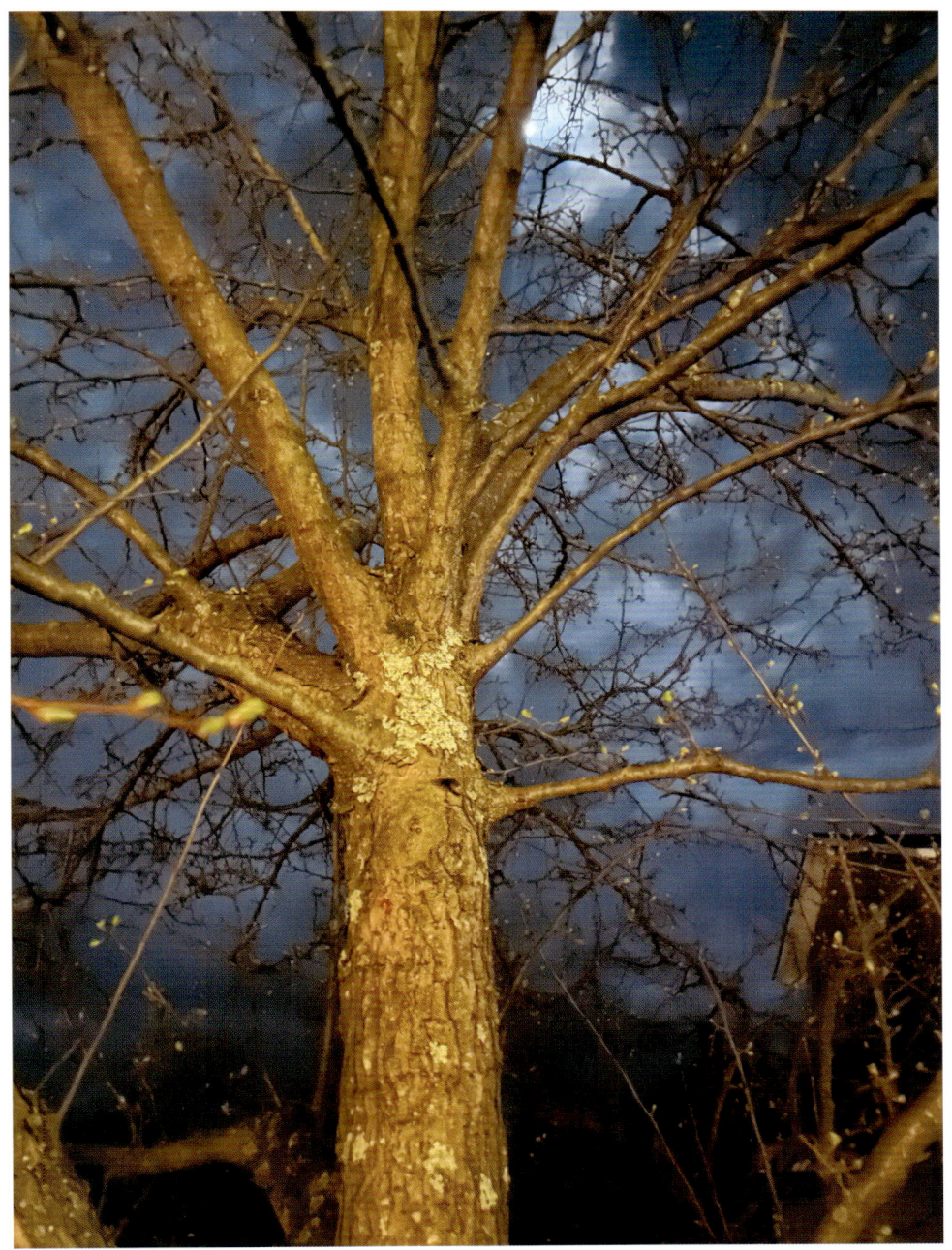

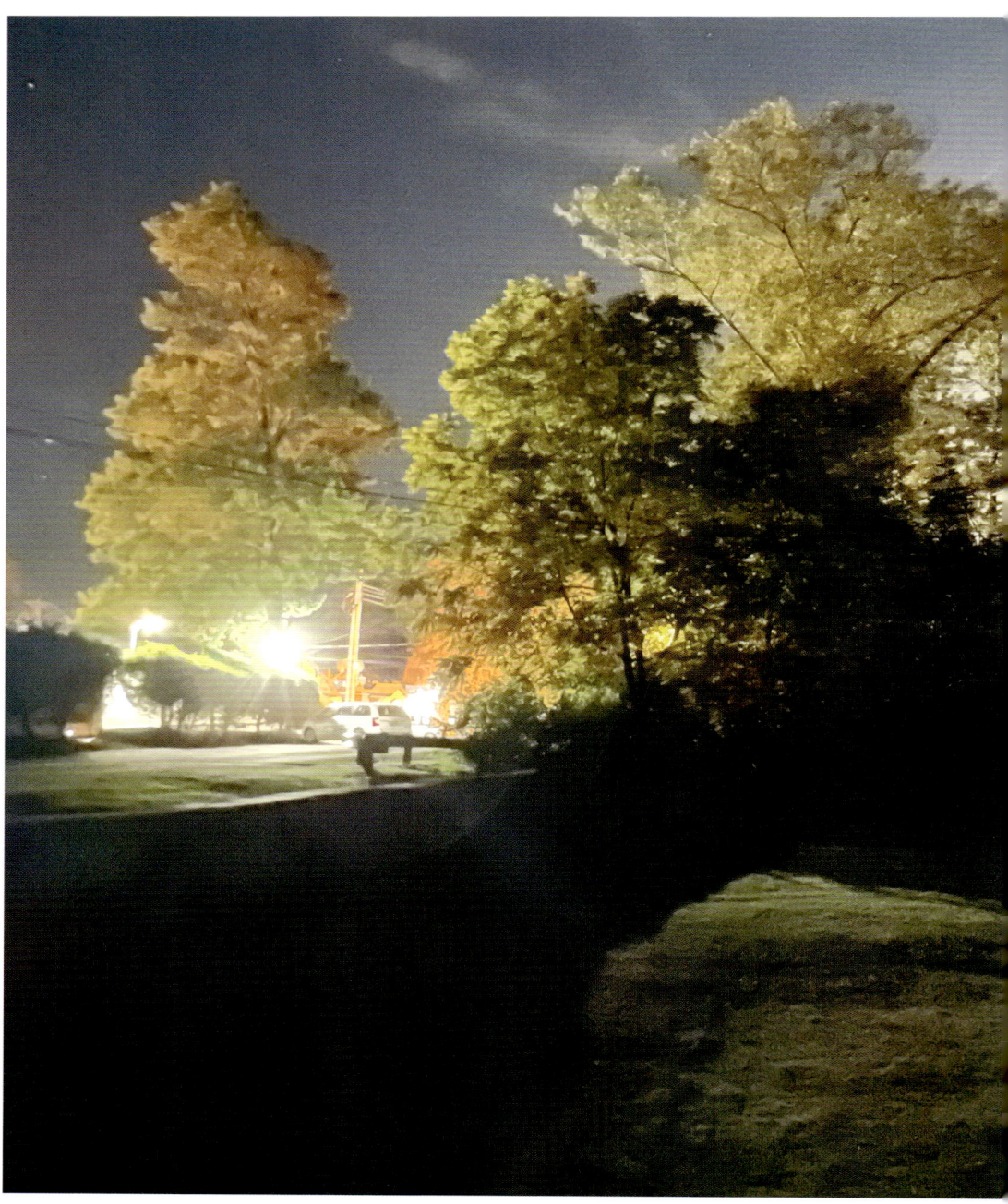

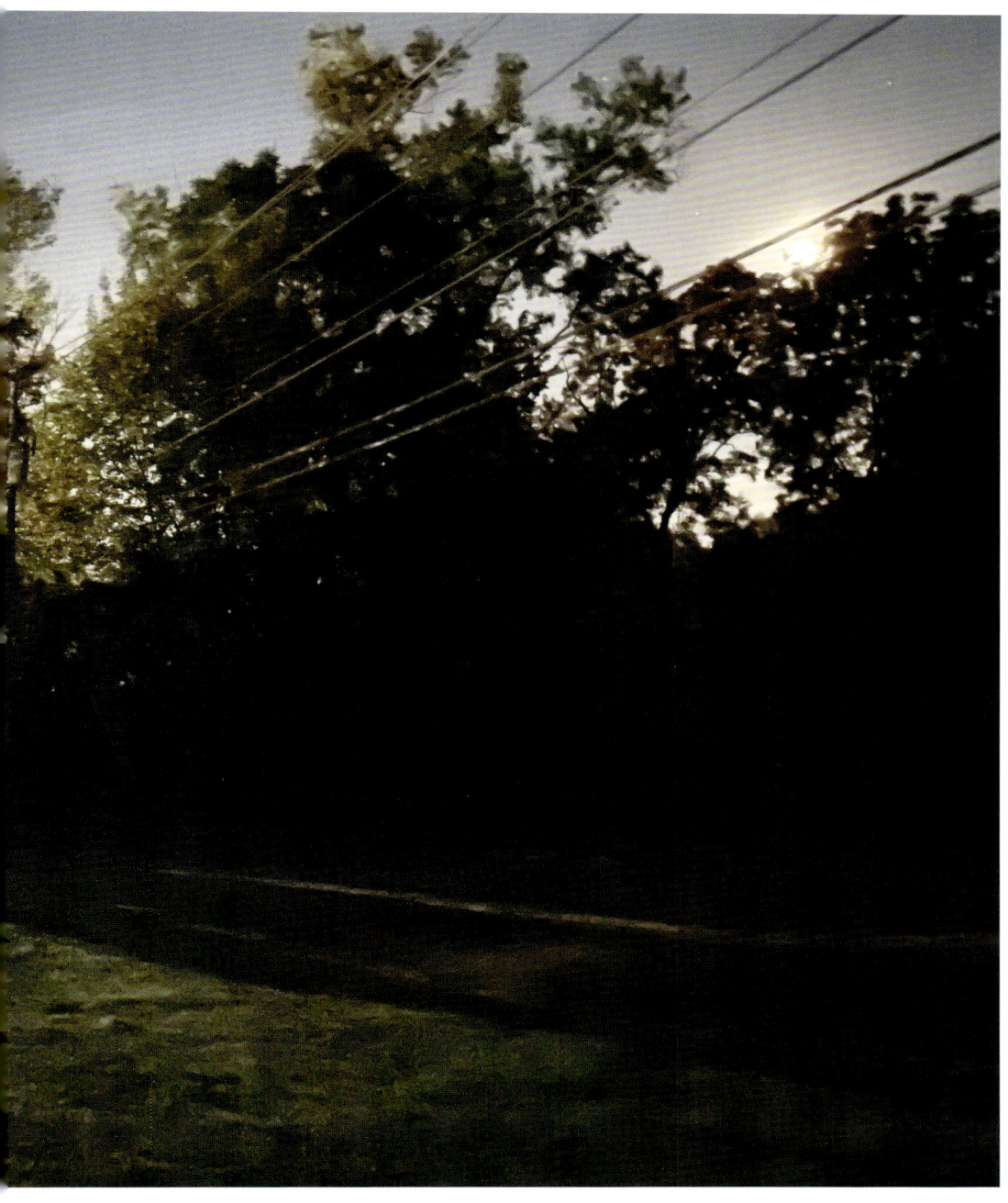

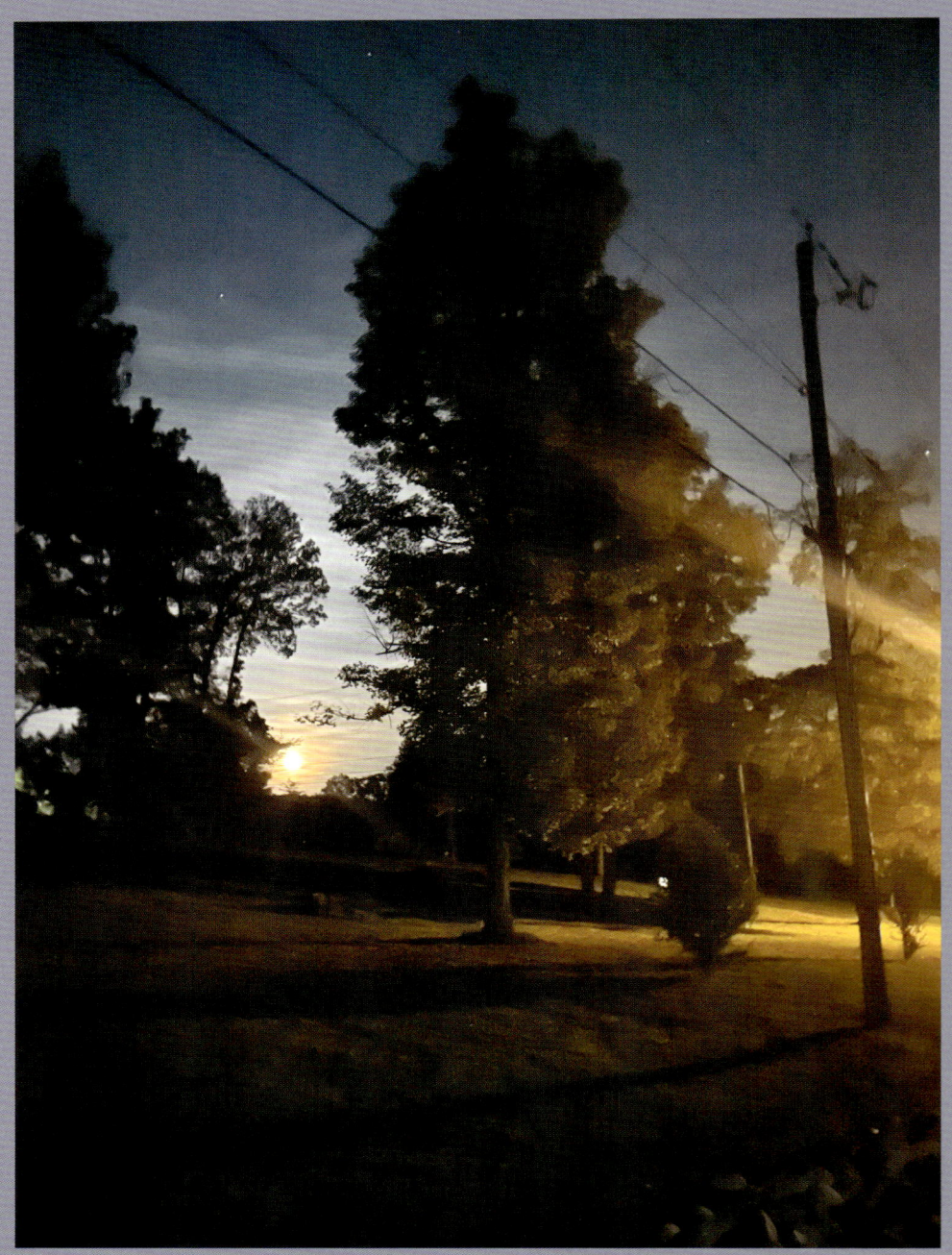

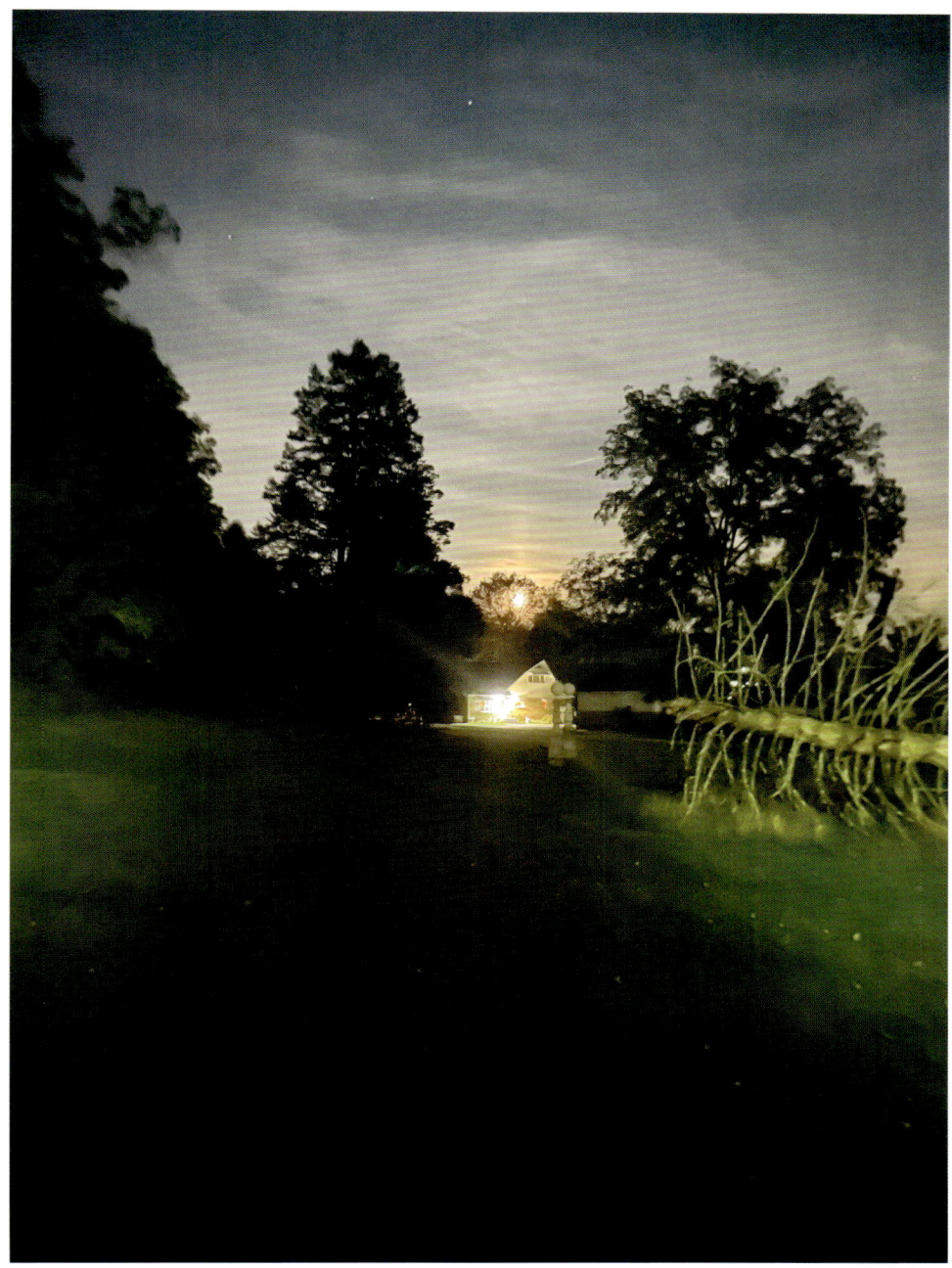

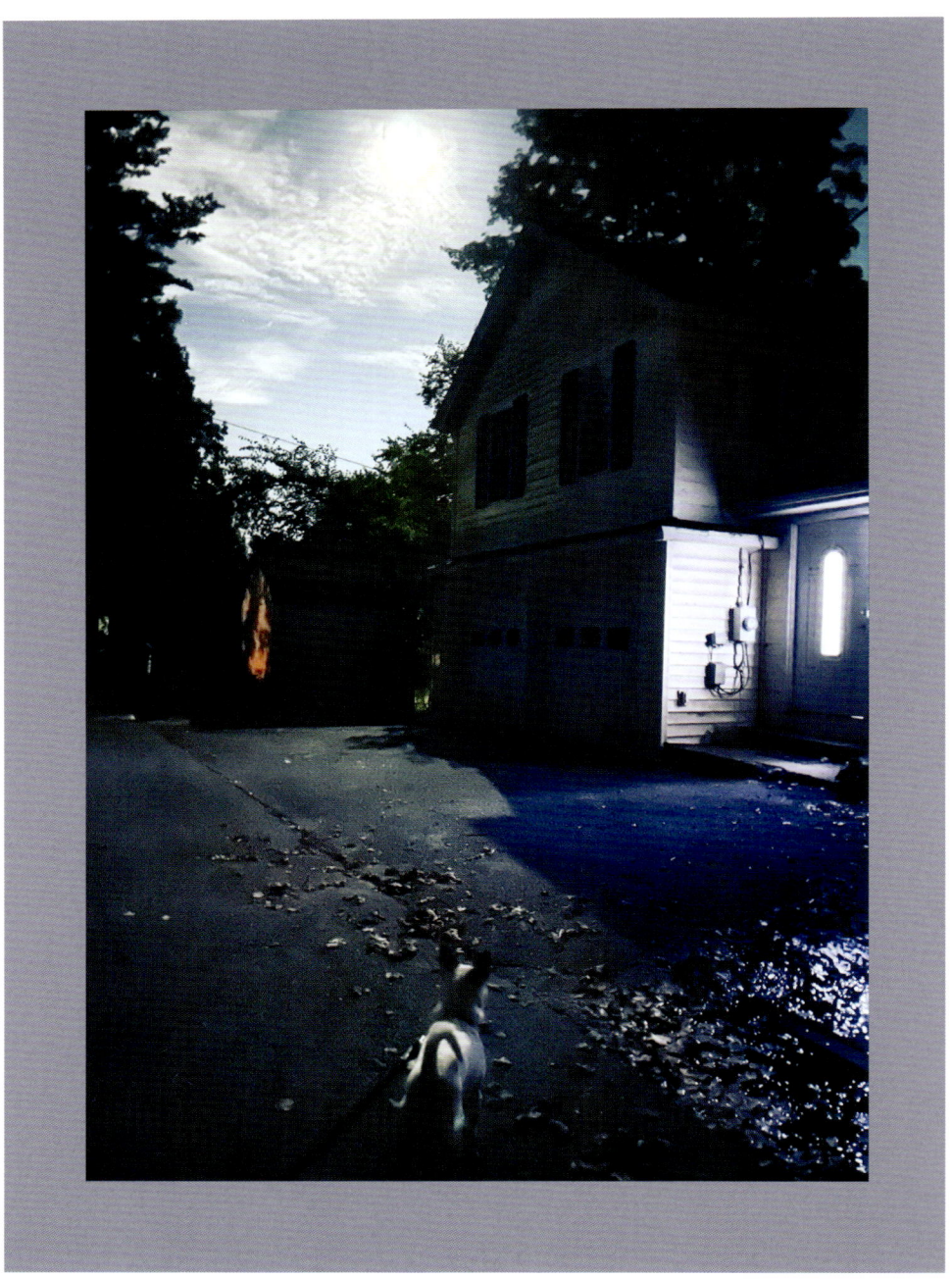

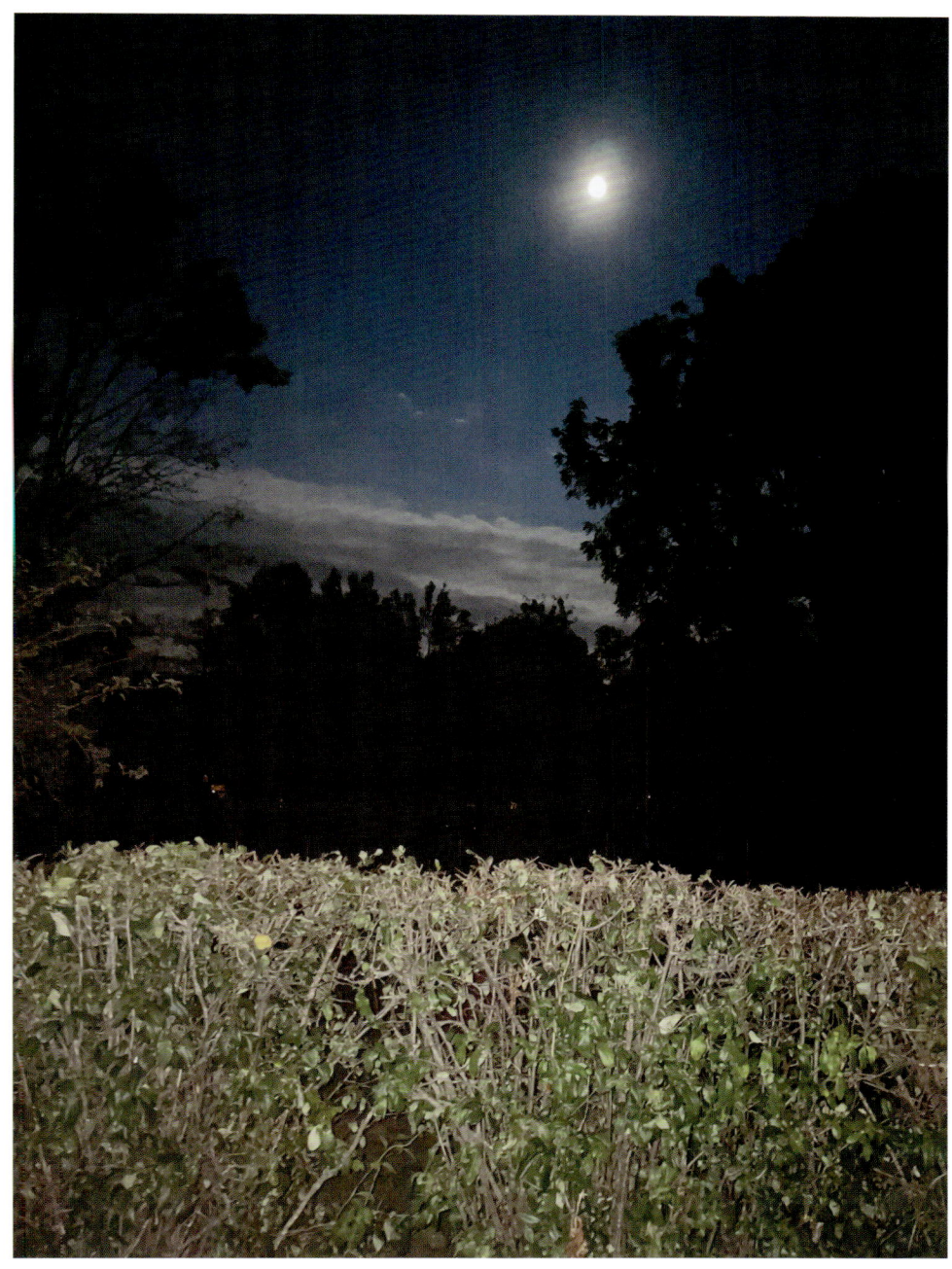

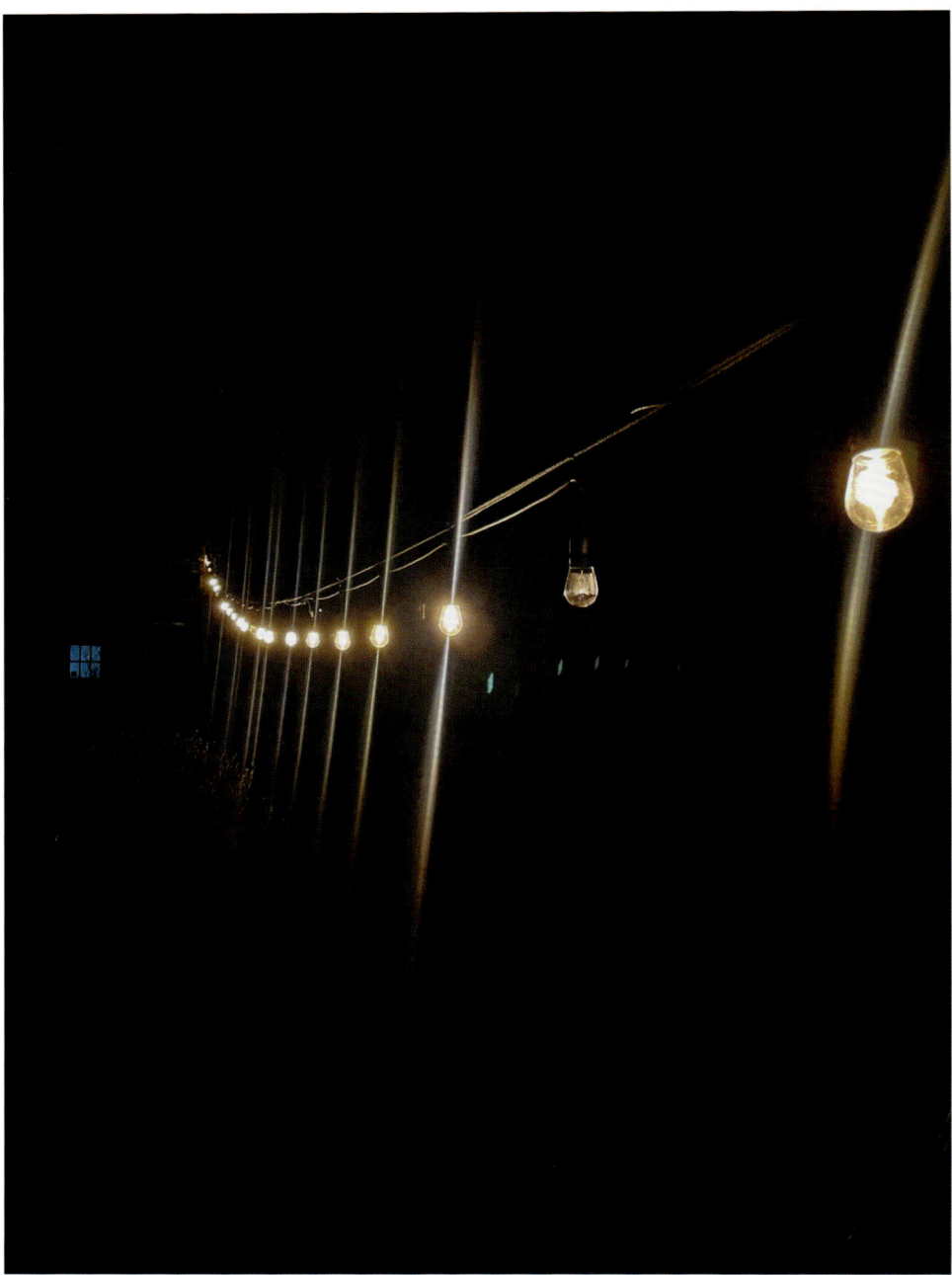

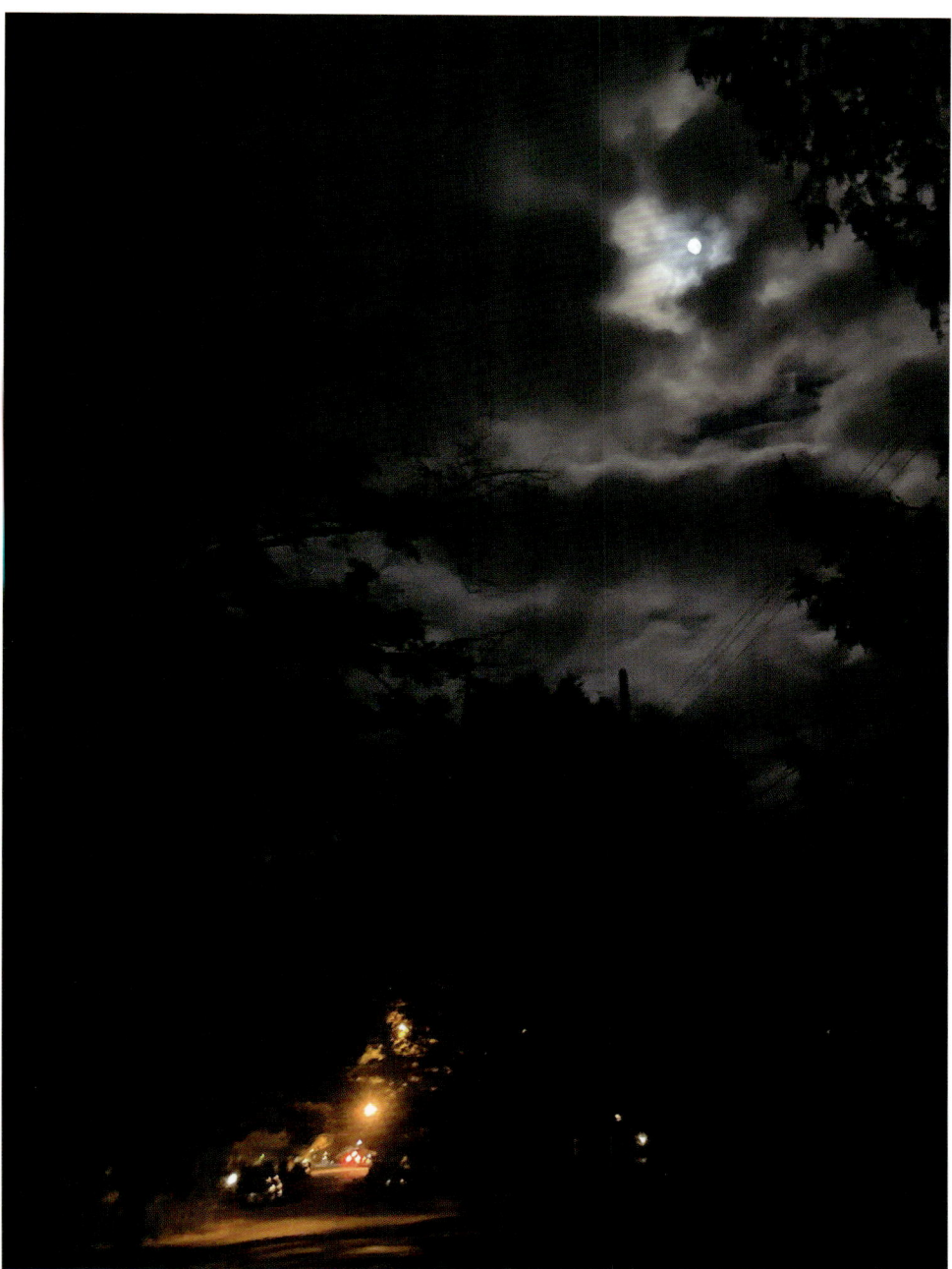

RENEWAL

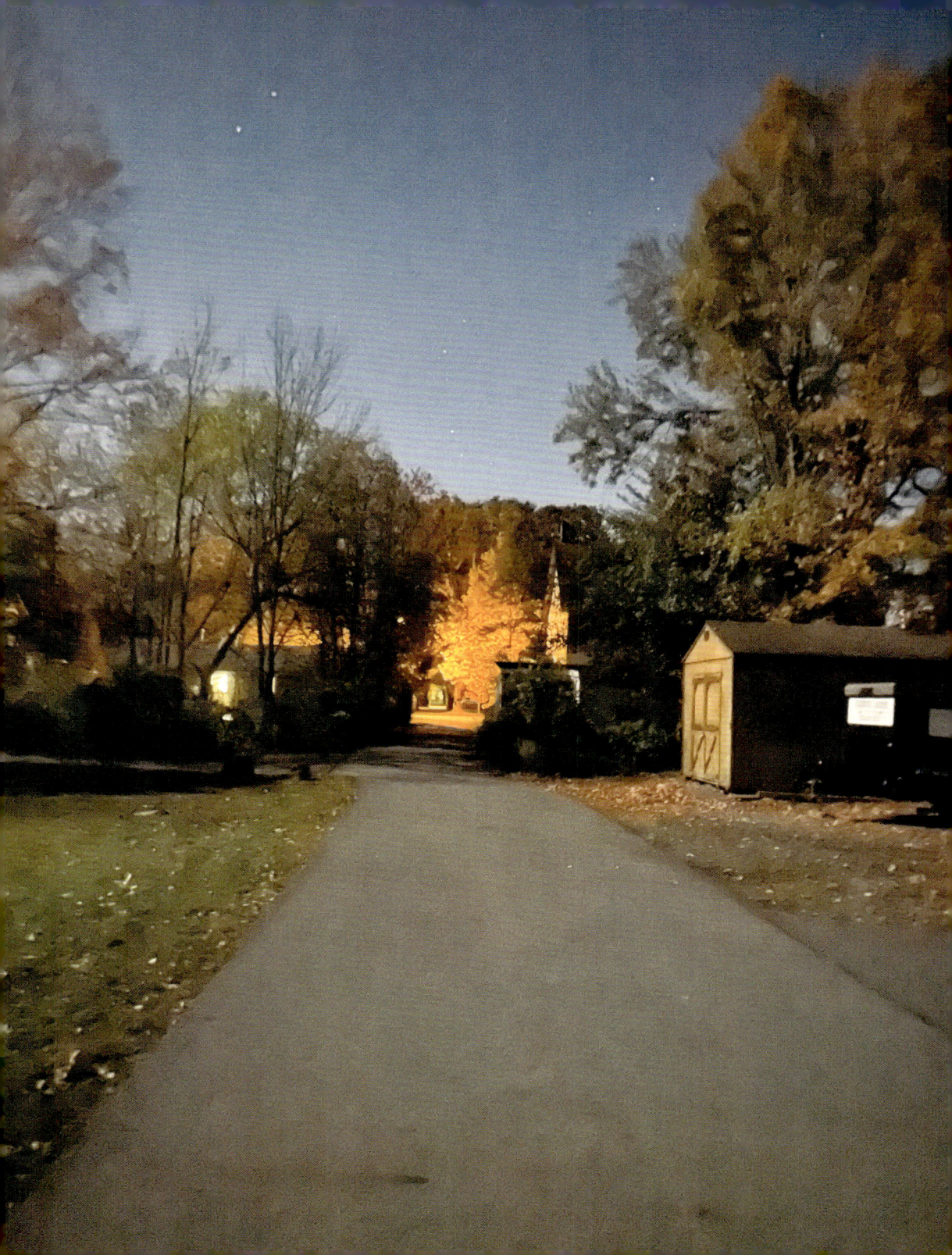

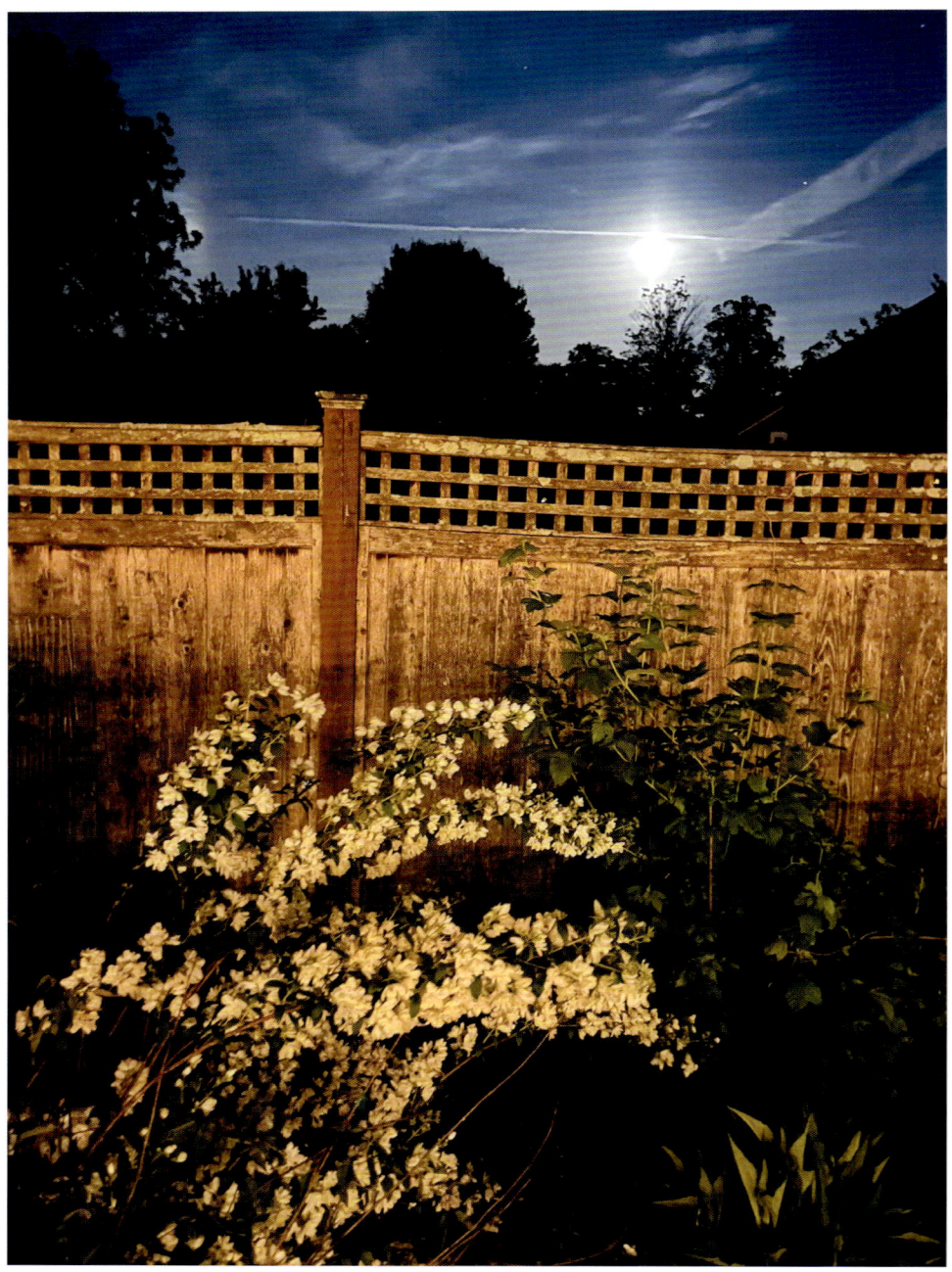

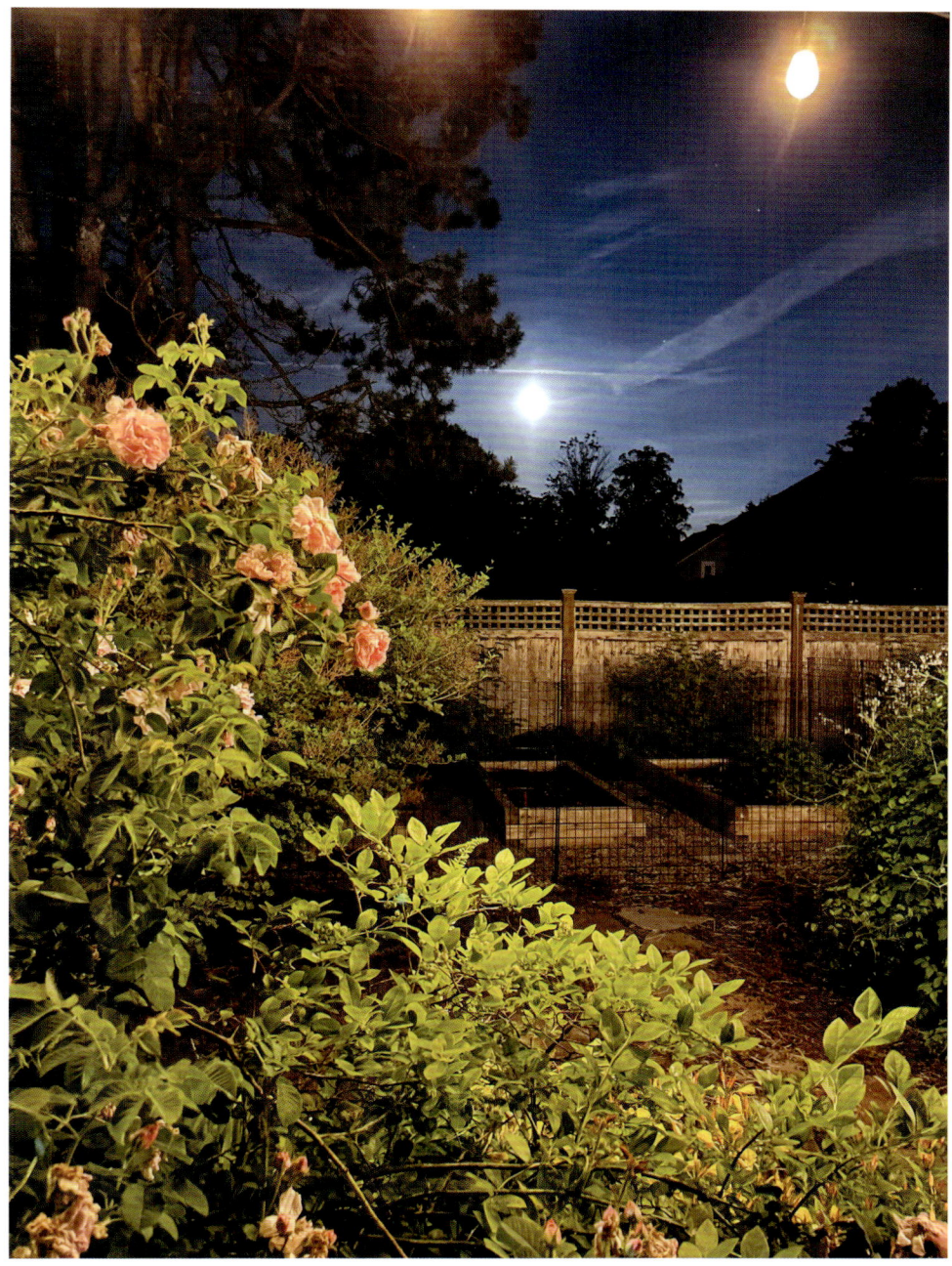

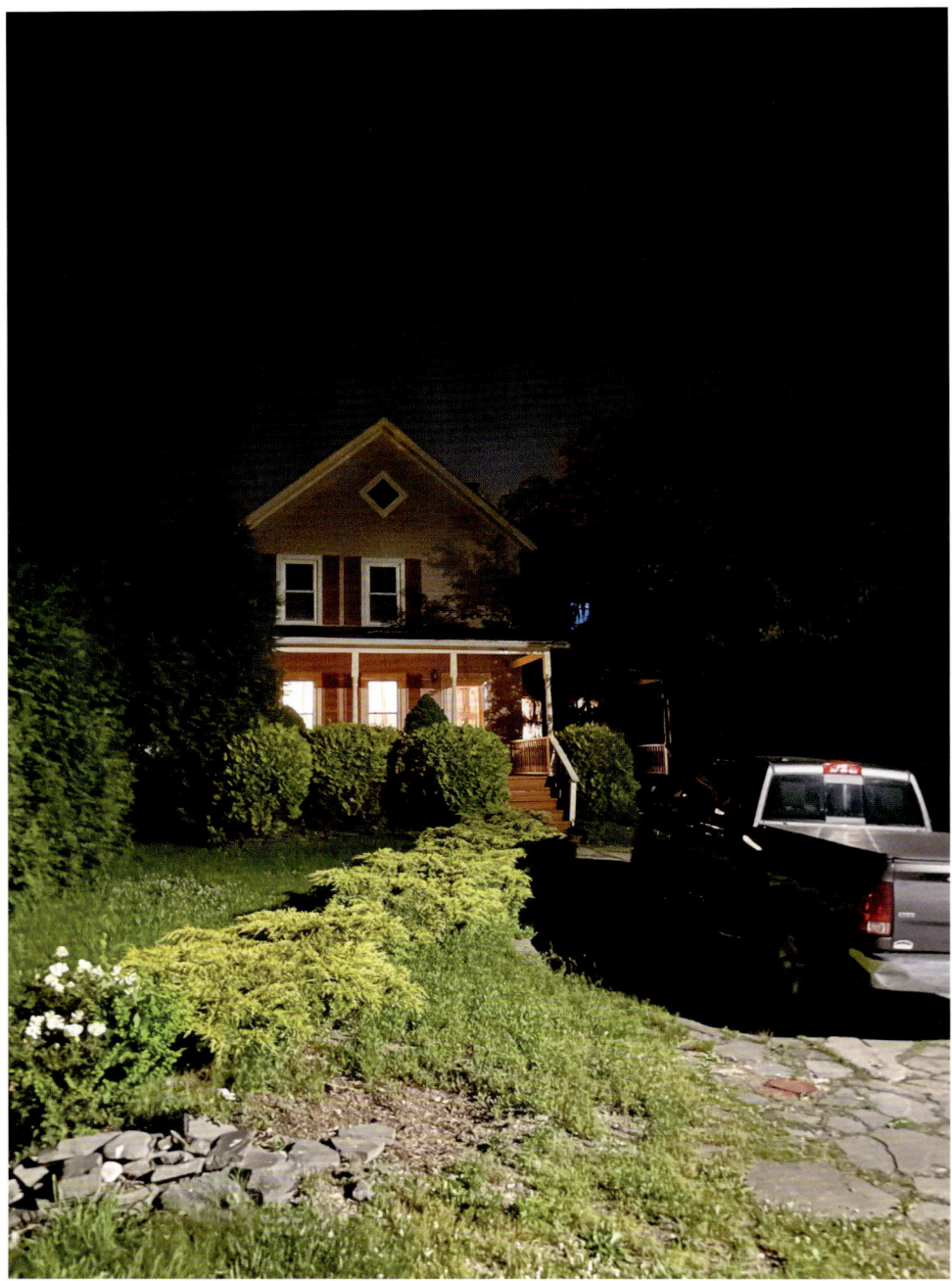

There is no time greater in Milford than spring and early summer. The darkness of winter has been chased away, life returns, and almost against our will, the inexhaustible drive of life propels us forward, just as waves, pulled by the powerful gravitational force of the moon, are always drawn to the shore.

In my case, it was not just the miracle of nature and life reasserting itself that filled me with renewal and hope; it was also the kindness of my neighbors. I cannot tell you how many times, alone with my self-absorbed thoughts, that the warm light of my neighbor's window reached out to me, providing me with comfort and solace. It was as if these bright panes of light and clarity, stretching out into the night, had been ordered by the full moon to do on a human scale what it did so grandly and majestically overhead.

Perhaps, not surprisingly, this image of the kind neighbor has also lived in my imagination for a long time. *Buddhaland Brooklyn* is my novel about a Buddhist priest who is forced by his Japanese superiors to open their first temple in America. The priest is painfully shy, an introvert, but he is forced by his Brooklyn neighbors to come out of his shell and embrace life. The transformation he undergoes shows up in the subtle way the haiku poetry he writes changes over the course of the year.

At the start of the book the priest writes the following poem—

> *Over Brooklyn*
>
> *The sliver moon of silver*
>
> *Reveals the jagged roof*

By the end of the book, he finds himself writing—

> *Over Brooklyn*
>
> *The sliver moon of silver*
>
> *Reveals my neighbor's roof*

That, too, is my Milford.

The harumphing and sometimes dour writer is inevitably, almost against his will, drawn out into the world by the light of the moon and by the warmth of his neighbors.

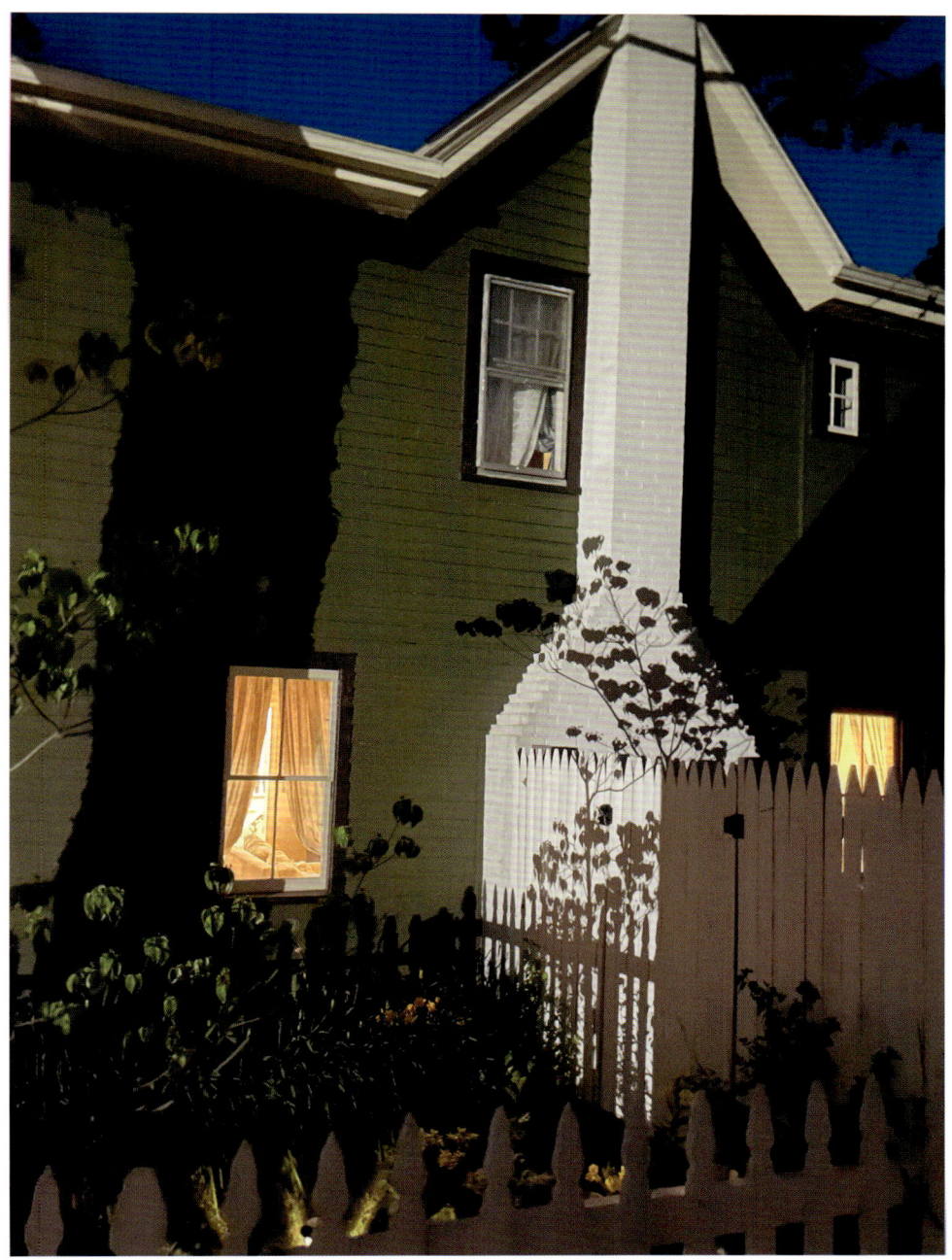

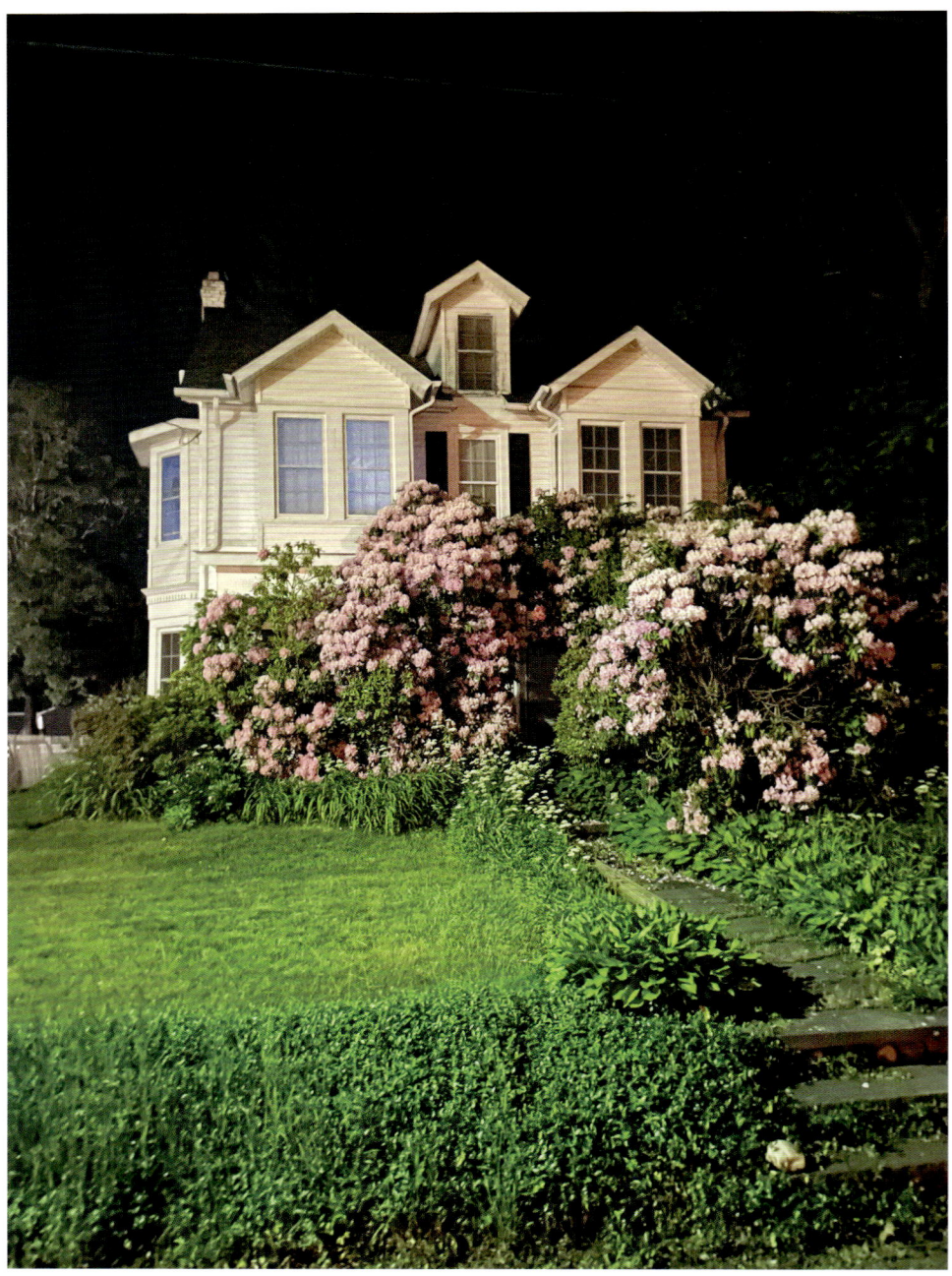

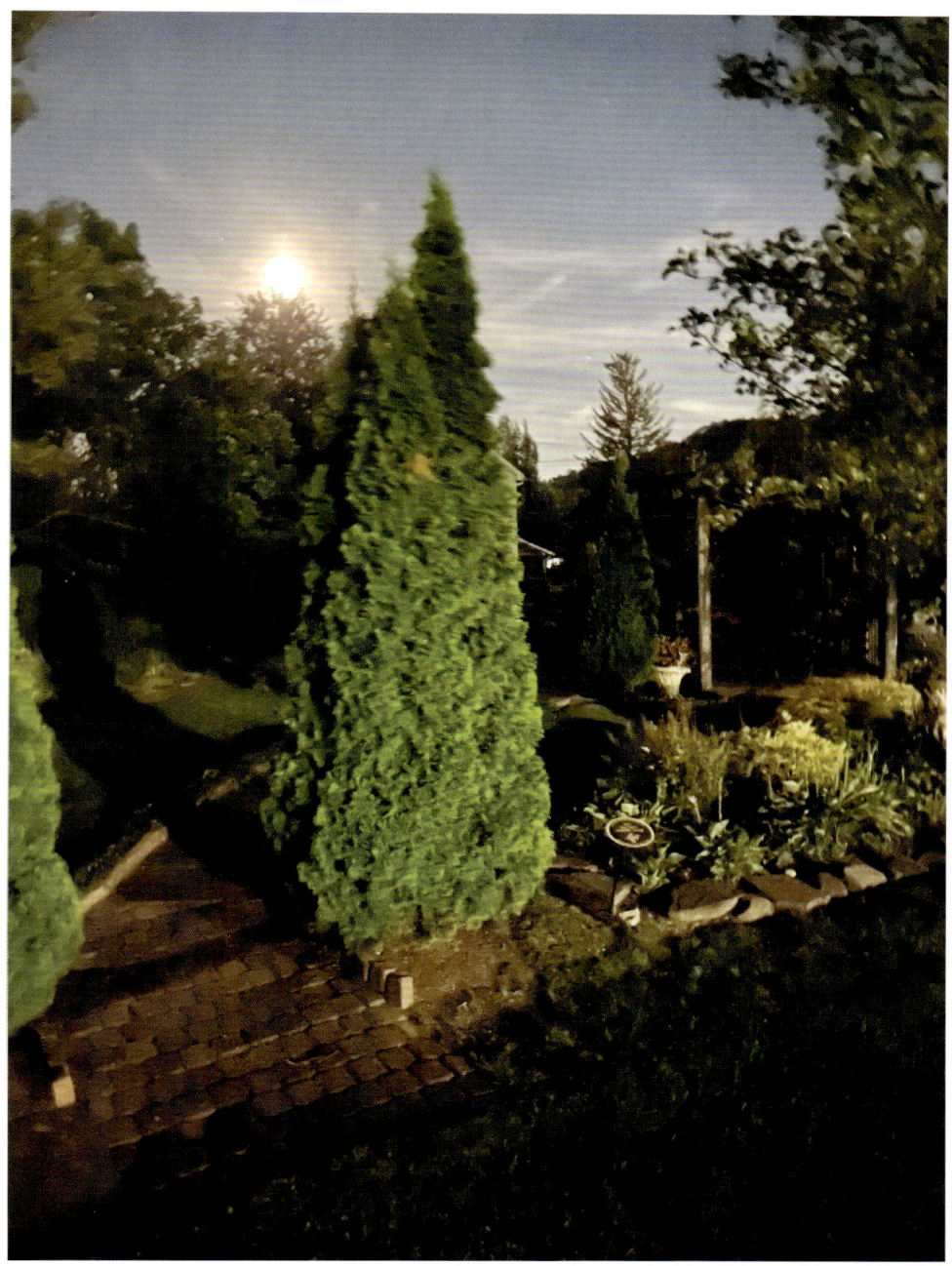

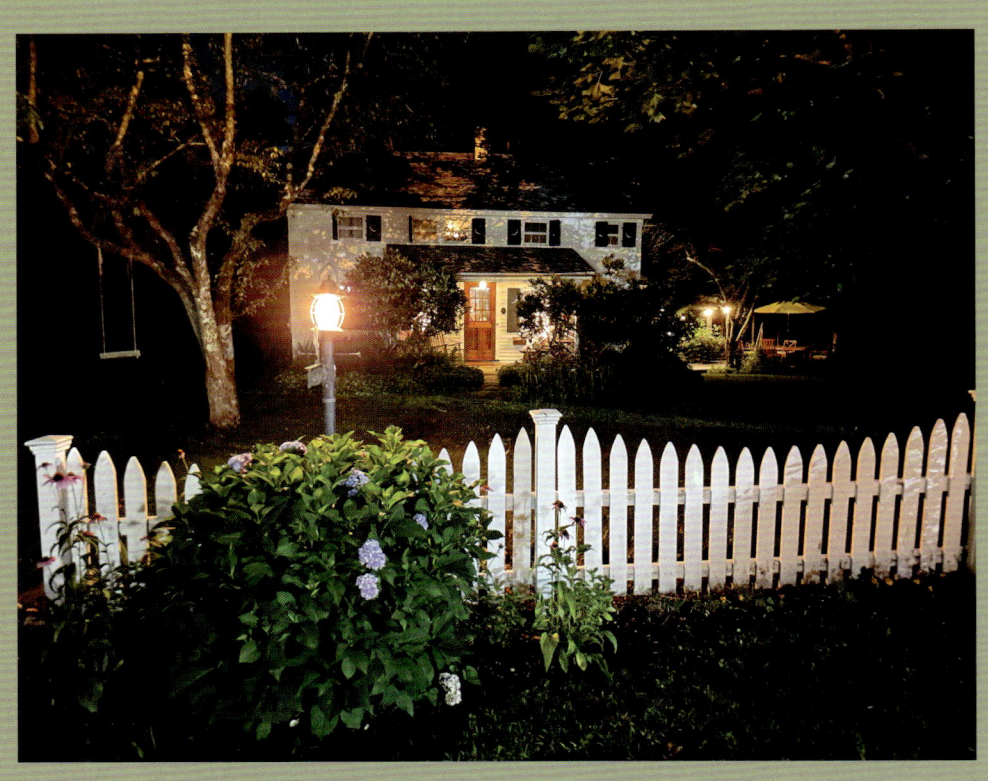

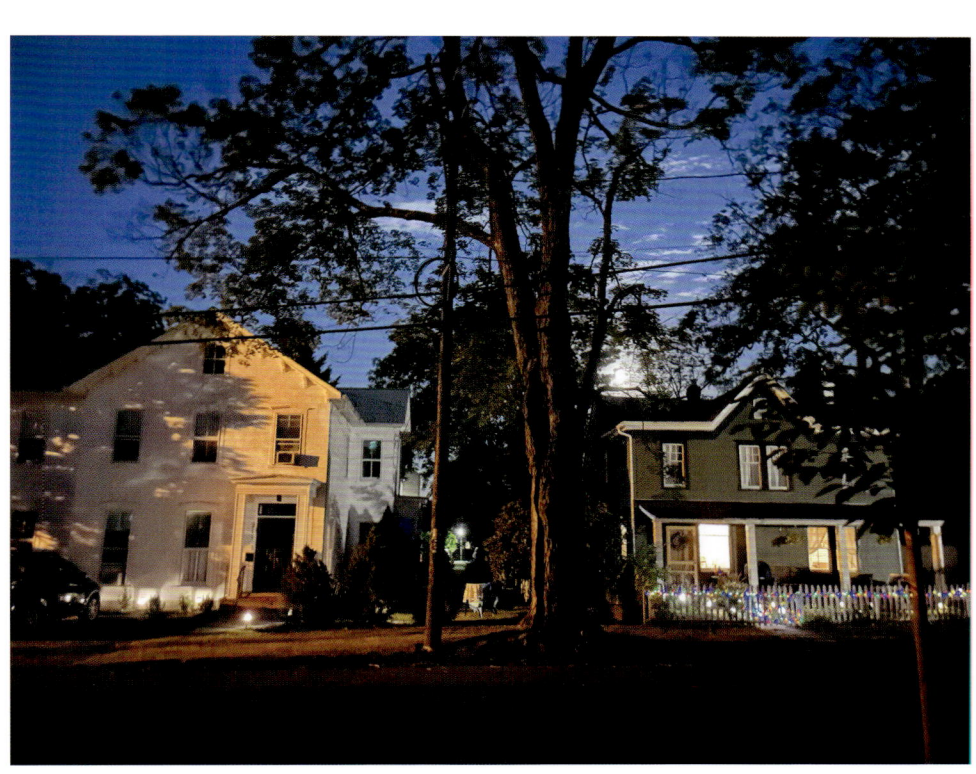

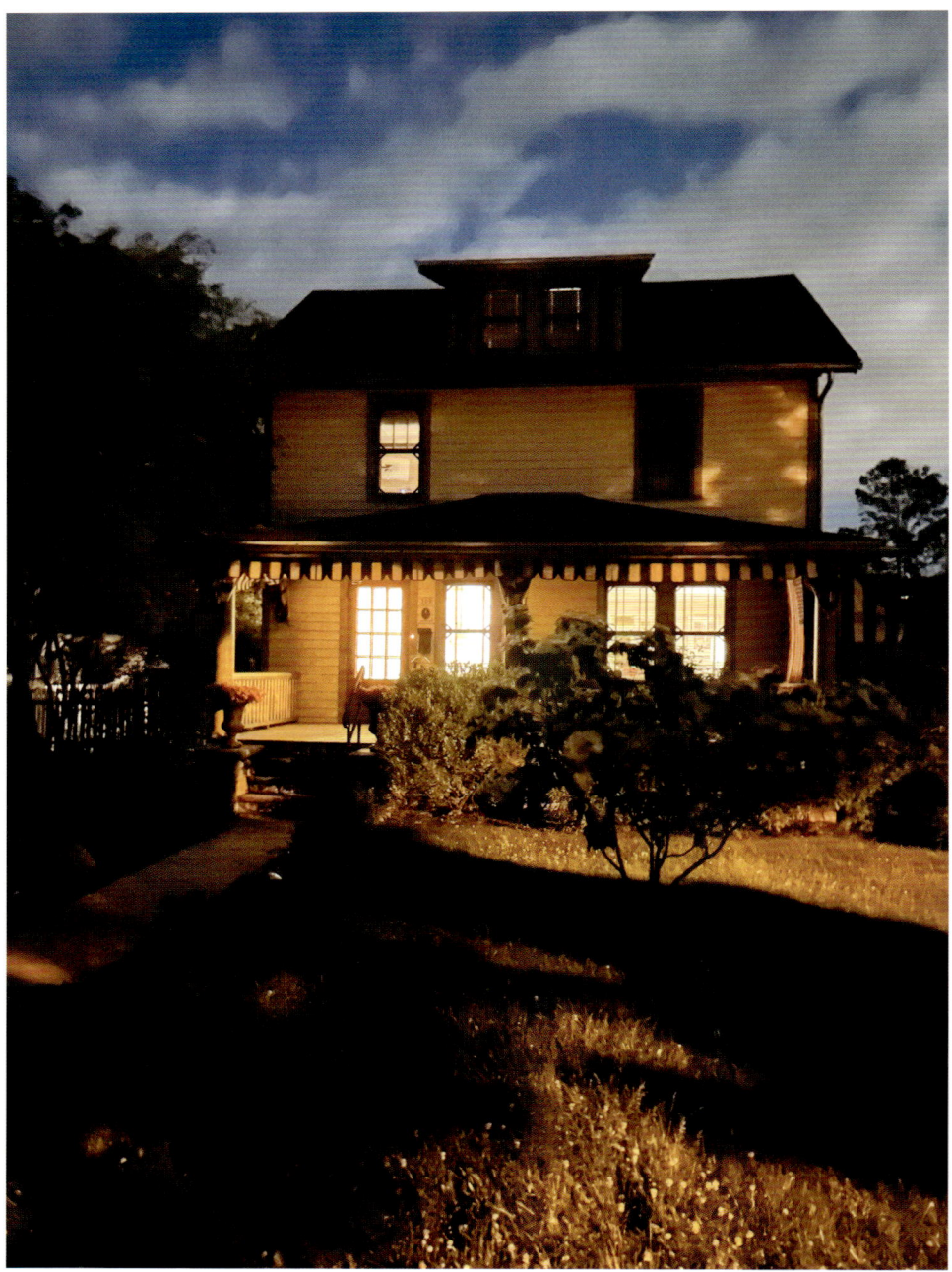

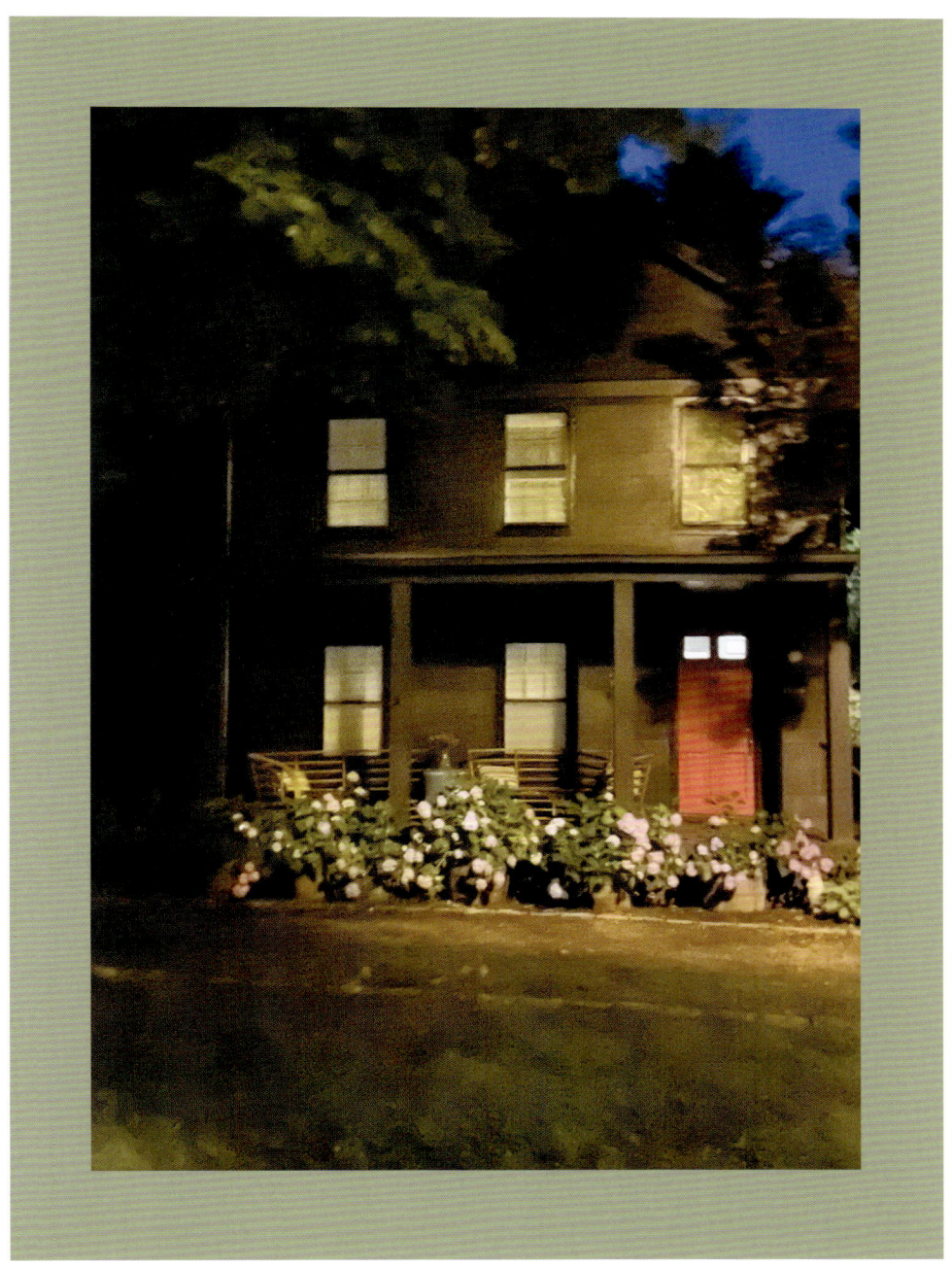

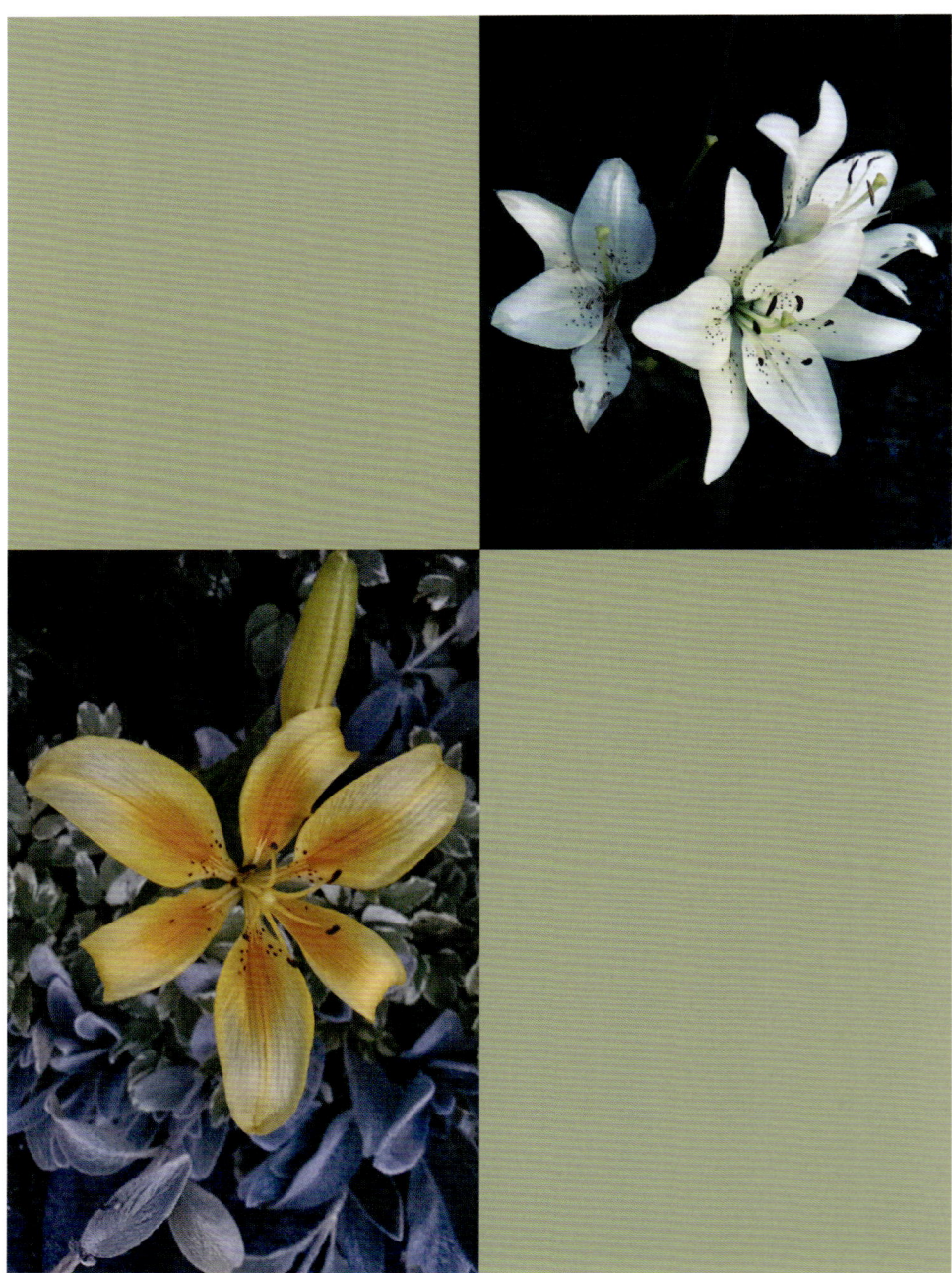

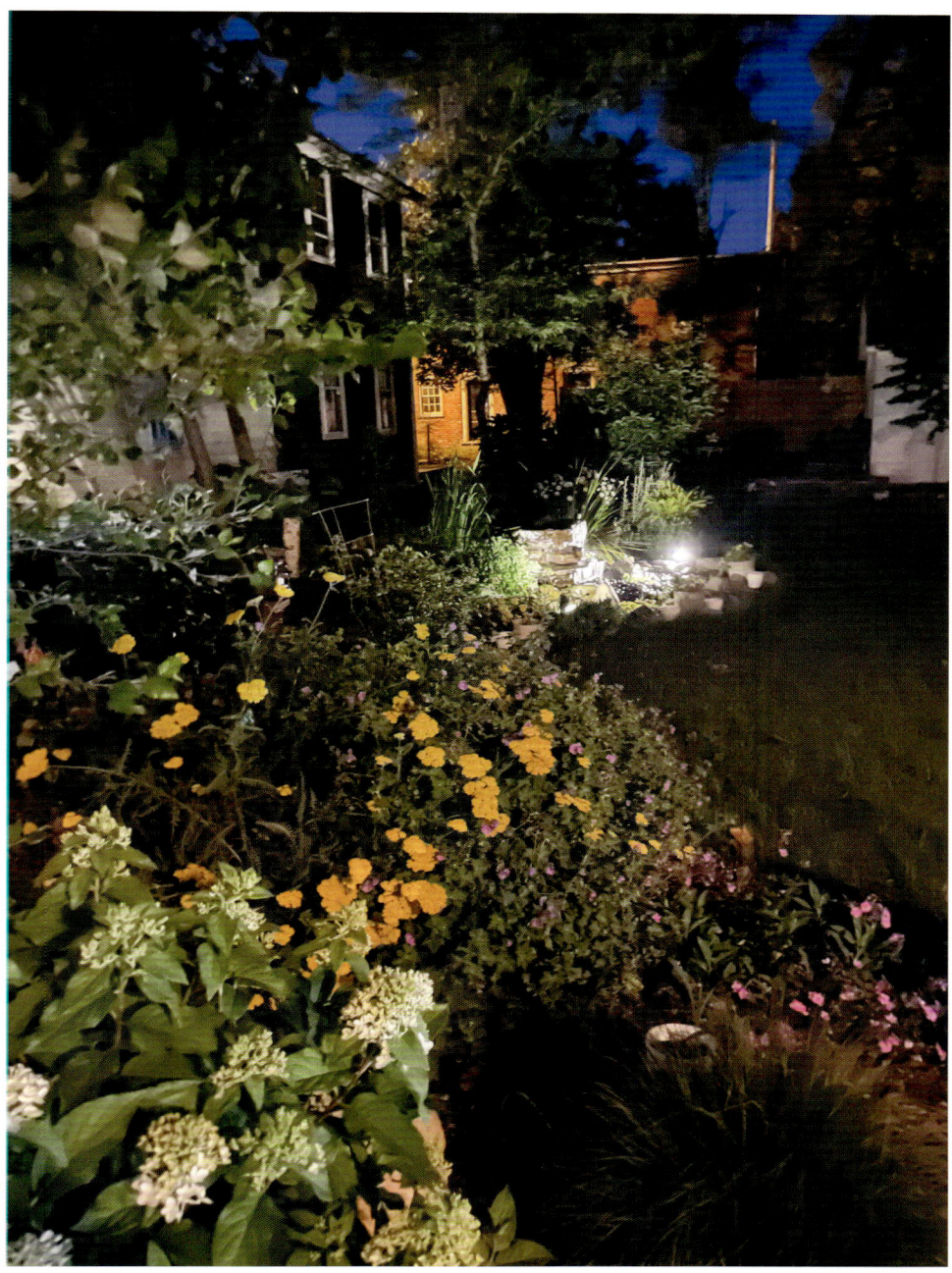

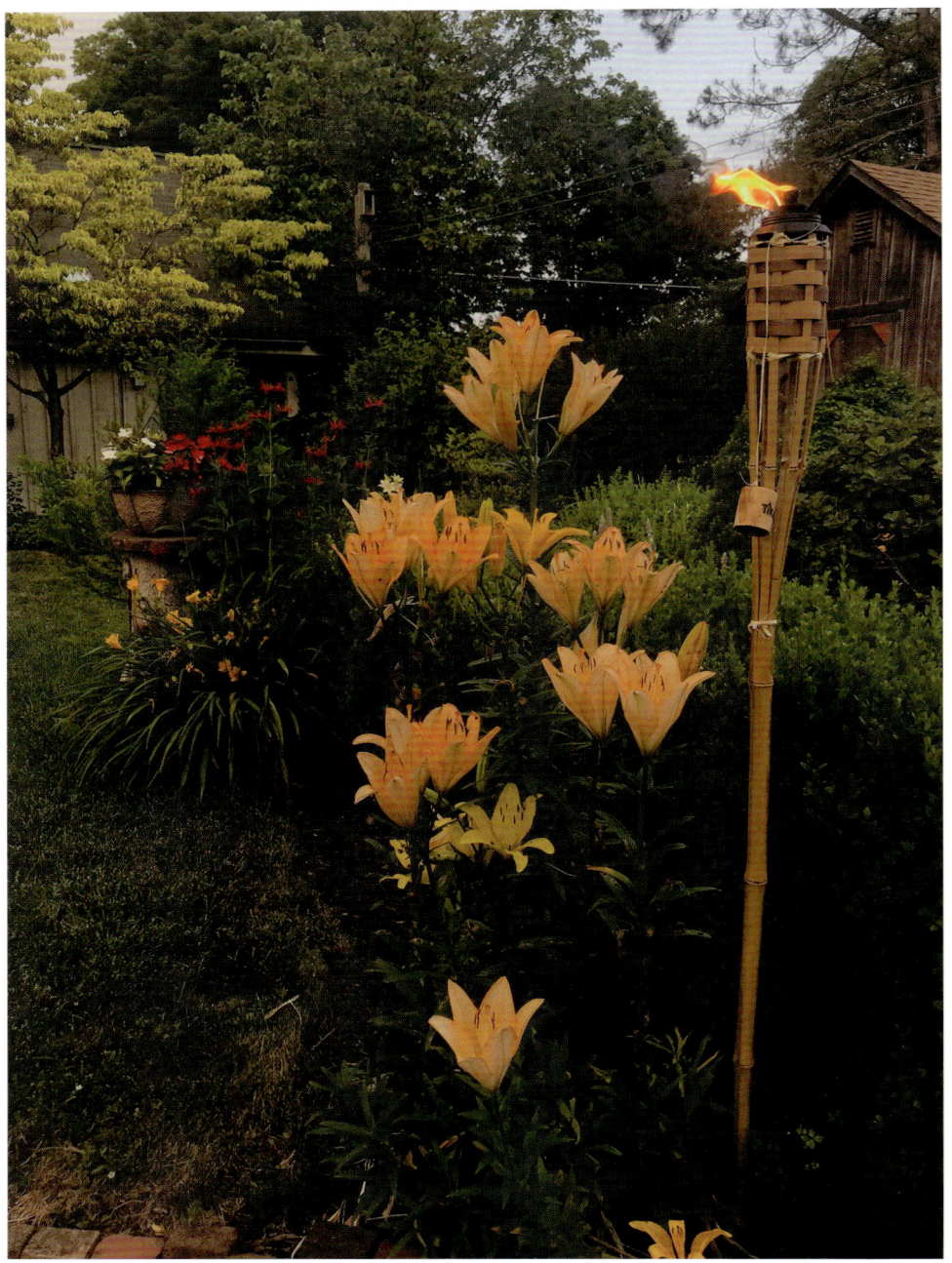

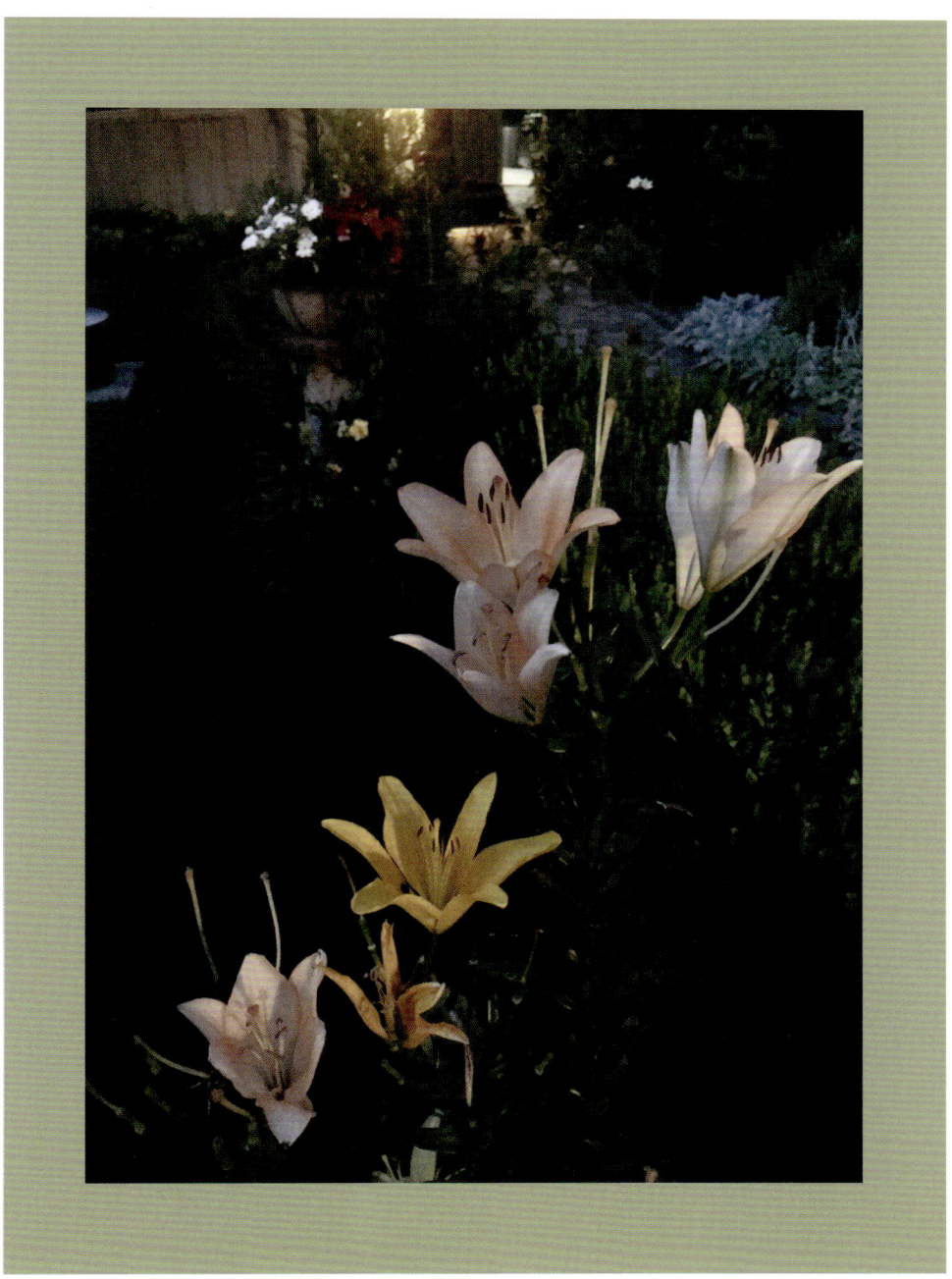

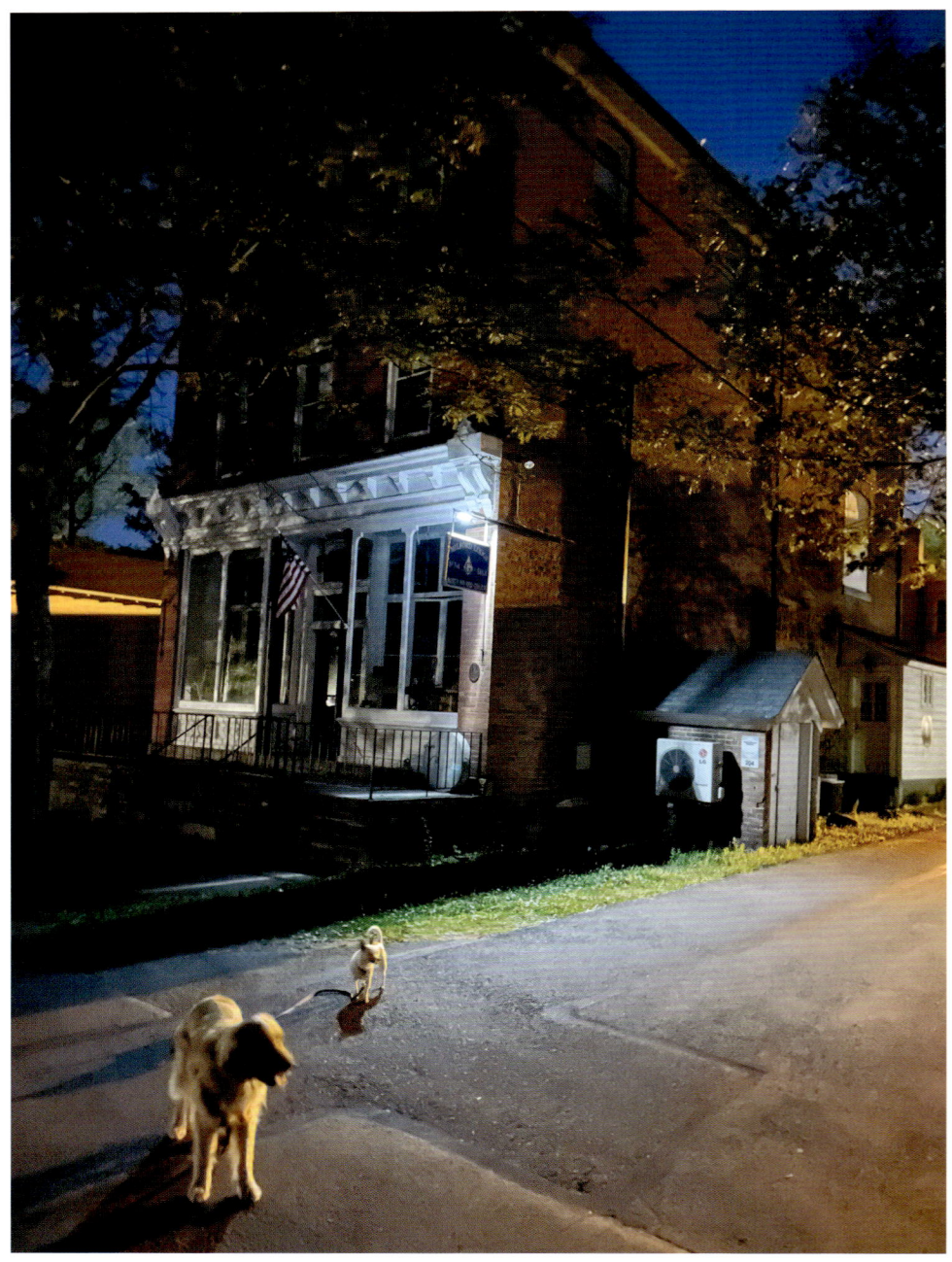

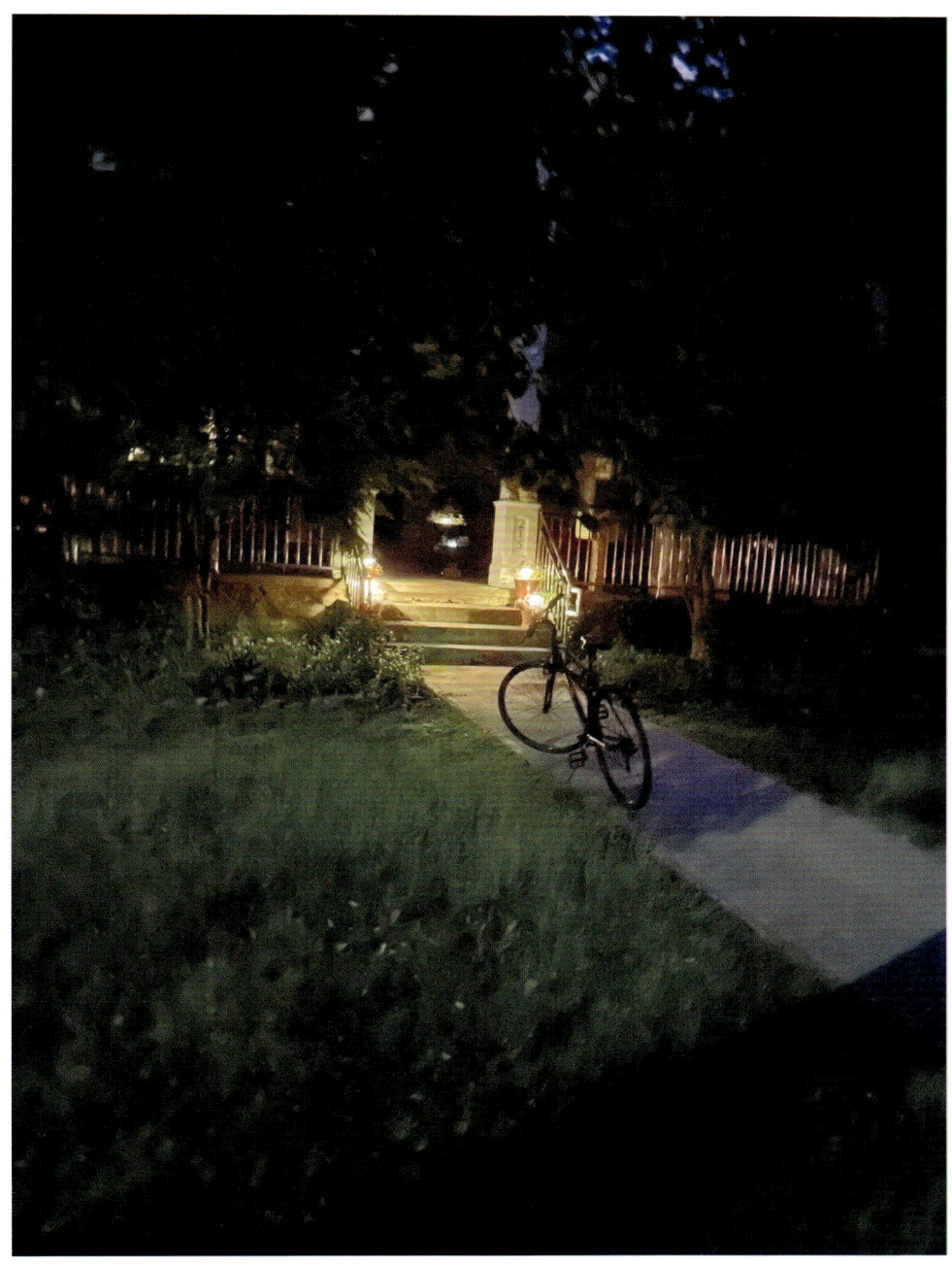

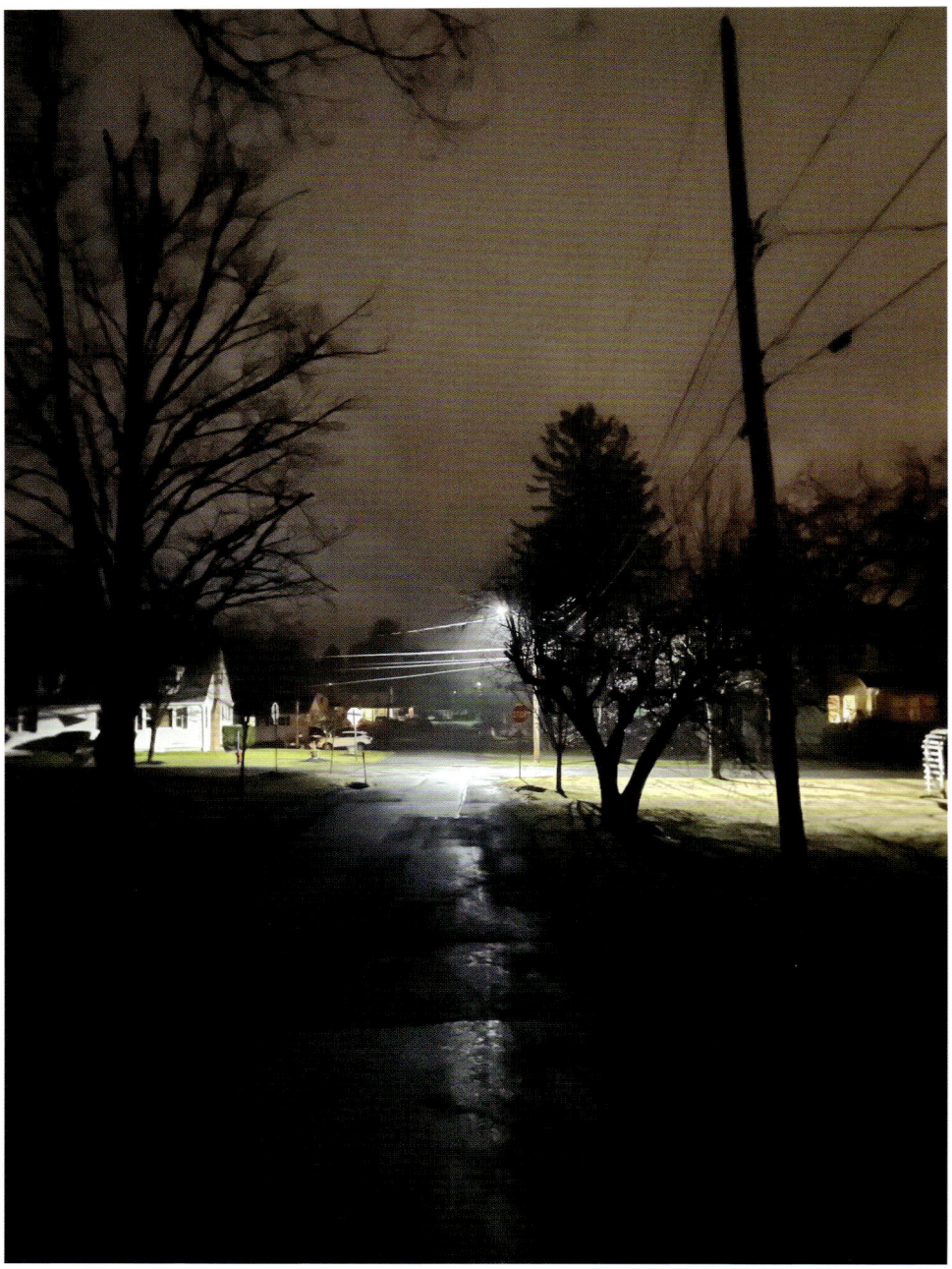

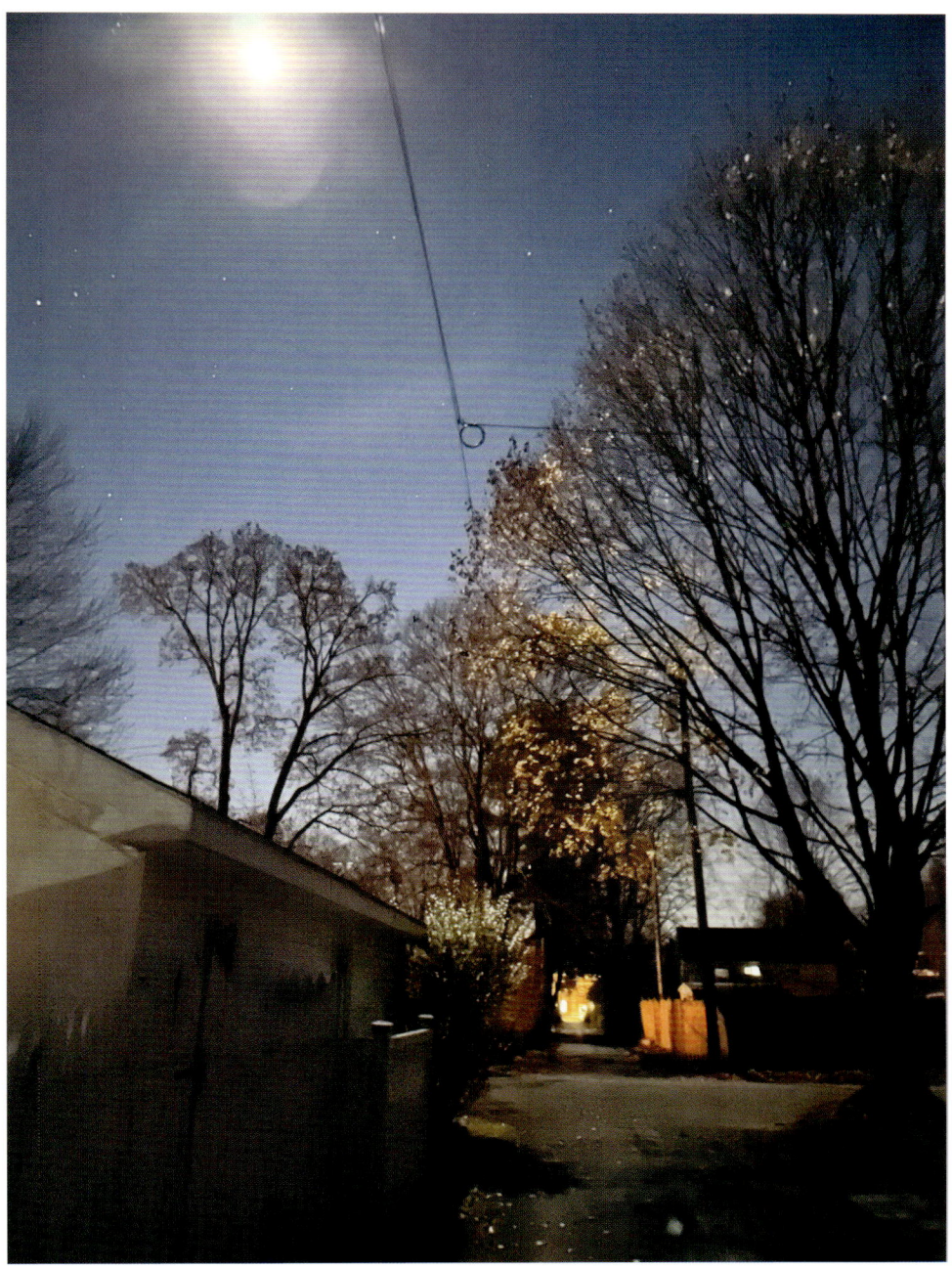

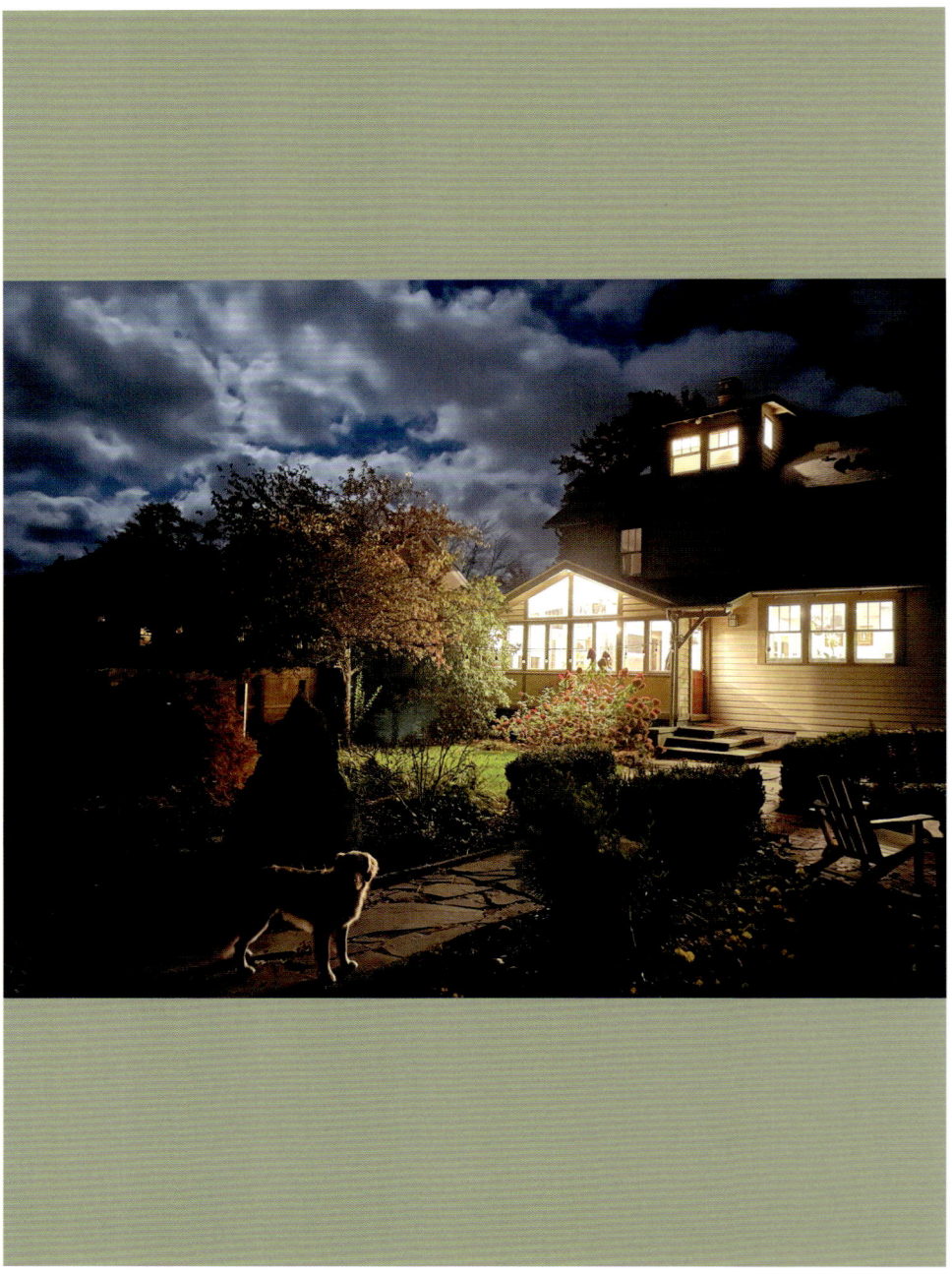

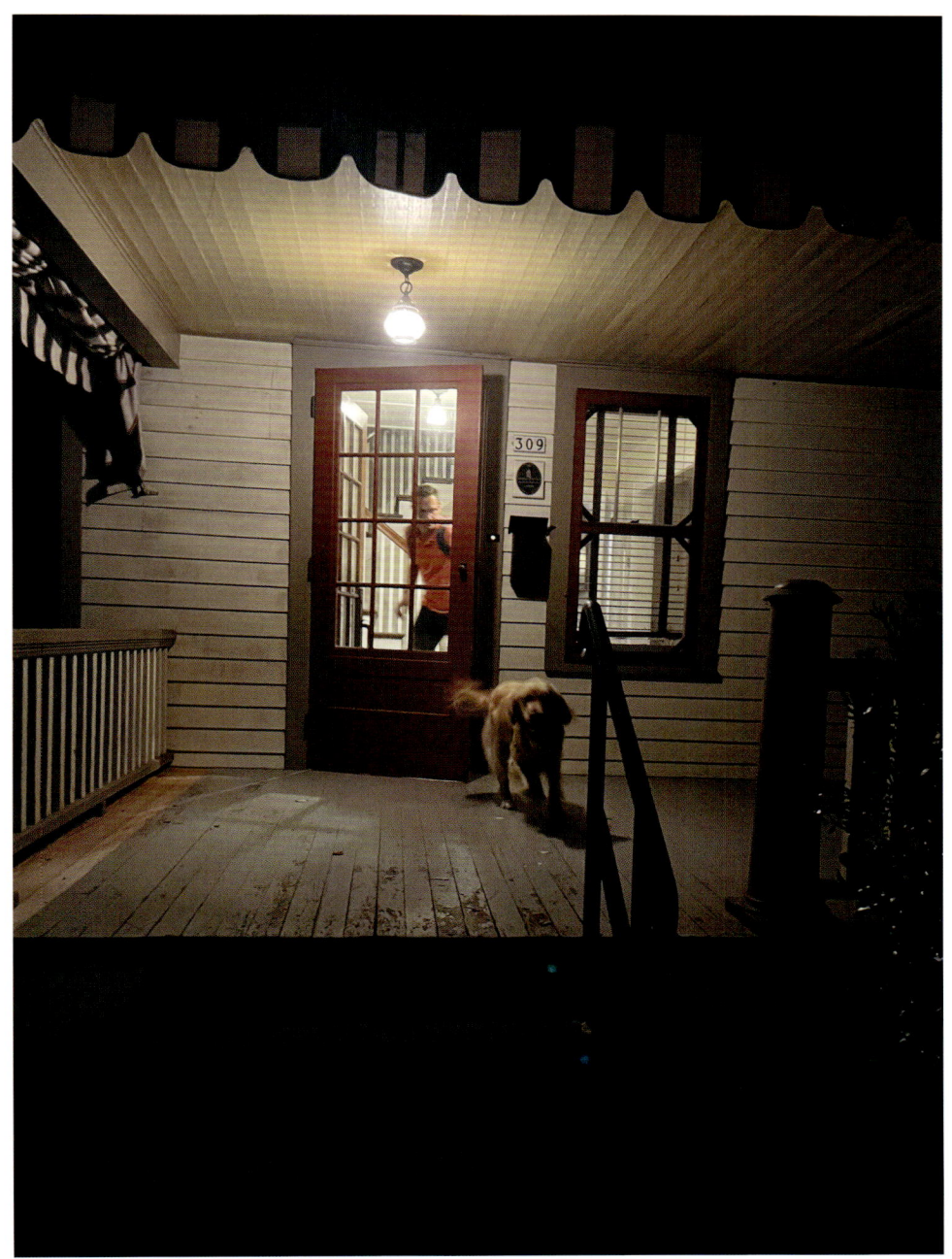

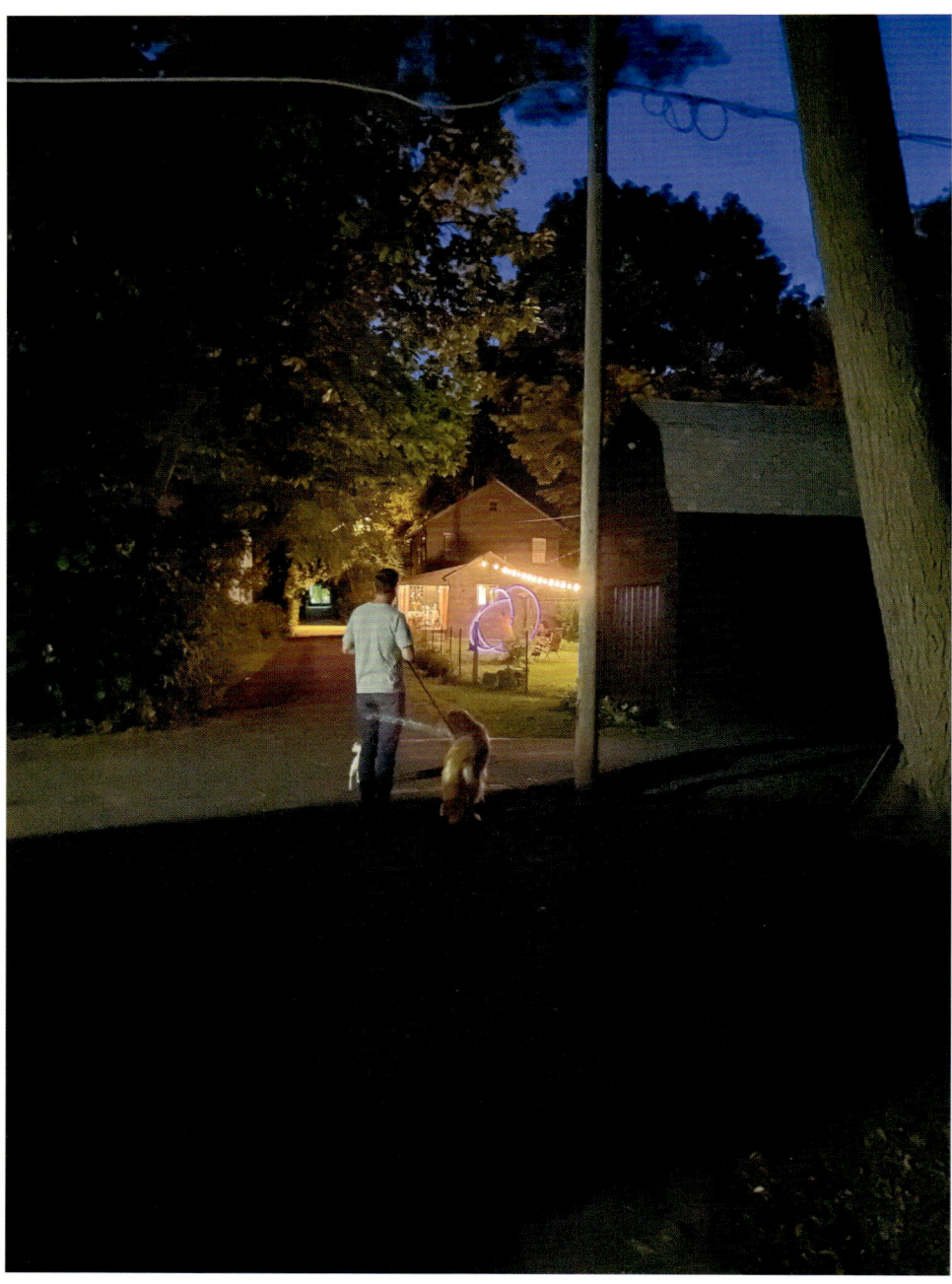

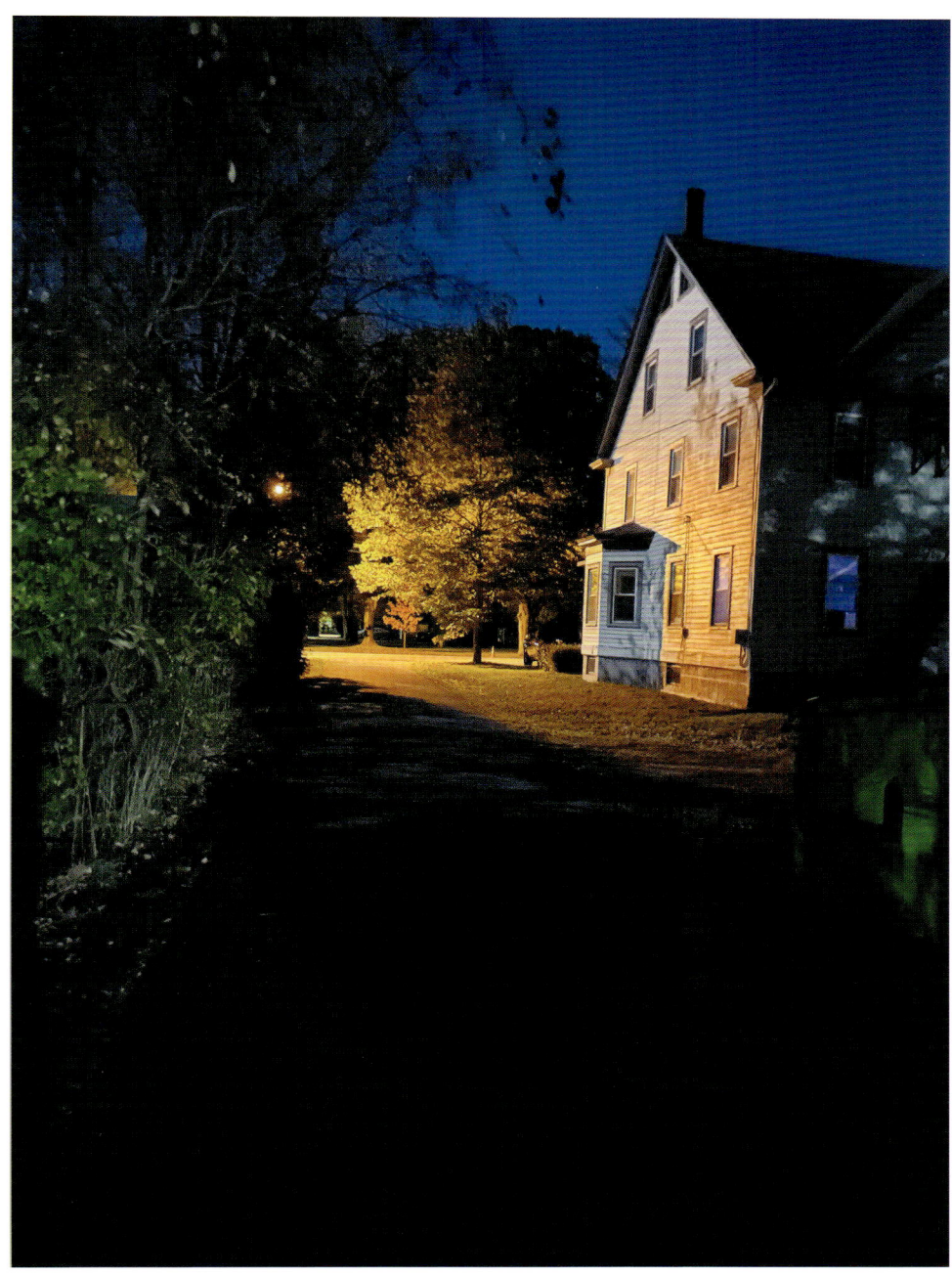

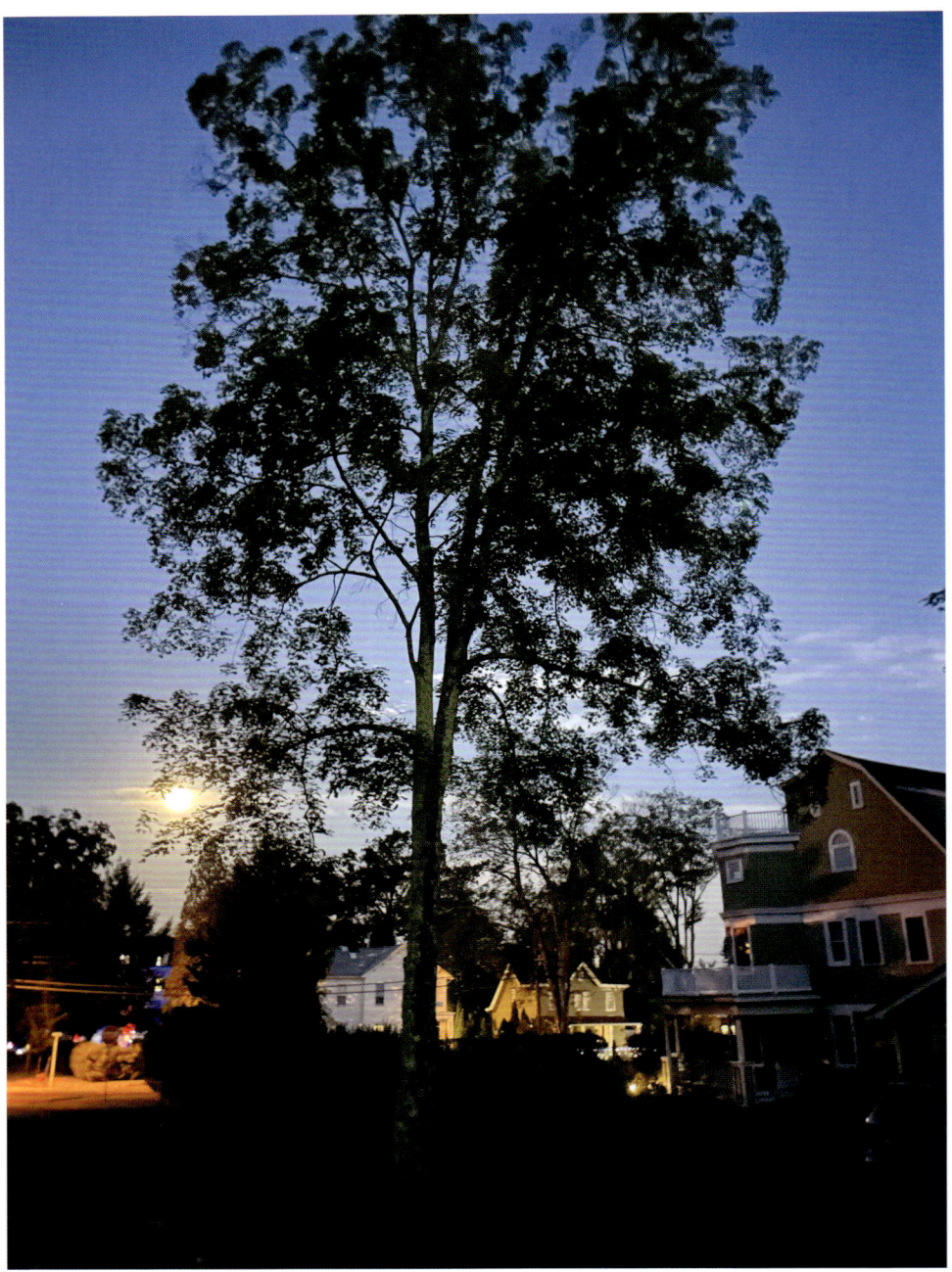

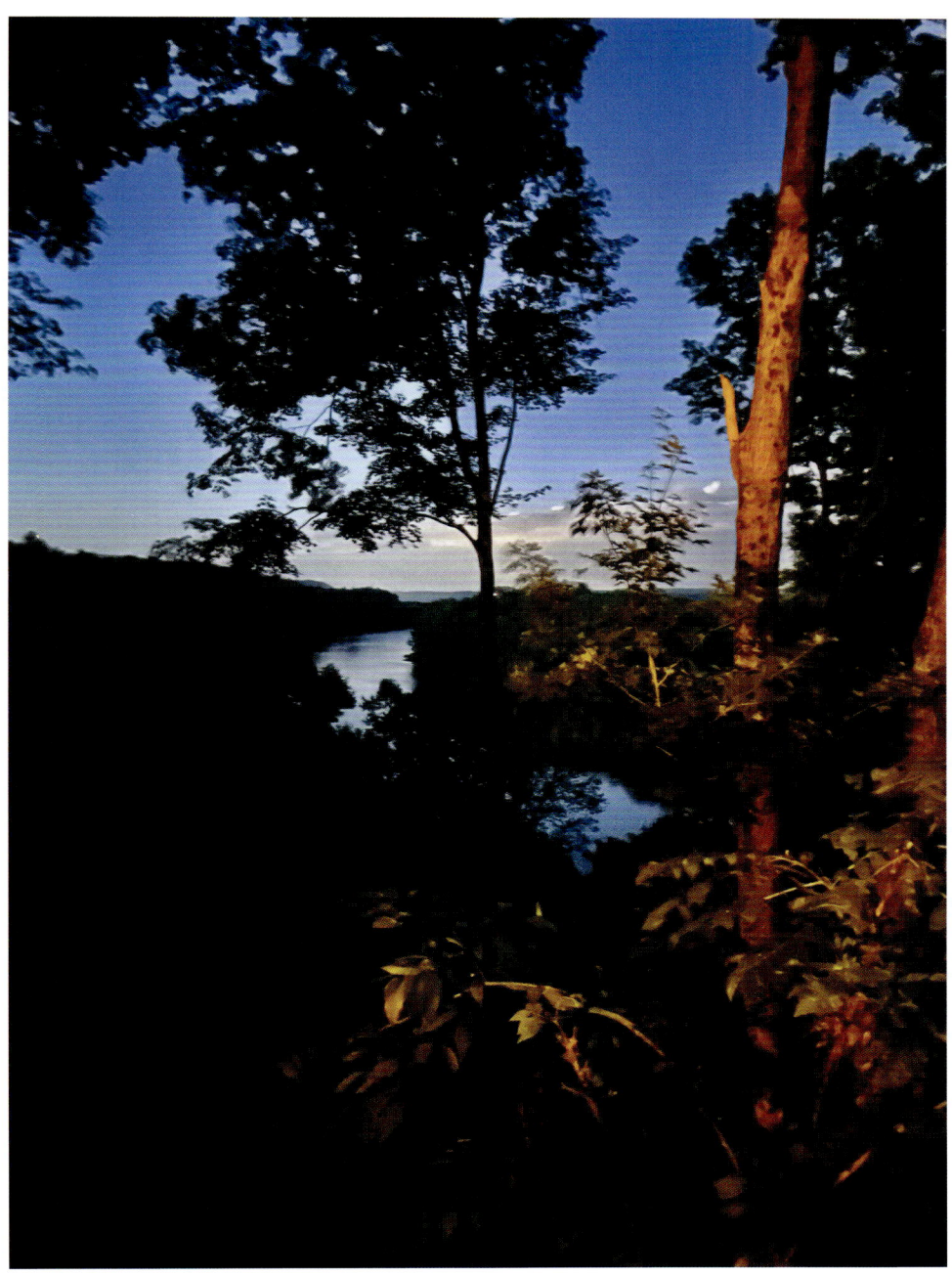

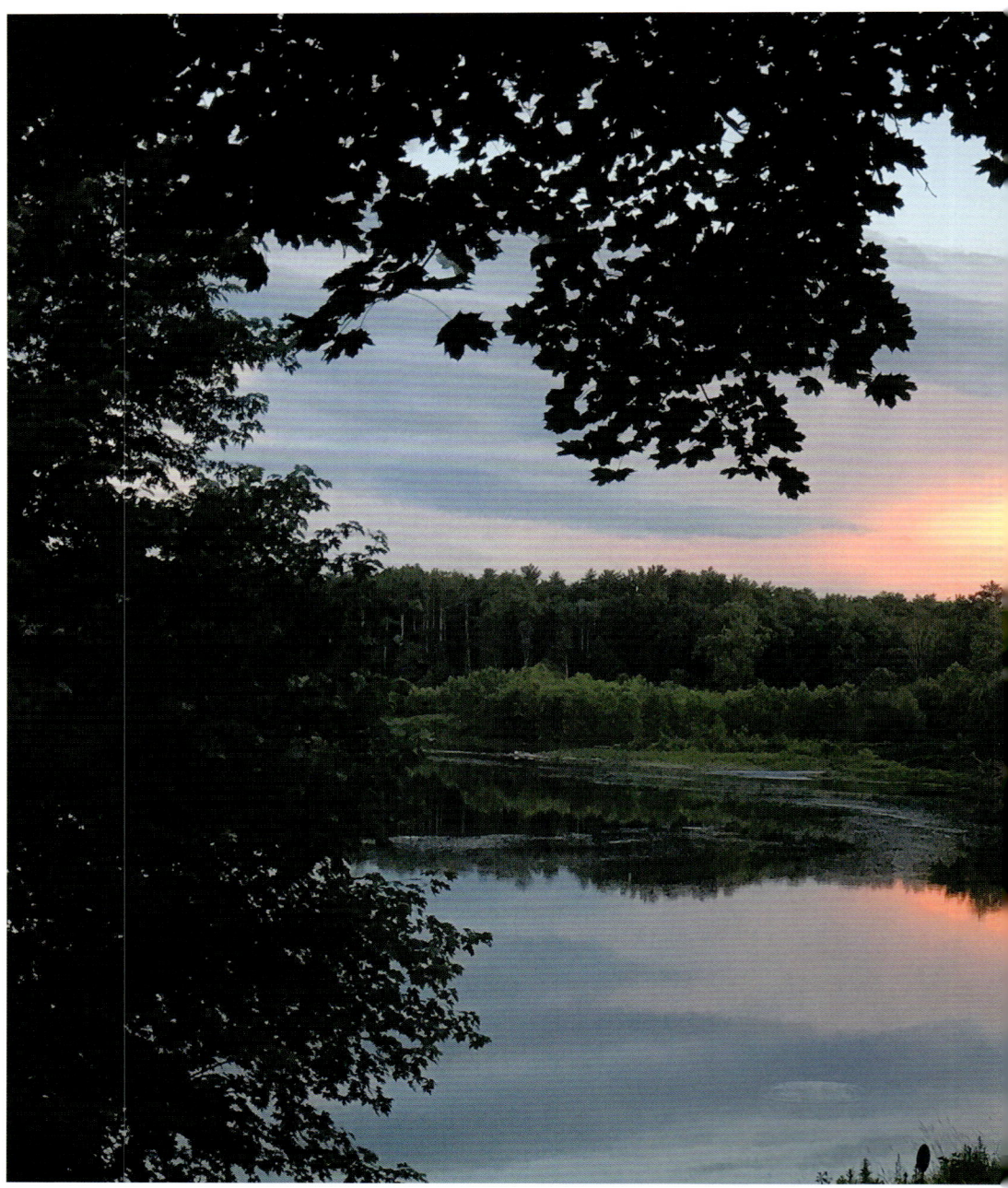

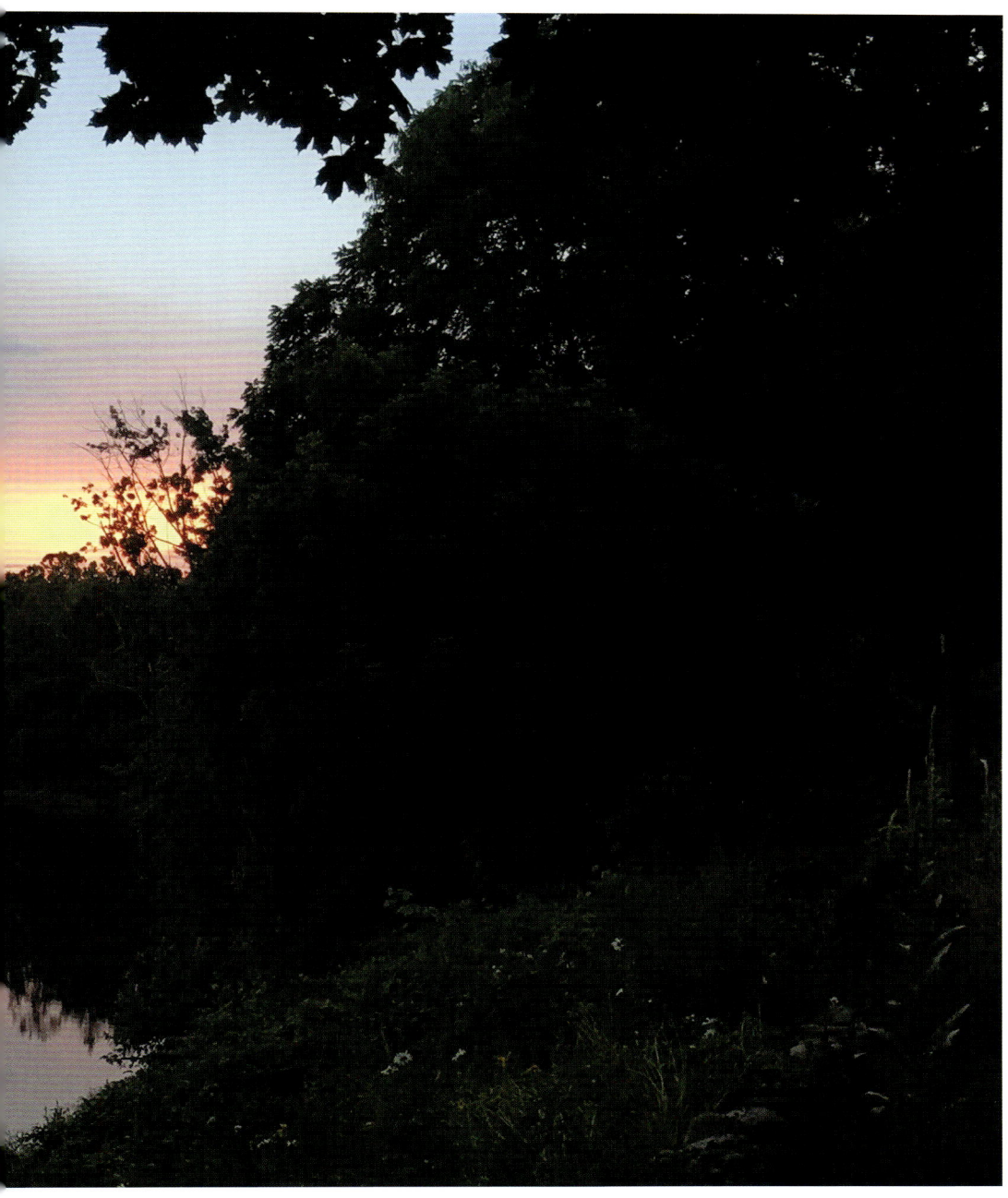

TRANQUILTY

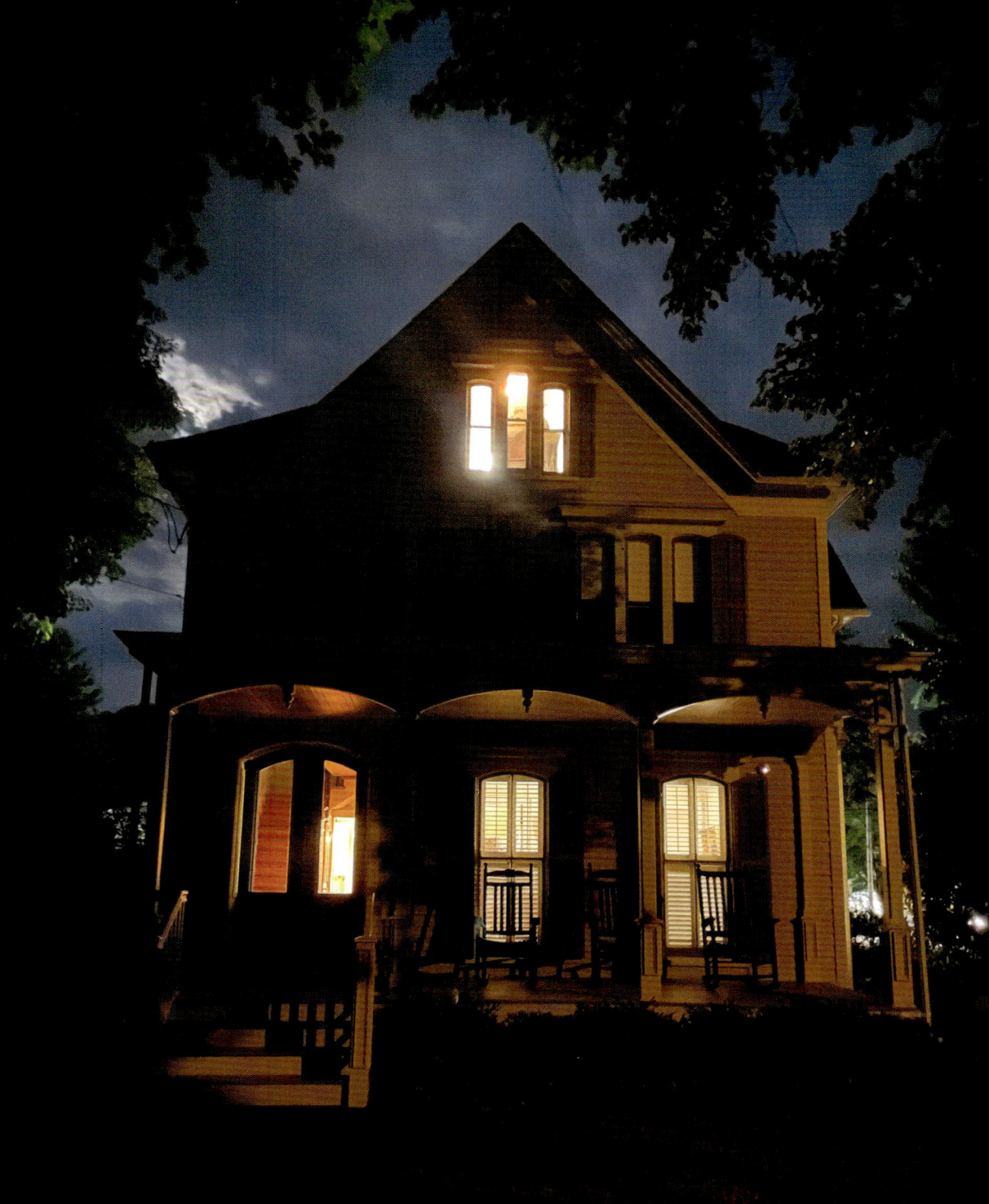

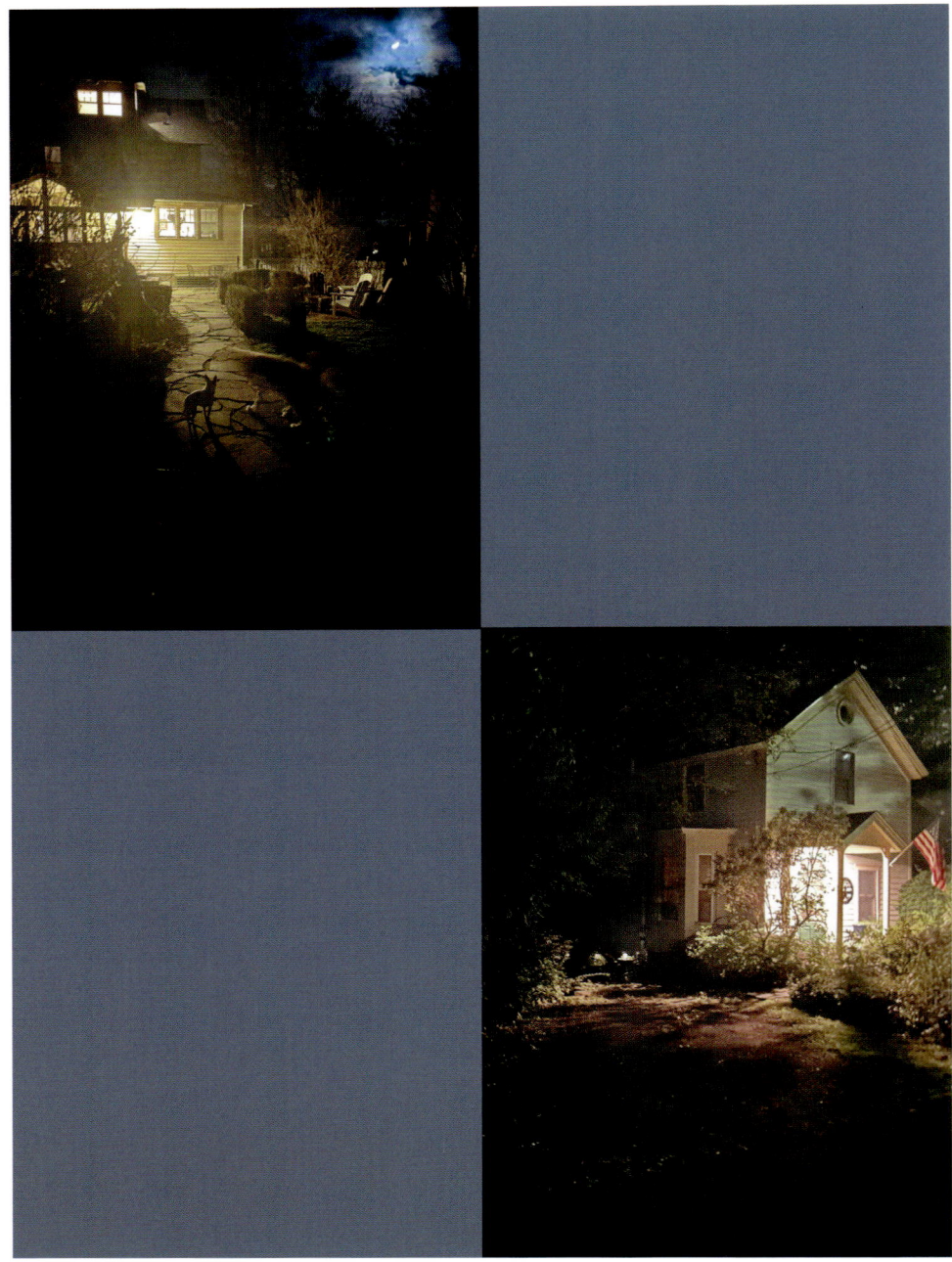

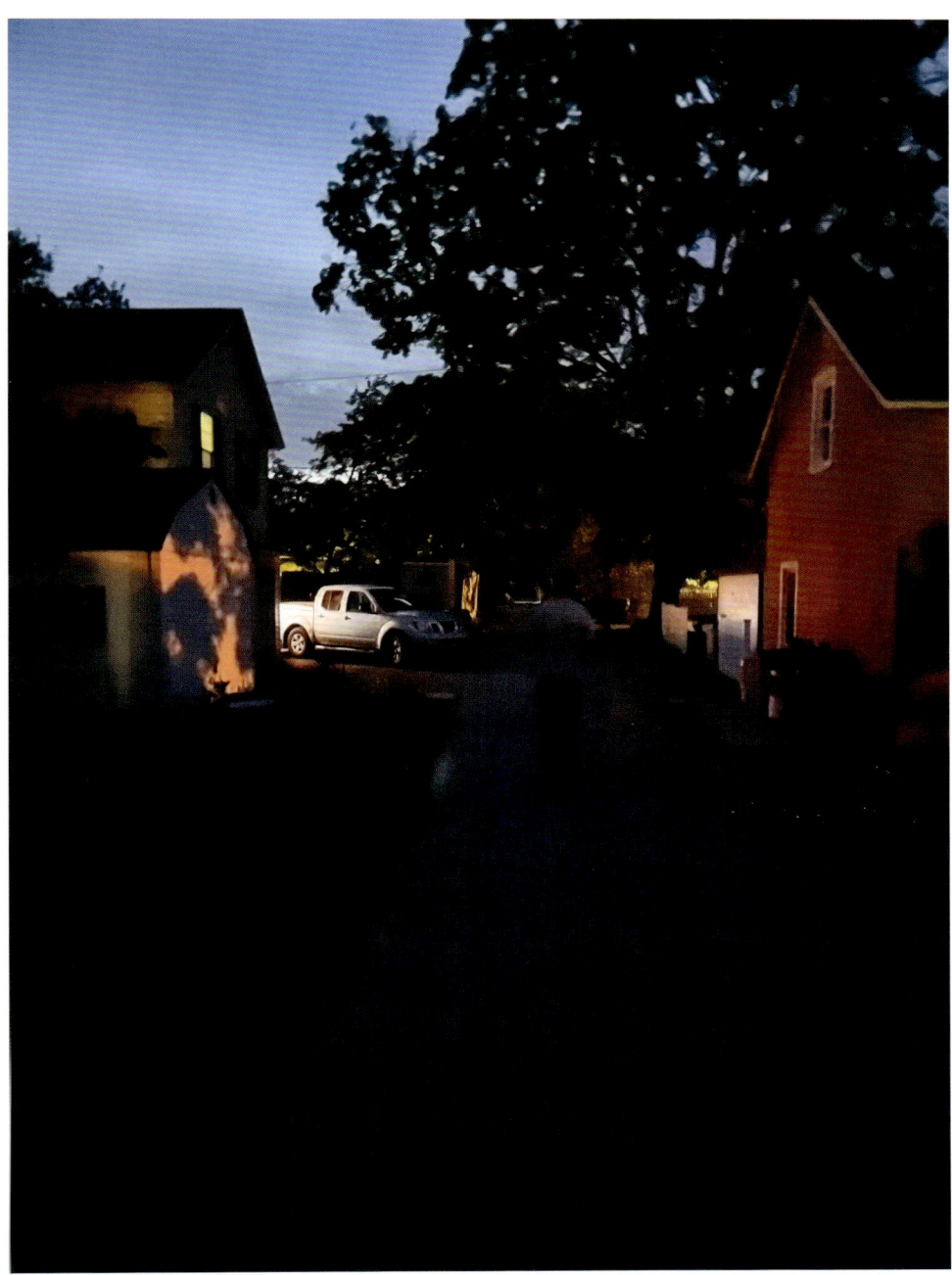

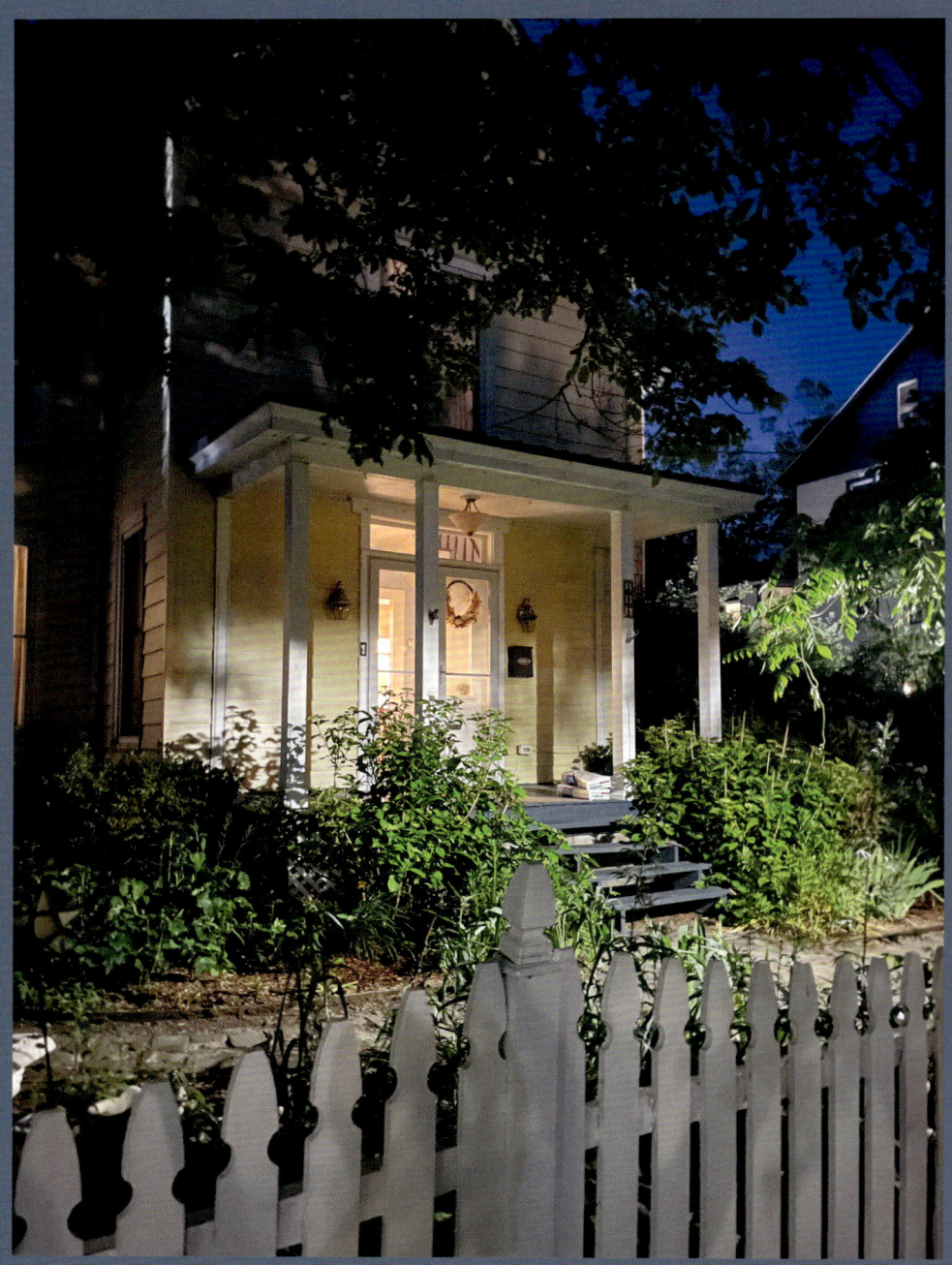

When I told my ex-wife, Susan, I was working on this book, she recalled something from our shared past and foraged in some boxes, unexpectedly retrieving my astrological chart, a report which she had commissioned on my behalf decades ago.

Astrology is not my thing, so I had long forgotten the report existed, and yet when I sat down to read the moon-related sections of my chart, I found my astrological signs reading like catalog copy for this book. I'm a Scorpio, and I was astounded to discover that because *la luna* "represents our upbringing and emotional background, the Moon denotes our sense of belonging and well-being (or not) and what we need in order to feel comfortable and content." As my chart advises me: "True gratification can be had only by feeding your Moon. The Feast of the Present is spread out and around you."

Wise words. Dylan Thomas, one of my favorite poets, famously penned "Do Not Go Gentle into that Good Night," a poem that exhorts us to *Rage, rage against the dying of the light*. But I find myself, at this stage of life, gravitating toward a different state.

I ache, not for the fight, but for the small pleasures of life: to reconnect, as my astrological chart says, to my "upbringing and emotional background;" to the moon over Milford, which mysteriously enhances my "sense of belonging and well-being" and is undeniably what my soul needs "to feel comfortable and content."

So, on this evening, as I draw to a close my work on this book and begin the final phase of my life, I grab Sherry's leash and once again we head out for our evening stroll. We are on our eternal search for that fat and full moon, our reliable friend, always there to show us our platinum path forward into the unknown.

It is during this nocturnal hunt that Sherry and I listen hard to the cicadas, who, on this balmy late-summer night, are chanting their prayers—for all of us.

And I find myself content. Finally at ease.

For Milford and its Moons—

They soothe my soul.

They are the tonic I drink.

They are the ground and sky where my ancestors and I live.

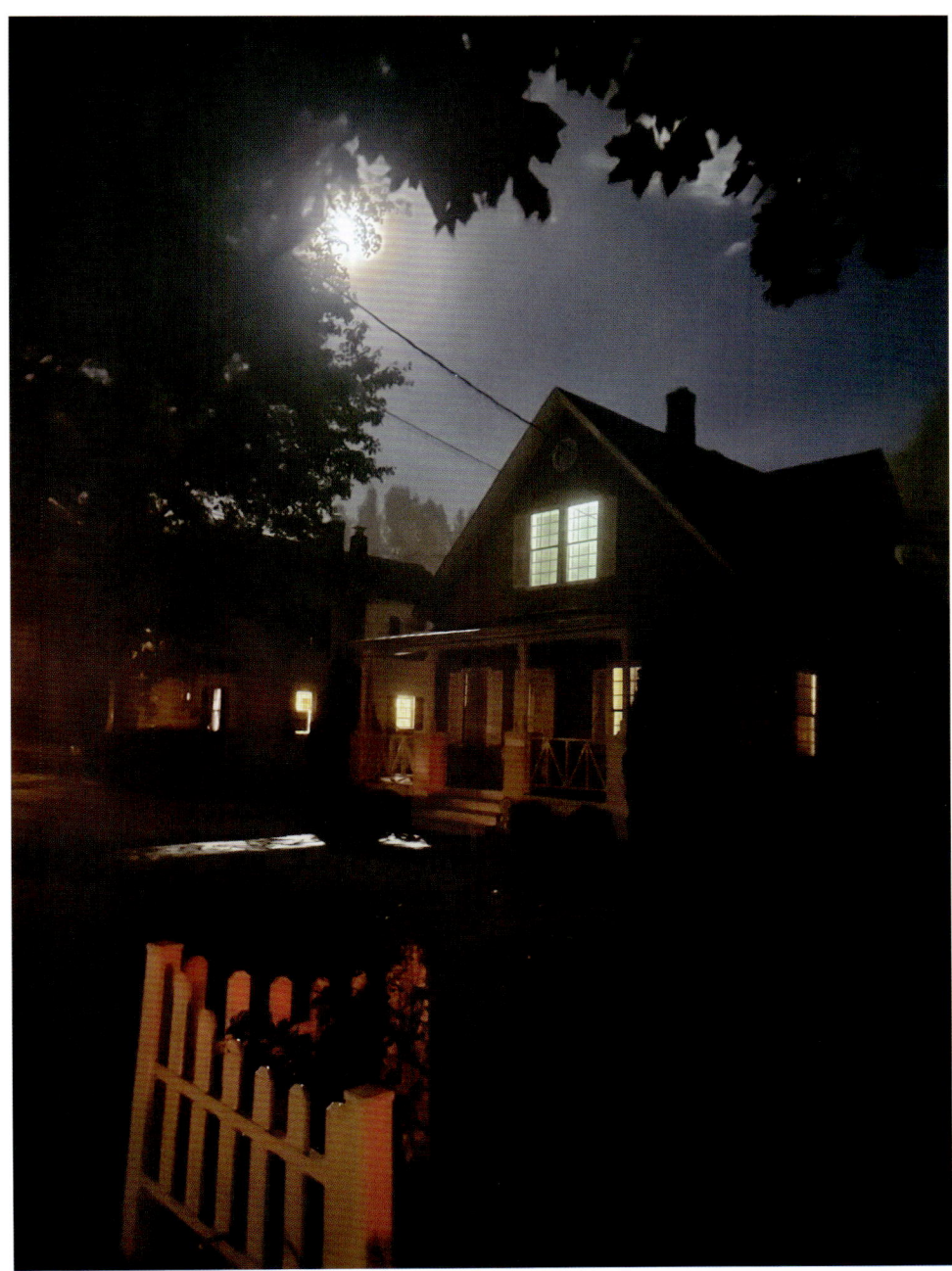

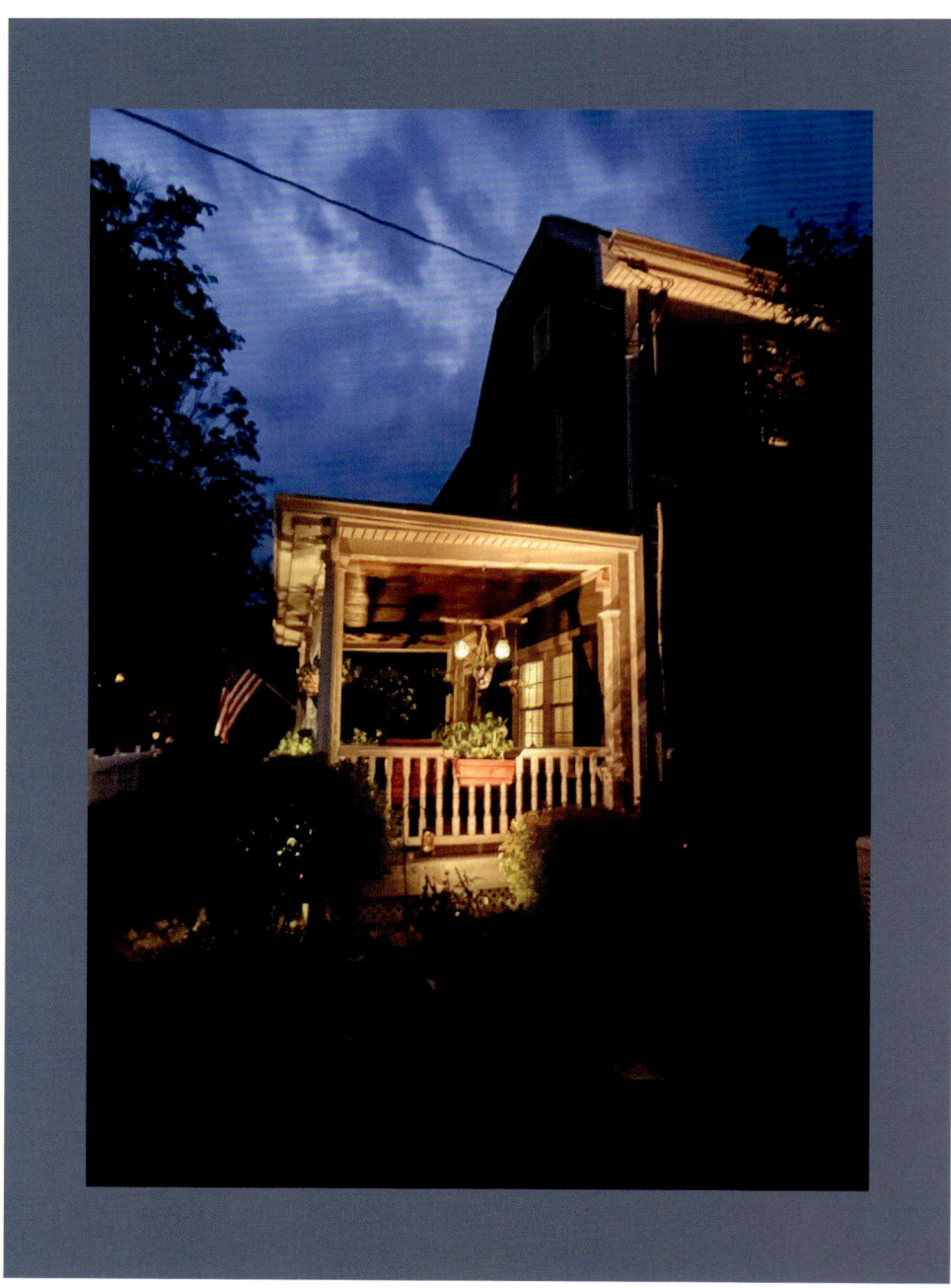

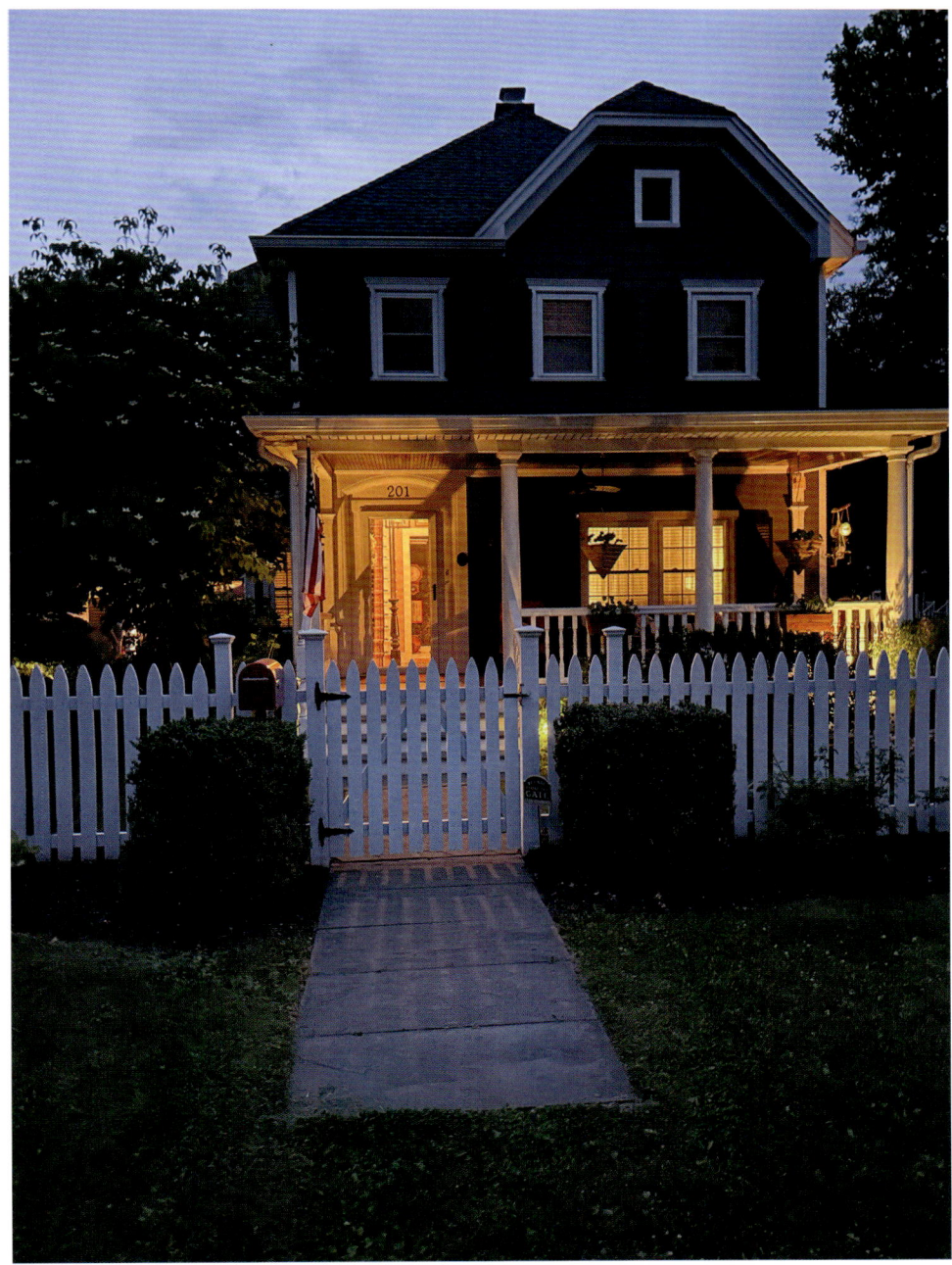

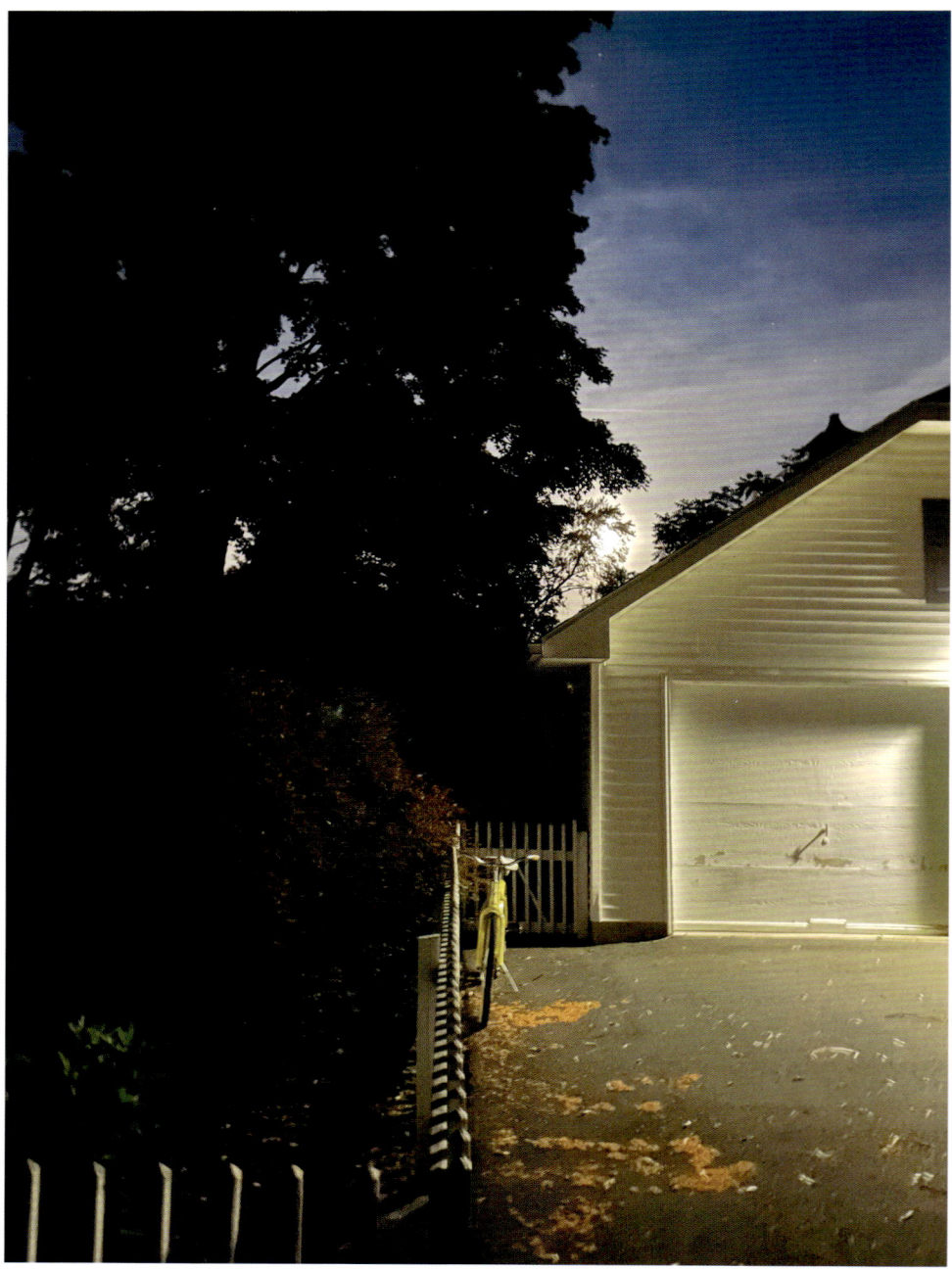

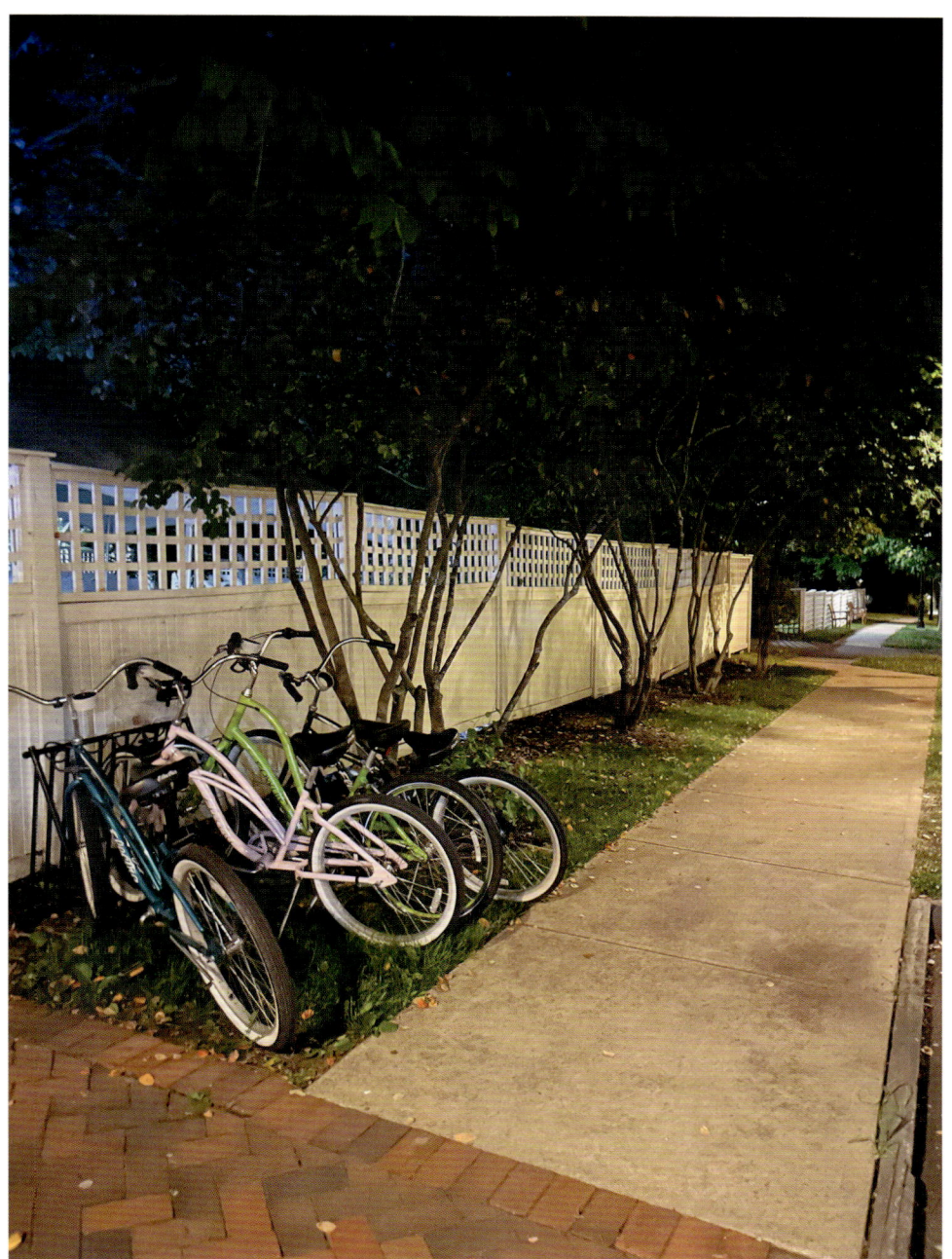

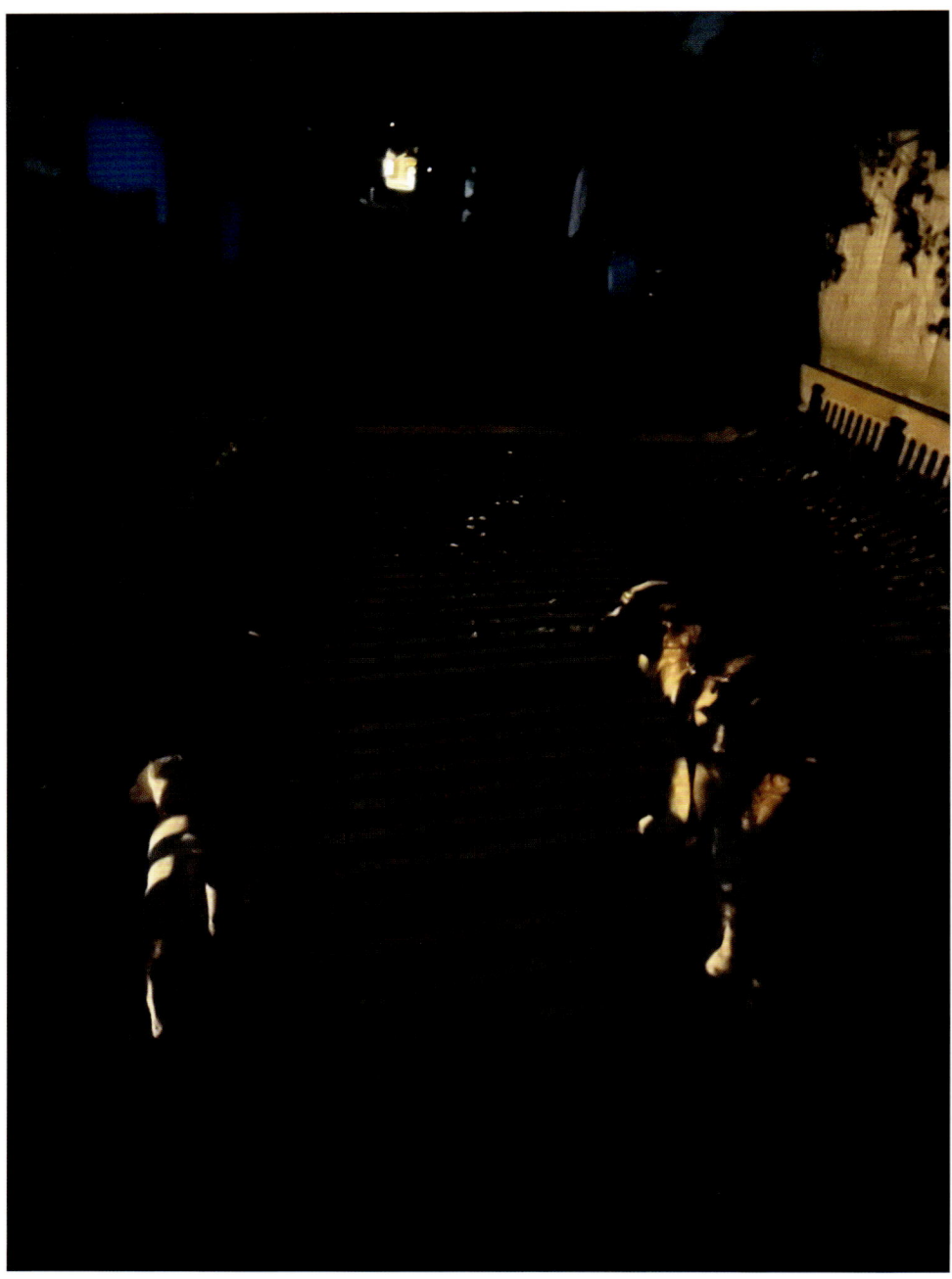

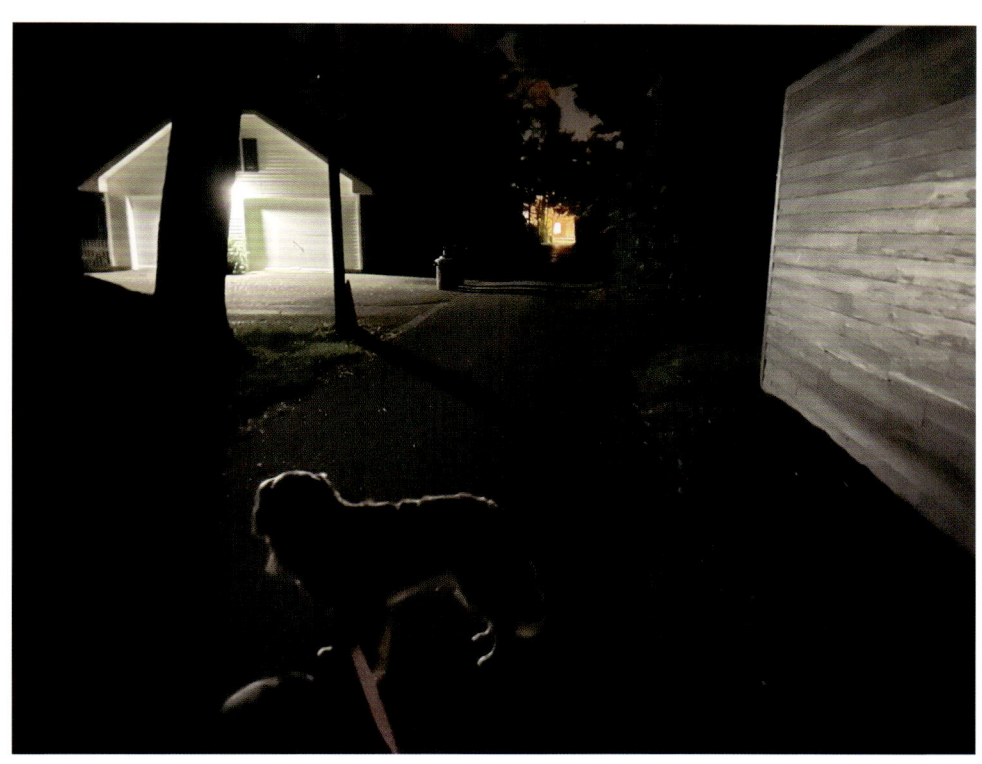

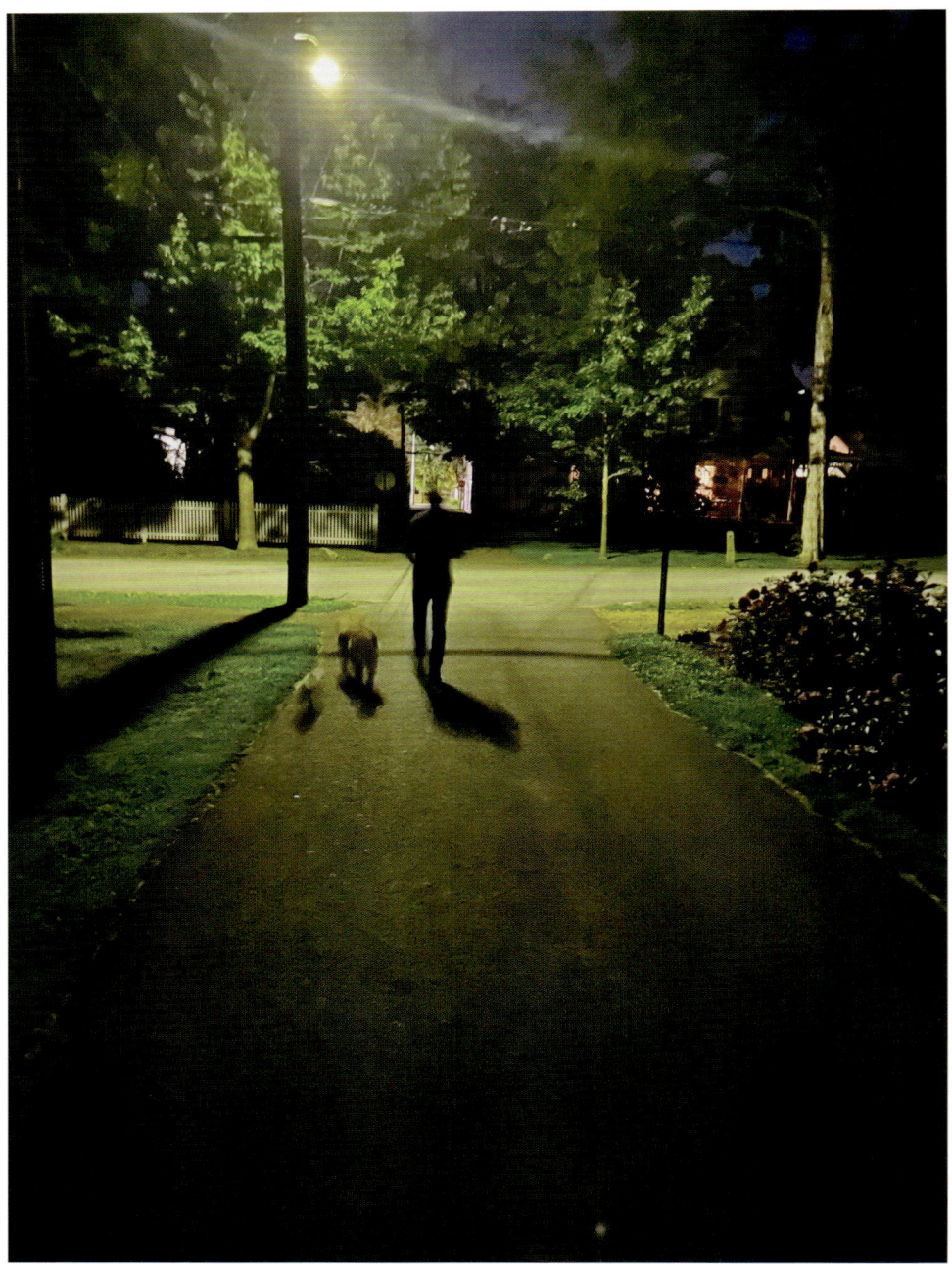

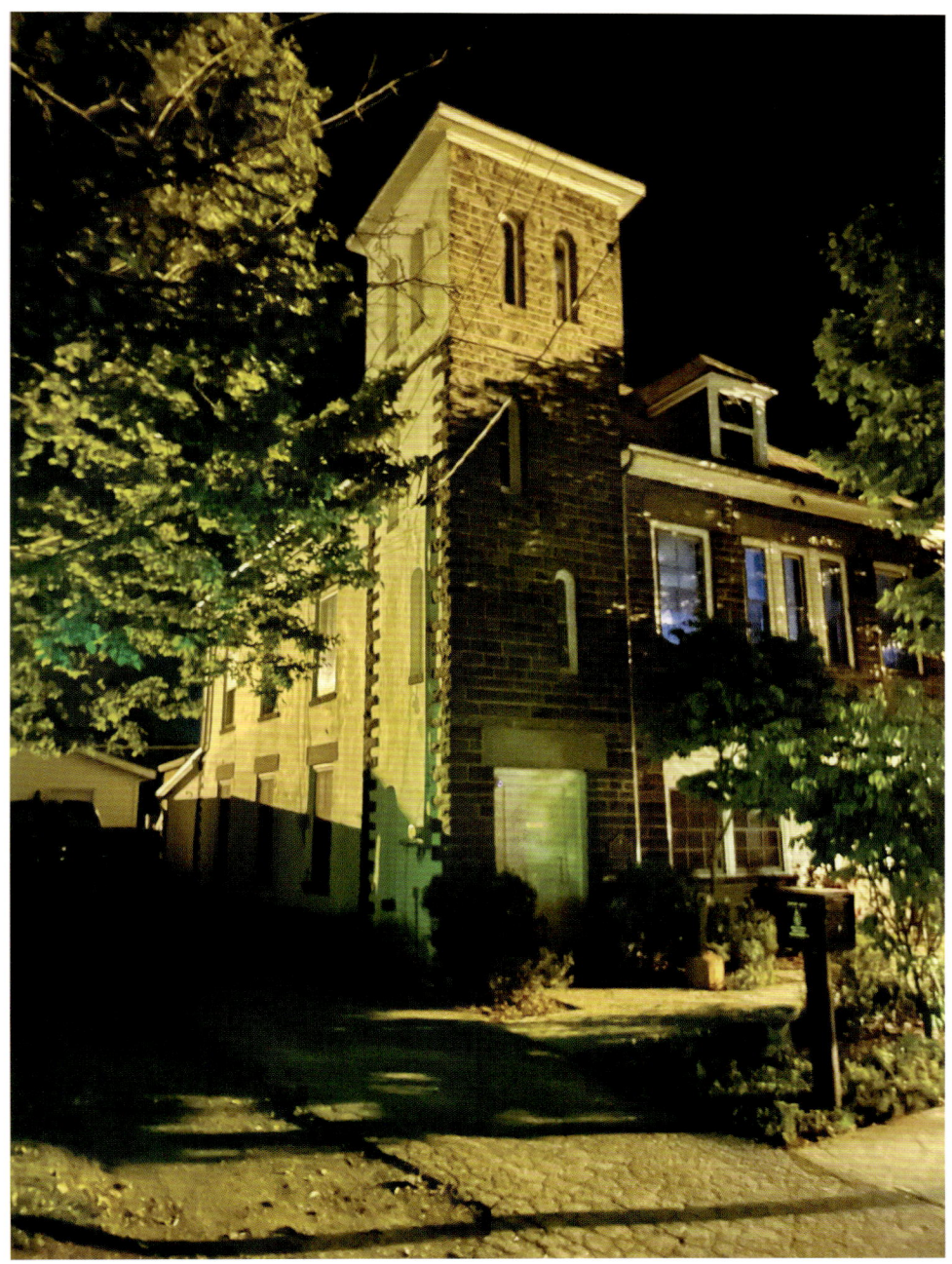

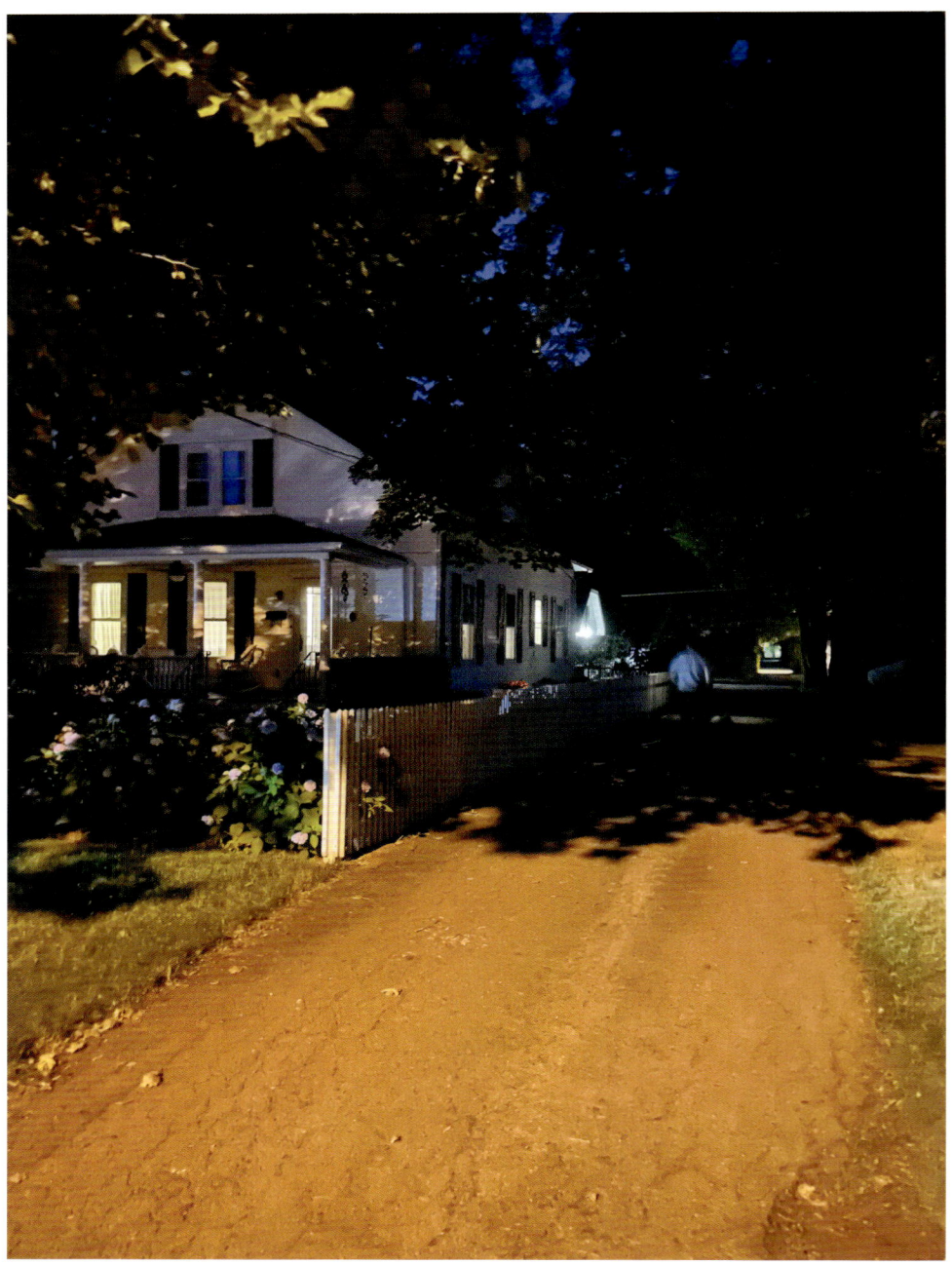

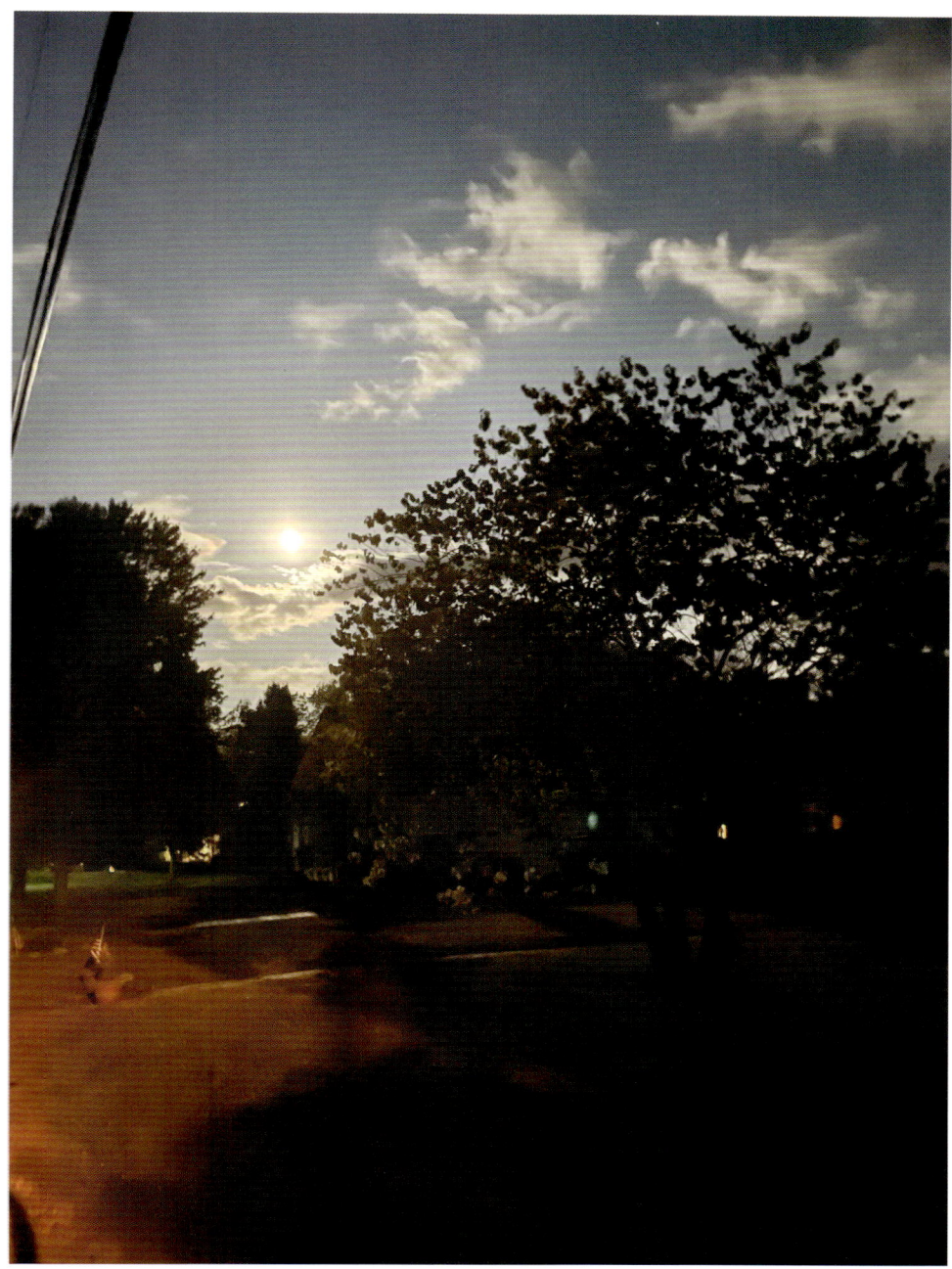

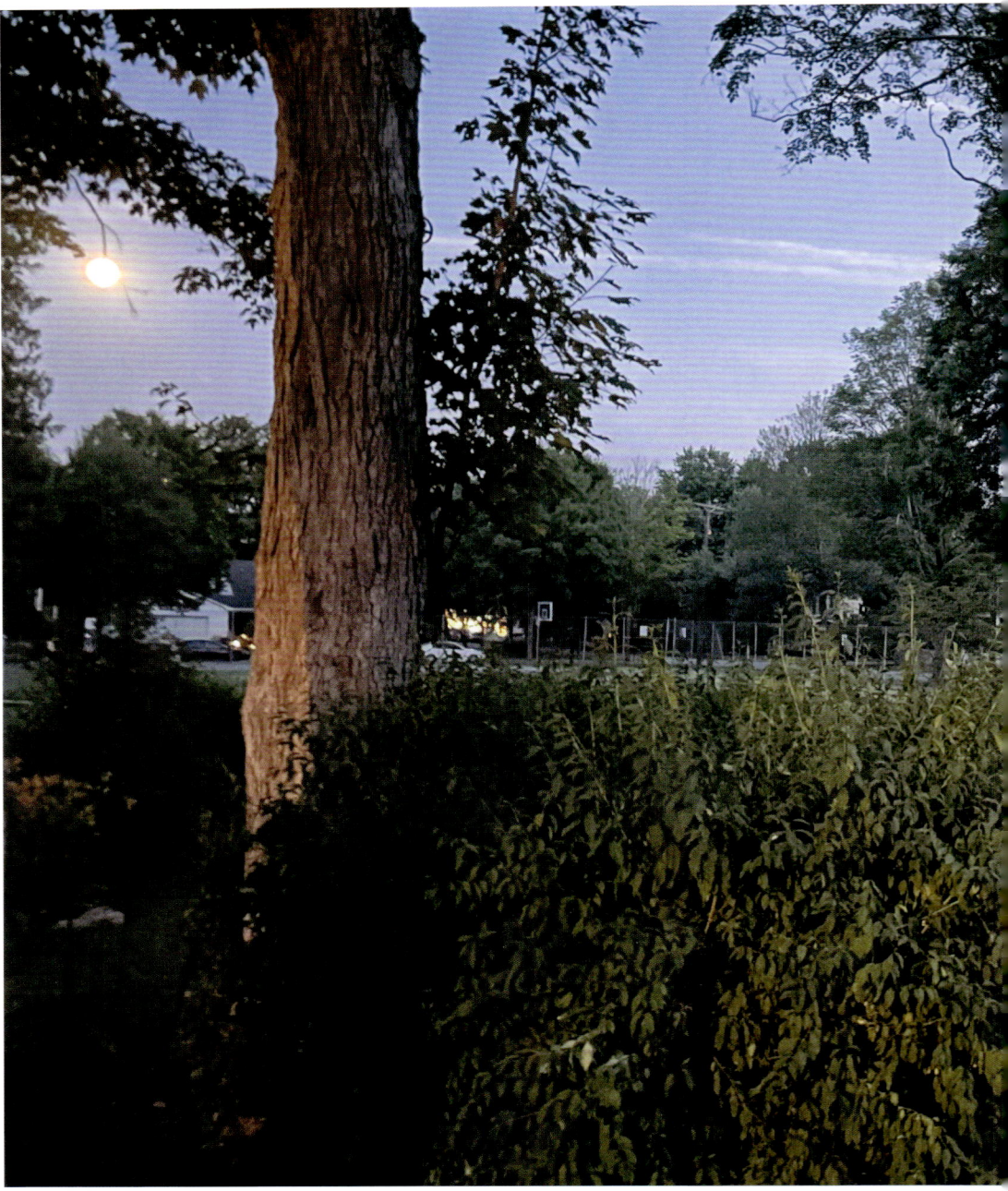

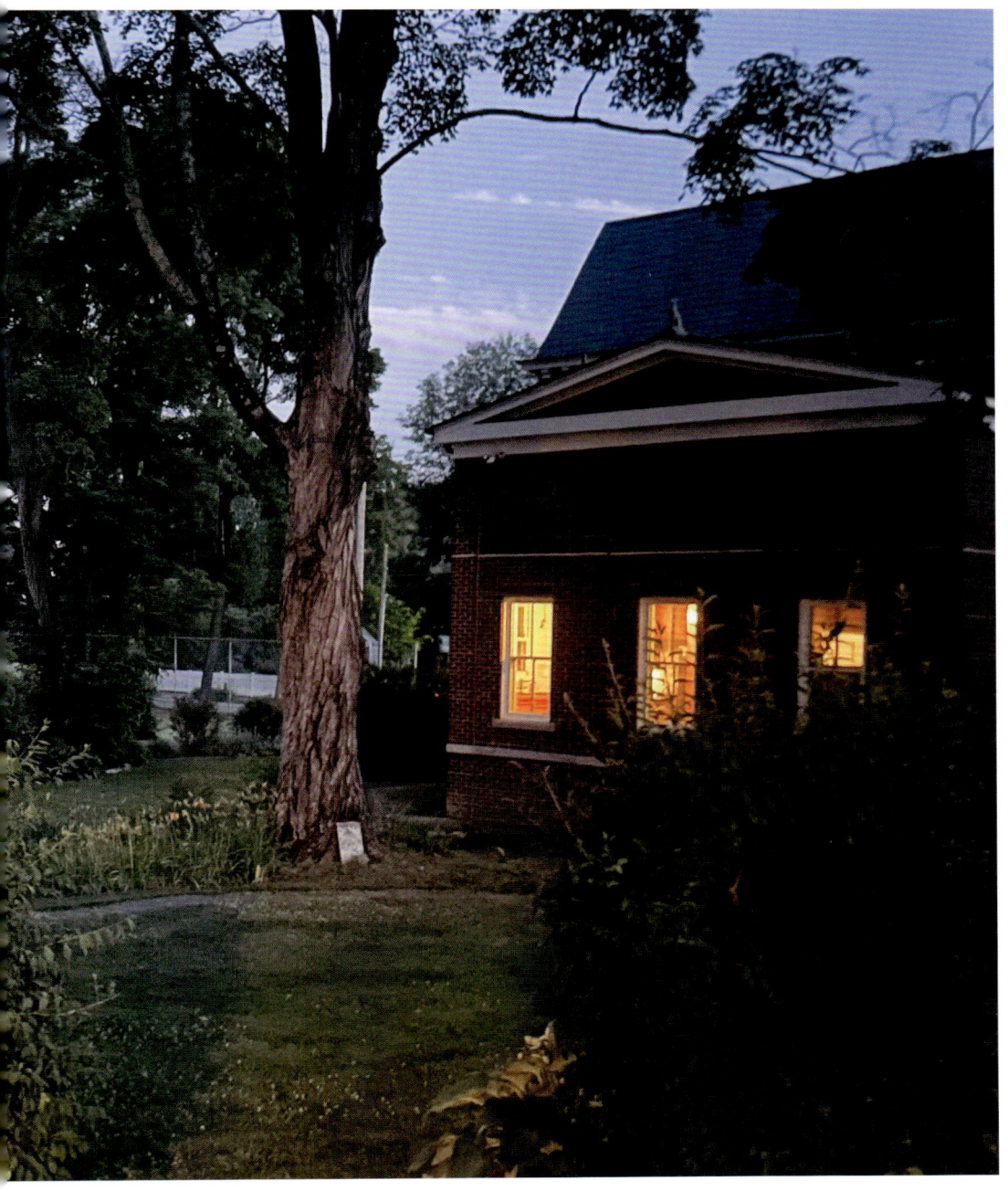

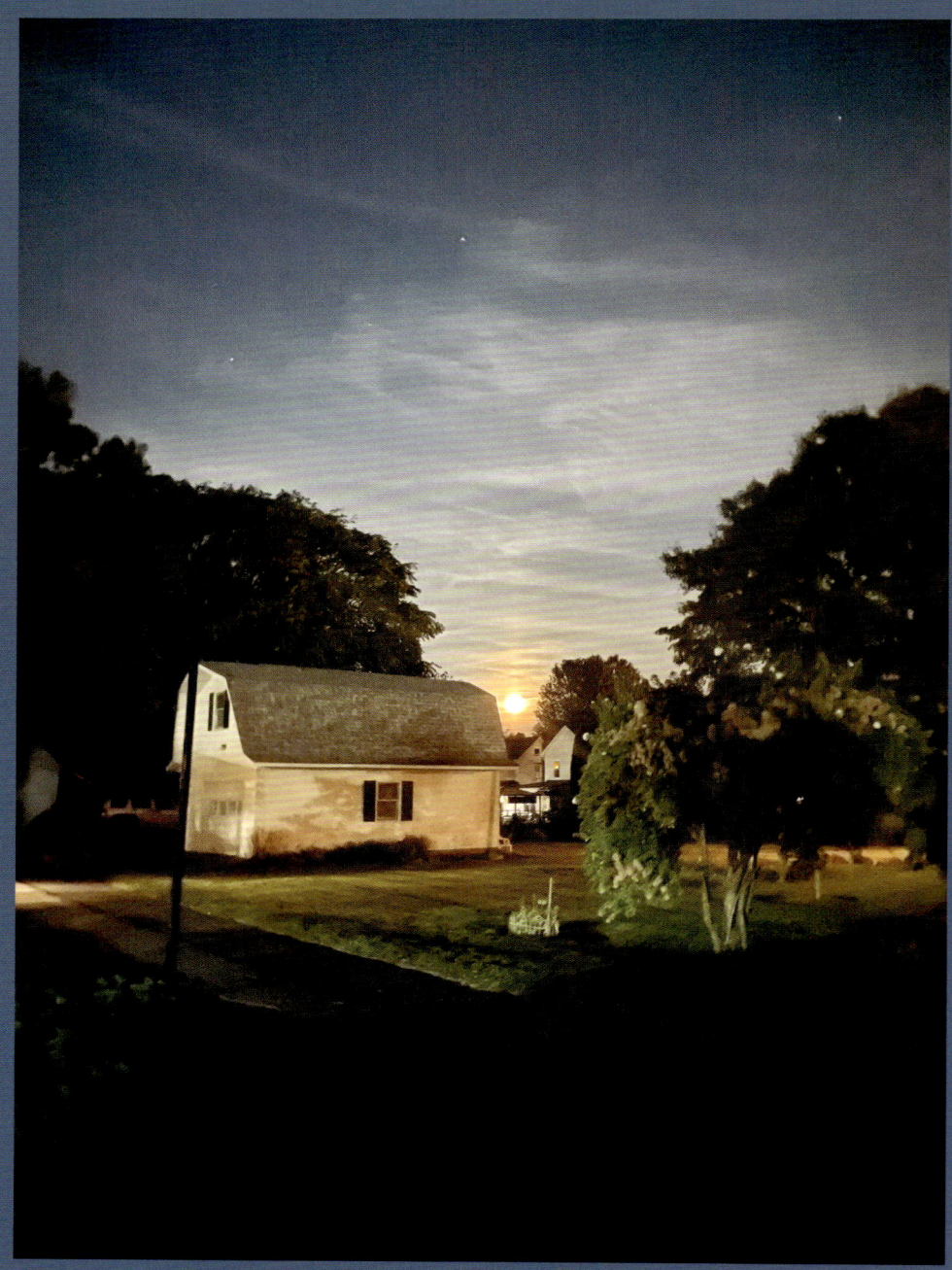

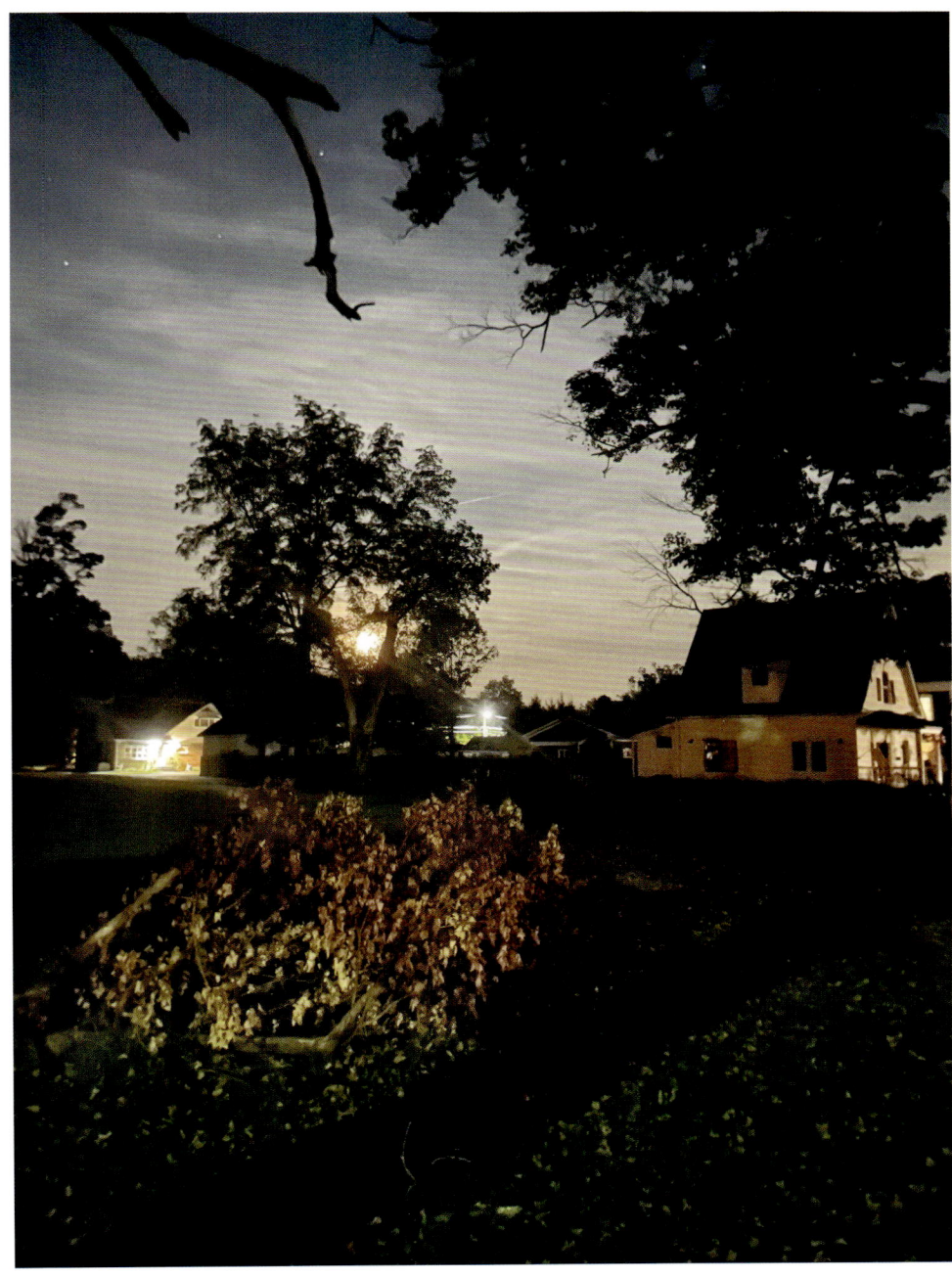

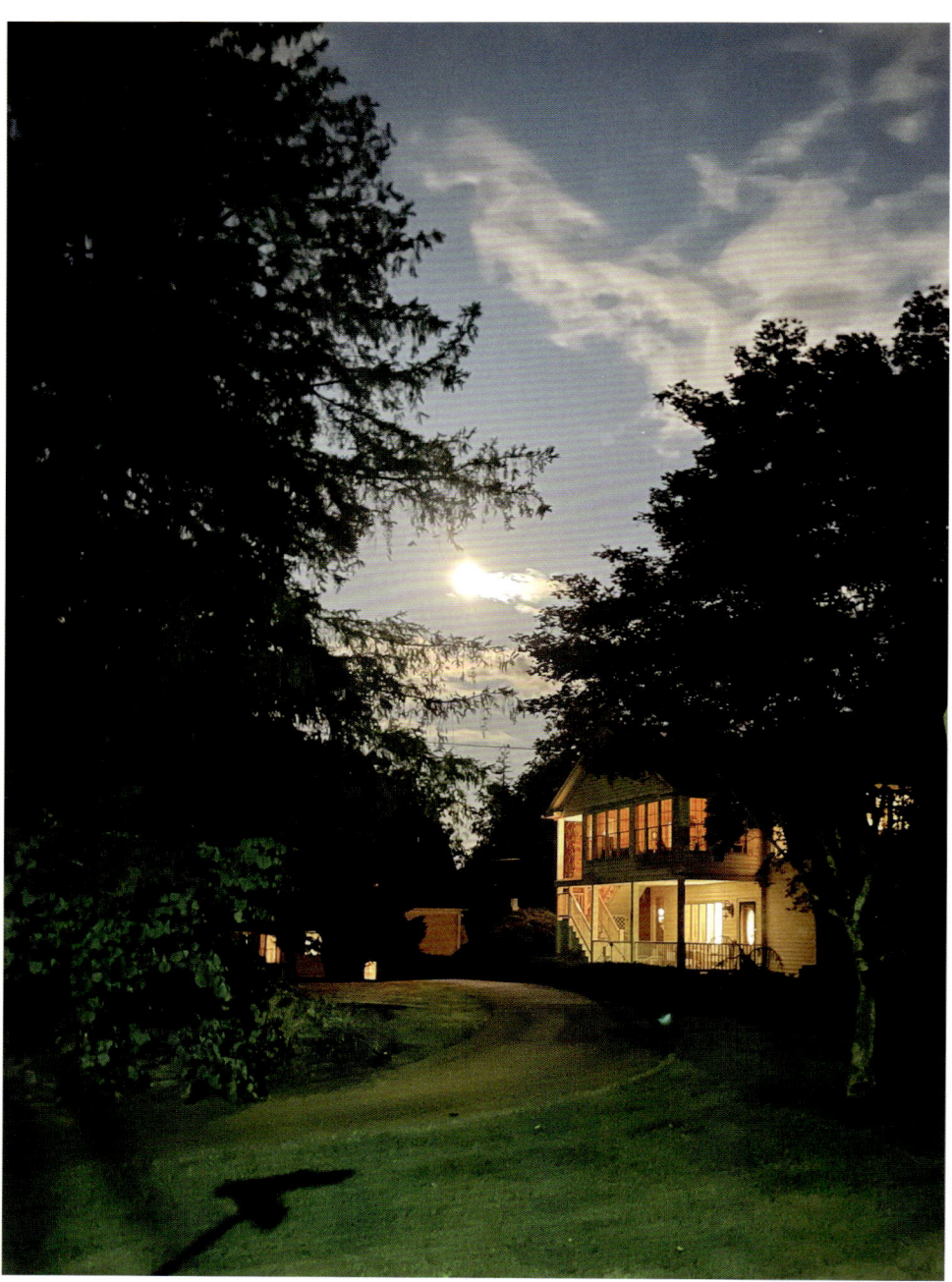

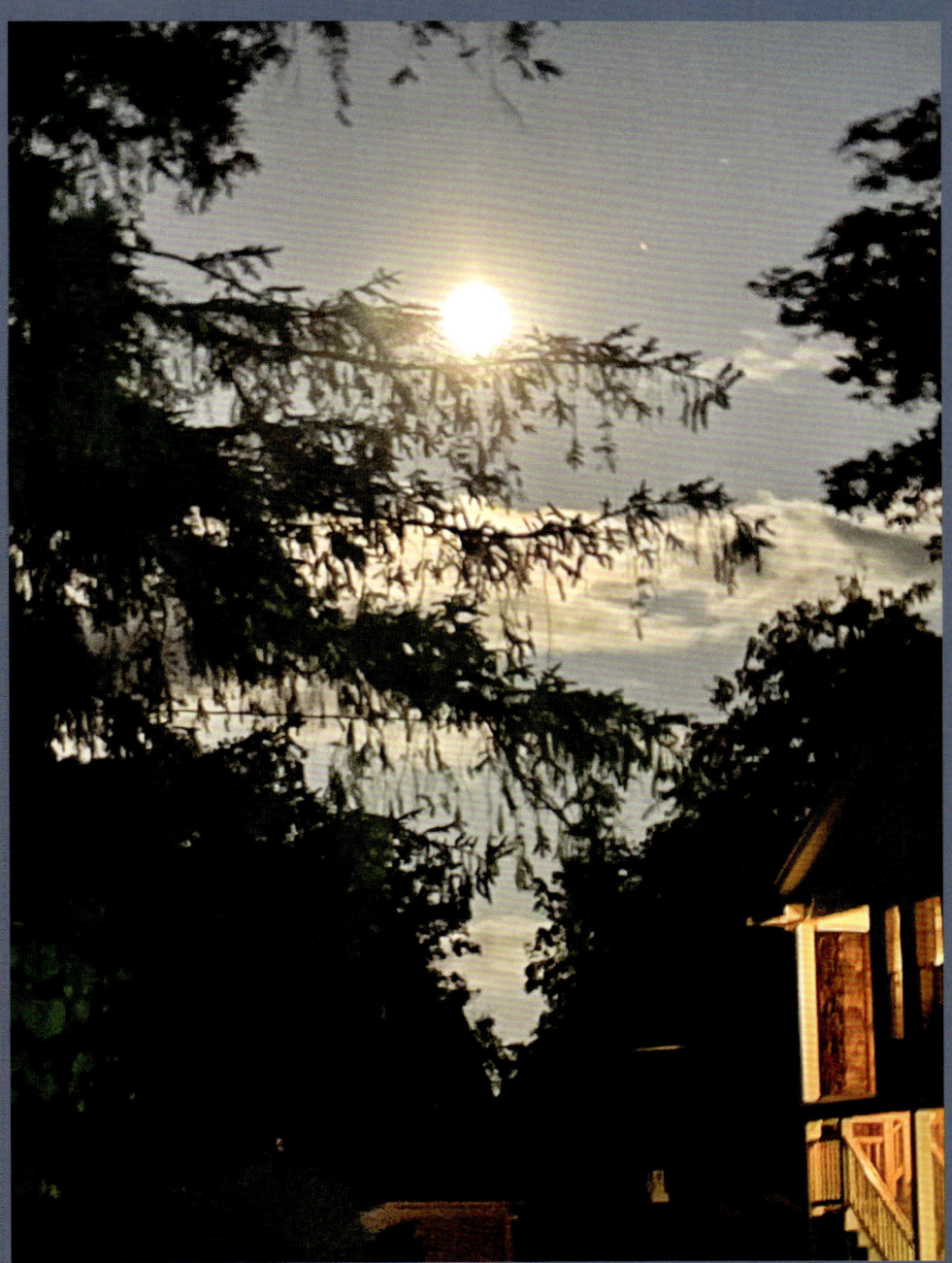

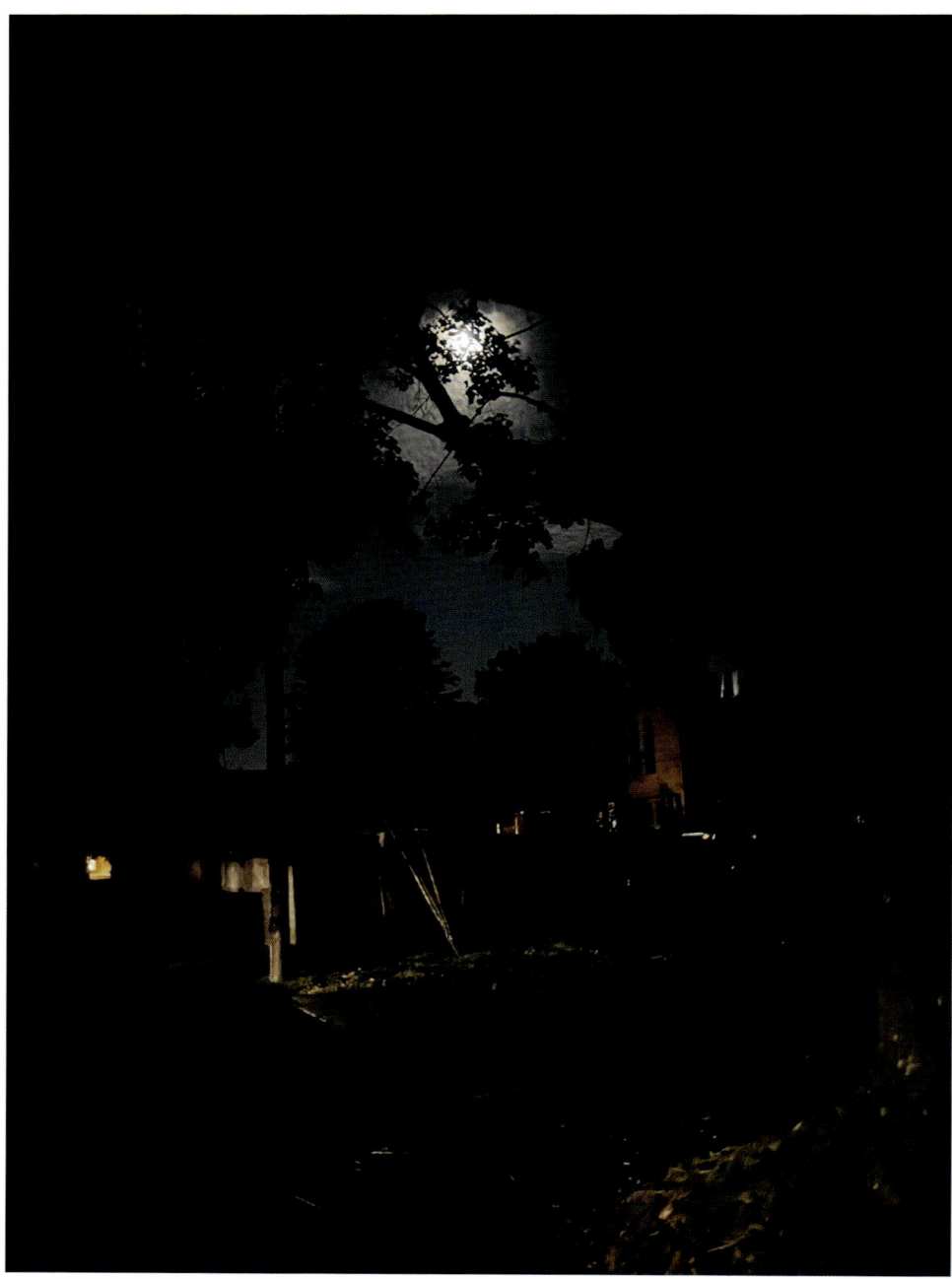

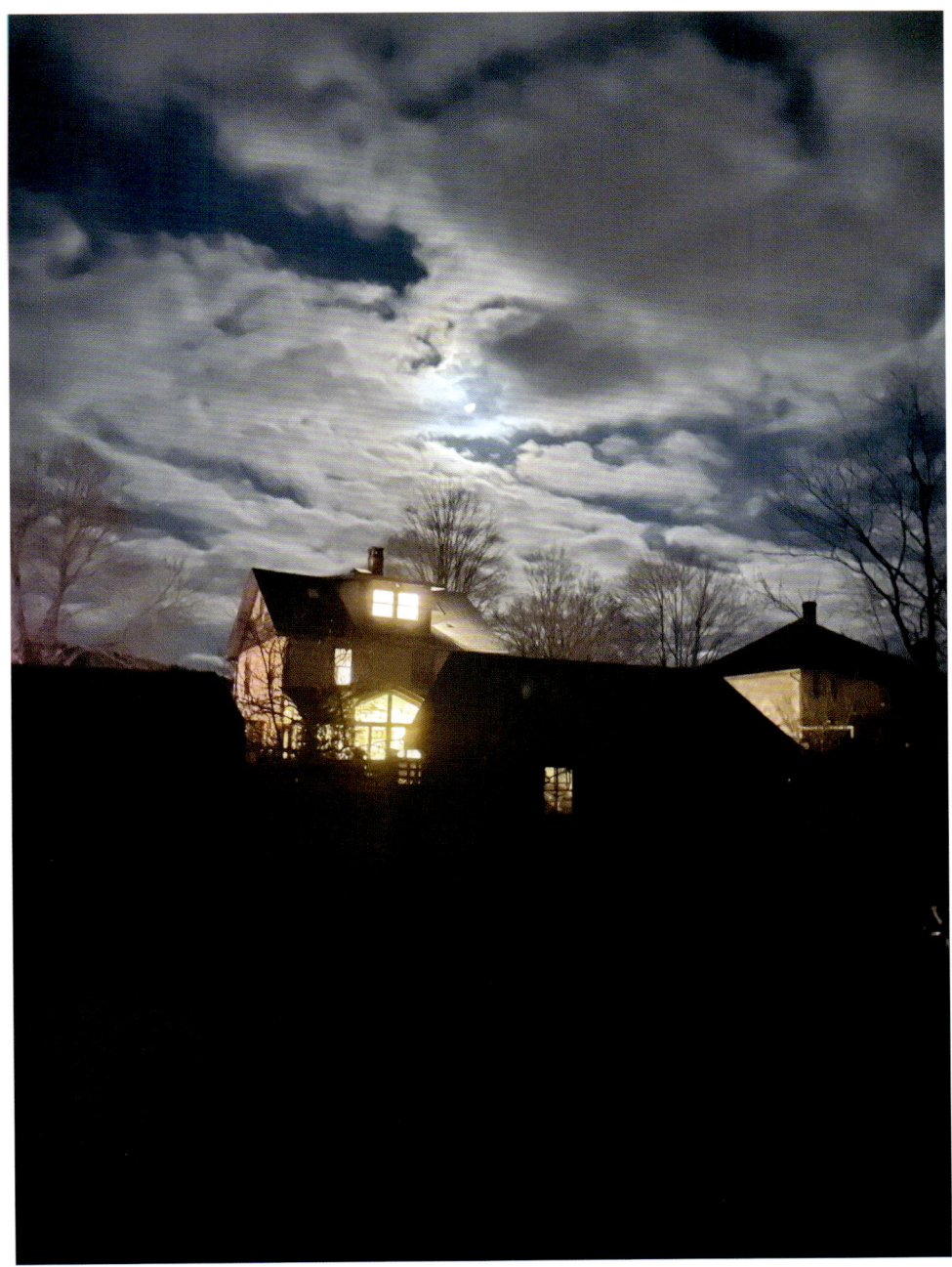

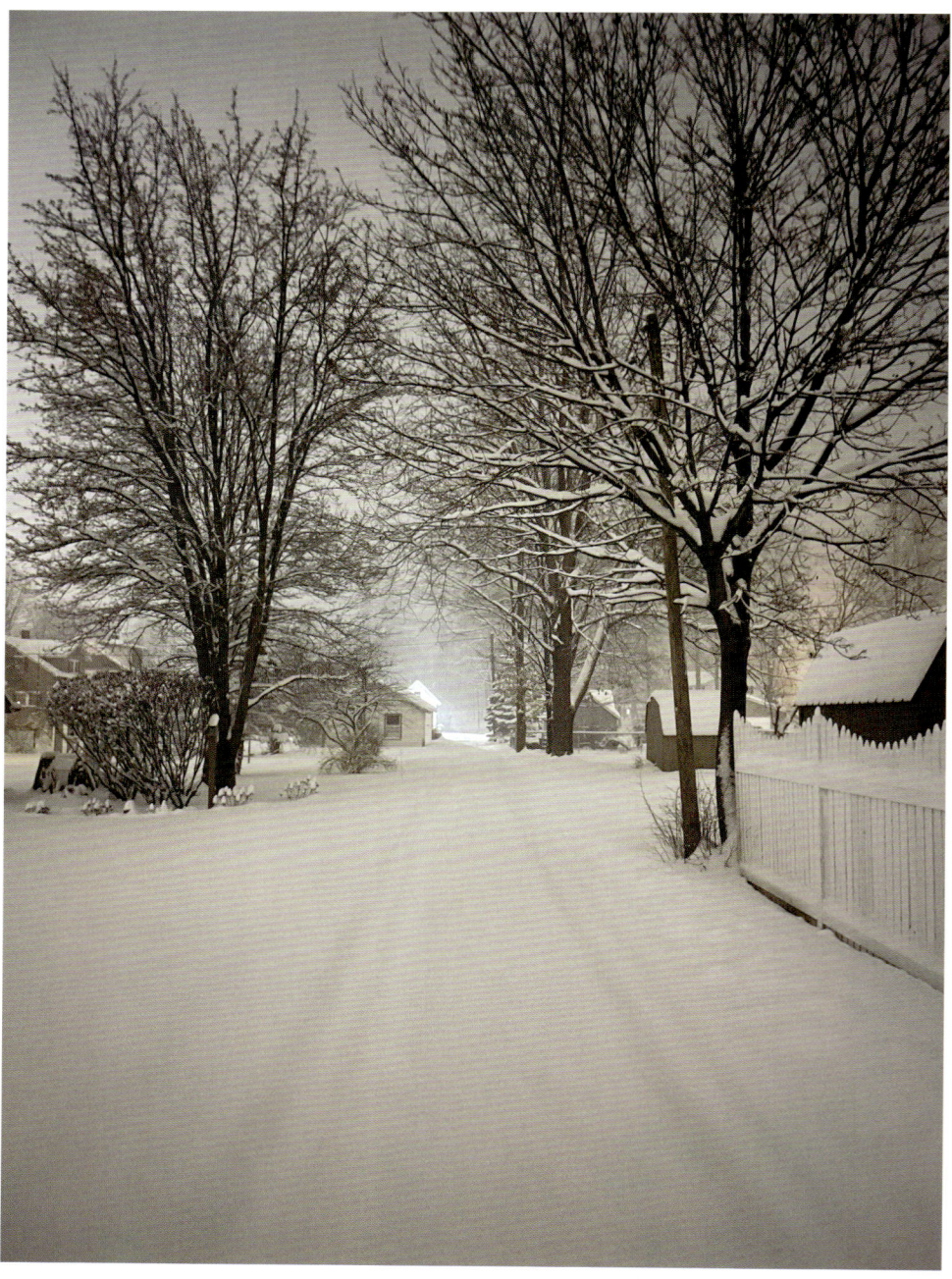

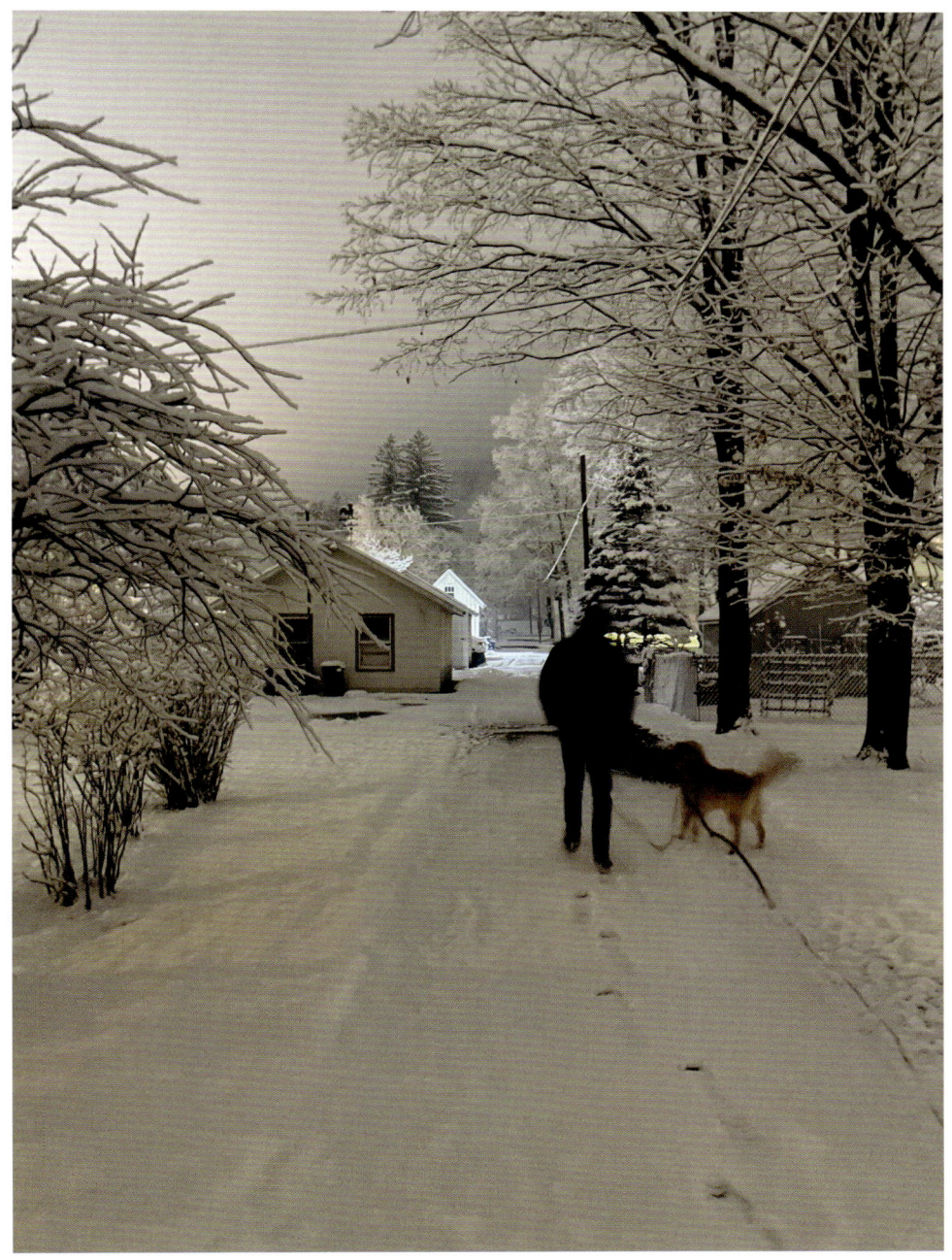

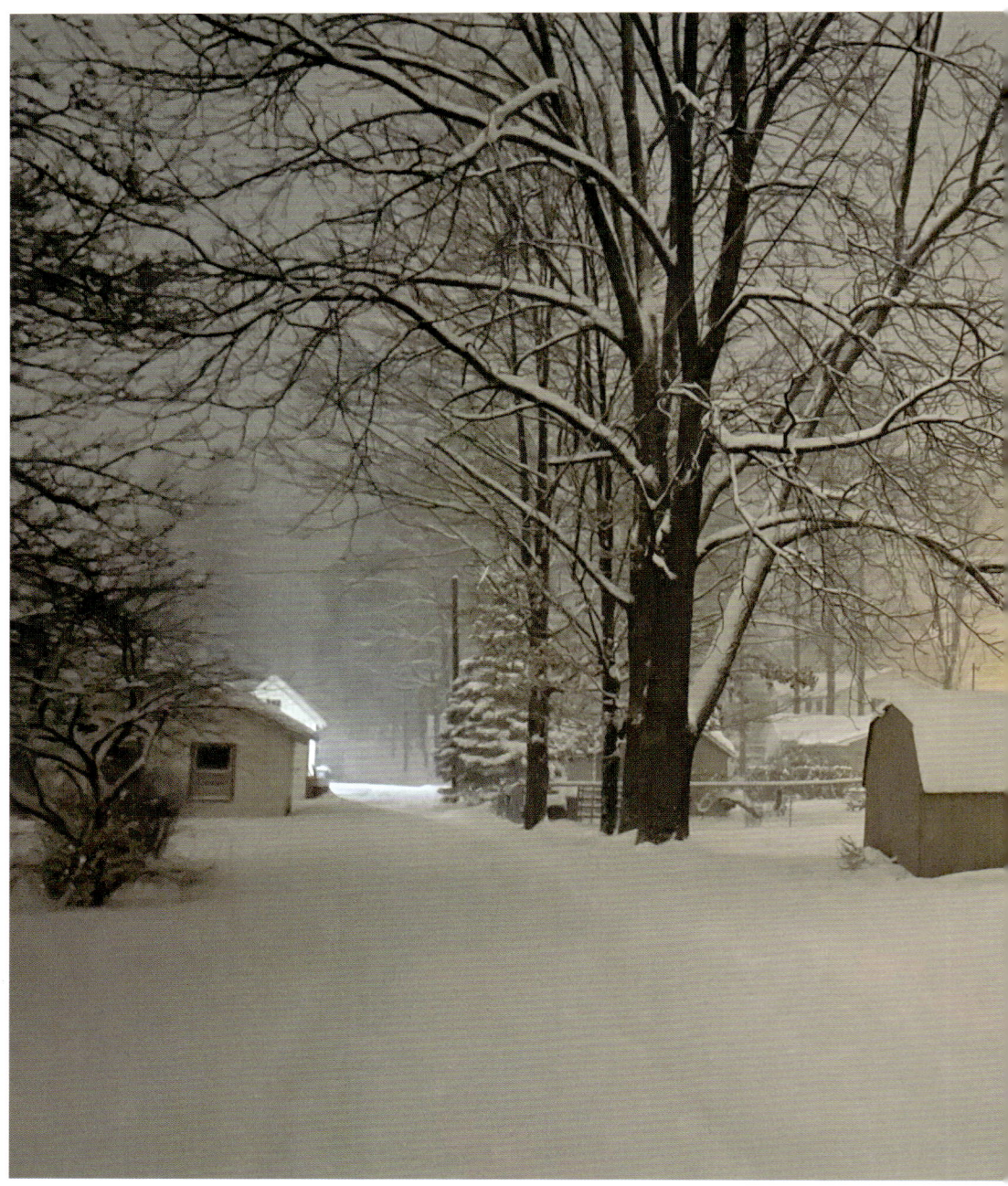

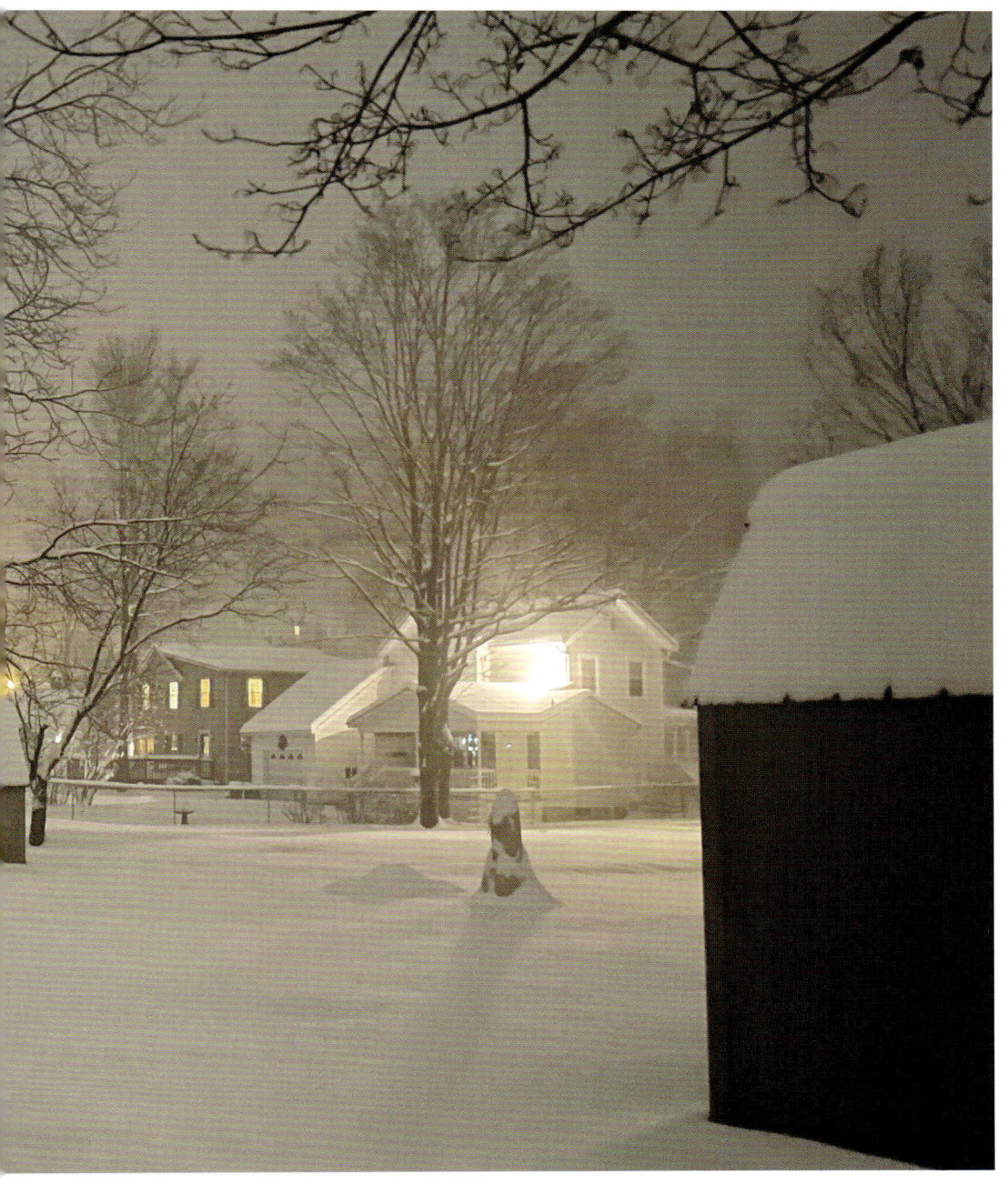

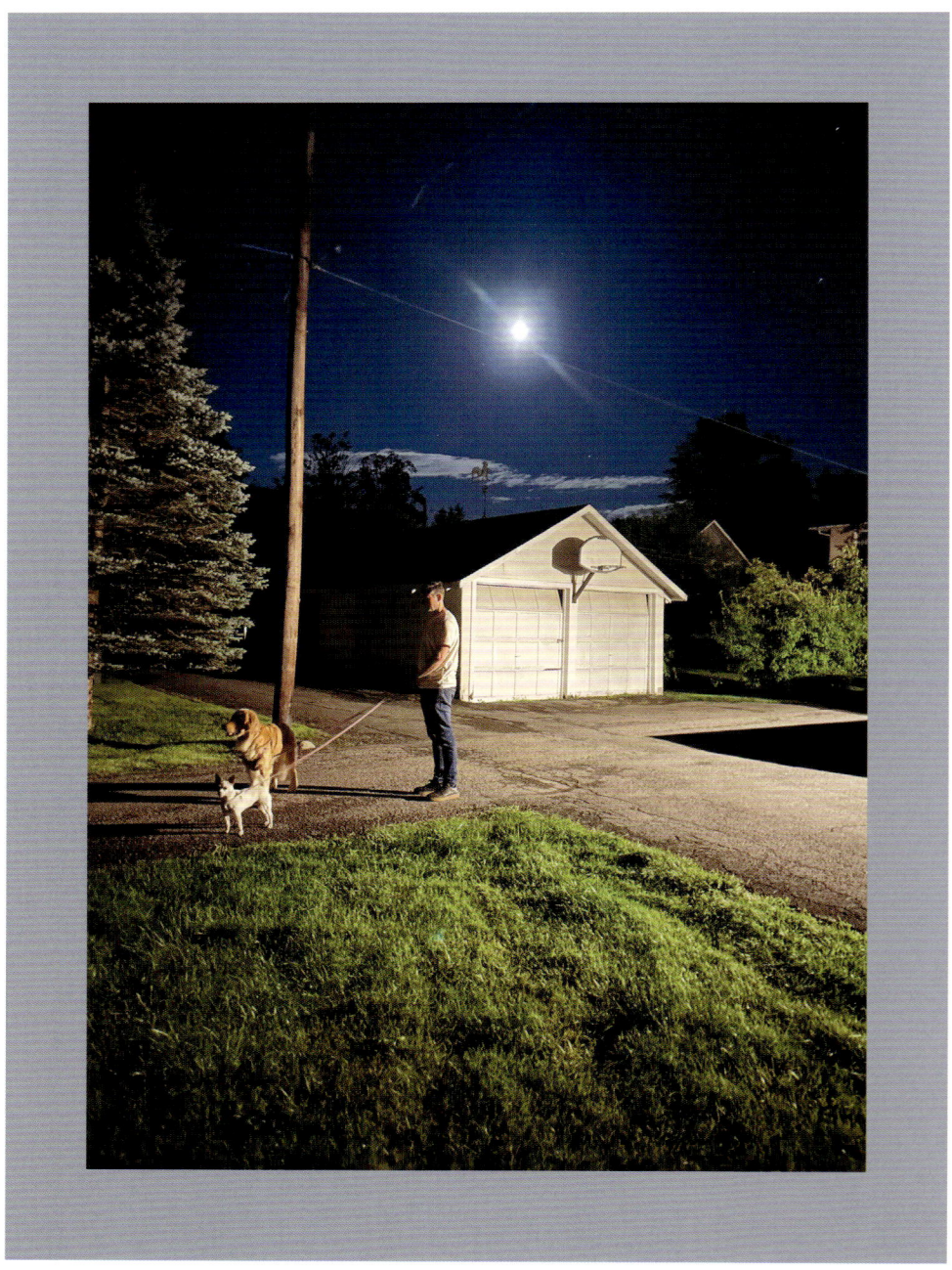

ABOUT THE AUTHOR

Richard C. Morais is an award-winning American novelist and journalist. He is the author of *The New York Times* and international bestseller *The Hundred-Foot Journey*, a novel that follows the life of an Indian chef as he conquers the rarified world of French haute cuisine. The novel sold in thirty-five territories across the globe, and in 2014, Steven Spielberg, Oprah Winfrey, and Juliet Blake released *The Hundred-Foot Journey* as a much-loved film directed by Lasse Hallström and starring Dame Helen Mirren and Om Puri.

Morais is also the author of novels *The Man With No Borders* (2019) and *Buddhaland Brookland* (2012) in addition to the critically acclaimed biography *Pierre Cardin: The Man Who Became a Label* (1991). He recently co-wrote *The New Rules of Investing* (2024) with UBS' Global Chief Investment Officer Mark Haefele.

He was previously both the editor of Barron's *Penta* magazine, and as *Forbes'* European Bureau Chief, the magazine's longest-serving foreign correspondent, stationed in London for eighteen years.

Morais has uniquely won three awards and six nominations as the Business Journalist of the Year. His literary works, meanwhile, were semifinalists shortlisted for multiple awards. He was named the 2015 Citizen Diplomat of the Year, "for promoting cross-cultural understanding in all of his literary work."

He lives in Milford, Pennsylvania.

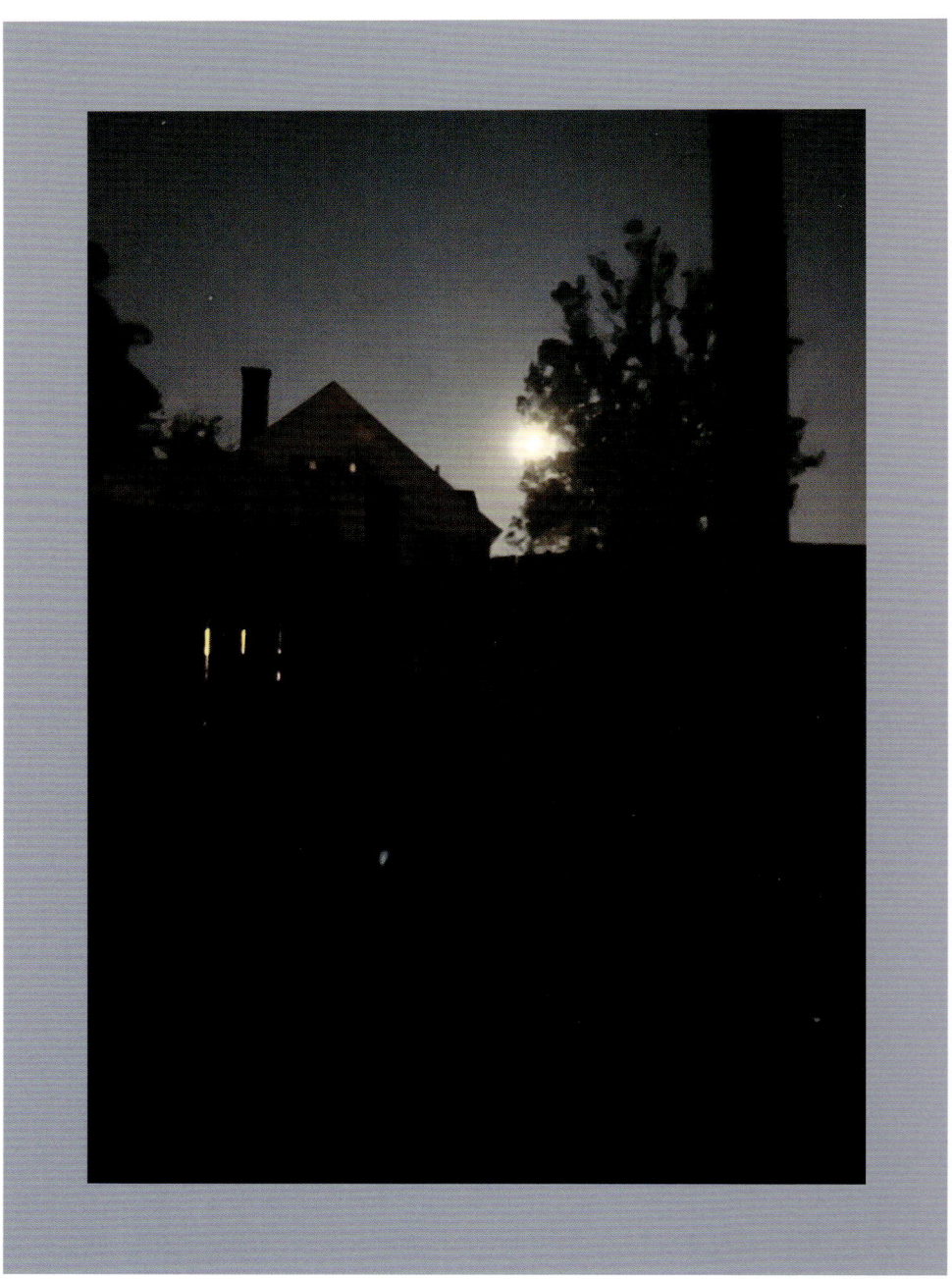

ABOUT SEAN STRUB

Sean Strub served as mayor of Milford, PA from 2016 to 2024. For twenty-five years he helped lead the Milford Enhancement Committee's restoration of Milford's bluestone sidewalks and pedestrian-oriented hardscapes to their Gilded Era prime.

He is a long-time activist and writer who is the founder of *POZ* Magazine, the leading independent global source of information about HIV, is a popular speaker, and is frequently cited in the media as an HIV expert on prevention and treatment policy.

He has also been active in environmental protection, historic preservation, and community redevelopment efforts in Rural Pike County, Pennsylvania, and in 2007 produced *Nature's Keepers*, a documentary about the conservation and land stewardship history of the region.

His book, *Body Counts: A Memoir of Politics, Sex, AIDS, and Survival* was published by Scribner in 2014. A native of Iowa, Strub attended Georgetown and Columbia Universities.

He lives in Milford, Pennsylvania.

ACKNOWLEDGMENTS

I first, foremost, and predominantly must thank Marta Hallett—an innovative, risk-taking publisher in a world where few still exist.

Marta is, of course, ably backed by a team of professionals. Most of all I must thank Liz Trovato, for so artistically assembling the photographs in this book, seeing themes and recurring images that I so frequently overlooked. Another shoutout goes to Charlene Iacocucci, who looked over our shoulder and made sure we weren't coloring outside the lines.

I must also thank Mayor Sean Strub, for encouraging me whenever I dropped a moonlit Milford photo onto my Instagram page. It was Sean's comments that made me believe I was on to something, despite my patently amateurish efforts at taking nocturnal photographs.

Finally, my heartfelt thanks to Robert, Sherry and Maya, my beloved Milford family; my daughter Kate, and my ex-wife Susan; and our good and kind neighbors who live with us in the village. You all—along with the moon—enrich and enliven my solitary search for meaning down Milford's hidden paths and alleyways.